# SITTING ON THE FENCE: NEGOTIATING ARCHAEOLOGY, ANTHROPOLOGY AND PHILOSOPHY

# SITTING ON THE FENCE: NEGOTIATING ARCHAEOLOGY, ANTHROPOLOGY AND PHILOSOPHY

## Festschrift for Prof. Dr Raymond H.A. Corbey in celebration of his 70th birthday

edited by
S.T. HUSSAIN AND G.L. DUSSELDORP

ANALECTA PRAEHISTORICA LEIDENSIA 54

Published by Sidestone Press, Leiden
www.sidestone.com
E-mail: info @ sidestone.nl
Phone: (+31)(0)71-7370131

Series: Analecta Praehistorica Leidensia
Series editors: Victor Klinkenberg, Carol van Driel-Murray, Richard Jansen, Nathalie Ø. Brusgaard

Lay-out & cover design: Sidestone Press

Cover illustration: Two Laughing Jesters, sculpture by Pieter Xaveri, Leiden 1673. Collection and photo: Rijksmuseum, Amsterdam BK-NM-5667.

ISBN 978-94-6426-320-6 (softcover)
ISBN 978-94-6426-321-3 (hardcover)
ISBN 978-94-6426-322-0 (PDF e-book)

ISSN 0169-7447 (Print)
ISSN 2665-9573 (Online)

DOI: 10.59641/uu901xg

Universiteit Leiden

# Contents

In Hussain, S.T. and G.L. Dusseldorp (eds) 2025. Sitting on the fence: Negotiating archaeology, anthropology and philosophy. Festschrift for Prof. Dr Raymond H.A. Corbey in celebration of his 70th birthday. *Analecta Praehistorica Leidensia* 54. Leiden: Sidestone Press, pp. 7-10.

# Raymond Corbey: A philosophical thorn in the side of archaeologists and much more

## Gerrit L. Dusseldorp, Shumon T. Hussain

### CAPTURING THE FENCE-SITTER

Who knew that "Sitting on the fence" could lead to such a versatile and inspiring academic biography? Raymond Corbey has moved across so many different areas of research that few of his colleagues realise the enormous scope and productivity of this epistemologist's life. A retrospective and a celebration are thus, we think, in order.

Raymond's academic career can be characterised via three main spatiotemporal nodes: Nijmegen, Tilburg, and Leiden. His disciplinary trajectory spans a wide array of fields with main foci on anthropology, archaeology, and philosophy. A single description can hardly do justice to Raymond's scientific history and hence this volume takes a multi-angled and deliberately multi-vocal approach to the complicated task. A notable historical perspective and personal contextualisation is offered by Roebroeks (this volume), while a conceptual sketch of Raymond's idiosyncratic scientific style is provided by Hussain (this volume). But can these descriptions really capture the man, the style, and the science? Here we propose a more intuitive and fairly pragmatic approach to the jubilarian consisting of some personal recollections, a few selected photographic illustrations, and a more artistic rendering of Corbey provided by Dersjant (see below). The rest of this celebratory *Festschrift* serves as a mosaic of diverse forms of engagement with Raymond's wide-ranging scientific interest and influence collated by some of his close colleagues, companions (including nonhuman companion species in the sense of Donna Haraway), and intellectual followers.

### THE LIMINAL ARCHAEOLOGIST

With his academic arrival in archaeology, Raymond literally managed to turn his hobby into his profession! Still, as a philosopher-anthropologist, he remained a liminal figure in the Dutch archaeological world (his arrival also, funnily, coincided with the increasing "hipness" of the concept of liminality in archaeology, so in a way his liminality embodies an important theoretical performance, perhaps even *performance art*).

This had some amusing reverberations (at least we students at the time thought so): When Raymond was first appointed professor at the Faculty of Archaeology in Leiden, the magazine for the archaeology profession in the Netherlands, *Archeobrief*, duly took notice and reported his arrival (Anonymous 2005). The editor even added a portrait picture, and laughter rang the halls of the faculty, as the printed image was of a completely different person! This aptly illustrates how Raymond has been an integral figure of the Faculty of Archaeology, yet flew under the radar in archaeology at large.

**Shumon T. Hussain**

Center for Multidisciplinary Environmental Studies in the Humanities (MESH) & Institute for Prehistoric Archaeology, University of Cologne, Germany
s.t.hussain@uni-koeln.de
ORCID: 0000-0002-6215-393X

**Gerrit L. Dusseldorp**

Faculty of Archaeology, Leiden University, The Netherlands
g.l.dusseldorp@arch.leidenuniv.nl
ORCID 0000-0001-6147-710X

Figure 1. Raymond with René Descartes, Oegstgeest, The Netherlands, June 2018. Photograph: Dmitri De Loecker.

## NOT SO LIMINAL NOW!

To archaeology students from the late 1990s onwards, Raymond is far from a liminal figure, however. PhD students and those enrolled in the Master's program were exposed to and influenced by the in-house philosopher as he taught the formative archaeological theory courses. But especially his long-running epistemology course, mandatory for RMA and PhD students, made waves. It inspired many of us to take new avenues of research (see for example Mol, this volume) but the relentless questioning of supposed certainties and the at first sight haphazard organisation of topics was also disliked by some. Even though some alumni would never again adopt the "view from the fence", they could not escape the faculty without at least indulging it briefly.

Although always friendly and approachable, Raymond is unfazed by occasionally awkward situations. Regardless of seniority, he will voice brusque interjections during lectures to "speak louder!" as well as raise incisive questions and sometimes adamant objections. This is always done with a good dose of often implicit humour though. At the defence of Dusseldorp's MA-thesis his opening remark was to encourage him to take a sip of water followed by the words "You'll need it when I ask my first question". The question that followed was probably tricky to answer but by now long-forgotten – not Raymond's prefacing of it though.

## CAPTURING THE EMBEDDED PHILOSOPHER

Still, although pulling the rug from under students' feet to force them to examine treasured assumptions and *idees reçus* was important to at least some of us, Raymond had far more on his mind. He has always been highly productive in terms of academic papers, books, and reviews reflecting his wide range of interests – despite or perhaps precisely because of his apparent liminal positionality within the field. More importantly, titles such as *Vuistbijlen en Cadillacs – Reflecties over het verzamelen* ("Handaxes and Cadillacs, reflections on collecting") and *The Acheulean handaxe: More like a bird's song than a Beatles' tune?* not only reference the one topic that keeps returning to the forefront in his career, they also illustrate his highly original and often provocative style of reasoning and argumentation, which will continue to shape the tone and academic legacy of the Faculty of Archaeology.

To capture this quirky originality, one of the *Festschrift* contributors decided to adopt a similarly original approach, creatively mapping the contours of Raymond's scholarly persona:

> *Raymond*
>
> always
> *wondering about*
> *wandering on*
> *all ways*
> *ways*
>
> always
> *dialogue*
> *internal*
> *external*
> *cutting sharply*
>
> always
> *im Grund*
> *εἰς Δυνατότητα*
> *in efficacia*
> *dans l'histoire*
>
> always
> *primum non nocere*
>
> *Corbey*[1]

- Paul J. Dersjant (Leiden, December 2022)

Figure 2. The bird-friend: Raymond and Marina Elliott at the George C. Reifel Migratory Bird Sanctuary during a visit to Vancouver, Canada in 2006. Photograph: Mark Collard.

## RAYMOND – A HOMMAGE

The following pages are a *hommage* to an important, widely cherished, and always approachable and kind colleague, supervisor, and academic. They can never hope to capture the breadth and richness of the jubilarian personality and academic endeavour, as a *Festschrift* is always, before anything else, a community artefact and not a mirror of life, intention, or personal priorities. It largely reflects the attitudes, agendas, and beliefs of those contributing to and assembling the *Festschrift* more so than the purport of its receiver. What we, humble workers being observed from atop the fence, do with the wisdom imparted to us may amuse or even annoy the fence-sitter and unvoluntary subject of this volume. Yet, to complement the diverse contributions, considerations, contextualisations, interpretations, and reflections that follow, an overview of Raymond's published work, as complete as possible, is offered below, a body of work that stands as a reflection of his many intellectual wanderings (see Geurds, this volume) and lasting academic achievements.

The passing of time that archaeologists are so obsessed with ultimately affects all human endeavour and also this volume. One of the planned contributions has unfortunately not materialised due

---

1    The text is written as a sediment of conversations with Raymond during our many walks in and around Leiden, and not least on terraces of the cafés along the way.

to unforeseen circumstances,[2] and other intended reflections had to be abandoned or redirected because of the complexities and mangle of practice that is everyday life. We hope that the present volume, with all its partiality and historicity, still succeeds in documenting and commenting on the academic life of the jubilarian. Just like archaeology, the *Festschrift* represents merely a fragmentary, imperfect record of Raymond's life and efforts, but this is perhaps precisely its beauty.

## ACKNOWLEDGEMENTS

We thank all those who shared photographic memories on the jubilarian with us, especially Dimitri De Loecker, Marina Elliott, and Mark Collard.

## REFERENCES

Anonymous, 2005. "Corbey benoemd tot bijzonder hoogleraar archeologie." *Archeobrief* 9 (2), 40.

Geurds, A. this volume. "Better divergent than aligning: An argument in favour of the 'shaken-bookcase syndrome' in archaeological theory-building." In *Sitting on the fence: Negotiating archaeology, palaeoanthropology, anthropology and philosophy* edited by S.T. Hussain and G.L. Dusseldorp, 45-54. Leiden: Sidestone Press (Analecta Praehistoric Leidensia volume 54).

Hussain, S.T. this volume. "'Intentions do not fossilize' – Unpacking persistent but problematic domain-assumptions in Pleistocene lithic studies." In *Sitting on the fence: Negotiating archaeology, palaeoanthropology, anthropology and philosophy* edited by S.T. Hussain and G.L. Dusseldorp, 103-114. Leiden: Sidestone Press (Analecta Praehistoric Leidensia volume 54).

Mol, A.A.A. this volume. "Epistemology on Acid: Is Darwinism really such a dangerous idea?" In *Sitting on the fence: Negotiating archaeology, palaeoanthropology, anthropology and philosophy* edited by S.T. Hussain and G.L. Dusseldorp, 85-94. Leiden: Sidestone Press (Analecta Praehistoric Leidensia volume 54).

Roebroeks, W. this volume. "Towards an archaeology of an epistemologist's epistemology." In *Sitting on the fence: Negotiating archaeology, palaeoanthropology, anthropology and philosophy* edited by S.T. Hussain and G.L. Dusseldorp, 19-28. Leiden: Sidestone Press (Analecta Praehistoric Leidensia volume 54).

---

2    *"Early in the preparation of my contribution to the present Festschrift, my physician said that dr Alzheim had come my way. I shall therefore have to restrain from writing a notice, regrettably. My plan was to write on the two adjacent and rather similar LBK early farmers' villages of Janskamperveld and Sittard (at only 3 km one from the other, on the same side of the Geleenbeek in Raymond's home province of Limburg).*

*For long times Raymond and I have done things together, walked the Leiden vicinity, discussed his and my ideas, certainly not only on academical questions but also on broader topics. Given the verdict, I regret very much to have to abstain from a contribution to this Festschrift.*

*However, I take this opportunity to wish him all the best, now and further on.*

*Piet"*

(Pieter van de Velde 20 December 2022)

In Hussain, S.T. and G.L. Dusseldorp (eds) 2025. Sitting on the fence: Negotiating archaeology, anthropology and philosophy. Festschrift for Prof. Dr Raymond H.A. Corbey in celebration of his 70th birthday. *Analecta Praehistorica Leidensia* 54. Leiden: Sidestone Press, pp. 11-18.

# The (Almost Complete) Bibliography of Raymond Corbey

## 1983

Corbey, R.H.A. 1983. "Max Schelers onmachtsthese." *Tijdschrift voor Filosofie* 45, 363-387.

Corbey, R.H.A. 1983. "Vuistbijlen en Cadillacs – Reflecties over het verzamelen." *De Gids* 146, 792-797.

## 1985

Corbey, R.H.A. 1985. "Over de menselijkheid van vroege Hominidae." *Algemeen Nederlands Tijdschrift voor Wijsbegeerte* 77 (2), 65-76.

## 1986

Corbey, R.H.A. 1986. "Plessner, Scheler en de menselijke geest." *Tijdschrift voor Filosofie* 48 (1), 49-65.

## 1987

Struyker Boudier, C.E.M., and R.H.A. Corbey. 1987. "Zur Scheler-Rezeption in den Niederlanden und in Belgien." *Phänomenologische Forschungen* 20, 150-161.

Struyker Boudier, C.E.M., and R.H.A. Corbey. 1987. "Review of 'Uit de ban van de rede: Een confrontatie tussen de cultuur- en kennissociologische visies van Max Scheler en Max Weber', B.E. van Vucht Tijssen, 1985." *Tijdschrift voor Filosofie* 49 (1), 141-142.

## 1988

Corbey, R.H.A. 1988. *De mens een dier? Scheler, Plessner en de crisis van het traditionele mensbeeld*. PhD thesis. Nijmegen: Katholieke Universiteit Nijmegen.

Corbey, R.H.A. 1988. "Alterity: The colonial nude." *Critique of Anthropology* VIII (3): 75-92.

Corbey, R.H.A. 1988. "Aapmensen, mensapen, primitieven." *De Gids* 151 (7-8), 504-513.

## 1989

Corbey, R.H.A. 1989. *Wildheid en beschaving: De Europese verbeelding van Afrika*. Baarn: Ambo.

Corbey, R.H.A. 1989. "Review of 'Schriften aus dem Nachlass (Gesammelte Werke Bd. 3: Philosophische Anthropologie)', M. Scheler, 1987." *Tijdschrift voor Filosofie* 51, 353-354.

## 1990

Corbey, R.H.A. 1990. "Fetisj/rariteit/kunst/artefact: Tribale objecten in westerse context." In *Natuur en cultuur: Beschouwingen op het raakvlak van antropologie en filosofie: Liber amicorum voor Ton Lemaire*, edited by R.H.A. Corbey and P.M.F. van der Grijp, 256-270. Baarn: Ambo.

Corbey, R.H.A., and F. Melssen. 1990. "Paters over Papoea's: Narratio, macht en ideologie in Kaiser Wilhelmsland, 1896-1914." *Antropologische Verkenningen* 9 (1), 11-27.

Corbey, R.H.A., and P. Van der Grijp, eds. 1990. *Natuur en cultuur: Beschouwingen op het raakvlak van antropologie en filosofie: Liber amicorum voor Ton Lemaire.* Baarn: Ambo.

### 1991
Corbey, R.H.A. 1991. "Freud's phylogenetic narrative." In *Alterity, identity, image: Selves and others in society and scholarship.* edited by R.H.A. Corbey and J.T.L. Leerssen, 37-56. Amsterdam/Atlanta: Rodopi.

Corbey, R.H.A. 1991. "Kant als Erblasser der philosophischen Anthropologie." In *The quest for man: The topicality of philosophical anthropology,* edited by J. van Nispen and D. Tiemersma, 21-26. Assen: Koninklijke Van Gorcum.

Corbey, R.H.A. 1991. "Review of 'Op verhaal komen: Over narrativiteit in de mens- en cultuurwetenschappen', F.R. Ankersmit, M.C. Doeser, and A. Kibédi Varga, 1990." *Antropologische Verkenningen* 10 (3), 75-76.

Corbey R.H.A. 1991. "Review of 'Op verhaal komen: Over narrativiteit in de mens- en cultuurwetenschappen', F.R. Ankersmit, M.C. Doeser, and A. Kibédi Varga, 1990." *Algemeen Nederlands Tijdschrift voor Wijsbegeerte* 83 (4), 309-311.

Corbey, R.H.A. 1991. "Review of 'Waarneming en interpretatie: Vergaring en gebruik van etnografische informatie in Nederlands Nieuw-Guinea, 1950-1962', S.R. Jaarsma, 1990." *Antropologische Verkenningen* 10: 75-76.

Corbey, R.H.A and J.T.L. Leerssen, eds. 1991. *Alterity, identity, image: Selves and others in society and scholarship.* Amsterdam/Atlanta: Rodopi.

### 1992
Corbey, R.H.A., and J. Sleutels. 1992. "Darwin, Dilthey and beyond." *Tractrix* 4, 114-125.

### 1993
Corbey, R.H.A. 1993. "Ethnographic Showcases, 1870-1930." *Cultural Anthropology* 8 (3), 338-369.

Corbey, R.H.A. 1993. "Freud et le sauvage." In *Des sciences contre l'homme, Volume II: Au nom du bien,* edited by C. Blanckaert, 83-103. Paris: Autrement.

Corbey, R.H.A. 1993. "Ambiguous Apes." In *The great ape project: Equality beyond humanity,* edited by P. Cavalieri and P. Singer, 126-136. London: Fourth Estate.

Corbey, R.H.A. 1993. "Burgers en wilden: Negentiende-eeuwse interpretaties van cultuur, ras en evolutie." In *Denken over cultuur: Gebruik en misbruik van een concept,* edited by A.J.J. van Breemen, 159-182, Heerlen: Open Universiteit.

Corbey, R.H.A. 1993. "Etnografische verzamelingen: Retoriek en politiek, koloniaal en postkoloniaal." In *Denken over cultuur: Gebruik en misbruik van een concept,* edited by A.J.J. van Breemen, 445-470. Heerlen: Open Universiteit.

Corbey, R.H.A. 1993. "Review of the 'Schriften aus dem Nachlass (Bd. 4: Philosophie und Geschichte)', M. Scheler, 1990." *Tijdschrift voor Filosofie* 55, 353-354.

### 1994
Corbey, R.H.A. 1994. "Gift en transgressie: Kanttekeningen bij Bataille." *Tijdschrift voor Filosofie* 56 (2): 272-312.

Corbey, R.H.A. 1994. "Wie zijn wij? Archeologie en identiteit." *Spiegel Historiael* 29 (7-8), 272-275.

Corbey, R.H.A.1994. "Review of 'Filosofische wegwijzer: Correspondentie van F.J.J. Buytendijk met Helmuth Plessner', H. Struyker Bouddier, 1993." *Tijdschrift voor Filosofie* 56 (1):154-156.

Corbey, R.H.A. and P. Mason. 1994. "Limited company." *Anthrozoös: A Multidisciplinary Journal on The Interaction of People and Animals and Nature* VII (2), 90-102.

### 1995
Corbey, R.H.A. 1995. "Explaining human origins: An archaeological dialogue with Wiktor Stoczkowski." *Archaeological Dialogues* 2 (1), 57-66.

Corbey, R.H.A. 1995. "Ethnographic showcases." In *The decolonization of imagination: Culture, knowledge and power,* edited by J. Nederveen Pieterse and B. Parekh, 57-80. London & New Jersey: Zed Books.

Corbey, R.H.A., and W. Roebroeks. 1995. "Comment on M. Chazan, 'The language hypothesis and lithic analysis'." *Current Anthropology* 36 (5), 759.

Corbey, R.H.A., and B. Theunissen, eds. 1995. *Ape, man, apeman: Changing views since 1600.* Leiden: Leiden University Press.

Corbey, R.H.A., and B. Theunissen. 1995. "Introduction: Missing links, or the ape's place in nature." In *Ape, man, apeman: Changing views since 1600,* edited by R.H.A. Corbey and B. Theunissen, 1-10. Leiden: Leiden University Press.

## 1996

Corbey, R.H.A. 1996. "Roots, backgrounds and contexts of primatology: A bibliographic essay." *Primate Report* 45, 29-44.

Corbey, R.H.A. 1996. "Asmat in Berlin." *Anthropology Today* 12 (3), 21-23.

Corbey, R.H.A. 1996. "De bedreiging van het menselijke monopolie." *Filosofie Magazine* 11 (9), 44-45.

Corbey, R.H.A. 1996. "Aapmens, mensaap, mens." In *Het raadsel in de wetenschap*, edited by F. Cannegieter, 5-8. Leiden: Bureau Studium Generale.

Corbey, R.H.A. 1996. "Review of the 'Helmuth Plessner oder die verkörperte Philosophie', H. Redeker, 1993." *Algemeen Nederlands Tijdschrift voor Wijsbegeerte* 88 (1), 73-76.

Corbey, R.H.A. 1996. "Review of 'Les frères ennemis: René Caillois et Claude Lévi-Strauss', M. Panoff, 1996." *Journal of the Royal Anthropological Institute* 2 (1), 178.

## 1997

Corbey, R.H.A. 1997. "De prehistorie van het menselijk samenleven." *Facta: Sociaal Wetenschappelijk Magazine* 5 (7), 2-6.

Corbey, R.H.A. 1997. "Beschaving is meer dan mes en vork: De civilisatietheorie van Norbert Elias." *NRC Handelsblad*, 8 November 1997.

Corbey, R.H.A. 1997. "Inventaire et surveillance: l'Appropriation de la nature à travers l'histoire naturelle." In *Le Museum au premier siècle de son existence*, edited by C. Blanckaert, 541-557. Paris: Muséum d'Histoire Naturelle.

Corbey, R.H.A., and W. Roebroeks. 1997. "Ancient minds." *Current Anthropology* 38 (4), 917-921.

## 1998

Corbey, R.H.A. 1998. "Theoretische Probleme zur Kognition, Sprache und Gesellschaft bei frühen Hominiden." *Ethnographisch-Archäologische Zeitschrift* 39, 321-333.

Corbey, R.H.A. 1998. "De l'histoire naturelle à l'histoire humaine: Comment conceptualiser les origines de la culture?" In *La culture est-elle naturelle? Histoire, épistémologie et applications récentes du concept de culture*, edited by A. Ducros, J. Ducros and F. Joulian, 223-238. Paris: Éditions Errance.

Corbey, R.H.A. 1998. "Review of 'Heidegger en de wereld van het dier', B. Blans and S. Lijmbach, 1998." *Algemeen Nederlands Tijdschrift voor Wijsbegeerte* 90 (2), 158-159.

## 1999

Corbey, R.H.A. 1999. "African art in Brussels." *Anthropology Today* 15 (6), 11-16.

Corbey, R.H.A. 1999. "Archeologie en filosofie: Conceptuele problemen met betrekking tot cognitie, taal en cultuur bij vroege hominiden." *Algemeen Nederlands Tijdschrift voor Wijsbegeerte* 91 (2), 95-111.

Corbey, R.H.A. 1999. "Periodisations and double standards in the study of the Palaeolithic." In *Hunters of the Golden Age: The Mid-Upper Palaeolithic of Eurasia, 30.000-20.000 BP*, edited by W. Roebroeks, M. Mussi, J. Svoboda and K. Fennema, 77-86. Leiden: Sidestone Press (Analecta Praehistorica Leidensia 31).

## 2000

Corbey, R.H.A. 2000. *Tribal art traffic: a chronicle of taste, trade and desire in colonial and post-colonial times*. Amsterdam: Royal Tropical Institute.

Corbey, R.H.A. 2000. "Arts premiers in the Louvre." *Anthropology Today* 16 (4), 3-6.

Corbey, R.H.A. 2000. "Musée Chirac: Het Louvre toont uitheemse kunst." *De Volkskrant*, 20 April 2000.

Corbey, R.H.A. 2000. "On becoming human: Mauss, the gift and social origins." In *Gifts and interests*, edited by A. Vandevelde, 157-174. Leuven: Peeters.

Corbey, R.H.A. 2000. "Review of 'Interculturele communicatie en multiculturalisme: Enige filosofische voorbemerkingen', J. van Brakel, 2000, and 'Culturen bestaan niet: Het onderzoek van interculturaliteit als het openbreken van vanzelfsprekendheden', W.J.M. van Binsbergen, 1999." *Algemeen Nederlands Tijdschrift voor Wijsbegeerte* 92 (1), 112-113.

## 2001

Corbey, R.H.A. 2001. "ExitCongoMuseum: The travels of Congolese Art." *Anthropology Today* 17 (3), 26-28.

Corbey, R.H.A. 2001. "Un bouclier Trobriandais un Westphalie." *Tribal* VI (5), 132-133.

Corbey, R.H.A. 2001. "Apes might well be self-conscious, free agents and more like us than we might think." In *New and old world philosophy: Introductory readings*, edited by V. Luizzi and L. McKinney, 47-51. Hoboken: Prentice Hall.

Corbey, R.H.A., 2001. "Negotiating the ape-human boundary." In *Great apes and humans: The ethics of coexistence*, edited by B. Beck, A. Arluke and E.F. Stevens, 91-103. Washington: Smithsonian Institution Press.

Corbey, R.H.A. 2001. "Tijger, varken, baviaan: Mens-dier relaties in (inter-) cultureel perspectief. [Review of 'Het verbond met de tijger: Visies op mensetende dieren in Kerinci, Sumatra', J. Bakels, 2000]." *De Academische Boekengids* (27), 7-8.

Corbey, R.H.A., and J.W.M. Roebroeks, eds. 2001. *Studying Human Origins: Disciplinary history and epistemology*. Amsterdam: Amsterdam University Press.

Corbey, R.H.A., and W. Roebroeks. 2001. "Does disciplinary history matter? An introduction." In *Studying human origins: Disciplinary history and epistemology*, edited by R.H.A. Corbey and J.W.M. Roebroeks, 1-7. Amsterdam: Amsterdam University Press.

Corbey, R.H.A., and W. Roebroeks. 2001. "Biases and double standards in palaeoanthropology." In *Studying human origins: Disciplinary history and epistemology*, edited by R.H.A. Corbey and J.W.M. Roebroeks, 67-76. Amsterdam: Amsterdam University Press.

## 2002

Corbey, R.H.A. 2002. "Objects-in-motion: Collectors, dealers, missionaries and artists." In *Tales from academia: History of Anthropology in the Netherlands*, edited by H. Vermeulen and J. Kommers, 995-1014. Saarbrücken: Verlag für Entwicklungspolitik (Nijmegen Studies in Development and Cultural Change).

Corbey, R.H.A. 2002. "From Lake Toba to Lake Sentani." In *Treasure hunting? Collectors and collections of Indonesian artefacts*, edited by R. Schefold and H. Vermeulen, 289-301. Leiden: Research School of Asian, African and Amerindian Studies (Medelingen van het Rijksmuseum voor Volkenkunde).

Corbey, R.H.A. 2002. "Image breaking on the Christian frontier." In *Iconclash: Beyond the Image Wars in Science, Religion and Art*, edited by B. Latour and P. Weibel, 69-71. Cambridge: Centre for Art and Media.

Corbey, R.H.A. 2002. "Vitrines ethnographiques : Le récit et le regard." In *Zoos humains, XIXe et XXe siècles*, edited by N. Bancel, 90-98. Paris: Éditions la Découverte.

Corbey, R.H.A. 2002. "Naäpen bij mensapen. [Review of the 'The ape and the sushi master', F. de Waal, 2001]." *De Academische Boekengids* (32), 4-6.

Corbey, R.H.A. 2002. "Review of 'Hunting the Gatherers: Ethnographic Collectors, Agents, and Agency in Melanesia 1870s-1930s', edited by M. O'Hanlon and R. Welsch, 2001." *Bijdragen tot de Taal-, Land- en Volkenkunde* 158, 104-105.

## 2003

Corbey, R.H.A. 2003. "Destroying the graven image: Religious iconoclasm on the Christian frontier." *Anthropology Today* 19 (4), 10-14.

Corbey, R.H.A. 2003. "Vetrine ethnografiche: Il racconto e lo sguardo." In *Zoo Umani: Dalla Venere ottentotta ai reality show*, edited by S. Lemaire, *et al.* 81-90. Verona: Ombro Corte.

Corbey, R.H.A. 2003. "Het '*Homo symbolicus*' mensbeeld in de culturele antropologie." In *Denken over cultuur*, edited by P. van Zilfhout, 279-304. Heerlen: Open Universiteit.

Corbey, R.H.A. 2003. "Iconoclasm and conversion: Ritual riddance on the Christian frontier." In *Verhandelingen KITLV*, edited by G. Persoon and P. Nas, 113-132. Leiden: KITLV.

Corbey, R.H.A. 2003. "Review of 'The ape and the sushi master', F. de Waal, 2001." *International Studies in the Philosophy of Science* 17 (1), 103-106.

Corbey, R.H.A. 2003. "Darwin voor de socioloog [Review of 'The blank slate: The modern denial of human nature', S. Pinker, 2002; 'Why some apes became human: Competition consciousness and culture', P. Slurink, 2002; 'Genes, memes and human history: Darwinian archaeology and cultural evolution', S. Shennan, 2002; 'Voorbij het rationele model: Evolutionaire verklaringen van gedrag en sociaal-economische instituties, J. van den Bergh and D. Fetchenhauer, 2001; and 'Culturele vernieuwing en de grondslagen van de geesteswetenschappen', G.H. de Vries, 2002]." *De Academische Boekengids* (40), 14-15.

## 2004

Corbey, R.H.A. 2004. "The authenticity of Kamoro and Asmat art" *Tribal Art* 35 (Summer), 72-75.

Corbey, R.H.A. 2004. "Neandertal e Cro-Magnon: Due pesi e due misure?" *Il Bollettino di Clio* 92 (15), 37-44.

Corbey, R.H.A. 2004. "Review of 'Why some apes became humans: Competition, consciousness and culture', P. Slurink, 2002." *Algemeen Nederlands Tijdschrift voor Wijsbegeerte* 96 (2): 162-163.

Corbey, R.H.A., R. Layton, and J. Tanner. 2004. "Archaeology and art." In *A companion to archaeology*, edited by J. Bintliff, 357-379. London/ New York: Blackwell.

2005

Corbey, R.H.A. 2005. *The metaphysics of apes: Negotiating the animal-human boundary.* Cambridge: Cambridge University Press.

Corbey, R.H.A. 2005. "Snelnaam en doopnaam, of de ambivalentie van de vooruitgang bij de Marind Anim." *Durante Magazine* 1, 40-42.

Corbey, R.H.A. 2004. "The authenticity of Kamoro and Asmat art." *Tribal* 35 (Summer), 72-75.

Corbey, R.H.A. 2005. "*Homo reciprocans*: Hoe uitwisseling de samenleving constitueert [Review of 'Engendering Objects: Barkcloth and the dynamics of identity in Papua New Guinea', A.-K. Hermkens, 2005; and 'Social solidarity and the gift', A.E. Komter, 2005]." *De Academische Boekengids* 53 (November), 9-10.

2006

Corbey, R.H.A. 2006. "Laying aside the spear: Hobbesian w a r r e and the Maussian gift." In *Warfare and society: Archaeological and Social Anthropological Perspectives*, edited by T. Otto, H. Thrane and H. Vandkilde, 29-36. Aarhus: Aarhus University Press.

Corbey, R.H.A. 2006. "Gorillas as Others." *Gorilla Journal* 32, 23-24.

Corbey, R.H.A. 2006. "Doden doet leven: De kunst van mammoetsteppe en regenwoud in biologisch perspectief [Review of 'Iban art: Sexual selection and severed heads', M. Hepell and L.A. Melaka, 2006; and 'The nature of paleolitic art', D. Guthrie, 2005]." *De Academische Boekengids* 59 (November), 22-23.

Corbey, R.H.A. 2006. *Homo reciprocans: Mauss, Hobbes en Darwin.* Leiden: Leiden University, Inaugural Lecture.

2007

Corbey, R.H.A. 2007. *Snellen om namen: De Marind Anim van New Guinea door de ogen van de Missionarissen van het Heilig Hart, 1905-1925.* Leiden: KITLV, Koninklijk Instituut voor Taal-, Land-, en Volkenkunde.

Corbey, R.H.A. 2007. "Cultural Heritage: Trade." In *New Encyclopedia of Africa*, edited by J. Middleton and J.C. Miller, 458-461. New York: Charles Scribner's Sons and Thomson Gale.

Corbey, R.H.A. 2007. "Anthropology." In *Imagology: The Cultural Construction and Literary Representation of National Characters – A Critical Survey*, edited by M. Beller and J. Leerssen, 98 – 108. Amsterdam: Rodopi.

Corbey, R.H.A. 2007. "Menschen, Menschenaffen, Affenmenschen." In *Tierrechte – Menschenpflichten*, edited by Heidelberg Interdisziplinäre Arbeitsgemeinschaft für Tierethik, 64-70. Erlangen: Harald Fischer Verlag.

Corbey, R.H.A. 2007. "Bilderwelten, Mischwesen, Metamorphosen." In *Ganz Alt: Wie bunt war die Vergangenheit wirklich? Die Archäologie des Eiszeitalters*, edited by S. Gaudzinski-Windheuser, R. Hoefer and O. Jöris, 12-13. Mainz: Verlag des Römisch-Germanischen Zentralmuseums.

Corbey, R.H.A. 2007. "Comment on 'The once and future "apeman"'." *Current Anthropology* 48 (5), 645-646.

Corbey, R.H.A. 2007. "Review of 'Evolutionair denken: De invloed van Darwin op ons wereldbeeld', C. Buskes, 2005." *Algemeen Nederlands Tijdschrift voor Wijsbegeerte* 99 (2), 165-166.

Corbey, R.H.A. 2007. "De mens werd een heerser, of: Stop fout vlees." *Trouw*, 13 April 2007.

Corbey, R.H.A., and W. Roebroeks. 2007. "From shell beads to syntax [Conference report of 'The Cradle of Language', University of Stellenbosch, November 2006]." *Anthropology Today* 23 (4), 24-26.

2008

Corbey, R.H.A. 2008. *Metafisiche delle scimmie: Negoziando il confine animali-umani.* Torino: Bollati Boringhieri.

Corbey, R.H.A. 2008. "Marcel Mauss." In *Kritisch Denkerslexicon*, edited by J. Sperna Weiland and H. Achterhuis, 1-14. Diemen: Veen.

Corbey, R.H.A. 2008. "Honderdduizend doden." In *Tijdreizigers: Op zoek naar archeologische sensatie*, edited by L. Amkreutz and A. Willemse, 24-25. Leiden: Rijksmuseum van Oudheden.

Corbey, R.H.A. 2008. "Ethnographic showcases." In *Human Zoos: Science and spectacle in the age of colonial empires*, edited P. Blanchard and T. Bridgeman, 95-103. Liverpool: Liverpool University Press.

Amkreutz, L., and R.H.A. Corbey. 2008. "An eagle-eyed perspective. *Haliaetus albicilla* in the Mesolithic and Neolithic of the Lower Rhine Area." In *Between Foraging and Farming: an extended broad spectrum of papers presented to Leendert Louwe Kooijmans*, edited by H. Fokkens, B. Coles, A. van Gijn, J. Kleijne, H. Ponjee and C. Slappendel, 167-180. Leiden University, Faculty of Archeology (Analecta Praehistorica Leidensia 40).

*2009*

Corbey, R.H.A. 2009. "The folk zoology of Southeast Asian wildmen [Review of 'Images of the wildman in Southeast Asia. An anthropological perspective', G. Forth, 2008]." *The Newsletter – International Institute for Asian Studies* 2009 (52), 31.

Corbey, R.H.A. 2009. "Natuurlijke historie als exploratie en exploitatie." In *De exotische mens: Andere culturen als amusement*, edited by A.P. Sliggers, 67-76. Tielt: Lannoo.

Roebroeks, J.W.M., and R.H.A. Corbey. 2009. "Review of 'Axe age: Acheulian tool-making from quarry to discard', N. Goren-Inbar and G. Sharon, 2006." *Lithic Technology* 34 (1), 53-59.

*2010*

Corbey, R.H.A. 2010. ""Thou shall have no other Gods before me!": Iconoclasm on the Christian frontier." In *Christianity in Indonesia*, edited by S. Schroter, 159-174. Münster: LIT Verlag.

Corbey, R.H.A. 2010. "Etno-esthetica tussen geestes- en levenswetenschappen." *Dante Magazine* 2 (2), 4-5.

Corbey, R.H.A. 2010. "De mens blijft verborgen: Helmut Plessner laveerde tussen Kant en Darwin. [Review of 'Philosophische Anthropologie: Eine Denkrichtung des 20. Jahrhunderts', J. Fischer, 2008; 'Nachgeholtes Leben, Helmuth Plessner 1892-1985', C. Dietze, 2006; 'Philosophische Anthropologie als Grundlagenwissenschaft? Vergleichende Studiën zur Aufgabe der Philosophischen Anthropologie bei Max Scheler und Helmuth Plessner', P. Wilwert, 2009; 'Philosophische Anthropologie im Aufbruch: Max Scheler und Helmuth Plessner im Vergleich', R. Becker and J. Fischer, 2009; and 'Natur und Geschichte: Helmuth Plessners in sich gebrochene Lebensphilosophie', O. Mitscherlich, 2007]." *De Academische Boekengids* 79, 9-11.

Corbey, R.H.A. 2010. *Headhunters from the swamps: The Marind Anim of New Guinea as seen by the Missionaries of the Sacred Heart, 1905-1925.* Leiden: KITLV.

*2011*

Corbey R.H.A. (2011), "Woeker en verbijstering." In *Th.C.W. Oudemans 60*, edited by H. van Kampen and T.E. Jaroszek, 64-66. Leiden: Wallenbeeks Nieuwsbrief.

Corbey, R.H.A., and A. Jagich. 2011. "Acheulean." In *Wiley-Blackwell encyclopedia of human evolution*, 5-6. Chichester: Wiley-Blackwell.

Corbey, R.H.A., and A.A.A. Mol. 2011. "'By weapons made worthy': a Darwinian perspective on Beowulf." In *Creating consilience: Integrating the sciences and the humanities* edited by M. Collard and E. Slingerland, 342-367. Oxford: Oxford University Press.

Corbey, R.H.A., and N. Stanley. 2011. "The Asmat Art project / Proyek Kesenian Asmat" In *Asmat: arts, crafts and people: a photographic diary, 1969-1974*, edited by J. Hoogerbrugge, 6-21. Leiden: C. Zwartenkot Art Books.

*2012*

Corbey, R.H.A. 2012. "*Homo habilis*' humanness: Phillip Tobias as a philosopher." *History and Philosophy of the Life Sciences* 33, 103-116.

Corbey, R.H.A. 2012. "Ethnograpische Schaukästen: Multimediale Erzählmuster." In *MenschenZoos*, edited by P. Blanchard, N. Bancel, M. Boëtsch, E. Deroo and S. Lemaire, 117-135. Hamburg: Les Éditions du Crieur Public.

Corbey, R.H.A. 2012. "'Aping humans' en 'minding animals'." *De Academische Boekengids* 93, 6-8.

*2013*

Corbey, R.H.A. 2013. "Habermas, Jürgen." In *Theory in social and cultural anthropology: An encyclopedia*, edited by R.L. Warms and R.J. McGee, 371 – 374. Sage: Thousand Oaks.

Corbey, R.H.A. 2013. "Ethnographic showcases, 1870-1930." In *SAGE Benchmarks in Social Research Methods*, edited by B. Smart, K. Peggs and J. Burridge, 338-369. Sage: Thousand Oaks.

Corbey, R.H.A. and A. Lanjouw, eds. 2013. *The politics of species: Reshaping our relationships with other animals*. Cambridge: Cambridge University Press.

Corbey, R.H.A. 2013. ""Race" and "species" in the post-World War II United Nations discourse on human rights." In *The Politics of Species: Reshaping our Relationships with Other Animals*, edited by R.H.A. Corbey and A. Lanjouw, 67-76. Cambridge: Cambridge University Press.

Corbey, R.H.A. and A. Lanjouw. 2013. "Between exploitation and respectful coexistence." In *The politics of species: Reshaping our relationships with other animals* edited by R.H.A. Corbey and A. Lanjouw, 1-16. Cambridge: Cambridge University Press.

## 2014

Corbey, R.H.A. 2014. "Crows and jays [Review of 'The Accidental Species: Misunderstandings of Human Evolution', H. Gee, 2013, and 'The Gap: The Science of What Separates Us from Other Animals', T. Suddendorf, 2013]." *The Times Literary Supplement* 2014 (5799).

## 2015

Corbey R.H.A. 2015. "Review of 'Aap zoekt zin: Waarom wij bewustzijn, vrije wil, moraal en religie hebben', P. Slurink, 2015; and 'The hermeneutic niche: Language within Darwinism', M. in 't Veld, 2015." *Algemeen Nederlands Tijdschrift voor Wijsbegeerte* 107 (4), 466-469.

Corbey, R.H.A, and K. Weener. 2015. "Collecting while converting." *Journal of Art Historiography* 12 (June): Article 12/RCFW1.

Corbey, R.H.A., and W. van Damme, eds. 2015. "Special issue: The European scholarly reception of 'primitive art' in the decades around 1900." *Journal of Art Historiography* 12 (June 2015).

Corbey, R.H.A., and W. van Damme. 2015. "Introduction: European encounters with 'primitive art' during the late nineteenth century." *Journal of Art Historiography* 12, Article 12/vDC1.

## 2016

Corbey, R.H.A. 2016. *Of jars and gongs: Two keys to Ot Danum Dayak cosmology*. Leiden: C. Zwartenkot Art Books.

Corbey, R.H.A., A. Jagich, K. Vaesen, and M. Collard. 2016. "The acheulean handaxe: More like a bird's song than a beatles' tune?" *Evolutionary Anthropology: Issues, News, and Reviews* 25 (1), 6-19.

## 2017

Corbey, R.H.A. 2017. *Raja Ampat ritual art: Spirit priests and ancestor cults in New Guinea's far West*. Leiden: C. Zwartenkot Art Books.

Corbey, R.H.A. 2017. "Review of 'A history of anthropology as a holistic science', G. Custred, 2016." *Anthropos* 2017 (112), 660-661.

## 2018

Corbey R.H.A. 2018. *Jurookng: Shamanic amulets from Southeast Borneo*. Leiden: C. Zwartenkot Art Books.

## 2019

Corbey, R.H.A. 2019. *Korwar: Northwest New Guinea ritual art according to missionary sources*. Leiden: C. Zwartenkot Art Books.

Corbey, R.H.A. 2019. "Wilfried van Damme: Kunsthistoricus en antropoloog." *VVE Jaarboek (Vereniging Vrienden van Etnografica)* 7, 20-27.

## 2020

Corbey, R.H.A. 2020. "Baldwin effects in early stone tools." *Evolutionary Anthropology: Issues, News, and Reviews* 29 (5), 237-244.

Corbey, R.H.A. 2020. "Snelnaam en doopnaam bij de Marind-Anim van Nieuw-Guinea." *Tribale Kunst en Cultuur* 2020, 8-13.

## 2021

Corbey R.H.A. 2021. "Foreword." In *The dialectical primatologist: the past, present and future of life in the hominoid niche*, edited by N. Malone, v-ix. Abingdon: Routledge.

## 2022

Corbey R.H.A. 2022. "Foreword." In *World archaeoprimatology: interconnections of humans and non-human primates in the past*, edited by B. Urbani, D. Youlatos and A. Antczak, xvii-xix Cambridge: Cambridge University Press.

## 2024

Corbey, R.H.A. 2024. *Death and display: Kuba funerary art from the Congo River Basin*. Leiden: Sidestone Press.

Corbey, R.H.A. 2024. "Negeren filosofen de prehistorie? Een reactie." *Algemeen Nederlands Tijdschrift voor Wijsbegeerte* 116 (4), 407-414.

In Hussain, S.T. and G.L. Dusseldorp (eds) 2025. Sitting on the fence: Negotiating archaeology, anthropology and philosophy. Festschrift for Prof. Dr Raymond H.A. Corbey in celebration of his 70th birthday. *Analecta Praehistorica Leidensia* 54. Leiden: Sidestone Press, pp. 19-28.

# Towards an archaeology of an epistemologist's epistemology

Wil Roebroeks

ABSTRACT

This contribution presents some time-ravaged personal memories from and reflections on more than four decades of interactions with the Festschrift's "target" – from our first encounter in the late 1970s to the present. The philosopher was an observer from the very beginning. He apparently feels most comfortable "on the fence", observing the empirical work of others, including his archaeology colleagues in field- and laboratory work, and commenting on the theory-ladenness and the implicit assumptions underlying their observations. He proves to be very consistent in his various passions, centered around (indeed) fence sitting, identifying the construction and role of "boundaries" (human-animal/sapiens-Neanderthal) through time, studying their underlying values and exploring the many beauties, hauntings, and mysteries of handaxes and tribal art. The contribution provides some (admittedly: half-baked) building stones for an archaeology of the epistemological *Werdegang* of this epistemologist.

*Keywords: Philosophy of science, history of archaeology, epistemology, Palaeolithic, handaxes, tribal art*

INTRODUCTION

Around 1978, a very energetic philosophy student – Raymond Corbey – burst into my student digs on the Professor Bromstraat in Nijmegen, notified by a mutual acquaintance – the (in the Netherlands famous) amateur-archaeologist Ad Wouters (1917-2001) from nearby Lent – that there was another Palaeolithic afficionado in Nijmegen, namely me. And this one was living in the same student housing complex as the young philosopher; so, he immediately had taken action.

We proved to be very different kinds of students. Already then, Raymond was an ultra-intellectual wide-ranging book devourer, studying philosophy, cultural anthropology, and, for a short period also psychology. In contrast, I was a (admittedly: dedicated) student of social-economic history, heavily engaged in the 1970s political activities in Nijmegen (aptly nicknamed then "Havana on the Waal"), whereas Raymond showed very little interest at all in the student movement nor its various by-products (strange music and squats) that I was deeply involved in. Already by that time, he was a sort of distanced observer, an early fence sitter, staying away from any political involvement.

Despite our differences, we connected from the beginning because of our common interests, which were heavily centered on cultural anthropology, geology, and Palaeolithic archaeology. The latter two I kept mostly on a slow burner in my early university years in Nijmegen. Born close to the Neolithic flint mines of Ryckholt-Sint Geertruid, I had collected flint artifacts (including a few handaxes)

**Wil Roebroeks**
Faculty of Archaeology, Leiden University, The Netherlands
w.roebroeks@arch.leidenuniv.nl
ORCID 0000-0002-5075-6899

near my home in southern Limburg in my early teens, and as a high school student I participated in the excavations of the Ryckholt mines. In his teens, Raymond also had collected fossils and flint artefacts in the chalk region where I grew up; though he was from a bit further north, just north of the *Feldbiss* fault. Raymond was a keen member of the *Netherlands Geological Society*, in which some of the Ryckholt excavation team members were active, such as the Felder brothers, two well-known geologists in the Limburg area (Jagt *et al.* 2011). He even visited the Ryckholt excavations in the early 1970s, so we may have crossed paths before we really met in person in Nijmegen; he visiting, me excavating – a familiar and recurrent theme in our relationship, as illustrated by what follows.

My first Nijmegen encounter with Raymond was soon followed by many informal Palaeolithic archaeology "tutorials": in-depth stone artefact identification and description sessions in his student room. With Francois Bordes' *Typologie du paléolithique ancien et moyen* always close at hand, the two of us doggedly studied original French Palaeolithic material that Raymond had amassed through his remarkably extensive social network of amateur archaeologists. We focused on typology, technology, and surface modifications, highly aware of the possibility of encountering "faked pieces" – triggered by the so-called Vermaning-affair, centered on a possible forgery of Middle Palaeolithic stone tools in the northern Netherlands (*e.g.*, Stapert 1986; de Vries *et al.* 2022). We also used to discuss in great detail lithic objects recovered from various parts in the Netherlands by amateur-archaeologists, interpreted as testifying to the existence of an early Pleistocene "Chopper-Chopping tool-complex". In our view these objects were simply "geofacts", produced by natural processes and very similar to flint pieces central in the late 19th century "eolith" debates. We regularly embarked on fieldtrips to geological exposures where such objects could be found in large numbers, *e.g.*, in the Lunteren Quarry within the ice pushed ridges of the central Netherlands or in Tertiary sediments in southern Limburg and its immediate surrounding Belgian and German areas.

It was while writing this short "personal reflection" piece that I came to fully realize that my late 1970s archaeology interactions with Raymond were instrumental in rekindling my own interest in the Palaeolithic, and thus, in retrospect, were key in my decision, after graduating in history, to return to my high school interests, instead of continuing my academic journey in social-economic history. I decided to dive deeper into Palaeolithic archaeology, an excitingly broad field at the interface of geology, archaeology, biology, and cultural anthropology, and holding the promise of extensive fieldwork activities. I thus enrolled for a second MA (in Leiden) and in parallel set up my own fieldwork project in the southern Netherlands, under the supervision of Leiden Professor Pieter Modderman and supported by the *State Geological Survey*, where several of my former co-flint miners worked.

## LOESS HEAPS AND GRAVEL QUARRIES

When I moved to Maastricht in 1980 to carry out my PhD research fieldwork, the project soon hit Palaeolithic gold at the Maastricht-Belvédère loess and gravel quarry, when the geologist Werner Felder, my tutor in the Ryckholt excavations, discovered the first flint artifacts in the exposures there late in the year 1980. Raymond became a regular visitor of the year-round excavations conducted in the pit between 1981 and 1989. Our professional observer, however, never even once held a trowel in his hands, despite his many visits, as he jokingly admitted himself in a 2020 interview:

*"Already during Roebroeks' 1980s fieldwork in a quarry near Maastricht I used to sit on a heap of loess, smoking cigars, observing, joking, instead of digging. Some found this amusing, others thought I was a lazy nuisance" (Leiden University, 2020).*

I indeed assume that no future archaeologist will be able to retrieve his DNA from a trowel or any other excavation gear that survives from the Maastricht-Belvédère project to "prove" his attendance, despite the recent progress made in such forensic investigations (see *e.g.*, Essel *et al.* 2023).

From my Maastricht base, we undertook several long-weekend visits to the famous Aisne Valley in northern France, a three and a half hours' drive from Maastricht, where small-scale gravel quarrying had exposed thousands of Lower and Middle Palaeolithic stone tools, including beautiful Acheulean handaxes that quarry workers collected in massive numbers (Kelley and Joulie 1961; Tuffreau 1982; figure 1). Visiting these quarries and inspecting the handaxe collections of the workers there in the early 1980s, I witnessed the philosopher's strong passion and fascination for these objects. I admit that some of the

Figure 1. A postcard picture of a gravel pit in Raymond Corbey's beloved Aisne Valley (northern France), early 20th century. The postcard was stamped a few weeks after the beginning of World War 1, and two weeks before the Battle of the Aisne valley commenced, which led to a four year-long trench warfare in the area, the unfathomable massive loss of human lives, and to the terrible devastation of this part of France.

Aisne valley handaxes were very impressive artefacts indeed, occasionally reaching extraordinarily large dimensions and often testifying to high levels of craftmanship: "beautiful" objects, which now, four decades later, are regularly offered for sale by art dealers at the Maastricht TEFAF art fair. Raymond's *"amour de l'objet"* also entailed long, persistent, and often emphatic reflections about the significance of these early stone tools as "fossilized" intentions and proxies for past hominin cognition, which, more than 30 years later, would resurface as the core subject of one of his most successful papers (Corbey *et al.* 2016).

Our discussions about and disagreements on such shared interests proved to be formative for us both, or at least for me. Debating various schools and viewpoints in the philosophy of science, the value of accuracy in describing archaeological phenomena, to take nothing for granted and keep pressing for the basic questions, while at the same time acknowledging the importance of Hilary Putnam's (1981) "internal realism" and the theory-ladenness of all observation. In the late 1970s, Raymond had gotten me in touch with the cultural anthropologist Ton Lemaire, himself an avid collector of flint artefacts. In his work, popular amongst Nijmegen students in the late 1970s, Lemaire argued that in Western thinking, "distant" people had often functioned as a kind of projection screen – a "foil" – upon which Western discontent with their own cultures, nostalgia, and our ingrained ideologies of superiority had been projected. Archaeology,

we surmised, to some degree at least, operated in a comparable way, with interpretations of the sparse archaeological record adding a substantial time dimension to this issue of "distance". We agreed that archaeological deep-time narratives often reflected the archaeologist's own preoccupations and mirrored broader historical conditions, often more than that they informed about life in the past.

## TRIBAL ART AFICIONADOS

Our shared interest in material culture was not limited to Palaeolithic stone tools: from Raymond's general cultural anthropological background and my own readings of (mainly: hunter-gatherer) ethnographies, we gradually developed a strong interest in the more recent and dazzlingly rich material cultures of various populations in Africa (Raymond) and Oceania (both of us). Contacts with museum curators such as Dirk Smidt at Leiden, and especially with former missionaries in these areas and the collections they had established in the Netherlands and elsewhere were instrumental for developing hands-on experience, getting in touch with the "real stuff", and developing our own expertise. Raymond's connections with the *Missionaries of the Sacred Heart* (MSC) at Tilburg, who provided us access to their archives and to their collections, proved to be invaluable here. And (almost literally): blessed by these contacts, we got in touch with other collectors, for instance the New Guinea veteran Jac Hoogerbrugge who would become a close friend of both of us, and whom Raymond would decades later help to produce

Figure 2. Raymond Corbey (left) and Gerard Zegwaard MSC, summer 1995, discussing the meaning of the decoration on a 1950s fighting shield from Atsj, in the Asmat area of western New Guinea.

Figure 3. Raymond Corbey (left) and the author in Berlin visiting the Asmat exhibition in the *Museum für Völkerkunde* in 1995 (see: Corbey 1996).

a voluminous book on his ethnographic work and his famous Asmat collection (Hoogerbrugge 2011).

The various interactions with these fascinating people and their object collections proved to be a catalyst for continuing debates about the (im) possibilities of assigning "meaning" to prehistoric artefacts: the bewildering variety both in "tribal art" and in the "meaning" assigned to material culture, possibly only a bleak remainder of the cultural diversity that once existed in the past, minimally called for great care when using archaeological data to make inferences about cultural or symbolic dimensions of past human behaviour. To illustrate this thorny issue and confront it with our Leiden students in a class on Upper Palaeolithic art, Raymond and me once invited Gerard Zegwaard MSC (1919-1996) (figure 2), a missionary who had lived with the Asmat people of south-west New Guinea in the 1950s. Zegwaard had documented their cosmology, including their "headhunting" practices (Zegwaard 1959), collected their material culture for several museums and had extensive field notes about the various meanings of the decorations on the objects he collected. He was the ideal person to discuss the problems encountered when trying to assign meaning to objects when one is no longer able to directly interact with their original producers and users, as with Palaeolithic art. However, the bulk of the problem, as we quickly learned, would not even disappear when one could actually live with and talk to the objects' original producers and owners and ask them directly, as vividly illustrated by the discussion generated around the Asmat art objects that Zegwaard brought into the class.

In recent years, Raymond has embarked on a research and publication trajectory which may be taken to suggest that his strongest passion is indeed the study of ethnographic "art" objects. His work on various books on "tribal art" from Indonesia and New Guinea (*e.g.*, Corbey 2016; 2017; 2018; 2019) clearly testifies to his love for these artefacts and their former ritual contexts. These publications illustrate his fascination for how they moved from their original cultural settings in often complicated ways to European museums abroad and Western collectors (Corbey 2000), and currently how many of them return to their areas of origin through repatriation measures.

The speed at which he has been producing these books and the almost visceral attention to large numbers of high-quality full color illustrations of the study objects included in them, are in my view a clear symptom of what motivates his current research: a passionate interest in a recent past full of "unspoiled" distant cultures and their cosmologies and how these changed through time. In this past, "tribal art" objects were vibrantly alive and central in rituals and everyday life. His recent work moves on to highlight the role of colonial governments in the destruction of these societies, the often-ambiguous role of missionaries, some intentionally destroying "heathen" objects in the wake of attempts to destroy the belief systems in which they operated, others making careful efforts to document, save, and collect them. In more general terms, Raymond is documenting the many ways in which these objects came to be into the possession of museums, dealers, and collectors, and how they played a role in Western visions of "the other". His voluminous *Korwar: Northwest New Guinea ritual art according to missionary sources*" provides a good example of this fascination and vigorously showcases his signature "brand" (figure 4), well summarized and qualified in a review by French anthropologist Pierre Lemonnier:

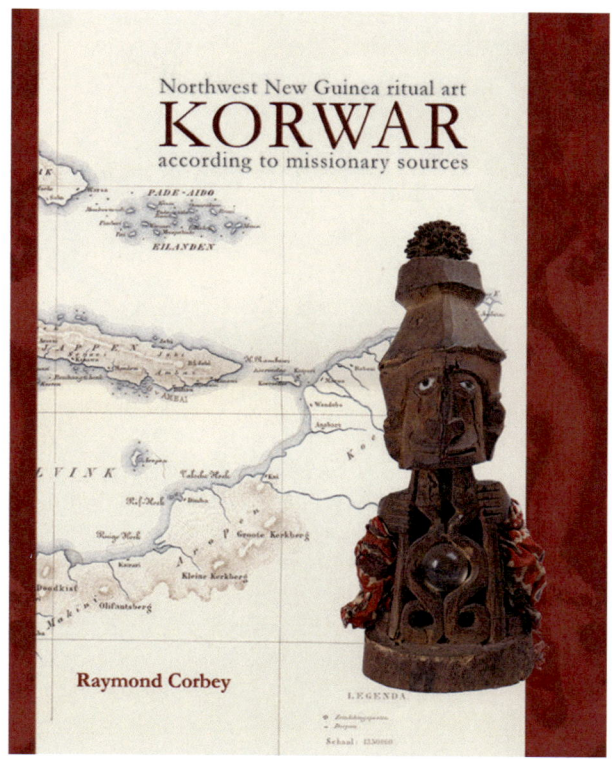

Figure 4. A "korwar" ancestor sculpture from Northwest New Guinea, as displayed on the cover of Raymond's 2019 book on the topic (Corbey 2019).

"[...] *Korwar is a beautiful piece of work, consisting of a mixture of the author's three preferred themes of study: the art and the material culture of west New Guinea, formerly under Dutch colonial rule – but since annexed by Indonesia under the name Papua Barat (West Papua); the ancient ethnography of its populations; and with a focus on the role of missions in the second half of the nineteenth century and the first decades of the twentieth, catholics in the south of the island (Corbey 2010), protestants on the north coast, as in the Geelvink Bay, the area at stake in this volume," Lemonnier (2022; translation WR).*

### LEIDEN PIONIER PROJECT YEARS: 1994-1999

In 1983 I had obtained a part-time lecturer position at the *Instituut voor Prehistorie* in Leiden, headed by Modderman's successor Professor Leendert Louwe Kooijmans, while Raymond became a lecturer at the Department of Philosophy at Tilburg University, as a self-declared "anthropologist" amongst philosophers. In 1994, Tilburg University "lent him out" to my

N.W.O.-funded so-called PIONIER project ("Changing Views of Ice Age Foragers"), on a part-time 5-year "lease". The project was to focus on the Pleistocene occupation history of Europe, and both empirically grounded and epistemologically informed: one part of the project was explicitly addressing the fact that many of the debates in palaeoanthropology seemed more steered by (usually implicit) assumptions than by empirical data. In the spirit of what Ernst Mayr had called "Problematic histories", one of the sub-projects focused on the history of our discipline, acknowledging the stubborn longevity of concepts used in ongoing research, and hence treating disciplinary history as an important source of evaluating current conceptual structures and research practices. The sub-project was supervised by Raymond, and our friendship thus morphed into a professional, hierarchical relationship. Among other topics (*cf.* Corbey 2005; Van Reybrouck 2000), the project involved tracking the history of core concepts, which were not so much a reflection of archaeological data, but developed a repetitive life of their own, recycled from one generation of researchers to the next, sometimes clearly deriving from "pre-scientific" ways of Western thinking, as well illustrated by Wiktor Stoczkowski's *Anthropologie naïve, anthropologie savante* (Stoczkowski 1994), which appeared in English eight years after the French original was published (Stoczkowski 2002). Seen from this perspective, studying the history of a discipline can function as inspiration for alternative approaches and as a means of "denaturalizing" current opinions and practices, as discussed in great detail by Tim Murray (2001) in an edited volume resulting from this sub-project. The compilation of this volume, *Studying Human Origins*, the outcome of a Leiden Workshop on the theme, was fruitful and its contribution well-received. To quote from Ian Tattersall's (2002, 275) review:

> *"Instead of rounding up the usual suspects to rehash the sparse, though expanding base of information on human emergence, Corbey and Roebroeks have chosen to ask their contributors to look at how we approach (and have approached) the question of our own origins [....] The book has something to engage or infuriate everyone. Once in a while, it is salutary to step back a bit and engage in the exercises of its contributors, even those that skate on the edge of our well-known tendency to narcissism when it comes to our own species*

*Homo sapiens. Anyone with an interest in how our egotistical species studies itself would do well to browse this book."*

I am strongly convinced that tracing the history of the concepts scientists work with should be an integral part of any academic curriculum, and that a historical perspective can be very illuminating for one's own research. As an example: while writing this essay, I am working on a paper that discusses the field's ideas about Neanderthal local group sizes, generally thought to be much lower than the modern hunter-gatherer "average" number of 25 (Churchill 2014), as well as long-standing and persistent views regarding their presumed highly mobile lifestyles. The literature routinely emphasizes a local group size in the range of 11-16 individuals (Churchill 2014). These small numbers, however, are not rooted in archaeological, but in comparative ethnographic data, already influencing late 19th-century and early 20th-century views of Palaeolithic hunter-gatherers, with an influential role also played by the 1968 "Man the Hunter" conference papers. These ethnographic data originate from a biased sample of hunter-gatherers, excluded from highly productive environments now occupied by industrial societies, which may have blurred original ecologically-determined variation in mobility and local group size (*cf.* Singh and Glowacki 2022). As a caveat against too easily extrapolating ethnographic data into the Pleistocene past, Birdsell (1968, 235-236) already stressed half a century ago that "[...] where large food resources are concentrated either regionally or seasonally, local groups take on a very different nature", and display such a wide range of adaptive behavior "[...] that Pleistocene reconstructions will largely depend upon archeological evidence" – evidence which has virtually been non-existing.

This "small group size" mantra is just another illustration of the power of repetition, and the important yet treacherous role of ethnographic data in giving flesh, blood, and meaning to a meagre record. Beyond being identified by studying the history of our disciplinary conceptual toolkit, such powerful mantras and sometimes deeply hidden assumptions can simply be falsified by empirical studies of the archaeological record. There is for example now sufficient archaeological evidence demonstrating that the Middle and Late Pleistocene hominins we tend to call Neanderthals varied substantially in behaviour from region to region over their ~10 million km$^2$ range and from period to period during the ~400,000 years of their existence (Roebroeks and Soressi 2016), including data suggestive of (at least temporarily) substantially large local group sizes (Gaudzinski-Windheuser *et al.* 2023) .

## SITTING ON THE FENCE

This brings me to our long-running bone of contention, how to use ethnographic data and analogies when interpreting the deep past, already somewhat touched upon before. In my view, the "embedded" philosopher exhibits some notable ambiguity in this respect, as aptly illustrated by Raymond's inaugural lecture. There he enthusiastically dived into the relevance of the work of French sociologist Marcel Mauss for interpreting archaeological deep-time data, pointing out that Mauss has been used in very different, but nonetheless productive ways by diverse archaeologists. In the 2020 interview referenced above he said:

*"I stress Marcel Mauss' theorizing from the 1920s on the reciprocal exchange of gifts, services and courtesies as constitutive of social formations and identities. Mauss has proven immensely valuable in archaeology," (Leiden University, 2020).*

However, Raymond also repeatedly agreed with Tim Murray's critical stance against "normalizing" the past – *i.e.*, using ethnographic data to turn a very much unknown and enigmatic past into something more familiar and "normal" – when he warns that uncritically applying Mauss' work to archaeological evidence is at odds with the time-averaged structure of the archaeological record:

*"Archaeology is a discipline with a long-term perspective, focused on processes of change. Given the scarcity, low resolution and ambiguous character of many archaeological data the danger looms of reading* (hineinlesen) *favourite points of view into those poor data. The danger is that the past becomes "normalized". Archaeologists have to work with data that are very different from the ones ethnographers work with [...]," Corbey (2006, 12; translation WR).*

In this case, our philosopher seems happy with simply observing players on the field, without – in my view – taking a clear position. He is indeed, in his own words, sitting

*"[...] on the fence, as it were, focusing on my own data: the discourse of these archaeologists. Analysing it I talk about theory-laden observation, paradigms, incommensurability, or abduction as a type of argument," (Leiden University, 2020).*

From my experience, this is Raymond's preferred position, the safe space in which he can emphasize and bring to bear, say, Mauss as being immensely valuable for archaeology, and at the same time pointing out that the structure of the archaeological record may be incompatible with the grain of such ethnographic phenomena. Using ethnographic observations, theories, and models to make sense of the archaeological record in an uncritical way can thus easily lead to "reconstructions" in which the past has become a mirror image of one's favorite ethnographies.

Raymond may be comfortable with sitting "on the fence", and may even be content, perhaps even proud, about some of ambiguities in his writings and contestations from the fence (a "fence point of view"). Here again, we differ: I like to take a stand, get involved in debates, dive in the mud of empirical observations and argue and defend my position. As an old-fashioned Popperian (as he would qualify me), I like testable hypotheses – and of course I have been shown wrong many times, sometimes being too quick with my judgment and conviction. The scientific process thrives on dialogue, disagreement, and debate, while Raymond's contribution may often appear as "reflection(s)" from a distance. At the same time, as was the remit of the PIONIER project, such reflection allows one to better grasp and chart the disputed territory in debates, where lack of empirical data is not rarely overtaken by "[...] obsolete assumptions inherited from the origins of the discipline and by the social/cultural context of knowledge production," (Zilhão 2020, 85).

Reflection indeed was at the core of his epistemology classes in Leiden, where he obtained the freshly created chair of "Epistemology of Archaeology" some years after the end of the PIONIER project. He likes to study the activity of researchers in the broader field of archaeology, without choosing sides or advocating specific approaches – "Grundlagenforschung" so to say. Admittedly, such a stance can be a bit annoying when one is in the middle of a fierce debate, but at the same time, such a reflective attitude may help to put things into broader perspective, both scientifically and in terms of "toning it down", potentially finding a new middle ground, by taking some critical distance and time to analyze the larger context and re-consider pros and cons.

A rare example of Raymond getting of the fence is his 2016 paper on the possible factors governing the shapes of Acheulean handaxes (Corbey *et al.* 2016), the beloved pet objects he so diligently chased in the gravel pits of the Aisne valley in the early 1980s:

> *"The goal of this paper is to provoke debate about the nature of an iconic artifact – the Acheulean handaxe. Specifically, we want to initiate a conversation about whether or not they are cultural objects. The vast majority of archeologists assume that the behaviors involved in the production of handaxes were acquired by social learning and that handaxes are therefore cultural. We will argue that this assumption is not warranted on the basis of the available evidence and that an alternative hypothesis should be given serious consideration. This alternative hypothesis is that the form of Acheulean handaxes was at least partly under genetic control," Corbey et al. (2016, 6).*

With the evocative title "The Acheulean handaxe: More like a bird's song than a Beatles' tune?", this paper generated a fiery debate about the character of early stone tools as "fossilized" behaviour and proxies for cognition, and specifically on the possibility of at least some degree of genetic control on such tool-making. While still residing in the realm of "reflection" about what anthropologists are doing, and what the basic assumptions (cultural versus genetic control) are, in this paper he explicitly took a *position* that had to be defended against many disagreeing archaeology colleagues.

The philosopher came down from the comfortable, safe space of the fence – an exceptional occurrence. To the excavators being observed from the top of the spoil heap (as during the Maastricht-Belvédère excavations), his observer stance could be – as he noted himself – a nuisance indeed (see quote above). After all, the metaphorical loess heaps our philosopher decided to sit on to observe us archaeological excavators from were not natural, preexisting observation points – they were actually *created* by the field crew working in the sweltering summer heat in the 20 m deep wind-protected Maastricht-Belvédère quarry. The same heaps were subsequently perused by our philosopher and used to observe us from a comfortable position.

Where do these choices come from, what do they say about our philosopher himself? Not taking a position *is*, as our philosopher would aptly agree, *also a position*. But what is this philosopher's motivation to mostly remain merely observant, as he himself characterized the kind of work he does? Might his "fence sitting" be a product of his unique philosophical-anthropological background and specific scholarly trajectory? His philosophy of science training emphasizing the unattainability of objective knowledge and the impossibility of a "God's eye point of view" (*cf.* Putnam 1981)? Reflections which to some degree resonate with cultural anthropologists' insistence on the challenges of obtaining deep, "emic" knowledge of other cultures.

On top of these major epistemological concerns, Raymond was also heavily influenced by Ton Lemaire, whose many publications, and especially *De Indiaan in ons bewustzijn* (Lemaire 1986), sketch Lemaire's attempts to reach out to the idealized native Americans of his childhood. His attempts failed, and in the end, his 1986 book stresses that travelling to "The Other", "The Wild", "Nature", or "The Past" is a doomed enterprise, which alienates the voyager from the present, cherishing romantic images of the past and ideals for the future that ultimately only allow one to travel in ones' own mind. Any voyage, any attempt to escape from the present and from mass tourism into an "unspoiled" world is doomed, the traveler in this case being an archaeologist in search of a single vanished past.

Is Raymond, given this prospect of cultural (Lemaire) and epistemological (Putnam and others) "doom", simply more "relaxed" in (archaeological) debates, more meticulously covering all possible bases and vantage points, remaining in the safe and grey area of "on the one hand … on the other …"? I realize very well that framed as it is here, this question gives a very crude and perhaps somewhat naïve summary of a de facto complex issue. But after more than four decades, such questions still puzzle me.

## CORDIALLY DISAGREEING
With my focus on our joint interests in archaeology and ethnography, I have only – and superficially at times – addressed some aspects of Raymond's broad-ranging enthusiasm and academic output, there is of course much more to his research than the topics I have briefly highlighted here, as shown in this *Festschrift*. For example, he is one of the early explorers of animal-human boundary negotiations, a field in which he earned a track record by influential

publications such as *The Metaphysics of Apes* and *Politics of Species*, the latter reviewed as "[...] a book that should be required reading, cover to cover, not just for academics and researchers studying human – animal relationships, but for all *Homo sapiens* living and engaging with others in the Anthropocene" (Jost Robinson 2015, 201).

I have been engaging with this philosopher "other" for a big chunk of the Anthropocene (in its narrow definition). In his 2006 inaugural lecture, Raymond surmised that our 20 years of friendship and more than a decade of academic cooperation were characterized by constant disagreement, jubilantly adding "let us continue that way" ("laten we zo doorgaan"). We indeed disagreed (and still do) quite a lot and frequently, on various scientific issues, on assessments of ethnographic objects, and Palaeolithic stone tools, and also about what we consider to be proper ways to deal with colleagues and conflicts, we even debated the best ways (including footwear) to move through a forest making as little noise as possible, how to select optimal locations for observing wildlife, etc. What we share(d) was always stronger and more vital than our "ritual" fighting, so our friendship survived and lives on. It is, for sure, not only the scientific process that thrives on cordial disagreement...

## REFERENCES

Birdsell, J.B. 1968. "Some Predictions for the Pleistocene Based on Equilibrium Systems among Recent Hunter-Gatherers." In *Man the Hunter*, edited by Richard B. Lee and I. DeVore, 229-40. Chicago: Aldine.

Churchill, S. 2014. *Thin on the Ground: Neandertal Biology, Archeology and Ecology*. Ames: John Wiley & Son.

Corbey, R.H.A. 1996. "Asmat in Berlin." *Anthropology Today* 12 (3), 21-23.

Corbey, R.H.A. 2000. *Tribal Art Traffic. A Chronicle of Taste, Trade and Desire in Colonial and Post-Colonial Times*. Amsterdam: Royal Tropical Institute.

Corbey, R.H.A. 2005. *The Metaphysics of Apes: Negotiating the Animal-Human Boundary*. Cambridge: Cambridge University Press.

Corbey, R.H.A. 2006. *Homo Reciprocans: Mauss, Hobbes en Darwin*. Inaugural Lecture Leiden University. Leiden: Leiden University.

Corbey, R.H.A. 2016. *Of Jars and Gongs: Two Keys to Ot Danum Dayak Cosmology*. Leiden: C. Zwartenkot Art Books (2016)

Corbey, R.H.A. 2017. *Raja Ampat Ritual Art: Spirit Priests and Ancestor Cults in New Guinea's Far West*. Leiden: C. Zwartenkot Art Books.

Corbey, R.H.A. 2018. *Jurookng: Shamanic Amulets from Southeast Borneo*. Leiden: C. Zwartenkot Art Books.

Corbey, R.H.A. 2019. *Korwar: Northwest New Guinea Ritual Art According to Missionary Sources*. Leiden: C. Zwartenkot Art Books.

Corbey, R., A. Jagich, K. Vaesen, and M. Collard. "The Acheulean Handaxe: More Like a Bird's Song Than a Beatles' Tune?". Evolutionary Anthropology 25 (1), 6-19.

Corbey, R., and A. Lanjouw, eds. 2013. *The Politics of Species: Reshaping Our Relationships with Other Animals*. Cambridge: Cambridge University Press.

Corbey, R., and W. Roebroeks, eds. 2001. *Studying Human Origins: Disciplinary History and Epistemology*. Amsterdam: Amsterdam University Press.

De Vries, F., L. Postma, M. Postma, M. Niekus, H. de Kruijk, J. Timmner, and H. Kars 2022. *Valsheid in Gesteente : Waarom zijn de vuistbijlen van Tjerk Vermaning vals en wie zit er achter?* Assen: Koninklijke Van Gorcum, 2022.

Essel, E., E.I. Zavala, E. Schulz-Kornas, M. B. Kozlikin, H. Fewlass, B. Vernot, M.V. Shunkov, A.P. Derevianko, K. Douka, I. Barnes, M.-C. Soulier, A. Schmidt, M. Szymanski, T. Tsanova, N. Sirakov, E. Endarova, S.P. McPherron, J.-J, Hublin, J. Kelso, S. Pääbo, M. Hajdinjak, M. Soressi, and M. Meyer. 2023. "Ancient Human DNA Recovered from a Palaeolithic Pendant." *Nature* 618, 328-332.

Gaudzinski-Windheuser, S., L. Kindler, K. MacDonald, and W. Roebroeks 2023. "Hunting and Processing of Straight-Tusked Elephants 125.000 Years Ago: Implications for Neanderthal Behavior." *Science Advances* 9 (5), eadd8186.

Hoogerbrugge, J. 2011. *Asmat: Arts, Crafts and People: A Photographic Diary, 1969-1974*. Leiden: C. Zwartenkot Art Books.

Jagt, J.W.M., E.A. Jagt-Yazykova, and W.J.H. Schins. 2011. "A Tribute to the Late Felder Brothers – Pioneers of Limburg Geology and Prehistoric Archaeology; Introduction." *Netherlands Journal of Geosciences* 90 (2-3), 65-71.

Jost Robinson, C. A. 2015. "Review of Raymond Corbey and Annette Lanjouw (Eds.): The Politics of Species: Reshaping Our Relationships with Other Animals." *International Journal of Primatology* 36, (1), 197-201.

Kelley, H., and H. Joullie. 1961. "Recherches Récentes sur le Paléolithique de la région de Vailly-

Sur-Aisne." *Bulletin de la Société préhistorique française* 58 (7), 440-49.

Lee, R.B., and I. DeVore, eds. 1968. *Man the Hunter: The First Intensive Survey of a Single, Crucial Stage of Human Development – Man's Once Universal Hunting Way of Life*. Chicago: Aldine Publishing Company.

Leiden University. 2020. "Raymond Corbey's Leiden experience: Meet the 'embedded philosopher." *Leiden University – News.* https://www.universiteitleiden.nl/en/news/2020/04/raymond-corbeys-leiden-experience-meet-the-embedded-philosopher.

Lemaire, T. *De Indiaan in ons bewustzijn. De ontmoeting van de Oude met de Nieuwe Wereld.* Baarn: Ambo, 1986.

Lemonnier, P. 2022. "Review of Raymond Corbey, Korwar. Northwest New Guinea Ritual Art According to Missionary Sources. Leiden: C. Zwartenkot Art Book, 2019, Cartes, Photographies, Gravures, Bibliographie, 395 P." *Moussons. Recherche en sciences humaines sur l'Asie du Sud-Est* 39. DOI:10.4000/moussons.9659

Mayr, E. 1982. *The Growth of Biological Thought: Diversity, Evolution, and Inheritance.* Cambridge: Harvard University Press.

Murray, T. 2001. "On 'normalizing' the Palaeolithic: An Orthodoxy Questioned." In *Studying Human Origins. Disciplinary History and Epistemology*, edited by R.H.A. Corbey and W Roebroeks, 29-43. Amsterdam: Amsterdam University Press.

Putnam, H. 1981. *Reason, Truth and History.* Cambridge: Cambridge University Press.

Roebroeks, W. and M. Soressi. 2016 "Neandertals Revised." *Proceedings of the National Academy of Sciences* 113 (23), 6372-79.

Singh, M. and L. Glowacki. 2022. "Human Social Organization During the Late Pleistocene: Beyond the Nomadic-Egalitarian Model." *Evolution and Human Behavior* 43, 418-31.

Stapert, D. 1986. "The Vermaning Stones: Some Facts and Arguments." *Palaeohistoria* 28, 1-25.

Stoczkowski, W. 1994. *Anthropologie Naïve, Anthropologie Savante, De l'origine de l'homme, de l'imagination et des idées reçues.* Paris: CNRS.

Stoczkowski, W. 2002. *Explaining Human Origins: Myth, Imagination and Conjecture.* Cambridge: Cambridge University Press.

Tuffreau, A. 1982. "Aperçu sur le Paléolithique de la vallée de l'Aisne." *Revue archéologique de Picardie* 2 (1), 2-6.

Van Reybrouck, D. 2000. *From primitives to primates: A history of ethnographic and primatological analogies in the study of prehistory.* Leiden: PhD thesis Leiden University.

Zegwaard, G. A. 1959. "Headhunting Practices of the Asmat of Netherlands New Guinea." *American Anthropologist* 61 (6), 1020-1041.

Zilhão, J. "The Middle Paleolithic Revolution, the Origins of Art, and the Epistemology of Paleoanthropology." In *The Matter of Prehistory: Papers in Honor of Antonio Gilman Guillén*, edited by P. Díaz-del-Río, K. Lillios and I. Sastré, 85-104. Madrid: Consejo Supérior de Investigaciones Científicas, 2020.

In Hussain, S.T. and G.L. Dusseldorp (eds) 2025. Sitting on the fence: Negotiating archaeology, anthropology and philosophy. Festschrift for Prof. Dr Raymond H.A. Corbey in celebration of his 70th birthday. *Analecta Praehistorica Leidensia* 54. Leiden: Sidestone Press, pp. 29-44.

# Raymond Corbey, the embedded philosopher sitting on the fence: Making sense of a unique academic pursuit

Shumon T. Hussain

## ABSTRACT

In this introductory contribution, I attempt to embark on dedicated basic research (*Grundlagenforschung*) as to Raymond's scholarly existence. I explore the motivations, concepts, practices, and outcomes that together help to qualify Raymond's wide-ranging intellectual life and his many contributions from a critical-reflexive stance. This exploration centres on the figure of the 'embedded philosopher' as he self-identifies. I unpack his infamous self-localisation as 'sitting on the fence' and argue that the kind of 'embeddedness' Raymond pursued foreshadows developments in interdisciplinary science studies and philosophy of science alike, but takes 'ambivalence', 'emic observation', and 'boundary-work' more serious – all key tropes of his unique academic trajectory. 'Sitting on the fence' is not (always) a tacit excuse to withdraw from difficult debates or a cheap way to affirm impartiality but instead constitutes a distinct method of meta-scientific observation, description, and analysis. 'Fence-sitting', similarly, emerges as an inherently creative and potentially transformative scholarly practice. From this reconstruction, I then derive 'negotiation' – also found in the title of this *Festschrift* – as a core concern of his work and stress that 'dialogue' and epistemological 'diplomacy' are key components thereof. Raymond so comes into view as an early defender of scientific pluralism, sparked by his recognition of the irreducibly 'multiparadigmatic' nature of archaeological data, theory, and debate.

*Keywords: Embeddedness, fence-sitting, epistemology, interdisciplinarity, boundaries, multiparadigmatic science*

## SOME ERUDITIONS OF RAYMOND CORBEY

Already when I first met Raymond in Liège in 2012, when attending the UISPP congress *Modes de contacts et de déplacements au Paléolithique eurasiatique*, he was primarily interested in all things meta and in big questions of how the human deep past articulates with and informs present-day concerns, agendas, and the self-image of the human species – *i.e.* how we see ourselves in the treacherous mirror that is archaeology (and anthropology). It is certainly no caricature to say that Raymond's work always was, and continues to be, centred on *who* we are, qua human beings, what our place in the world is, and how we as reflexive creatures with 'excentric positionality' (Plessner 1975) continuously contrive ourselves and our place in history and evolution. Such a perspective necessarily implies a critical moment of self-distancing which is ambivalent in itself – qua human beings we cannot escape the situatedness of our premises and viewpoints, our *Geworfensein*

**Shumon T. Hussain**
Center for Multidisciplinary Environmental Studies in the Humanities (MESH) & Institute for Prehistoric Archaeology, University of Cologne, Germany
s.t.hussain@uni-koeln.de
ORCID: 0000-0002-6215-393X

(thrownness) to use the language of ontological hermeneutics (Heidegger 2006; Richardson 2003), but we coevally must recognise, acknowledge, and reflect on such positionalities, even if we can never hope to fully eclipse them. In classic humanist logic, this entails embracing admission of the complexities of human existence and knowledge but also humbleness and hope. As such *Geworfensein* is no excuse to *not* work on and better ourselves. The brutal fact of *Geworfensein*, in other words, must make us *realise* our difficult situation *and act on it*. Such ambivalence is indeed an important characteristic of Raymond's scholarly pursuit as a whole as we will see.

Raymond's fundamental interrogation of *who* we are as humans, I would argue, includes ontological (being-oriented), epistemological (knowing-oriented) and practical dimensions (action-oriented). These questions were already identified by Immanuel Kant as the core of philosophical curiosity (see below), and for Raymond they importantly involve academic science and the scholarly world. The question of who we are therefore acquires a *double* sense: we can ask who we are as a species, but we can also ask who we are as researchers, scholars, teachers, and intellectuals. Asking these two questions may indeed not be so different after all, as some humanists would argue that the academy *exemplifies* some of the potentials and ideals of what it means to be human, in literal reference to our genus identity, *Homo sapiens* (wise or knowledgeable human being). Academic life and pursuit, from this perspective, can be seen as a (particular) microcosm of being human, and studying the struggles and intricacies of academic knowledge-work thus promises sone general insight into the human condition. This is also an important sense of Raymond's obsession with the 'meta', illustrating that he has always tacitly bought into the idea that a defining feature of the human is its *self-reflexiveness* – i.e. the ability to constantly critique and re-think ourselves, and in doing so re-tailor action in the world. The inherent difficulties of domesticating the human within the boundaries of convincing self-definitions – reflected in the uncountable set of *Homo* epitheta (*Homo faber, ludens, deus*) – is thereby evidence for precisely this: our ability qua being human to constantly *re-invent* ourselves and so to escape fixation. Childe (2003), although in a different context, has famously referred to this idea as 'man [*sic*!] makes himself'. This sense of 'meta' foreshadows a key conceptual struggle in Raymond's scholarly work: to reconcile the bodily with the cognitive.

I still remember vividly from our conversations how sympathetic Raymond was of the idea of humans inhabiting a distinct 'hermeneutic niche' emerging from natural evolution (In 't Veld 2015), underscoring the promise of integrating conflicting portrayals of the human as animal and more-than-animal. This problem is surveyed and explored in-depth in *The Metaphysics of Apes* (Corbey 2005), re-kindling all kinds of problems tied to the clash between naturalising the human in evolutionary thought and the emphasis on human exceptionality (language, morality, culture) in Western humanist thinking. Even though Raymond primarily dissects the meta of this debate in his landmark publication – its assumptive structures, discursive dynamics, and historical roots – one nonetheless cannot escape the impression that Durkheim's *Homo duplex* and Nietzsche's 'definition-open' animal (*nicht-festgestelltes Tier*) survive the exercise almost unharmed. To put it differently, it seems to me that Raymond's almost life-long confrontation of explanatory evolutionary and interpretive human sciences on questions of human origins and the nature of human beings did *not* result in him taking any side, but in the proposal of a somewhat Salomonian division of labour. As such, it is implicitly recognised that reducing the richness of humanist qualifications of the Anthropos by means of conventional evolutionary analysis is almost certainly misleading, in a similar way as the *a priori* rejection of evolutionary reasoning is. With Raymond, what needs to be acknowledged instead is that *being* and *becoming* are not the same but too often confused. Being refers to what we are as humans in the here and now, what we have become as biocultural beings over the course of many millennia, and to describe and make sense of it is the expertise of the human sciences. These sciences have often little to say, however, as to how and why we have become what we are. This is the domain of the evolutionary and comparative behavioural sciences. The question, then, is perhaps not so much what field, perspective, or epistemology can deliver the ultimate description of the human – as such endeavour may be misguided and unattainable in the first place – but rather how they can come to terms with and inform each other, as they may contribute different insights. This may in turn lead to new questions, for example how to explain the emergence of a distinctly human 'hermeneutic niche' in evolutionary terms and our ability of radical self-revision. An important point here is hope understood as future-openness.

To safeguard ourselves and the planet as a whole, we may indeed need to fundamentally re-imagine ourselves, and this may require the cultivation of a novel self-image with distinct behavioural and normative ramifications. Casting the Anthropos as a 'definition-open' animal, in other words, critically secures human *responsibility* and *accountability*. How we live together with other animals is part of that inescapable human responsibility and non-coincidentally forms another recurrent focus of Raymond's scholarship (*e.g.*, Corbey and Lanjouw 2013).

We then also possess responsibility for how we look at our scholarly pursuits as human endeavours, and that we look at them in a self-distanced manner at all (as best we can). In this sense, Raymond's scholarly efforts table an *ethical* dimension, even if he would probably hesitate to admit and embrace it. Recognising the overriding *humanity* of academic scholarship and the scientific enterprise writ large can indeed be seen as a precondition of doing justice to and fulfilling our human condition. We may distil a normative residue of what it may then mean to do 'good' research, namely research that is self-conscious, self-critical, and non-dogmatic insofar as it acknowledges the plurality and 'multiparadigmatic' constitution of academic pursuits *as human projects*. Fierce defenders of a single universal view of science and the scientific method typically deny this humanity (or seek to overcome it). However, good science, in this view, cannot resort to spurious attempts of getting rid of the human, for example by eliminating the 'mark of the human' found in supposedly subjective interpretations and methodologies, as such attempts turn out to be delusional. This does not lead to an everything-goes relativism, however, as collective standards of knowledge can still be defended, but only *within* a certain way of doing science and its social environment (*e.g.*, as *Denkkollektive*: Fleck 1983: 87ff.) – pluralism here comes with *internalism*.

This brings us to Hilary Putnam who provides his guiding hand to much of Raymond's work and, inter alia, influentially developed an internalist view of science and reality. Again, Putnam's role – alongside influences by people such as Imre Lakatos, Thomas Kuhn, Ian Hacking, and Nelson Goodman – testifies to an overriding concern with who we are as humans because being human also means to be a historical, sociocultural, and political creature. Better understanding ourselves and our humanity therefore calls for a *historical* analysis of scientific practice in the broadest possible and most comprehensive sense. Raymond in fact never gets tired of insisting on the research historical angle of his work, for example, when distinguishing his project from the philosophy of science *sensu stricto*. He would rather align himself with the British project of 'history and philosophy of science' and even with continental European historical epistemology (*e.g.*, Rheinberger 2008), even though he has rarely confessed the latter in public. This brings into focus Raymond's cosmopolitan scholarship and intellectuality, de facto interlacing the 'analytic' and the 'continental' tradition of inquiry (Friedman 2000) at the science-philosophy interface, drawing explicitly on thinkers such as Kuhn and Putnam, but also being cognizant about, and sometimes implicitly deploying the achievements of, German and French epistemological traditions. Given Raymond's sometimes idiosyncratic scholarship and his interest in the human, it is thereby somewhat ironic that he rarely built on ideas developed by francophone science scholars such as Canguilhem, Foucault, or Derrida, even though their work provided key impetus and some fundamental insights into the historical, cultural, and political framings of science and human knowing more generally. Raymond's approach to the humanity of science may thus appear 'analytic' in some respects, for example when concentrating on specific disciplines and even problems or debates. At the same time, it appears to be decisively 'holistic', for example when acknowledging the inner logic (*Eigenlogik*) of particular fields of research and their discourses, especially with regard to distinctive batteries of concepts and biases – what Raymond elegantly referred to as the study of 'domain assumptions'. The domain-specificity of scholarly work, although perhaps captured in some sense by the notion of expertise more generally, when linked to particular 'modes of being' a scientist, scholar, or teacher becomes a genuinely French figure of thought with references to Souriau, Simondon, Latour, and even Descola. This, to me, is still puzzling at times, as to not emphasise and foreground these thinkers seems to be a conscious choice and in structural terms mirrors Wil Roebroek's intimate familiarity with the details of French lithic technological and typological research without explicitly deploying it.

## QUOTING RAYMOND TO SET THE SCENE FOR INVESTIGATING HIS SCHOLARSHIP

Raymond's work has always been chiefly conceptual, as his characterisation of his own work in his 2020 interview in the 'Pass on the trowel' series clearly illustrates. When asked how he would define epistemology, his principal domain of expertise and research, he said:

> "*Analyzing knowledge: methods, validity, scope, and what distinguishes justified belief from mere opinion. [...] It comprises the study not so much of archaeological, stratigraphical, or palaeoanthropological data as such, but of the ways these data are handled conceptually, in terms of basic assumptions. The idea of "ways of worldmaking" (Nelson Goodman), or "conceptual schemes" (Hilary Putnam, also a favourite of Dean Kolen), is an excellent tool for archaeology students to take a step back and reflect on what they are doing,*" Corbey (2020a).

The interview gives a good impression of Raymond's scholarly persona and the kind of intellectuality he espouses. When asked about 'sitting on the fence', his pet slogan of sorts, he responded:

> "*I sit on the fence, as it were, focusing on my own data: the discourse of these archaeologists. Analysing it I talk about theory-laden observation, paradigms, incommensurability, or abduction as a type of argument. In my epistemology classes the students are invited to sit on the fence with me and put on a philosophy hat. Reflection presupposes distance, taking a step back!,*" Corbey (2020a).

He goes even further and embraces 'sitting on the fence' as a particular meta-disciplinary practice and a distinct scholarly way of being, in a hands-on and almost hyper-figurative manner:

> "*[...] [I]n fact, yes, indeed, [I] quite literally [sit on the fence]! I love to visit ongoing excavations. In the field I learned a lot from our Caribbean colleagues, from Peter Akkermans and his team in Syria, and in particular from palaeolithic archaeologists in France. Already during Roebroeks' 1980s fieldwork in a quarry near Maastricht I used to sit on a heap of loess, smoking cigars, observing, joking, instead of digging. Some found this amusing, others thought I was a lazy nuisance,*" Corbey (2020a).

This almost praxeological rendering of 'sitting on the fence' at first sight starkly contrasts with Raymond's conceptual, abstract, and at times almost intellectualistic approach to academic research and knowledge production. The notion of the 'embedded philosopher' that the interview invokes similarly suggests a contrast between the detached 'armchair' philosopher interested in processes of science and Raymond's own approach to such matters. I suggest that this tension is indeed quite characteristic of Raymond's academic and personal project and captures another facet of the inherent ambivalence that permeates his work and life.

Also because Raymond has never openly sympathised with the 'practice turn' in the philosophy of science and wider science studies (Soler *et al.* 2014), which posits that rather than focusing on the supposedly cognitive ongoings in science we should pay more attention to situated and often messy academic practices as they unfold in the lab, field, and so forth, I will in the following examine Raymond's scholarship from such a practice-oriented perspective. This introduces yet another 'meta'-level as, in doing so, I apply some of the methods and practices Raymond uses to study other discipline-bound scholars and researchers to his own work. My goal is to clarify key concepts such as embeddedness and fence-sitting and to show how they inform the unique academic lifeform that is Raymond Corbey. I thereby argue that ambivalence, quasi-emic observation, and boundary-work are key components and practices of this embedded philosopher. The latter, in this way, emerges as an endangered species with its own intellectual niche. As such, the embedded philosopher should be cast not as an erratic, elusive, and puzzling figure but as the crystallisation of a coherent strategy of meta-scientific inquiry with a distinct potential for advancing our knowledge about knowledge, be it archaeological or otherwise. My point is not that the total configuration that is the embedded philosopher is the result of conscious decision-making or a particular self-image but rather the contingent outcome of *trying to be the embedded philosopher*, and continuously enacting and re-enacting such scholarly life. Put provocatively, I am interested in the existential strains of this scholarly life, as I – at least methodologically – adopt an existentialist perspective: that *existence precedes essence* (Kierkegaard 1985; Sartre 2012), also, or perhaps especially, in the conduct we call science (and science about science).

## THE 'EMBEDDED' PHILOSOPHER

The embedded philosopher as embodied by Raymond Corbey differs from the ordinary philosopher but also from the historian and philosopher of science or the historical epistemologist. The ordinary philosopher engages in the art of philosophy and primarily addresses genuine philosophical questions, with the aim to advance general philosophical knowledge. The ordinary philosopher can be portrayed with reference to Kant's (1998) four big questions formulated in *The Critique of Pure Reason*, broadly characterising the nature and goals of general philosophical knowledge. Such knowledge, then, responds to the questions: 1) what can I know?, so 2) what may I hope?, and 3) what is the Anthropos (the human), so 4) what ought I to do? The ordinary philosopher's peers are clearly circumscribed and defined: other trained philosophers.

Practitioners of the history and philosophy of science and historical epistemologists are special kinds of philosophers; some are trained historians, and very few had any training in the empirical sciences they study. Indeed, they ask philosophical questions *about* such observational sciences, but they do not normally engage in the latter's discourses or try to answer their questions. They publish their research in specialised journals of philosophy or history of science. Their peers are other philosophers of science or historians of science, and they attend scientific conferences to observe the ongoings without the urge to engage with the empirical issues at hand. Distancing themselves from existential concerns and emotion-laden debates, from the specific perspectives that clash and strife for authority, and from the struggles of reputation, even from the details of the empirical evidence, is a precondition of the work they do. This reflects the idea that as scholars *of science*, specific scientific fields are taken up as 'objects of study' and as such cannot be encountered as 'subjects', otherwise neutrality or impartiality would be forfeited. The latter are epistemic virtues in their fields, contributing to the dominant scholarly identities and key ingredients of the research methodologies respectively adopted. Much recent philosophy of science thereby also seeks to resolve long-standing *philosophical* issues by drawing on the historical developments and/or insights of the special sciences, for example vis-à-vis 'realism' (Turner 2012; Massimi 2022), 'objectivity' (Daston and Galison 2010), 'knowledge' (Renn 2020) or 'observation' (Daston and Lunbeck 2011).

The embedded philosopher is a different beast altogether. He deliberately 'embeds' himself in a living and breathing community of empirical scientists and, ideally, interacts with them on a near-daily basis, even works within the confines of their faculties and departments. The embedded philosopher does not despise immersivity, he rather embraces it and draws inspiration and insight from the constant, even if at times demanding, *exposition* with the 'other'. This 'other' is whatever he was not originally trained in, and so aspires to better understand. In other words, the embedded philosopher throws himself into the unknown and seeks intellectual and academic 'culture shock' in order to learn about other academic fields, their practices, concerns, debates and daily pursuits. As a consequence, the embedded philosopher does not refrain from questions pertaining to empirical evidence of the field he immerses himself in. By means of his ongoing acculturation in the at first alien fields, he gradually adopts, pursues, and appropriates their domain-specific questions and problems *as his own*. The embedded philosopher is so ready, and often develops an ambition, to *contribute* to the very fields of research he takes to be his objects of study. The boundaries between attending to these fields as 'objects' or 'subjects' of study is thereby rendered increasingly ambivalent. The embedded philosopher, because of this configuration of his native habitat, is 1) an invasive academic species and 2) typically a lone wolf without any natural peers or community. The embedded philosopher may therefore regularly re-configure who he considers 'peer' and freely moves between different peer communities as a function of evolving research interests, enthusiasms, and concerns.

The embedded philosopher is therefore also an inherently transdisciplinary creature – he has no clearly defined disciplinary home and this is reflected in a wide-ranging academic biography and focus of inquiry. The embedded philosopher freely and deliberately transgresses disciplinary boundaries, often messily so, and excels in what Britta Padberg (2014, 103-106) calls 'interdisciplinary metadiscourse'. Interdisciplinary metadiscourse describes a form of cross-disciplinary collaboration aimed at "exchange about paradigmatic developments within and between the disciplines and the discussion of research results relevant for our conception of the world [...] without expecting consensual results" (Padberg 2014, 104). In contrast to historians and philosophers of science proper, the embedded philosopher thereby acquires part of his conceptual and analytical prowess by firmly tethering himself to a specific disciplinary place (both cognitively and spatially), even if only for a while, rather than cherishing and practicing detached forms of science observation. 'Embeddedness' can therefore be understood as etiquette for a special form of scholarly life and academic endeavour, and is shorthand for a special way of working *within*, *on*, and *about* empirical fields of research and the questions and contributions they table.

## Ambivalence

A few ruminations on the notion of 'embeddedness' may be helpful to further unpack the so tethered philosopher. We can bring in the Austro-Hungarian economist and anthropologist Karl Polanyi (1944, 44-49) here, as his arguments about embeddedness in the formative formalist-substantivist debates in economic anthropology help to understand what it means to be embedded. Polanyi (1968) opposed a formalist rendering of the economy as a separate realm of reality – for example as a subsystem of human society with distinct organisational and operational rules and dynamics – and instead argued that the economy and economic activity are always *embedded* in their specific socio-political context. Embeddedness in this sense can be understood as a measure of the degree to which economic activity is constrained by non-economic institutions and practices within a given context. As such, embeddedness is a key concept of substantivist views of human economic behaviour, rejecting the universalist stance of opposing formalists who sought to develop explicit, formal descriptions and models to quantify and compare economic behaviour across societies. Formalists in this way attempted to defend a general canon of context-independent economic laws, principles, and logics – a conviction which in archaeology resonates with attempts of so-called 'New' archaeologies to render the discipline a more 'scientific' project (Binford and Binford 1968; Binford 2016; Clarke 2015). Embeddedness, contrary to such formalist inclinations, signals interlacing and cross-pollination between economic and non-economic spheres, maintaining that there can be no 'pure' economic behaviour which can be quantified and modelled independently of its broader socio-political framings. The assumption of pure reason and a shared, universal form of economic rationality mirrored in the figure of the *Homo oeconomicus* is therefore generally challenged by those who defend embeddedness. Mark Granovetter (1985, 481/487), a leading theorist of economic embeddedness, for example argues:

*"Much of the utilitarian tradition, including classical and neoclassical economics, assumes rational, self-interested behavior affected minimally by social relations, thus invoking an idealized state not far from that of [...] thought experiments. [...] [Yet] [a]ctors do not behave or decide as atoms outside a social context, nor do they adhere slavishly to a script written for them by the particular intersection of social categories that they happen to occupy. Their attempts at purposive action are instead embedded in concrete, ongoing systems of social relations."*

Embeddedness, in this view, posits a condition of ambivalence vis-à-vis dominant registers of explaining human cognition and behaviour. The latter can neither be usefully approximated by reducing them to ahistorical, asocial rules of rationality, nor is it helpful to regard them as largely socially determined. Both positions are idealisations of what is actually going on in situated human lives, when individuals seek to *negotiate* agency in relation to the institutions, material resources, norms, and values provided to them by their larger social context.

This has a number of bearings on our understanding of the embedded philosopher: i) he embeds himself purposefully to constrain his philosophy by the target fields of empirical science he is interested in; ii) his embeddedness necessitates re-negotiation of taken-for-granted concepts and ideas; and iii) his embeddedness leaves him in an ambivalent position as he is neither a truly distanced philosopher nor fully trained, and to this effect immersed, practising domain-expert. But there is also a reflexive, meta-philosophical implication. Interestingly, as 'embedded' philosopher, our protagonist – perhaps inevitably so – becomes iv) a substantivist observer of science, his thinking is neither reducible to philosophy/history of science categories, nor can it be fully consonant with how the concepts under scrutiny are currently understood and used in the observed sciences.

The embedded philosopher therefore evades philosophical and disciplinary fixation and becomes an *agent provocateur* by definition. This substantivist meta-stance – qua 'embedded' philosopher – leads him to sometimes *take position*, if often only tacitly and mostly momentarily. Such leanings, I would argue, are reflected for example in Raymond's continued emphasis on Marcel Mauss' socio-anthropology and especially the Maussian theory of the gift

(Corbey 2006a; 2000; 2006b; Corbey and Mol 2012). The *Essai sur le don* (Mauss 1990) ranks among the key readings of substantivist economic anthropology and emphasises distributive (unbalanced) exchange and reciprocity rather than generalised rationality, self-interest, and idealized principles of the market.

This being said, the ambivalence that comes with the embedded form of life that the philosopher has chosen proffers multiple identities – a sort of intellectual identity crisis – and creates the constant tension between going fully substantivist (and thus to go beyond both his original field of training and his field of observation) and shifting the perspective back and forth between the different fields of reference (in Raymond's case: philosophy/philosophy of science, cultural anthropology, archaeology). The relationship between, and status of, the alternating perspectives is an ongoing concern and an open-ended issue, and to the external observer thus sometimes evokes evasiveness – a symptom of *not* committing to any position. Such epistemological 'commitment issues' – as I have termed similar ambivalence in the broader context of more recent archaeological theorising (Hussain 2025) – are, however, often symptomatic for deeply interdisciplinary research orientations and the kind of 'interdisciplinary metadiscourse' highlighted above. Raymond adds another dimension to this ambivalence, however, linked to his distinct personality and particular style of scholarship: he tends to instrumentalise the inherent ambivalence of his being and observational analysis and turns it into a virtue. Raymond's (2020a) self-chosen metaphor here is that of the jester or trickster:

> "[...] *I cannot help but see the structural similarity between my position and that of the Renaissance court jester, or the trickster character in myths and rituals: stand-offish, ambiguous characters who do and don't belong at the same time, who joke and provoke. Go-betweens between social categories, betwixt-and-between, marginal and yet in some sense central and crucial to what is going on.*"

Another analogy that we can draw on to better understand this form of provocative criticality is the mockingjay. The mockingjay is a fictional bird from the Hunger Games series created through the accidental mating of jabberjays and mockingbirds. Mockingjays, black birds with white patches on the underside of their wings, are infamous for their ability to mimic a wide range of sounds produced by humans. They are liminal beings – *Grenzgänger* in German – and are neither jabberjays nor mockingbirds. They are betwixt and between and neither-nor, and their mimicry challenges the purity and reliability of inter-species communication. They unsettle the order of things, we may say. They are almost post-colonial to this effect and it is no coincidence that the mockingjay serves as a symbol of rebellion in the Panem dystopia. In post-colonial theory, too, *mimicry* is deployed (Bhabha 1984; GoGwilt and Holm 2018) but it has a teasing, mocking, and at times sarcastic undertone, as mimicry is understood as an imitative tactic employed by the 'other' in the face of the powerful, typically Western colonial powers. Mimicry thereby attests to an unbalanced power dynamic and entails a critical although not immediately obvious metacommentary on this powerful. It is deployed within asymmetric power-relations to de-stable them from within but without open opposition. It is, in other words, an embedded way of challenging the established. The embedded philosopher essentially aspires to do the same, by mimicking the disciplinarily established and the given authorities (notably theories) in these fields. Just like the fictional mockingjay, he learns the domain-specific language of the professional other, and through his constant questioning and deeper-digging – to use an archaeological metaphor – even or perhaps especially if perceived as nuisance, challenges the premises of the disciplinary powerful, slowly degrading and possibly destabilizing configurations of assumptions and concepts. The embedded philosopher, just like the jester, thereby does essential work that nobody else dares (or is allowed) to do and because of his liminal status evades serious punishment. As such, this work is considered constructive, functional, and ultimately necessary within a disciplinary system of knowledge production, not least as a way of breaking free of entrenched debates.

As Orr and Orr (2022) remind us, deceit and deception generally play important roles as 'catalysts of knowledge production' in human societies. They argue that Western scientific experimental rationality and processes are based on the deliberate deception of subjects in order to elicit insight into causality. The trickster is also an important Indigenous figure and playfully opens-up spaces of knowing. More broadly speaking, deceit is often used in conjunction with assuming the perspective of prey animals and this is not just for strategic reasons in relation to the hunt itself, but also because engaging in animal-oriented empathetic imitation is inherently dangerous, and deception and mockery help to shield against this (Willerslev 2004). The embedded philosopher follows a similar logic when deploying deception. He must imitate in order to be recognised as a worthy interlocutor in the first place, but walking among specialists is risky and potentially costly as his disguise may be unveiled, so mockery, irony, and an attitude of being serious *but not too serious* emerge as suitable strategies to alleviate this situation and shield oneself against foundational critique.

### Quasi-emic observation

As a proxy for this scholarly life, 'embeddedness' implies (often uncomfortable) *exposure*. This has an almost Heideggerian touch. The philosopher is 'thrown into' (*Geworfensein*, see above) a materially and cognitively pre-furnished world (the target empirical sciences), and has to develop his mode of being in relation to such disciplinary *Gestell(e)*. As indicated before, this kind of always precarious exposure promotes unique ways of accessing, observing, and understanding the empirical sciences as objects of study. The notion of embeddedness here draws attention to the dialectic between closeness and distance. The embedded philosopher is subject to the constant urge to integrate himself into his empirical fields of concern and thus runs the risk of being fully absorbed by them. He therefore must ensure that he can always pull himself out again to re-establish some form of critical distance. The ongoing oscillation between becoming a true practitioner and falling back to the austere, detached philosopher therefore emerges as a diagnostic lifestyle and mode of inquiry. The perpetual creation of radical exposure to the disciplinary 'other' thereby serves to ensure that this 'other' is described from *within*, in terms of its own standards and preoccupations, rather than from a supposedly neutral position. This radical exposure is also a means to provoke illuminating cathartic experiences. Catharsis refers to a process of intellectual self-purging. Such 'intellectual catharsis' – as we may call it – is almost a method of investigation and insight. Catharsis, from the original Greek for 'purification' or 'cleansing', consists of an excreting act following a radically confrontative experience (thrownness into the studied academic fields as 'other') during which the mind is cleared from any apparent preunderstandings, conceptual distortions, and/or *a priori* biases. The exposure to actually lived practice within a given field of empirical research is cathartic because it helps to lay bare prejudices about this field and its practices and knowledges, and so to sharpen the sensitivity and understanding of domain and field-specific modes of academic thought. Only by cleansing himself in this manner can the philosopher, in a second step, gain direct access to the distinct prejudice structure of knowledge cultivated by different fields of research.

The catharsis metaphor also draws attention to another key pillar of the kinds of embedded philosophical investigation Raymond has conducted over the years: that the respectively observed and theorised empirical fields of scientific research are treated as quasi-anthropological field sites. The talk of 'otherness' initiated before is therefore not coincidental. The embedded philosopher throws himself into the disciplinarily alien by spending time 'in the field', literally acquaints himself with this other, learns to think and act like the other, and ultimately learns to speak the same (academic) language. He therefore draws on the methods of classical cultural anthropology in which catharsis is also a key component – to truly get to know the radical (cultural) other, the anthropologist must 'cleanse' himself from the baggage of the Western gaze and its cognitive frames of reference. I suggest that this import looms particularly large in Raymond's work due to his anthropological background and interest. The embedded philosopher, from this perspective, brings forth a quasi-ethnographic mode of observation to properly engage with and learn about other situated academic disciplines and their knowledge systems. Understood as such, we can specify what the constant movement between closeness and distance entails. Distance is ensured by the pre-empirical input of analysis provided by the history and philosophy of science, while closeness is produced by *participant observation*, pioneered by anthropologists such as Bronislaw Malinowski and Margaret Mead, and by cultivating an essentially *emic gaze*. Raymond has clearly expressed this aptitude himself in the earlier-referenced 'Pass on the trowel' interview, specifically describing his observational access as 'ethnographic' and as 'involved, yet at a distance' (Corbey 2020a).

The recurrent reference to Geertzian anthropology throughout Raymond's work can be seen as a reflection of this, as Geertz's famous essay 'From the Native's Point of View: On the Nature of Anthropological Understanding' (1984) was instrumental in developing a mature method of other-directed observation in anthropology. What shines through here is also Raymond's concern with Snow's (1968) polarisation of the 'Two Cultures' (human and natural sciences) within the academy, and the realisation that disciplinary endeavours are enwrapped by their own cultures of doing science and attaining knowledge. This 'cultural' condition of research supplies the analogy to engage in qualitative-interpretive forms of conceptual analysis to recover their logics. The *Metaphysics of Apes* (Corbey 2005) can in this way be read as a conceptual examination of data collected during quasi-emic fieldwork among Palaeolithic archaeologists and human origins researchers. An important complementary dimension of this quasi-ethnographic understanding of the embedded philosopher's observational work is that field sites need to be escaped from time to time in order to prevent complete immersion (to become the 'other'), and to organise and confront gained insights within current debates and identify matters of concern. Leaving such ecologies of the other, if only briefly, is thereby easily understood by practitioners as a withdrawal from difficult debates.

The embedded philosopher's quasi-emic form of observation sets him again apart from classical historians and philosophers of science who regard their project mostly as etic. It is notable that the embedded philosopher so charts interesting parallels to the so-called 'empirical' and 'anthropological turns' in more recent philosophy of science and interdisciplinary science studies (*e.g.*, Shapin and Schaffer 1985; Latour and Woolgar 1986; Galison 1997; Soler *et al.* 2014). The motivation of these projects is the emancipation from idealised views of science and to pay more attention to the details and complexities of scholarly practice as it unfolds in the lab, office or in the field. The embedded philosopher shares this motivation but has developed his own form of academic life to take stock of and productively engage with such matters 'on the ground'. Arguably, his main influence for quasi-emic observation thereby derives from continental *Lebensphilosophie* and its body-centric practices, however, which, as charted by Lipowsky (2020), provided key impetus for a methodological framework of observation placing central emphasis on the immersion of a researcher into the social or cultural setting chosen for intense and detailed study. In this sense, embedded philosophizing inscribes into the broader 'turn to life' which re-modelled early-twentieth century anthropology. Implicit in this approach is certainly also a sort of 'ethnomethodology' as proposed by Garfinkel (1984) to re-appraise scholarly life and work as a deeply social and interactive affair.

## Boundary-work

The notion of 'embeddedness' further helps to explain why the embedded philosopher is so prone to engage in boundary-work. Most importantly, the embedded philosopher is himself a border-crosser, and his own scholarly identity thus needs to be constantly re-negotiated (see above), and so critically depends on active boundary-work. Another reason is that ambivalence features prominently in the work and life of the philosopher (see above), focalising the construction of binaries and boundaries and their role in scholarly cognition. In Raymond's case, this is enforced by the ongoing tension between an emphasis on human exceptionalism in Western philosophy and cultural anthropology (his background) and the empirical challenges raised against such views by palaeoanthropology and deep-time archaeology (his field of study). This is fostered by his early engagement with the German philosophical anthropologists Max Scheler and Arnold Plessner (Corbey 1986; 1998; 2005), who were themselves boundary workers at the crossroads of the humanities and the natural sciences, especially biology. The kind of boundary-work – chiefly conceptual – that the embedded philosopher is mostly interested in is thereby perhaps best reflected in *The Metaphysics of Apes* (2005), *Politics of Species* (Corbey and Lanjouw 2013: human-animal boundary), and 'Theoretische Probleme zur Kognition, Sprache und Gesellschaft bei frühen Hominiden' (Corbey 1998: mind-body boundary/problem). Qua 'embedded' philosopher, he is primarily interested in how long-standing philosophical debates feed into conceptual binaries, and how these are policed – and thus *constrained* and *reconfigured* – by the relevant empirical sciences such as archaeology and cognitive science. The philosopher's boundary-work therefore reflects his own positionality; he works at a sort of 'contact zone' where data, concepts, theories, and larger research paradigms collide. The focus on 'domain-assumptions', 'implicit ontologies', 'double standards', and similar pre-configurations of situated scholarly inquiry (Corbey and Roebroeks 2001) illustrates this concern. Boundary-work is also foregrounded by how the philosopher makes sense of his own role as an intermediary, mediator, and arbitrator at the interface of different domains of knowing. He may thus cast himself as an epistemological diplomat of sorts who freely shifts between, and thereby performatively triangulates, various emic and etic standpoints. Boundary-work in this sense, I would argue, is part and parcel of the embedded philosopher's designated 'style of reasoning' (Hacking 1994), it exemplifies what he tries to achieve, and so defines his designated mode of scholarly existence. Because of this constant and always precarious boundary-traversing, the philosopher seems to lack scholarly essence in the sense of a coherent set of concepts and positions, but again: his existence qua strategic ambivalence precedes his essence. Just like the Anthropos itself, the embedded philosopher is 'definition-open' and as such constantly re-invents himself. The concern with boundary-work is recursive in the sense that the embedded philosopher is a boundary-worker himself but also remains chiefly interested in the *boundary work of others*. To put it more poignantly, boundary-work firmly points to our *conditio humana* and as such is practically inescapable, also – or *especially* – for scientists and scholars. To identify, map, and belabour it – engaging with it epistemologically – therefore certifies the humanity of academic research and science in general, thus closing the circle.

## SITTING ON THE FENCE

Raymond describes himself as a fence-sitter (see above). Colloquially, the English idiom of 'sitting on the fence' is commonly used to point to a person's lack of decisiveness, neutrality, or reluctance to choose between two sides within a debate. The phrase is similarly employed to critique a problematic delay in decision-making, for example as 'you cannot sit on the fence any longer and now need to take a side!'. The connotations of such understandings are overwhelmingly negative. Fence-sitting is constructed as something that needs to be overcome – sitting on the fence in this sense can only be a temporary state, if at all, and it impedes further action and progress.

But this apprehension may be misleading when applied to the embedded philosopher. The notion of fence-sitting that can be recovered from his specific form of intellectual life, I would argue, instead reflects the kind of ambivalence and boundary-work that he grapples with. Fence-sitting, in this view, is tied to a specific observational technique and promotes a unique form of 'negotiative' analysis rooted in the ongoing, dialectic cross-adjustment between emic and etic insights. The image of the 'fence' then literally stands for a boundary demarcation itself, and 'sitting on it' literally means to be on neither side properly. Fence-sitting, therefore, affords observational and analytical possibilities unavailable for those who do not sit on the same fence, let alone for those who never sat on *any* fence. The fence is *simultaneously* within and outside the observed disciplines.

Fencing (erecting between-disciplinary boundaries), conversely, is a precondition for the kind of transdisciplinary work pursued by the philosopher. This is why, in principle, the embedded philosopher cannot afford to fully immerse himself in his fields of study and allow these to crystallize fully as 'subjects', as this would undermine the very basis of his existence. As a practice, fence-sitting, at the same time, recognizes the unattainability of what Putnam has called 'God's eye point of view' (Putnam 1981) or what has been termed 'view from nowhere' (Wylie 2002; 2015) – views which have often been criticised as underpinning the self-declared 'objective' data-driven sciences. The embedded philosopher, by sitting on the fence, does clearly not deploy a view from *nowhere* but he simultaneously does not adhere to radical versions of standpoint epistemology either (Harding 1991; Gurung 2020). The 'view from the fence' is a view from *somewhere*, and it recognises the situatedness of knowledge (Haraway 2016), but rather than being interested in radical domain-specificity and the relationality of objectivity, the 'view from the fence' seeks to *triangulate* between different scholarly fields and to so reveal conceptual friction points. The fence affords a privileged position to engage in such confrontation and triangulation, precisely because of the ambivalent positionality of the observer – as an observer from *within* and from *outside* for each disciplinary context so triangulated. Triangulation in this sense simply means to rely on multiple perspectives, data resources, or interpretive registers to develop a comprehensive understanding of phenomena, especially on the level of 'interdisciplinary metadiscourses'. Such triangulation amounts to foundational boundary-work itself – what the embedded philosopher has called basic research (*Grundlangenforschung*) in epistemology (Corbey 1998). The fence is an appropriate metaphor for this kind of work: it bespeaks of the ambivalent position of the practitioner and the constant boundary-work required to maintain the fence as a vantage point of observation and analysis. The fence therefore ultimately acquires the status of a 'habitat', describing the knowledge ecology and potential that defines the embedded philosopher as a species. The fence, in other words, is a key component of his *Umwelt* – to speak with von Uexküll (2004) – and thus plays an elementary role in the distinct form of intellectual life that is the embedded philosopher. The fence stands for a distinct technology of knowing and fence-sitting is a unique meta-discursive practice.

The fence is also the reason why the embedded philosopher may appear with many faces. Sometimes as a pseudo-detached philosopher of science and historical epistemologist, at other times as a pseudo-engaged archaeologist, art historian, or cultural anthropologist. His fence-positionality allows him both to be critically distanced from and existentially engaged with the disciplinary discourses he is interested in. The perhaps best example in Raymond's case is the iconic Palaeolithic handaxe, which he continues to belabour in his academic work, especially in terms of its cognitive ramifications, most recently arguing for ethological rather than cultural explanations of the millennial-scale persistence of handaxes in the archaeological record (Corbey *et al.* 2004; Roebroeks and Corbey 2009; Corbey *et al.* 2016; Corbey 2020b). This at first glance bewildering inconsistency and heterogeneity of perspectives in fact bespeaks of an impressive and rarely encountered capacity to switch perspectives and to contribute meaningfully to different academic pursuits, while remaining faithful to the embedded philosopher's unique style of reasoning and knowledge production. The embedded philosopher is therefore akin to a chameleon, momentarily capable to become one of his studied practitioners before retreating to his original habitat again – the fence. This is only possible because of the extended exposition and quasi-emic mode of investigative research described before. It is tempting to interpret this as a salute to Raymond's spiritual mentor, Hilary Putnam, who productively reconfigured his own views and arguments on key themes of his work again and again over the course of his professional career rather than stubbornly defending a single point of view, for example reflected in Putnam's (1981; 1983; 1987; *cf.* Rochefort 2021) life-long struggle to come to turns with realism (*e.g.*, his move from externalist to internalist positions, and then possibly even beyond the latter).

Fence-sitting, notwithstanding all criticism, can then be recognised as an extremely productive, creative, and potentially transformative scholarly way of being. Partly because of this, fence-sitting does not always contribute to the relevant disciplinary discourses by advancing them in classical fashion, for example by *resolving* pressing questions and issues, but rather by means of deliberate provocation. Similarly, progress is not necessarily regarded as a matter of definitively answering specific questions but is frequently identified with revealing the conceptual preconditions to ask them in the first place, and in this way to unmask *why* they are so difficult to answer. This may involve but is not limited to the realisation that the questions themselves rely on problematic assumptions and overcoming these assumptions may require posing different questions. As briefly explored above, neutrality or impartiality are not a primary concern of the embedded philosopher as these are recognised as sources of bias and misunderstandings themselves. For the embedded philosopher, impartiality can only emerge from bringing together different views, by confronting and triangulating them, even if the incommensurabilities can never be resolved. This suggests that the embedded philosopher is an epistemological diplomat and moderator, who ultimately engages in foundational negotiation work. Such 'negotiation' is based on the reconstruction, explanation, and exchange of contrasting views in order to foster critical dialogue and better mutual understanding of the involved parties and perspectives. Just like in the political arena, such diplomacy must recognise the *irreducible diversity* of so belaboured viewpoints. Fence-sitting helps to acquaint these viewpoints with one another and to showcase their respective strengths and weaknesses, but also their radicalities and at times absurdities. Paired with the image of the jester or the fictional mockingjay, the embedded philosopher's method is almost Platonian: dialogical and not necessarily about giving away the right answers, but to supply important pointers, questions, and clues to tackle them better. The goal is to make the disciplinary natives themselves (the domain-experts) think, and to unroot their certainties to catalyse progress, but the responsibility to answer the questions remains with them. The ambiguity of fence-sitting ultimately undermines the authority of having the final say. But it also testifies to the virtue of humbleness sketched in the beginning, as providing answers, yet alone final answers, would be intellectual hubris and ultimately self-undermining.

## ARCHAEOLOGY AS A FORMATIVE EXPERIENCE

It is no coincidence, I believe, that the academic lifeform that is Raymond Corbey emerged at the intersection of philosophy, (cultural) anthropology, and archaeology. While the former two, grosso modo, supply the conceptual, observational, and interpretive tools to study archaeologists in practice and in discourse, archaeology as a field of research is itself deeply ambiguous. The ecological niche of the embedded philosopher, as it were, is as such fundamentally framed by the problems and inherent struggles archaeology faces as a disciplinary human endeavour. The humanity of the archaeological project can thereby easily become overwhelming. This has mainly to do with the field's precarious source conditions including the fragmentary, highly selective survival of archaeological evidence, which render almost all archaeological interpretations contested. Bruce Trigger (2017, 1) has poignantly described this situation as follows:

*"Archaeology might have been invented as a case study for the philosophy of science [...]" [as] [t]he paucity of evidential constraint renders [it] a very revealing example of how data are interpreted by social scientists."*

With Wittgenstein, one is therefore tempted to conclude that the 'language games' of archaeologists are only weekly constrained by the evidence they retrieve from the ground. Some of these language games also seem to be played by only a few individuals. Because of this, archaeologists can sometimes appear to be exceptionally *opinionated*. To put it differently: because of the inherent difficulties to decide between alternative interpretations merely on the basis of the available, limited archaeological evidence, practitioners can easily retreat to gross dismissal of the respectively contra-positions based on *general* epistemological and even political grounds. These can at times be arbitrary because the point is not to have good grounds but simply to reject the non-shared views. Archaeological data in themselves play hardly any role in this dynamic (see *e.g.*, Hussain 2019 for an in-depth case study). Again, the reality of the game shows that it often makes little difference to critique a contested view from the outside – *i.e.* by means of non-shared resources and standards of knowledge – but that change can most successfully be enacted from *within*. This knowledge internalism, following Putnam and others, is taken seriously by the embedded philosopher as his immersive method of becoming the 'other' coupled with sophisticated tricksteresque mimicry of disciplinary practice and thought, in a liminal space between sharp analytical sincerity and playful provocation and irony, testifies. Ultimately, this is perhaps the main difference to other observers of science who typically believe in the capacity of the detached gaze to spur change. Raymond, by contrast, puts his stock into embeddedness as a precondition for such transformative impact. Scientific communities are thus clearly modelled as micro-societies with their own 'culture'.

Raymond continues to highlight the 'multiparadigmatic' nature of archaeological research, in which diversity and division sometimes seem to be more pervasive than the primarily puzzle-solving 'normal science' that Kuhn proclaimed. In fact, the *normalisation* of research as 'normal science' may precisely be a quality that the humanities have traditionally resisted, in part because of their reflexivity and acknowledgement of the inescapable humanity of inquiry. Archaeology is a boundary discipline, charting a somewhat uncanny valley between what is now known as HAS (humanities and social sciences) and STEM fields (natural/life sciences, technology, engineering, and mathematics) within the academy. It may have thus inherited part of this reluctance from HAS, while coevally striving to cultivate the disciplinary homogeneity and normality that STEM values. This is perhaps nowhere as recognisable as in human origins research and Palaeolithic archaeology, which, at least in the English-speaking world, have now developed firm leanings towards STEM logics of research. Nonetheless, even within STEM it is now increasingly recognised that paradigms do not merely follow each other in time (vertical Kuhnian structure of paradigm shifts) but forcefully co-exist (horizontality, pluralism), and that such antagonistic cohabitation is an important source of intra-disciplinary innovation and change (Kellert, Longino, and Waters 2006). It is the (quasi-anthropological) *encounter* with this distinct disciplinary fabric of archaeology, I would argue, that has shaped the life and project of the embedded philosopher.

The inherent liminality and ambiguity of archaeology *as a discipline between disciplines* without much disciplinary unity *calls* for boundary-policing and the recognition of residual knowledge ambivalence. There is thus a recursive relationship between the constitution of archaeology as an academic discipline and the kind of work the embedded philosopher does (another 'meta' if you will). At the same time, the plastic coexistence of radically antithetic, paradigmatic ways of doing research, sometimes within the same university department or faculty (archaeology is a comparatively small field with only so many practitioners), seem to have triggered a classic philosophical reflex – to assume the role of a meta-scientific mediator who somehow stands outside of practiced science, yet again introducing a difficult-to-resolve ambivalence of positionality. Given all of this and what has been said before, it is somewhat surprising that Raymond, as a recursive manoeuvre of sorts, has never cast archaeological practices as gift-giving or costly display, in a similar fashion as he has read the *Beowulf* together with Agnus Mol (2012) against the grain. Gift-giving as a relevant frame of analysis has at least entered contemporary science studies now, for example when Martus and Spoerhase (2022) explore the role of the *Sonderdruck* in early humanities practices.

In total, I would argue that the archaeological encounter has therefore substantially catalysed the making of the embedded philosopher and his distinct behavioural and cognitive niche. The encounter has certainly fostered an overriding sensitivity for open-endedness and the impossibility of finding easy (final) answers with observer-independent value. There simply is no, and can never be a, 'God's eye point of view' (Putnam 1981) or 'view from nowhere' (Wylie 2015). Archaeology as an empirical field site has thus brought the urgency of developing a clearer sense of pluralism in human knowledge production endeavours more generally to the fore. *The ambivalent positionality of the embedded philosopher thereby mirrors the ambivalent positionality of archaeology itself.* This is also why *negotiation* of assumptions, arguments, and theories emerges as a key concern. As such, the lifeform that is Raymond, even though rare to spot in its natural habitat, can be regarded as an early defender and mediator of scientific pluralism and as an ambassador of interdisciplinarity.

## Acknowledgements

This contribution is my personal homage to Raymond's inspiring scholarship. My portrayal is certainly not comprehensive and in many ways filtered by my own experiences, perspectives, and interests. I nonetheless hope that, overall, the image I outline helps to throw the academic lifeform that is Raymond Corbey into clearer focus. I realise that I am perhaps not the first person that comes to mind to write such a piece and I acknowledge my partiality, but similarly I maintain, again, that capacity is perhaps not as important as action. In any case, I dedicate these explorations to the support and mentorship that I have received throughout the years from Raymond.

## References

Bhabha, H. 1984. "Of Mimicry and Man: The Ambivalence of Colonial Discourse". *October* 28, 125-129. DOI: 10.2307/778467.

Binford, L.R. 2016. *Debating Archaeology: Updated paperback edition*. Abingdon: Routledge.

Binford, S.R., and L.R. Binford. 1968. *New Perspectives in Archeology*. Chicago: Aldine Publishing Company.

Childe, V.G. 2003. *Man Makes Himself*. Nottingham: Spokesman.

Clarke, D.L. 2015. *Analytical Archaeology*. London: Routledge (Routledge Library Editions Archaeology 13).

Corbey, R.H.A. 1986. "Plessner, Scheler En De Menselijke Geest". *Tijdschrift Voor Filosofie* 48 (1), 49-65.

Corbey, R.H.A. 1998. "Theoretische Probleme Zur Kognition, Sprache Und Gesellschaft Bei Frühen Hominiden". *EAZ – Ethnographisch-Archäologische Zeitschrift* 39, 321-33.

Corbey, R.H.A. 2000. "On Becoming Human: Mauss, the Gift, and Social Origins". In *Gifts and Interests*, edited by T. Vandevelde, 157-74. Leuven: Peeters.

Corbey, R.H.A. 2005. *The Metaphysics of Apes: Negotiating the Animal-Human Boundary*. Cambridge/New York: Cambridge University Press.

Corbey, R.H.A. 2006a. *Homo Reciprocans: Mauss, Hobbes En Darwin. Inaugural Lecture*. Leiden: Leiden University.

Corbey, R.H.A. 2006b. "Laying aside the Spear: Hobbesian Warre and the Maussian Gift". In *Warfare and Society: Archaeological and Social Anthropological Perspectives*, edited by T. Otto, H. Thrane, and H. Vandkilde, 29-36. Aarhus: Aarhus University Press.

Corbey, R.H.A. 2020a. "Raymond Corbey's Leiden Experience: Meet the "Embedded Philosopher"'. *Pass on the Trowel*, 6 April 2020. https://www.universiteitleiden.nl/en/news/2020/04/raymond-corbeys-leiden-experience-meet-the-embedded-philosopher.

Corbey, R.H.A. 2020b. "Baldwin Effects in Early Stone Tools". *Evolutionary Anthropology: Issues, News, and Reviews* 29 (5), 237-44. DOI: 10.1002/evan.21864.

Corbey, R.H.A., A. Jagich, K. Vaesen, and M. Collard. 2016. "The Acheulean Handaxe: More like a Bird's Song than a Beatles' Tune?" *Evolutionary Anthropology: Issues, News, and Reviews* 25 (1), 6-19. DOI: 10.1002/evan.21467.

Corbey, R.H.A., and A. Lanjouw, eds. 2013. *The Politics of Species: Reshaping Our Relationships with Other Animals*. 1st ed. Cambridge: Cambridge University Press. DOI:10.1017/CBO9781139506755.

Corbey, R.H.A., R. Layton, J. Tanner, and J. Bintliff. 2004. "Archaeology and Art". In A companion to archaeology, edited by J. Bintliff, 357-379. Oxford: Blackwell. https://hdl.handle.net/1887/43057.

Corbey, R.H.A., and A. Mol. 2012. ""By Weapons Made Worthy": A Darwinian Perspective on Beowulf". In *Creating Consilience: Integrating the Sciences and the Humanities*, edited by E. Slingerland, and M. Collard, 342-67. Oxford: Oxford University Press.

Corbey, R.H.A., and W. Roebroeks. 2001. "Biases and Double Standards in Palaeoanthropology". In *Studying Human Origins: Disciplinary History and Epistemology*, edited by R.H.A. Corbey, and W. Roebroeks, 67-76. Amsterdam: Amsterdam University Press.

Daston, L., and P. Galison. 2010. *Objectivity*. 1. paperback ed. New York: Zone Books.

Daston, L., and E. Lunbeck, eds. 2011. *Histories of Scientific Observation*. Chicago/London: The University of Chicago Press.

Fleck, L. 1983. *Erfahrung und Tatsache: Gesammelte Aufsätze*. Introduction by L. Schäfer and T. Schnelle. Frankfurt am Main: Suhrkamp.

Friedman, M. 2000. *A Parting of the Ways: Carnap, Cassirer, and Heidegger*. Chicago: Open Court.

Galison, P. 1997. *Image and Logic: A Material Culture of Microphysics*. Chicago, IL: University of Chicago Press.

Garfinkel, H. 1984. *Studies in Ethnomethodology*. Cambridge, UK: Polity Press.

Geertz, C. 1984. "From the Native's Point of View: On the Nature of Anthropological Understanding". In *Culture Theory: Essays on Mind, Self, and Emotion*, edited by R. Shweder, and R.A. LeVine, 123-36. New York: Cambridge University Press.

GoGwilt, C.L., and M.D. Holm, eds. 2018. *Mocking Bird Technologies: The Poetics of Parroting, Mimicry, and Other Starling Tropes*. First edition. New York: Fordham University Press.

Granovetter, M. 1985. "Economic Action and Social Structure: The Problem of Embeddedness". *American Journal of Sociology* 91 (3), 481-510.

Gurung, L. 2020. "Feminist Standpoint Theory: Conceptualization and Utility". *Dhaulagiri Journal of Sociology and Anthropology* 14 (December), 106-15. DOI:10.3126/dsaj.v14i0.27357.

Hacking, I. 1994. "Styles of Scientific Thinking or Reasoning: A New Analytical Tool for Historians and Philosophers of the Sciences". In *Trends in the Historiography of Science*, edited by K. Gavroglu, J. Christianidis, and E. Nicolaidis, 31-48. Boston Studies in the Philosophy of Science. Dordrecht: Springer Netherlands.

Haraway, D. 2016. "Situated Knowledges: The Science Question in Feminism and the Privilege of Partial Perspective". In *Space, Gender, Knowledge: Feminist Readings*, edited by L. McDowell, and J. Sharp, 53-72. London: Routledge.

Harding, S.G. 1991. *Whose Science? Whose Knowledge? Thinking from Women's Lives*. Ithaca, N.Y: Cornell University Press.

Heidegger, M. 2006. *Sein und Zeit*. 19. Aufl., Tübingen: Niemeyer.

Hussain, S.T. 2019. *The French-Anglophone Divide in Lithic Research: A Plea for Pluralism in Palaeolithic Archaeology*. Leiden: Open Access Leiden Dissertations. https://hdl.handle.net/1887/69812.

Hussain, S.T. 2025. "Strukturwandel und Wirksamkeit archäologischer Theoriearbeit". In  *kultURgeschichten: Ur- und Frühgeschichte aus historischer, methodischer und theoretischer Perspektive*, edited by M. Augstein, M. Halle, U. Kraus, K. Krüger, and M. Wöhrl, 539-562. Bielefeld: transcript.

In 't Veld, M.W. 2015. *The Hermeneutic Niche. Language within Darwinism*. Leiden: Unpublished Doctoral Dissertation, Leiden University.

Kant, I. 1998. *Kritik Der Reinen Vernunft*. Philosophische Bibliothek, Bd. 505. Hamburg: F. Meiner.

Kellert, S.H., H.E. Longino, and C.K. Waters, eds. 2006. *Scientific Pluralism*. Minneapolis, MN: University of Minnesota Press.

Kierkegaard, S. 1985. *Philosophical Fragments*. Kierkegaard's Writings 7. Princeton, NJ: Princeton University Press.

Latour, B, and S. Woolgar. 1986. *Laboratory Life: The Construction of Scientific Facts*. Princeton, NJ: Princeton University Press.

Lipowsky, A. 2020. "Lebensphilosophie and the Revolution in Anthropology: Uncovering the Original "Turn to Life"". *HAU: Journal of Ethnographic Theory* 10 (3), 800-812. DOI:10.1086/711881.

Martus, S., and C. Spoerhase. 2022. *Geistesarbeit: eine Praxeologie der Geisteswissenschaften*. Suhrkamp Taschenbuch Wissenschaft 2379. Berlin: Suhrkamp.

Massimi, M. 2022. *Perspectival Realism*. Oxford Studies in Philosophy of Science Series. New York: Oxford University Press.

Mauss, M. 1990. *The Gift: The Form and Reason for Exchange in Archaic Societies*. New York: Whitney Museum of American Art.

Orr, Y, and R. Orr. 2022. "Deception-Based Knowledge in Indigenous and Scientific Societies: American Indian Tricksters and Experimental Research Designs". *HAU: Journal of Ethnographic Theory* 12 (1), 46-62. DOI:10.1086/719574.

Padberg, B. 2014. "The Center for Interdisciplinary Research (ZiF)-Epistemic and Institutional Considerations". In *University Experiments in Interdisciplinarity: Obstacles and Opportunities*, edited by P. Weingart, and B. Padberg, 95-116. Bielefeld: transcript.

Plessner, H. 1975. *Die Stufen Des Organischen Und Der Mensch: Einleitung in Die Philosophische Anthropologie*. Berlin: De Gruyter.

Polanyi, K. 1944. *The Great Transformation*. New York: Farrar & Rinehart.

Polanyi, K. 1968. "The Economy as Instituted Process". In *Economic Anthropology: Readings in Theory and Analysis*, edited by E.E. LeClair Jr., and H.K. Schneider, 3-21. New York: Holt, Rinehart, Winston.

Putnam, H. 1981. *Reason, Truth and History*. Cambridge: Cambridge University Press.

Putnam, H. 1983. *Realism and Reason*. Philosophical Papers, v. 3. Cambridge/New York: Cambridge University Press.

Putnam, H. 1987. *The Many Faces of Realism*. The Paul Carus Lectures, 16th ser. (Dec. 1985). La Salle, Ill: Open Court.

Renn, J. 2020. *The Evolution of Knowledge: Rethinking Science for the Anthropocene*. Princeton: Princeton University Press.

Rheinberger, H.-J. 2008. *Historische Epistemologie zur Einführung*. 2. Aufl. Zur Einführung 336. Hamburg: Junius.

Richardson, W.J. 2003. *Heidegger: Through Phenomenology to Thought*. 4th ed. Perspectives in Continental Philosophy, no. 30. New York: Fordham University Press.

Rochefort, P.-Y. 2021. "Did Putnam Really Abandon Internal Realism in the 1990s?" *European Journal of Pragmatism and American Philosophy* XIII (2), DOI:10.4000/ejpap.2515.

Roebroeks, W., and R.H.A. Corbey. 2009. "Review of *Review of Axe Age. Acheulian Toolmaking from Quarry to Discard*, by Naama Goren-Inbar and Gonen Sharon." *Lithic Technology* 34 (1), 53-59.

Sartre, J.-P. 2012. *Being and Nothingness: An Essay on Phenomenological Ontology*. 23rd print. New York: Washington Square Press.

Shapin, S., and S. Schaffer. 1985. *Leviathan and the Air-Pump: Hobbes, Boyle, and the Experimental Life: Including a Translation of Thomas Hobbes, Dialogus Physicus de Natura Aeris by Simon Schaffer*. Princeton, N.J: Princeton University Press.

Snow, C.P. 1968. *The Two Cultures and the Scientific Revolution*. Martino Fine Books.

Soler, L., S. Zwart, M. Lynch, and V. Israel-Jost, eds. 2014. *Science after the Practice Turn in the Philosophy, History, and Social Studies of Science*. New York: Routledge.

Trigger, B. 2017. *Artifacts and Ideas: Essays in Archaeology*. First edition. London: Taylor and Francis.

Turner, D.D. 2012. *Making Prehistory: Historical Science and the Scientific Realism Debate*. Cambridge: Cambridge University Press.

Uexküll, J. von. 2004. *Mondes animaux et monde humain suivi de La théorie de la signification*. Agora 268. Paris: Pocket.

Willerslev, R. 2004. "Not Animal, Not Not-Animal: Hunting, Imitation and Empathetic Knowledge Among the Siberian Yukaghirs". *Journal of the Royal Anthropological Institute* 10 (3), 629-52. DOI:10.1111/j.1467-9655.2004.00205.x

Wylie, A. 2002. *Thinking from Things: Essays in the Philosophy of Archaeology*. Berkeley: University of California Press.

Wylie, A. 2015. "A Plurality of Pluralisms: Collaborative Practice in Archaeology". In *Objectivity in Science*, edited by F. Padovani, A. Richardson, and J.Y. Tsou, 189-210. Cham: Springer.

In Hussain, S.T. and G.L. Dusseldorp (eds) 2025. Sitting on the fence: Negotiating archaeology, anthropology and philosophy. Festschrift for Prof. Dr Raymond H.A. Corbey in celebration of his 70th birthday. *Analecta Praehistorica Leidensia* 54. Leiden: Sidestone Press, pp. 45-54.

# Better divergent than aligning: An argument in favour of the 'shaken-bookcase syndrome' in archaeological theory-building

Alexander Geurds

## ABSTRACT

This provocation suggests that an archaeologist's confrontation with philosophy, while hazardous like any boundary crossing, is ultimately a catalyst for creativity. And creativity is at the heart of archaeological storytelling. The paradox exposed along the way is that a scholar (let's call him Raymond) can be both disciplinary gatekeeper and archaeological adviser to the philosophically curious student. To archaeology, philosophy can be seen as an invitation to think differently and 'travel with' the epistemic views of a chosen author's work – French, German, or otherwise – that may have dropped from a bookcase under carefully randomized conditions. Such travels do not attest to a lack of disciplinary integrity but are arguably consistent with, and even strengthen, the continually emergent character of archaeological consciousness.

*Keywords: Archaeological consciousness, philosophy, Campari*

## INTRODUCTION

Theories and archaeology are what Raymond and I talk about. And we've done so principally either in the setting of undergraduate teaching at Leiden or while being coolly contemplated by Abyssinians. In this brief chapter, I argue that deep commitment in archaeological work to specific philosophical schools of thought is not preferred, *contra* various personal communications by Raymond. Instead, I will suggest that *theoretical wandering* – spurred on by academic curiosity – between a range of standpoints and their philosophical foundations is a preferred path to attain creative insights and producing archaeological knowledge. Such wandering mirrors long-standing practice-based insights in social science. Consider, for example, Michel de Certeau's *voyeur* (1984) or indeed Charles Beaudelaire's *flâneur* (2010 [1863]). Following a brief contextual sketch of archaeological theorizing in Leiden, I will conclude that theory is an ongoing process of argued theses and antitheses, resulting in increasing reflexivity and an archaeology discipline that is ever more aware of its location and consequence.

**Alexander Geurds**
Faculty of Archaeology, Leiden University, The Netherlands
a.geurds@arch.leidenuniv.nl
0000-0002-2418-2828

## THEORY AT LEIDEN

Writing about archaeological theory at Leiden is a hazardous path to go down. Indeed, the theoretical vignettes of the Leiden Faculty of Archaeology are decidedly less than clearly advertised. The informed reader might claim to have at least a preunderstanding of past or current archaeological theoretical signatures at respective departments in, for example, Ann Arbor, Cambridge, Kiel, Mexico-City, or Paris. But Leiden sits uncomfortably on that list. There is no chair in archaeological theory. Nor is there a postgraduate specialization in theory. And the undergraduate focus is decidedly limited, *mea culpa*. So, where are the Leiden-based ardent arguments on the nature and purpose of archaeological thinking?

The presently somewhat obfuscated theoretical landscape certainly did not always define the Leiden environment. During the 1980s and 90s, archaeological departments in the Netherlands increasingly tabled discussions about archaeological theory, for example, through an annual TAG-like symposium that rotated between universities, and the founding of the journal *Archaeological Dialogues* by several (junior) staff members, including some from Leiden. While clearly most of the debating tinder was lit in Amsterdam and Groningen, Leiden also played its part in this process (Slofstra 1994). One outcome of this period of internal interrogation and self-reflection were initial discussions on archaeology's role and responsibility in (Dutch) society. Subsequently, this provided an impetus for the further development of critical heritage studies – patterns still recognizable in the national archaeological landscape today. Indeed, one of those junior staff members is the present Dean of Leiden's Faculty of Archaeology!

The 1980s to 90s was also the period when Leiden undergraduates read Lakatos, Feyerabend, and Kuhn and produced essays discussing appropriate methodologies and frames of archaeological thought from Childe to Flannery. Four 12-week courses were explicitly theoretical and methodological in orientation and aim, ranging from an introduction to cultural anthropology (Claessen) to fundamentals of disciplinary methodology (Van de Velde); the history of archaeology (Fokkens), and indeed archaeological thought more broadly (Van de Velde). Further detailing is beyond the remit of this contribution, requiring a more comprehensive analysis of how commonality of one's conceptual framework is historically achieved by Leiden faculty members and students. For this, I refer the reader to Pieter van de Velde's (1994) insightful manuscript on a historical descriptive analysis of the development of archaeology in the Netherlands, and Leiden specifically.

I was one of those undergraduates during the mid-1990s and influenced by such emphases in the archaeology curriculum. Today, the course program and design contrast sharply, offering a single 7-week course in the sixth and final semester of a three-year degree – a course that I convened together with Raymond for several years. In this course, we try to engage students in some soul-searching for their ideas and plans, and to have them come out more aware and better prepared to ground their own thinking. That process is achieved in part by sketching epistemic extremes and historical trajectories in archaeological reasoning and providing an overview of key developments in archaeological thinking. Operating in Corbeyesque style, it's hard to forget the contemplative faces of Maarten Jansen ('The Phenomenologist') and Will Roebroeks ('The Empiricist') on a single slide, both presumed to bookend two sides of a scale of philosophical options. A scale on which students find themselves choosing their path to either hermeneutic understanding or positivist explanation. This may be provocatively intended, but I question if this is a fair way to confront students.

Can we discuss archaeological thinking in such binary terms and prevent this apparent crispness of polarity from outshining the complex entanglement of archaeology and philosophy? And if we leave the soothing empirical properties of the material record aside and assume for a moment that archaeology and philosophy are indeed deeply linked, how then do we advise students to proceed? If one enjoys political economic modelling of Late Bronze Age exchange networks, does one start with reading Late Marx? Surely a textbook on archaeological applications of those ideas will be sufficient (*e.g.*, McGuire 1992). Or not? And what is the exact grounding for even choosing this form of handling data (modelling) over, say, Malinowski's ethnographic focus on the role of magic in redistributive exchange relations that defy notions of property and the permanent control over resources? When asking such questions, we first show students that description and analysis are two different things, then argue that description itself is also theory-laden, showing them the dialectic process between observing, recognizing, and interpreting. In doing so, we demonstrate that the binary opposition between *Erklären* and *Verstehen* is a characterization of rhetorical convenience and has the potential to become dangerously confusing.

## THE SHAKEN-BOOKCASE-SYNDROME

Perhaps, then, binary views on archaeological theory do a disservice to the actual work it takes to epistemically consider one's archaeological materials (Shanks 2020), instead merely confusing students and cementing the believe that this is a matter of pledging allegiance to, say, post-processualism or not. As if the work required for theoretical positioning were to be accomplished by either a) seeking comfort in empiricism and not worrying about much other than observations in environments with controlled variables such as in, for example, new pragmatism, or b) deciding to take a birds-eye view and be convinced that material engagements are unpredictable and beyond human control and will therefore never be understood from a laboratory. While it is apparent that archaeology departments increasingly reflect this opposition between archaeological science and archaeology as a human endeavor, it is similarly clear that neither of the sketched extremes adequately portray the realities of how archaeological work comes about in a vast majority of cases (see Jones 2002, and a premonition in Snow 1959). Moving from *materials* to *evidence* entails the precondition to establish epistemic principles and finding a middle ground between, on the one hand, merely focusing on a minimal number of empirical correspondences and in the process losing sight of the reasons why archaeology is done at all, and on the other, to venture into apparent speculation (Chapman and Wylie 2016, 7; Shanks 2023).

The engagement with the philosophical foundations of archaeological research can be seen as a *process of growth* that is situational and depending on a wide range of potentially confusing situational factors. In turn, confusion is a breeding ground, and some would say critical vehicle, for creativity, and I suspect Raymond knows this when exposing his thinking to bachelor students. This is why he is known to throw small plastic balls into a room full of sleep-deprived undergraduates and why he does not shy away from treading along the boundaries of an anthropological archaeology and philosophy in his educational missioning (pun intended). This is also what makes talking about theory in archaeology so exciting; it is precisely the searching and grappling for recognition and utility of ideas that students and (mind you) colleagues need to contend with – if only for the sake of tempering and calibrating their own positions. For the processual-minded, it is the continuous flux of testing theory against data, and

for the broad church of post-processual approaches, the key is awareness of standpoint, and critical examination of historical context. We can see here that across such a wide field, the process of coming to an understanding is essentially *emergent*, defined by back-and-forth learning. By consequence, any binary sketch of archaeological theories amounts to a form of Othering. It forms ideological stereotypes and erases the continuous emergence of archaeological ideas. To illustrate by means of a colonial frame: It is as if a theory-missionary had stumbled across an uncontacted community amid a dense data forest and excitedly exclaimed: "Aha! Relativists!".

Even if temporary confusion can productively lead to unsuspected new insights, there can be no short-cuts according to Raymond. Like the labradorite in his mineral collection, he prefers his students to be illuminated in their thinking and polished in their reasoning. Quick fixes by means of jumping on passing bandwagons of philosophical thinkers *de rigueur* is not an elegant or preferable option for him. In fact, such fashionable opportunism runs the risk of combining archaeological materials and a philosophical influence-of-choice in an eclectic, almost random manner. Instead, I suspect Raymond would rather have his students and colleagues exhibit a deep *understanding* of how archaeological theory came to be where it is today: as being the result of a limited number of philosophical propositions that, in turn, arose from certain societal and intra-disciplinary problems. Merely grabbing one thinker (say, Bruno Latour) and applying the corresponding theoretical lens to one's archaeological problem(s) might be the equivalent of sporting black tie to a hunting party: it qualifies as clothing, but it makes little sense and lacks aptness and sophistication. This is the 'shaken-bookcase-syndrome' (SBS), as Raymond referred to it over Campari one evening. As far as I could ascertain, it is also a notion coined by him.

## THEORY-WORK IN ARCHAEOLOGY

Raymond Corbey lives in the borderlands of philosophical and archaeological schools of thought, equipping him with the rare positionality of someone whom students cannot easily pigeonhole. His SBS notion expresses a dislike for the capriciousness of archaeology in confronting its source materials with a range of thinkers and intellectual traditions from outside of the discipline. This is too straightforward and suspicious for him; overly opportunistic, perhaps even running the risk of being fashionable. It shows, in other words, a lack of deep engagement and commitment by the archaeologist. Simply shopping around for ideas and assembling publications by retrofitting, for example, aspects of sociological thinking to archaeological datasets, amounts, for Raymond, to a *modular* handling of archaeology and philosophy along an epistemological toolbox approach: see if it sticks and then run with it. Perhaps not even going back to the primary source and leaning on an oft-cited theoretically-inclined archaeologist. In short, shaking the book closet and seeing what falls off the shelf.

From this follows the question how and from where archaeology undergraduates acquire and distil their methodology. Is it from a deep study of social theorists that, in turn, anchor their work in 19th and 20th century Western philosophical traditions? To answer this, we take a step back (as Raymond often does by sitting on his proverbial fence) and ask what it is that archaeology tries to achieve. We can recognize that archaeology has different goals and ambitions than the respective disciplines borrowed from and needs to re-translate ideas and perspectives. Definitions of the archaeological project abound, one recent elegant formulation states that archaeology is a discipline that allows for an examination of the human past using the residual traces of human activities (Chapman and Wylie 2016, 6). Here we see that the discipline allows for a space to study human pasts, but this alone provides little in the way of guidance of *how* to do so. Key for students (and colleagues) is to find a position from which one can isolate one such way of productive examination. In this regard, undergraduate courses on field techniques may seem like a least likely candidate for learning and strategizing about the theory-laden nature of observation and recording, but one with significant potential. Students can develop a grasp of archaeological objects and sites within the constraints of a limited number of variables: point of view, methodology, and a commitment to observing the history inherent in the studied material traces (Barrett 2021).

Classes on archaeological method and theory generally hinge on two emphases: the history of thought and the intellectual undercurrents of that thought. This is indeed how Raymond and I would structure our classes: positing broader philosophical questions and confronting them with archaeological echoes, in part showing the meshwork that is philosophy and archaeological enquiry. Victimized in

this type of structure is the question of method. Class discussions on the philosophical groundings of certain field techniques are much rarer than broad-sweep issues of theoretical positionality, to the degree that students might be led to assume that archaeological field methods just 'are'; naturalized in their existence and impervious to the shifting sands of theory. Recent introductory textbooks underline this, with little to almost no reflection on the epistemology of archaeological work (*e.g.*, Flatman 2022; Grant *et al.* 2015; see also Shanks 2023). Yet we know that field methods are equally theoretically established; they represent an epistemic decision; a methodology, in short. Recent work has further foregrounded this by considering archaeological field sites as hyperobjects (Campbell 2021), following earlier work by Timothy Morton (2013). Kevin Greene and Tom Moore's *Archaeology: An Introduction* (2010) is an exception, making room for a joint discussion of the history of archaeological method and theory.

Even rarer is the inverse: how archaeological practice might inform philosophical insights, a major exception being R. C. Collingwood who argued that archaeological fieldwork was meaningless unless question-driven. This is the logic of Question-and-Answer, as also developed in Collingwood's methodology for historical work (Collingwood and Myers 1936; see also Lowther 1961). Such a question-driven approach is now a staple for undergraduate archaeology tutoring on essay and thesis writing. Archaeology teaching at Leiden may thus be at risk of forgetting that field and writing techniques are also theory-laden and require proper engagement. The use of Total Station surveying equipment, for example, may reinforce a view of sites as consisting of isolated components and finds (Hussain, pers. comm.). Many of these techniques saw their introduction during the advent of processual archaeology in the 60s and 70s but are today seen as natural ways to approach the residual traces of human activity in a way that was recently described as *"process after processualism"* (Evans 2023: 250).

Barrett's (2021) three variables of point of view, methodology, and history of objects are recurrent patterns in the history of archaeological thought. Initially, this remained largely implicit in regional archaeological work of the pre-World War 2 (WW2) era, although I would single out, for example, the later work of Gordon Childe (1956) as an emphatic conscious effort to reflect on conceptual underpinnings and scrutinize what archaeological studies tended to implicitly assume. Childe was not a philosopher (even if a keen reader of philosophy, including Marxist writings) though he was clearly a product of his time, as philosophers equally tend to be. Archaeologists today only infrequently cite Childe's work, and often as a methodological point of orientation, leaving him principally in the realm of Trigger's (1989) histories of archaeological thought. Yet there is a point of relevance here whether to determine your philosopher-of-choice, à la SBS, based in part on externally validating reasons or to adhere to a deep philosophical understanding, crafting an independent personal conceptual frame from which to build archaeological work. The archaeological interest in the pre-Kantian notion of the ontological turn, for example, may well be the product of the current surge in studies enticing more and more adopting by archaeologists, rather than being the result of more exposure to, say, philosophies of metaphysics.

The historical context of Western philosophical thinking is marked by rotating academic opinions that mirror the shifts between viewing the human past as either a process of *unifying progression* (consider mid-19th century Darwinian social evolutionism and mid-20th century New Archaeology) or one of *fragmentary divergence* with overall questionable progress (consider early 20th century Boasian culture history and late 20th century Hodderian interpretive archaeology). All these shifts strongly resonate with epistemological anxieties of what archaeological perspectives can reveal, and the 'truth-value' of the respective findings. Such theoretical discussions earmark the history of archaeology in North America and across Europe, often signposting the *Zeitgeist* in which debates emerge (see also Kristiansen 2011). These challenges to the foundational understandings of archaeology offer students the opportunity to critically consider where we currently stand (and on whose shoulders) – and where they wish to stand – on this alternating balance. The ambition to 'think differently' equally requires an understanding of the philosophical echoes that resonate in archaeological theory, in service of creating critical self-awareness to, first, develop theoretical scaffolding, then, approach archaeological materials and, lastly, be able to synthetically discuss knowledge of the human past.

## PERMEABLE DISCIPLINARY BOUNDARIES
Raymond and I speak to our students about the consciousness of our discipline, invoking its famous postlapsarian condition (Clarke 1973), and extending a call to critical reflection on the variables mentioned above, while still adhering to Childe's conviction to work towards a point of view and methodology that is internal to archaeology. I presume this is something all archaeologists, present generations of colleagues included, have at some point considered. Raymond and I try to show to students in our classes that such philosophical scaffolding was foregrounded not just in the advent of *seemingly* obfuscating and fieldwork-deficient post-processual studies from the 1980s onwards, but much earlier, for example by the New Archaeology as it rocked the proverbial archaeological landscape from the 1960s onwards. This is one shift where we witness a call to epistemic order to a degree Childe did probably not imagine, and which indeed also looked explicitly beyond disciplinary boundaries, even though, symptomatically, in a highly selective manner.

In North American New Archaeology specifically, views onto a foreign set of bookshelves are loosely connected to foundational theoretical discussions of a range of Western philosophers that strove toward systematic analysis along the lines of Bertrand Russell, Thomas Kuhn, and (prominently) the nomothetic deductive positivism of Carl Hempel (Leone 1972). The formal argument-building that is central to this body of philosophical treaties ran parallel to the increasing influence of natural scientific approaches as they began to attain a prominent position in North American academia in the post-WW2 period. This protrusion of advances in scientific method in archaeology has stirred internal debates on what goals to emphasize in the discipline on more than one occasion – the earlier mentioned current role of archaeological science in the discipline is no different, once again resurging discussions as to the primary objectives and epistemological alliances of the field.

Much earlier than the New Archaeology still, self-identifying archaeologists have searched for philosophical points of view since the 1930s (*e.g.,* Kluckhohn 1939). In the North American context of archaeological debate, the work of Alfred North Whitehead was drawn upon to push back against the antiquarian focus on objective classification: finding things, describing, and ordering them. The need for the archaeological practitioner to weigh and understand theories was also forcefully tabled by Clyde Kluckhohn and published, surprisingly perhaps, as a book chapter in a now classic volume in Mesoamerican archaeology entitled *The Maya and their Neighbors* (Kluckhohn 1960 [1939]). One could also mention the polemics between Albert Spaulding and James Ford revolving around the explanatory statistical potential to define archaeological types and link those types to past realities, or the all but assured failure to establish such links and the need for an epistemic stance that recognizes the agency of archaeological work itself, acknowledging John Dewey and Charles Peirce's philosophical pragmatism (Spaulding 1952; Ford 1954). These are all examples of early critiques by traditional archaeologists that would later be adopted by New Archaeologists. Likewise, early post-processual archaeological arguments rely on various continental European philosophical schools of thought, including the critical theory work of the Frankfurt School (Adorno, Habermas), and indeed also the broad school of Husserl's phenomenological thinking as well. Moments of large-scale consensus about approach and purpose of archaeology are rarely found and attempts at reconciliatory compromises receive relatively little following as shown by, for example, the proposal of *processual plus* for archaeological theory in North America (Hegmon 2003).

What the many explorations of philosophical schools of thought in archaeology have shown is the immense productivity and collaborative potential of an active drive to think differently and 'travel with' particular epistemic views, seeing theory as an open-ended and creative force. I consider what Raymond has at times called the 'multiparadigmatic' nature of the discipline an asset, one that is born from the necessity to acknowledge the nature of the source materials used and the inevitability of bringing assumptions to bear on those materials: all evidence for problem-driven and open-ended non-dogmatic research. Viewed in this way, the pluriform presence of philosophy in archaeology should not be equated to a problem of a lacking singular methodology (monism) for using residual traces to study the human past, but as evidence for an open and flexible disciplinary field, conscious of the continually changing and historically diverse contexts in which the (field)work takes place and fore-fronting the need to invite practices and ideas from other disciplines to engage with those residual (material) traces under varying conditions and with specific concerns.

This open character is also reflected in the institutional structure of Leiden University. Leiden University's organogram shows an apparent anomaly, with the Faculty of Archaeology being significantly smaller than most of the other six faculties. This is where the disciplinary boundaries of archaeology are also discussed, with the Faculty proving to be a possible organizational match to at least three of the Leiden faculties. At times this was considered a weakness of sorts, linked to anxiety more widely felt in the discipline, and an enduring identity crisis, being torn between the social sciences, humanities, or even the natural sciences (see also Yoffee and Fowles 2011, Smith 2017). Such quests for archaeological 'homelands' are divisive and ultimately unproductive – they cultivate antagonism and partisanship.

The open-ended and permeable view of the archaeological discipline needs to further be extended to include a student's search for philosophical grounding and orientation, best served by a form of methodological 'omnivory' (Currie 2018, 159) achieved by theoretical wandering. From this need for diversity of resources, it follows that there is merit in developing a theoretical praxis that can be seen as venturing into the open stacks and running your finger along the shelves of broader writings in the social sciences and humanities domain, that is, practicing SBS and allowing for shifts in one's fundamental theoretical position. I would further argue this on two grounds. My first contention is that such strolls away from the internal dialogues of archaeology lead to serendipitous fortunes, or 'happy little accidents' in popular vernacular: One can encounter a solution or way forward to a line of thinking for one's research problem that otherwise might have remained beyond a horizon of foundational ideas. Looking for a confrontation with different bookshelves invites creativity, friction, and doubt to define a point of view, perhaps also allowing more serious method-work that is not merely application-oriented and so trivializes methodological concerns in archaeology. My second contention is that this is a repeatable process, eschewing allegiance to a particular philosophical set of ideas until a point in time where a student finds the conceptual scaffolding that is sufficiently ample and applicable to the archaeological materials at hand and the context-specific practice that the student depends on. In sum, theoretical scaffolding in archaeology is seen here as a praxis of theorizing, marked by unforeseen but creative encounters with conceptual ideas.

## Conclusion

*"Young man, I don't know what you are talking about, and I don't think you do either."*

This statement was the spontaneous interjection offered by a member of the audience to the abovementioned American archaeologist James Ford during a lecture in 1938 (Ford 1954, 111). One key aspect of archaeology is continuous epistemic critique, that much is clear. This unrelenting emergence of archaeological theory begs a concluding consideration: whether a clear understanding of philosophical views is even relevant to students of archaeology today, given the conditions of the 'real world' outside the confinement of academic maisons, in which the majority who continues to practice archaeology following graduation do so by finding employment in the cultural resource management industry.

Archaeological theorists are at times accused of picking up on an idea by the time it is considered past its due date in philosophical circles or in the broader humanities, as happened, for example, with polemics surrounding the popularity of logical positivism among those writing about processual archaeology during the 1970s (*e.g.*, Fritz and Plog 1970; Morgan 1973; Levin 1976). By then, Hempelian emphasis on empiricism had lost much of its strength in the face of, among others, Kuhn's historical contextualization of seeing science as developing through a series of paradigmatic shifts and thus undermining the premise of an external empirical reality that scientists could always resort back to and insist on.

The earlier mentioned alternation between ways of regarding the human past as either convergent or divergent are generally accepted in the history of archaeological thought (Trigger 1989), and often cast as a struggle between commitments to particularism or universalism respectively. In fact, the historical succession of 'Culture History > New Archaeology > Interpretive Archaeology' is a common thread in university courses introducing and debating archaeological theory, like those convened by Raymond and myself. Such alternating shows that paradigmatic shifts in method and theory even implicitly underline the open-endedness of debating archaeological work. The irony then is that, when archaeologists adopted philosophical models to improve archaeological reasoning, the assumption was that such models themselves could be taken as final words, as authoritative and as such not themselves situated, wrongly rendering philosophy impervious to those same ongoing foundational discussions that dominate archaeology itself.

I suspect it is the long history of boundary crossing in archaeology that puts Raymond in a mood to challenge assumptions, and to hesitate in the face of a direct-line import of philosophical notions and perspectives into archaeology. This mirrors reflections on the relationship between anthropology and archaeology (Gosden 1999; Garrow and Yarrow 2010), where it is observed that the former is also often used as a reservoir of ready-for-use models for archaeological enquiry. Such observations on the co-opting of anthropological concepts are critically viewed as one-sided, thereby revealing a lack of positive consideration for creative disciplinary boundary crossing.

So, what is the archaeological *Denkstil* today (Fleck 2015 [1935])? Where do the concepts originate from that are mobilized in archaeological studies, and in how far should students be encouraged to reflect on how and where they philosophically anchor their work? These are questions not often tabled, but as is my impression, frequently contemplated by archaeology students themselves. This also opens the door to a worrying alternative interpretation of SBS. Perhaps it refers to an act of desperation, whereby those in search of philosophical grounding resort to grabbing the bookcase and violently shaking it to find an answer. This is of course ill-advised under any circumstance, not the least considering the infamous wrath of librarians it may conjure. But, more importantly, I do not suspect this is what Raymond has in mind, even if any archaeology student, compelled to work towards self-reflection and productive criticality, on occasion may become anxious from running a finger along the philosophy shelves. *Contra* Raymond's negative notion of SBS, what I hope to have argued is that archaeology is a discipline defined by shifting points of view and methodologies. Considering such openness, theoretical scaffolding is best seen as an emergent practice that wanders across disciplinary boundaries while critically conscious of one's goals and the larger purpose of our field.

## Acknowledgements

Over many years, Raymond has proven to be a thoughtful and stimulating colleague always in the mood to interact, whether talking about opaque aspects of antiquities trade in Europe, missionary ethnography across southeast Asia, or indeed archaeological epistemology. Not one to shy away from knocking on doors and combining conversation with food and drinks, Raymond regularly invited and, planning issues aside, afternoons or evenings were spent. This was also not a courtesy call – Raymond expected dialogue and at least some disagreement. That is something to particularly appreciate in times where Socratic dialogue at university has developed into something of a heritage concern: rare and in need of regulation. Looking forward to more. Lastly, thanks go to Shumon Hussain for identifying the terminological reference to the work of Fleck and the link to new pragmatism, and for stimulating suggestions that greatly improved the final text.

## References

Barrett, J.C. 2021. *Archaeology and its Discontents: Why Archaeology Matters*. London: Routledge.

Chapman, R., and A. Wylie 2016. *Evidential Reasoning in Archaeology*. London: Bloomsbury.

Childe, V.G. 1956. *Piecing Together the Past: The Interpretation of Archaeological Data*. London: Routledge.

Clarke, D. 1973. "Archaeology: the Loss of Innocence." *Antiquity* 47 (185), 6-18.

Collingwood, R.G., and J.N. Linton Myres. 1936. *Roman Britain and the English settlements*. Oxford: Clarendon Press.

Currie, A. 2018. *Rock, Bone, and Ruin: An Optimist's Guide to the Historical Sciences*. Boston: MIT Press.

Evans, C. 2023. "Redirecting the Field – Total Archaeologies, Flagships, and Sample Design." In *Sentient Archaeologies: Global Perspectives on Places, Objects and Practice*, edited by C. Nimura, R. O'Sullivan, and R. Bradley, 241-256. Oxford: Oxbow Books.

Flatman, J. 2022. *Becoming an Archaeologist: A Guide to Professional Pathways*. Cambridge: Cambridge University Press.

Fleck, L. 2015 [1935]. *Entstehung und Entwicklung einer Wissenschaftlichen Tatsache. Einführung in die Lehre vom Denkstil und Denkkollektiv*. Frankfurt: Suhrkamp.

Ford, J.A. 1954. "Spaulding's Review of Ford." *American Anthropologist* 56 (1), 109-114.

Fritz, J.M., and F.T. Plog. 1970. "The Nature of Archaeological Explanation." *American Antiquity* 35 (4), 405-412.

Garrow, D., and T. Yarrow. 2010. *Archaeology and Anthropology: Understanding Similarity, Exploring Difference*. Oxford: Oxbow.

Gosden, C. 1999. *Anthropology and Archaeology: A Changing Relationship*. Cambridge: Cambridge University Press.

Grant, J., S. Gorin, and N. Fleming. 2015. *The Archaeology Coursebook: An Introduction to Themes, Sites, Methods, and Skills. Fifth Edition*. London: Routledge.

Greene, K., and T. Moore 2010. *Archaeology: An Introduction*. London: Routledge.

Hegmon, M. 2003. "Setting Theoretical Egos Aside: Issues and Theory in North American Archaeology". *American Antiquity* 68 (2), 213-243.

Jones, A. 2001. *Archaeological Theory and Scientific Practice*. Cambridge: Cambridge University Press.

Kluckhohn, C. 1939. The Place of Theory in Anthropological Studies. *Philosophy of Science* 6 (3), 328-344.

Kluckhohn, C. 1960 [1939]. "The Conceptual Structure in Middle American Studies." In *The Maya and their Neighbors. Second Edition*, edited by C.L. Hay, R.L. Linton, S.K. Lothrop, H.L. Shapiro, and G.C. Vaillant, 41-51. New York: Appleton-Century Company.

Kristiansen, K. 2011. "Theory Does Not Die, it Changes Direction." In *The Death of Archaeological Theory*, edited by J. Bintliff and M. Pearce, 72-80. Oxford: Oxbow Books.

Leone, M.P. 1972. *Contemporary Archaeology: A Guide to Theory and Contributions*. Carbondale: University of Southern Illinois Press.

Levin, M.E. 1976. "On the Ascription of Functions to Objects, with Special Reference to Inference in Archaeology." *Philosophy of the Social Sciences* 6 (3), 227-234.

Lowther, G.R. 1961. "Relations between Historical Theory and Archaeological Practice in the Work of RG Collingwood." *Anthropologica* 3 (2), 173-180.

McGuire, R.H. 1992. *A Marxist Archaeology*. New York: Academic Press.

Morgan, C.G. 1973. "Archaeology and Explanation." *World archaeology* 4 (3), 259-276.

Morton, T. 2013. *Hyperobjects: Philosophy and Ecology after the End of the World*. New York: Columbia University Press.

Shanks, M. 2020. "The Archaeological Imagination." In *The Cambridge Handbook of the Imagination*, edited A. Abraham, 47-63. Cambridge: Cambridge University Press.

Shanks, M. "Social Theory in Archaeology". Accessed July 18, 2023. https://www.academia.edu/105380112/Social_theory_in_archaeology?email_work_card=title.

Smith, M.E. 2017. "Social Science and Archaeological Enquiry." *Antiquity* 91 (356), 520-528.

Snow, C.P. 1959. *The Two Cultures*. Cambridge: Cambridge University Press.

Spaulding, A.C. 1953. "Statistical Techniques for the Discovery of Artifact Types." *American Antiquity* 18 (4), 305-313.

Trigger, B.G. 1989. *A History of Archaeological Thought*. Cambridge: Cambridge University Press.

Yoffee, N., and S. Fowles. 2011. "Archaeology in the Humanities." *Diogenes* 58 (1-2), 35-52.

In Hussain, S.T. and G.L. Dusseldorp (eds) 2025. Sitting on the fence: Negotiating archaeology, anthropology and philosophy. Festschrift for Prof. Dr Raymond H.A. Corbey in celebration of his 70th birthday. *Analecta Praehistorica Leidensia* 54. Leiden: Sidestone Press, pp. 55-68.

# Why, throughout the universe, reason and 'civilization' are more the exception than the rule

Pouwel Slurink

## ABSTRACT

Can we ever communicate with other civilizations in the cosmos? The age and size of the universe suggests that it is teeming with life and consciousness, and perhaps even with advanced civilizations. Yet we hear nothing. Perhaps it is worth reviewing what we know and think about life, consciousness, morality and civilization, and their relationships. How do these complex entities relate to each other, and how can they emerge or evolve from each other? Which qualities are enduring at all levels, which are new, which are robust, and which are more fragile and much less likely to evolve? We must always strike the right balance between reductionism and holism, because the fragility of emergent properties can vary greatly at different levels or stages. On Earth, evolving systems have passed through a series of probability-reducing 'bottlenecks'. But is this planet an average planet in a habitable zone? It has a special moon, plate tectonics, a highly variable climate, and life on it has undergone periodic mass extinctions. Human evolution, too, has been made possible by a particular configuration of continents and a particular sequence of disasters and climate changes. Moreover, the moral evolution necessary for 'civilization' is a strange and paradoxical process with an endless trail of conflict and tragedy. Cooperation becomes more difficult as more parties are involved, and the whole process is inevitably driven at least in part by competition, with attitudes such as jealousy and revenge. Throughout the cosmos, life is ultimately governed by the laws of selfish genes and the fragility of cooperation. The ultimate reason we do not hear of extraterrestrial 'civilizations' may then be that technological cultures either fail to become sustainable and perish, or, conversely, manage to become sustainable but then have to abandon further space exploration.

*Keywords: Life, consciousness, culture, morality, civilization, extraterrestrial intelligence*

## FINE THINGS ARE OFTEN RARE AND DELICATE

### Introduction

Dear Raymond, over the last four decades we have talked about all sorts of things, in the mensa, in the pub, or on birding excursions. Among other things, we discussed the nature of consciousness, human beings, and the origin of values. The problem of *qualia* is very important to you, as well as the nature and position of humans. In fact, all issues came together in our different expectations about the nature of the universe. With Conway, you sometimes seemed to cherish the idea that there is some kind of necessity in the succession of living things: there are limited possibilities and

**Pouwel Slurink**

Lijsterbesstraat 98, 6523JW
Nijmegen, The Netherlands
p.slurink@kpnplanet.nl
ORCID 0000-0002-5971-3166

time seems relatively unlimited (Conway 2003). So, according to you it is quite likely that elsewhere in the universe there are also intelligent beings with human-like traits ('convergent evolution'). At least, I got the impression that you sometimes think along these lines...

In what follows, I will comment on this, and at the same time solve all associated philosophical problems, so that in future we can talk more about birds, those wonderful feathered dinosaurs. I will argue that it is unlikely that the universe is full of rational and logical thinking (let alone 'civilised') creatures. Life is likely to arise here and there. Primitive forms of consciousness, sentience, will also appear here and there. But real intelligence is likely to be incredibly rare, and reason and morality almost inevitably perish everywhere in all kinds of conflicts of interest, if not aggressive competition. Above all, the evolution of a technological culture is rather unlikely and easily leads to self-destruction, making creativity and intelligence scarce and brittle. This reduces the likelihood that carriers of technological cultures will encounter other contemporaneous kindred spirits in their cosmic environment. Given the long periods during which our planet was home to purely unicellular organisms, or reasonably 'simple' multicellular organisms, we are likely to find planets with this kind of life in the future. But it is much less likely that we will find real technological cultures or 'civilizations' in the rest of our galaxy or in other galaxies.

In turn, I will talk about life, consciousness, self-awareness, culture, morality, hominins, and the possibilities of 'civilization'. Some of these phenomena emerge from one another, acquiring new properties, but also retaining older ones. The emergence of new qualities does not imply transcendence or the breaking of laws. It requires a set of favourable conditions in the form of favourable conditions, resources and/or pre-existing genes that limit the range of possible evolutionary products. In effect, these factors act as bottlenecks or filters because they constrain and limit an infinite number of possible designs, of which only a limited number actually work and can therefore evolve under certain conditions. The big question is, what are the narrowest bottlenecks or filters in the evolution of thinking beings? I list six, but my choice is determined by philosophical rather than phylogenetic considerations. I will also devote some attention to the evolution of qualia and emotions. In my view, they form the basis of consciousness and, as biological signposts, remain as dominant as the co-evolving 'rational' faculties. This immediately explains why humans on

this planet often show more emotion than reason... After all, genes pull a lot of strings.

Moreover, many of the things we associate with wonderful achievements such as reason, morality and culture are, in terms of probability, at the top of a pyramid, much like a food chain. Such things are often fragile emergent gems, vulnerable to many bottom-up effects. A slight change in conditions on anyone planet could wipe them out in an instant. Throughout the universe, then, evolution remains infinitely branching rather than progressive. And every now and then there is another mass extinction, caused by plate tectonics, meteorites, cyanobacteria or other calamities, such as 'intelligent', technologically advanced organisms.

All in all, it is worth revisiting our usual talking points.

### What is life? Bottleneck 1: The origin of life and the emergence of purpose

No life has yet been found on another planet, although amino acids have been found on meteorites. This suggests that amino acids, the building blocks of proteins, are everywhere in the cosmos. But amino acids contain carbon and nitrogen, and these are forged in supernovas. These are crucial to the creation of life, but they can also easily destroy it. We humans are in a zone of the galaxy where there are neither too many nor too few supernovas, but that is pure luck. Most galaxies in the universe do not contain so many supernovas. As a result, they do not contain large amounts of the heavier elements and are therefore not as suitable for life (Preston 2016). Our own galaxy, the Milky Way, is quite large (100 billion stars) and has 'benefited' from collisions with other galaxies, which stimulate star formation. This results in several generations of stars and heavier elements. The small galaxy 'Sagittarius Dwarf' has passed through our galaxy up to three times in the last seven billion years, the first time possibly triggering the formation of the Sun and its planets (Macmillan 2022).

So whether life exists depends on which galaxy you come from – and, of course, on the nature of your star and its position in and passage through that galaxy. Our own relatively long-lived solar system is located in the Orion arm of the Milky Way and orbits its centre every 225-250 million years (every galactic year). Here and there, stars explode, forming huge bubbles. Our solar system has been in our local bubble for perhaps 5 million years, but sooner or later it will end up in a slightly different bubble. In particular, the edge regions between bubbles can be extremely dangerous (Gamillo 2022).

So not every galaxy is metallic enough, not every star burns long enough, and not every planetary system follows a safe path around the centre of its galaxy. Also, of course, not all planets are the right size and in the right place and go through a suitable series of cosmic catastrophes and other 'operations'. So the number of stars and planets alone can give a distorted picture of the likelihood of life. Sure, there are a hundred billion galaxies and tens of trillions of stars, but that does not necessarily mean, sadly, that convergent evolution will result in birds singing everywhere.

Our planet is not just any planet in the habitable zone. We seem to owe our moon to a collision with another planet, Theia. Our Moon initially caused very large tidal movements (3 kilometres), which provided a kind of biochemical laboratory in which life could (perhaps) arise relatively quickly (at least that is one theory). Without the Moon, the Earth would also spin much faster (Comins 1993). The Earth's interior also has a unique composition that may contribute to the unique rhythm of extinctions on its surface (Rampino *et al.* 2021). Other planets orbiting elsewhere in a zone of similar temperatures need not have undergone a similarly long evolutionary process with a similar rhythm of extinctions.

So what is life? Life must have begun as a process of self-replication. In the right environment, this led to an autocatalytic breeding process of replicators with favourable properties. Eventually this led to giant molecules with protein codes for organic vehicles such as birds and humans. Life is the endless programming, testing, and reprogramming of these vehicles. Life requires a rich chemical substrate and a lot of time. Numerous geological and geothermal conditions must probably be met, and a lot of energy is needed to fuel the process.

Organisms are thus 'code carriers', 'survival machines of genes', in which the emergent properties of combinations of codes are tested. Genes themselves are not directly visible to natural selection, only phenotypes. These phenotypes have to interact and nestle into the same kind of food chains everywhere. The options are limited: either you produce energy or you harvest it. Either way, in the form of phenotypes, combinations of 'selfish genes' are being tested. This was the point made by sociobiologists, although it was sometimes exaggerated and often misunderstood (Slurink 1994a). Life in the whole cosmos must be roughly like this.

## Problem 1: Life requires energy and always leads to competition

As a result of competing strategies, life is always wild proliferation (as you called it). This soon leads to efficient use of all available energy and competition for the last scraps: the basis of scarcity and selection. And these two factors are found wherever there is life. They also characterise human life.

All of this is highly relevant to philosophy. Our knowledge of evolution does away with what Ortega y Gasset called 'metaphysical optimism': the tradition, from Parmenides to Leibniz, of assuming that the world is essentially good and that the unpleasant aspects are by and large accidental side-effects (Ortega y Gasset 1975).

Modern evolutionary philosophy has also rediscovered two of Aristotle's four causes, namely formal and final causes (material and efficient causes live on as 'matter' and 'energy'). Today we have to link them with Darwin's notions of variation and selection. Organisms owe their superior *form* to a lengthy breeding process in which suboptimal forms continually perish. The result is a kind of ultralocal organic *teleology* in the form of a genetic programme. This is constantly reprogrammed by variation and selection. The genetic programme thus controls the growth, behaviour, and reproduction of organisms. Aristotle's all-encompassing global teleology must therefore be replaced by the local, temporal teleology and functionality of individual organisms in mutual competition. This kind of local, organic teleology, driven by the genetic programme, is what Mayr calls 'teleonomy' (Mayr 1988).

Teleonomy is thus local rather than a global goal orientation. It refers to the goals of individual organisms and their adaptations. To pre-Darwinian thinkers, adaptations can give the impression of conscious design, but we now know that they result from the incremental testing and selection of emergent features arising from genetic codes (in complex interaction, of course, with all the other organisms in the food chain that make up an ecosystem).

Emergence is thus not achieved by magic wings, but by a very specific genetic programme or 'recipe', the result of evolution. The natural purposefulness resulting from the genetic programme is not the result of providence, but of selective forces in specific ecological contexts. Nightingales do not sing to glorify God, but to demonstrate their vitality and the quality of their genes to rivals and potential mates.

This also means that another, more modern variant of metaphysical optimism is difficult to sustain: the belief in progress. If there are stable systems in nature, they must be constantly maintained by stabilising selection. Life always remains competitive and, in that sense, always has winners and losers. Extreme traits and qualities can emerge as a result of arms races, but most adaptive traits are actually compromises. The overall framework is set by the cosmic context, plate tectonics, and climate change. The overarching direction is one of almost infinite diversification, bounded only by the laws of chemistry and physics. Progress becomes a local and temporary phenomenon. It is often the improvement of a specialisation that eventually leads to extinction when the ecological context changes, showing that improvement or optimisation does not necessarily mean survival. Even the adaptations that make cumulative culture possible do not guarantee long-term evolutionary success.

### What is consciousness? Bottleneck 2: Consciousness is miraculous, but not a complete mystery

We currently have no idea how rare life and consciousness are in the universe. However, we can infer something from the timescale of the evolution of life on Earth. The Earth is 4.54 billion years old, and the first life may have appeared 3.7 billion years ago. Multicellular life did not appear until about 600 billion years ago, but the Cambrian explosion occurred only 553 million years ago. During (or slightly before) this latter phase, a variety of multicellular organisms with nervous systems appeared. Only after several waves of extinction did mammals get a chance to fill all the niches, and only recently have hominins arrived on the scene.

Although this is a very small sample, it may reveal how complicated the trial-and-error origin of multicellular life is. Recent research shows that there are quite a few stars with planets in our Milky Way (see for example NASA's Exoplanet Archive, Brenan 2020), but as we have seen, the age and nature of the planets in question are important, as is their nature and place in the planetary system to which they belong.

However, if complex multicellular and mobile organisms exist somewhere on a planet, there is a good chance that they will exhibit emotions and some form of consciousness. After all, animal behaviour that is rigid and automatic leads to many mistakes. Lifelong learning is much more adaptive in this respect and

may have evolved several times in longer-lived species. But learning requires trial and error and therefore a powerful feedback mechanism. That feedback mechanism, in my opinion, is pain and pleasure, the ability to feel, to be hurt. In my view, learning requires punishment and reward. Animals need to feel what is the best way to behave, what is 'right' and 'wrong' in the most primal sense.

Reward and punishment can only exist if there is a registering sensitivity, a sensitive subject or protosubject. Plants and relatively immobile animals do not need a subject. Their possibilities are limited anyway. That is why the larvae of pocket squirts (tunicates, very simple vertebrates) seem to have a notochord as a mini- or protobrain to find the place where they settle and then lose this 'brain' again.

The behaviourists were right to see that reward and punishment play an important role in animal behaviour, although they overestimated the role of learned behaviour. Above all, they were metaphysically biased in their interpretation, as if reward and punishment do not require feeling and are possible on a 'blank slate'. Reward and punishment require a special neural network in which positive and negative values are pre-programmed, enabling animals to understand their opportunities and dangers. This specialised network sets the general framework for behaviour to be considered harmful or beneficial. Consciousness thus appears to be part of a feedback network that learns or unlearns behaviour. It is likely to be a network with many feedback loops, or 'recurrent networks' (Churchland 1995).

It may well be that we will never fully understand how emotions (and therefore consciousness) arise in neural networks. After all, our minds are just products of evolution, not designed to understand the universe, but primarily to find shelter, food, friends, partners, and avoid predators and enemies. But I think we are quite capable of understanding the function of consciousness. Neural networks are built by an alliance of genes to serve them. Consciousness is the cognitive representation of the intensely individual interest perspective of the genetic vehicle.

I propose that our consciousness of the world is the sophisticated interaction screen that allows us the extreme flexibility acquired during our evolution from vertebrate to small mammal to monkey to great ape to hominin to human. It is the product of an evolutionary accumulation of sensors, senses, expectations, and their integration into a fluid picture of the world that guides our actions and plans. It is not really a mystery why we have it, but a source of wonder. We will probably never understand how the flashing fields of neural activity in the brain constantly manage to compose such an interactive, all-encompassing vision, but it is clear that we need it.

Consciousness is thus on the one hand so subjective and ultra-perspectivistic that we will never be able to experience what it is like to be a particular other animal. On the other hand, we can see the workings of underlying emotions directly in the behaviour of animals and humans. Because we share a greater arsenal of emotions with some animals than with others, we are likely to have a better understanding of the depth of their experience. So you may understand your cat's purring on the one hand, and his total lack of guilt when he knocks over his water bowl on the other. It remains to be seen whether our empathy will be sufficient to determine whether the first aliens we encounter are worthy of our trust.

## Problem 2: Cosmic conditions for the evolution of consciousness and intelligence

So if there is multicellular life on other planets, chances are there are also forms of life with consciousness. However, there is a high risk that these forms of consciousness will be quite inaccessible and alien, even if we could land on these planets. After all, our kind of intelligence is quite exceptional and the product of a tough and long selection process.

If we look at the last half a billion years of life on Earth (550 million years), there have been 5 major extinction waves. Such extinction waves provide a periodic 'cleansing' of niches, giving new biological designs a chance to emerge and thus creating new ecosystems. Such a complete innovation can also lead to a cognitive leap in the lung run, as gradually all niches fill up again and competition becomes fiercer. Cognitive abilities can then provide an important advantage, and new cognitive tricks can evolve beyond the initial niche requirements. This explains why, after the extinction of the dinosaurs, it was not until the Eocene that relative brain size finally increased in mammals (Smith 2022).

Thus, if we are to find life elsewhere in the universe with which to communicate, periodic extinction waves are likely to be required to allow such life to emerge in the first place. In the 1980s and 1990s, rhythmic extinctions on this planet were even linked to a mysterious 'death star' responsible for triggering periodic meteorite rains (Muller 1989). As many stars are born as twins, astronomers sometimes still search for a lost binary of our Sun, but the idea that it is still orbiting it has been abandoned (Siraj and Loeb 2020).

Most extinctions seem to have multiple causes. Sometimes volcanism is involved. This suggests that the magmatic and sedimentary composition of our planet has a major influence on its inhabitants, as geologists have recently argued (Rampino *et al.* 2020). Then there are the impacts of cosmic projectiles, such as the Chicxulub meteorite impact, which caused the extinction of most (but not all) of the dinosaurs. One wonders how likely it is that similar evolutionary experiments took place elsewhere in the universe.

## What is self-awareness? Bottleneck 3: Self-awareness is particularly useful for social animals

The universe is probably a very empty and very poor zoo. Here and there, among the mostly dead galaxies, there are a few galaxies with heavier elements. In some of these, there are probably a few star systems at the right distance from the galactic centre with planets and moons of the right size and position from their star, some of which have single-celled creatures or creatures with basic/primitive consciousness. Microbiologists, in particular, would be delighted to be able to travel faster than is currently possible. An extraterrestrial traveller who visited our solar system sometime in the last four billion years would most likely have encountered only single-celled organisms. The chances of finding trilobites or dinosaurs were much, much lower. But how common is a slightly deeper, broader consciousness and self-awareness? Why is self-awareness actually much, much rarer here on Earth than the simple forms of feeling outlined above?

In a sense, of course, the line between consciousness and self-awareness is not quite as sharp as is sometimes assumed. Nociception (the perception of pain), interoception (the perception of stimuli coming from one's own body), and proprioception (the perception of one's own spatial position) all lead to simple forms of self-awareness. The more such data flow together in an organism's cognitive apparatus, the more there is a need for central processing, a kind of dashboard on which everything comes together and needs to be organised, with some kind of decision-making authority 'behind it'.

One can also imagine that in an evolutionary arms race, there is generally an increasing need to represent one's body in relation to the environment and to possible predators. Even the sheer size of organisms plays a role. A squirrel jumping from branch to branch probably already has a basic awareness of its own weight and position, but a climbing orangutan cannot afford the luxury of a misstep – the cost, at least, seems to be higher. Is fear of heights not a form of self-awareness?

In the evolutionary 'battle' with predators, self-awareness actually seems useful. A woodpecker knows exactly which side of a tree to stay on when someone approaches. Cuttlefish, various fish, and chameleons can even blend into the background and 'disappear' if necessary. The question is how much self-awareness is needed to do this. Navigating in the social domain is a different problem altogether. Some herd animals, but especially cooperative hunters, benefit from close cooperation. Here it is important to explore each other's and your own strengths and loyalties.

The psychologist Gallup has operationalised self-awareness as the ability to recognise oneself in a mirror (Gordon 1970). Several animal species seem to possess this ability: not only chimpanzees, but also dolphins, Asian elephants, and magpies. Certainly, at least in most cases, the ability seems to be related to strategic spatial and social behaviour and complex forms of cooperation. Cooperation requires intelligence because it requires an understanding of the costs and benefits of social relationships, including friendship and membership of particular subgroups, and often requires or involves constant monitoring of loyalty and obedience.

As Trivers (1985) and Dunbar (2015; 2020) have pointed out, the need to cooperate not only increases social intelligence, but also the required brain capacity. Food-sharing bats (*e.g.* the common vampire bat) also have slightly larger brains than insectivorous or fruit-eating species of similar size (Wilkinson 2003). It is therefore probably no coincidence that great apes ultimately excel at social intelligence tasks. Many primate societies are crucially held together by grooming and complex networks of grooming relationships. (Meanwhile, of course, it is well known that in birds the increase in brain cells need not be accompanied by larger brains – brain cells can also become smaller.)

The ultimate refinement of reciprocal altruism is called 'indirect reciprocal altruism' (Alexander, 1987), which is argued to require, promote and generate self-awareness. Indirect reciprocity implies that cooperating individuals not only consider their own experience with their partner, but also rely on their partner's reputation. This very quickly leads to a complicated arena full of bluffing and exposure, lying and distortion, exposure and deception – what is often

referred to as a basic capacity for 'theory of mind', a response to the problem of other minds. Thus, at least some organisms begin to recognise the perspectives of others and begin to extrapolate, to recognise what is their own, what is 'secret' and what is shared with others. In children, this awareness usually breaks through somewhere between the ages of four and six, as illustrated by the now famous Sally and Anna experiments (Leslie and Frith 1987).

Self-awareness in other apes is certainly not that complicated. Although chimpanzees sometimes hunt together and sometimes invade neighbouring territories, we are the result of a much longer trajectory behind us of extreme dependence on cooperation in hunting and fighting. The evolution of language was the result and facilitated indirect reciprocity. Language makes it possible to gossip and thus keep track of the reputations of multiple individuals (Dunbar 1998).

## Problem 3: It takes more than social intelligence

Given the well-documented social intelligence of elephants, dolphins, and orcas, among others, socio-cognitive arms races obviously took place in several animal groups and probably even outside mammals. So somewhere in the universe, similar processes may well have taken place. But primates seem to occupy a special place. It seems no coincidence that somewhere in their adaptive radiation species with more self-awareness have emerged. Primates have the acrobatic skills that force them to be aware of their bodies, the fur that makes them dependent on grooming; they live in an environment that makes them dependent on each other's eyes and ears and on the safety of a relatively large group. Ultimately, their handy front paws, those controlled grippers, our hands, may well have been the deciding factor (Lorenz 1954). The brain as such cannot do much without hands and feet. It could have far-reaching consequences if you became increasingly handy with them. Could such limbs evolve anywhere?

## What is culture? Bottleneck 4: Does it require specialized limbs?

Bonner (1980) defined culture as the non-hereditary transmission of information between generations. Based on such a definition, it quickly became clear that many forms of culture do indeed exist in animals, even outside the hominin lineage (*e.g.,* Gardner *et al.* 1994). Indeed, chimpanzees maintain a variety of different cultures, and even killer whales exhibit at least five different cultures in different oceans around the planet, based on differences in food choices (Foote *et al.* 2016). Culture is sometimes passed on deliberately: orcas, for example, appear to actively teach each other the 'landing trick' (getting washed up among prey, sea lions), and young chimpanzees watch with excitement as their mothers work with hammer and anvil.

Lorenz thus speculated that primates had a huge advantage with their handy front legs. Seen in this way, our culture began with our hands, which are just a little more handy than an elephant's trunk, a dolphin's snout and a crow's beak. I suspect that the primate hand, combined with social intelligence, opened up a special evolutionary path. Once you can make things with your hands, you can suddenly arm yourself better and hunt different species. At the same time, you have to pass on the art of making such tools. So our handy forepaws may have predestined us for 'cumulative culture'. Looking at the long period during which our ancestors were content with the Acheulian hand-axe, this required a long period of gene-culture coevolution (Corbey *et al.* 2016). The evolution of hominins was anything but a fast track to engineering college.

## Problem: Did climate oscillations drive cognitive escalation?

All in all, the evolution of hominins was one of chance and experimentation. It all started with monkeys that were a little too big to hold on with their tails alone. They held on with their front limbs and lost their tails. Their hands became more important. That made it possible to move upright in trees and on the ground. *Danuvius guggenmosi* and *Graecopithecus* show the new possibilities (Böhme 2020). Competition with smaller primates that learned to digest unripe fruit drove the larger apes to the forest floor, where they could partly live off fallen fruit. To this we still owe the ability to digest alcohol (Carrigan *et al.* 2017). Perhaps even more important were the constantly shifting boundaries between forested areas and more open spaces, which may have led to different forms of bipedalism.

The aridification of East Africa due to plate tectonics and changing monsoonal winds around the Arabian Sea may have had a major impact on hominin diversification (Maslin 2017). The movements of the Nubic, Arabian, and Somali plates and the (further) cooling of the climate during the Pliocene thus contributed to the emergence of the genus *Homo*. In any case, hominins in this phase were constantly confronted with rapidly changing conditions:

sometimes more, sometimes less savannah, sometimes more, sometimes less fauna, and so on.

Richard Potts' (1996) 'variability selection hypothesis' suggests that the rapid climatic fluctuations of the Pleistocene forced at least some hominins to constantly adapt to new conditions. This process actually may have started in the late Miocene and in the Pliocene. Thus it is possible that our extreme reliance on culture is a direct result of climate variability and the consequent need for flexible means of 'extrasomatic adaptation' (Binford 1962). Increased reliance on culturally transmitted behaviours is the stop-gap solution of a lost anthropoid that has had to become increasingly dexterous, inventive and clever to survive, and material culture in particular allows behavioural plasticity and change with slightly less genetic and physical change than would otherwise be the case.

All this suggests that hominin culture is not the transnatural or supernatural phenomenon that some would like it to be. The brains of some species of hominins became suitable for cumulative culture only very gradually. Even orcas prove that evolution does not stop at culture. Orcas with different cultures develop genetically differently (Foote *et al.* 2016). In hominins, the use of tools probably coevolved with the hand and its control. The use of language has also driven human speech: this is why we have wider vertebrae, a lower larynx, a flexible tongue, a relatively short snout, and a keen sense of hearing. The importance of experience and cultural transmission has also contributed to an extended post-reproductive lifespan in both hominins and orcas (Bainbridge 2012).

Cultural evolution is always accompanied by biological change in the long run. Populations with livestock can digest milk, Inuit have fewer sweat glands, Ethiopians run faster. Above all, it appears that in different cultures there is still a correlation between success in that culture's main economic activity (hunting, fighting, trading) and reproductive success, with status also playing a role (Hopcroft 2002, Slurink 2002). Ortega y Gasset noted already that sexual selection is sometimes slightly 'conservative' (Ortega y Gasset 1960).

Cumulative culture is in many ways an odd biological specialisation. If we compare it with other specialisations in nature, we will find that most are actually quite 'ecologically specific'. For example, in competition with other species, many insect species specialise in eating, parasitising, or pollinating a particular type of plant. As a result, when that plant species goes extinct, the specialised insect often goes with it. Many parasites also specialise in a single host. If the host becomes extinct, so does the parasite. Only the cuckoo manages to change host from time to time, which is necessary when hosts start to distinguish cuckoos from sparrowhawks, or their own eggs from the slightly larger eggs of cuckoos.

However, technology and culture have enabled different species of hominins to achieve 'ecological generalism', or radical forms of adaptive flexibility. Ecological generalism characterises species that can easily adapt to major changes in their environment. Rats, some gulls, and crows are examples of such generalists: they are relatively eager to test new food sources and can therefore rapidly adapt their behaviour to a changing world. It is likely that all these species have been exposed to rapidly changing environments in the past. Opportunistic hominins benefited from their handy forelimbs and their ability to learn from each other.

In more stable environments, other populations of hominins may have been less opportunistic and inventive. They maintained more specialised lifestyles tied to more specific and less flexible niches. Possible examples include *Paranthropus, Australopithecus sediba, Homo naledi, Homo floresiensis*, and Neanderthals, although each of these cases is open to debate. Human evolution could even be described as a continuous split between more conservative, specialised populations and populations of innovative opportunists who often behaved like parasites and invasive exotics. Perhaps *Homo naledi* was at times so well adapted to its environment that it saw our ancestors as dangerous invaders or the ultimate pests.

But there were always populations that adapted with the help of more cooperation and more culture. These 'ecological generalists' became increasingly dependent on close cooperation and the transmission of complex skills and techniques.

### What is so special about Homo sapiens?
### Bottleneck 5. Ecological dominance results in niche independence

All in all, the question remains how likely it is that such a complex evolutionary process as the diversification of hominins could have taken place elsewhere in the universe. Two million years ago, a variety of bipedal hominins roamed Africa. Some may have been still partially arboreal, others adapted to dry savannas *(Paranthropus)*, while others were on their

way to becoming ecologically generalist opportunists *(Homo?)*. In an environment with so many predators, larger groups were adaptive. Some of these groups were better at working together than others, as different forms of sociality are favoured in different niches. Tool-based behaviour allowed hominins to add resources such as termites, honey, bone marrow or meat to their diet. Meat could be obtained by, for example, isolating calves (Guthrie 2007), 'power scavenging' (Bickerton 2009), or chasing and exhausting prey ('persistence hunting'). The evolution of the modern foot and generalised athletic anatomy may have made all these strategies more efficient (Bramble and Lieberman 2004). In any case, the bodies of *Homo ergaster* were already built to allow foraging over a larger area than the various *Australopithecus* species (Shipman and Walker 1989).

According to Bickerton (2009), this probably happened when the initial impetus for the evolution of true symbolic language was provided by the need to recruit help in defending large carcasses. In contrast to animal cries and calls, whose meaning is derived purely from their context, more specific referential utterances had to emerge when a reference was needed to a specific object and place beyond the immediate horizon. According to Bickerton, a group of bone marrow specialists gradually switched to 'confrontational scavenging' as their primary behavioural strategy (chimpanzees also occasionally chase leopards away from their prey, but this happens only situationally and is therefore not a specialisation).

Perhaps Bickerton's scenario is still a bit of a just-so story. But the evolution of language must have begun through an extreme reliance on 'precision collaboration': increasingly precise reference to far-flung resources, and more precise distribution and definition of tasks (gossip and reputation probably followed in the wake of this development).

All indications are that our ancestors gradually became more cooperative and incrementally more dependent on tricks and techniques. Possible steps may have included the maternal aid, the baby carrier (Taylor, 2010), tools for reaching bone marrow, tools for scraping flesh, stone throwing, and eventually the classic Acheulian hand axe. As further episodes of drought or other hardship followed, *Homo heidelbergensis* and/or *bodoensis* gradually became the inventive top predators who ended up at the top of the food pyramid. They discovered fire, language and the spear. In them, ecological generalism became 'ecological dominance' (Alexander 1990).

Ecological dominance means that there are no predators controlling the population of the candidate species. As a result, a population of the ecologically dominant species can grow beyond the carrying capacity of its environment, leading to expansion and migration, as well as to potential conflict within the species. Alexander (1990) argued that the resulting intergroup competition leads to social, cultural and moral arms races, resulting in distinctive human traits (see also Slurink 1993; 1994b).

It is sometimes thought that intergroup competition necessarily takes the form of large-scale warfare and thus leads to group selection (Vining 1981), but in chimpanzees we can already see how more limited forms of conflict involving a limited number of casualties can be adaptive. If taking over a territory means taking over the females living there, this is obviously not group selection. In chimpanzees, the leader is sometimes also killed, which triggers a very different process (Whyte 2017).

More recently, Boehm (2012) and Wrangham (2019) have highlighted the dynamics of within-group selection in the emergence and refinement of moral sentiments. Boehm (2012) shows that capital punishment is both ancient and ubiquitous, and thus may have had a real impact on early human populations. If violent and ruthless traits led to ostracism for thousands of years, a population may have gradually gained more control over its own 'aggressive' and 'tyrannical' traits. Fear of group judgement, and even exclusion and execution, could lead to the development of more empathy and compassion and the emergence of a true conscience. Indeed, these are effects of long-term indirect reciprocal altruism and these ideas are compatible with Dunbar's gossip hypothesis (1998).

Wrangham links Boehm's 'execution hypothesis' to the older domestication hypothesis, suggesting that humans belong to the exclusive club of domesticated animals (*cf.* Wrangham 2019; Lorenz 1954). There is an even more exclusive club of *self*-domesticated animals, which, according to Wrangham, includes not only humans but also the bonobo and, according to recent research, possibly the elephant (Wetzel 2023). Incidentally, it is well known that dogs are less intelligent than wolves and one can speculate that domestication can also lead to passivity, obedience, and herd behaviour.

In my view, the intergroup competition hypothesis, ideas about indirect reciprocity, the execution hypothesis and the domestication

hypothesis are not mutually exclusive. They probably all relate to aspects of 'moral evolution' in a species living under reduced predation pressure and trying to cope with increasing group size. Taken together, these ideas fit well with the notion that humans have been put in a special position by our increasing reliance on language and technology. It seems that our ape ancestors evolved into a somewhat bizarre artificial predatory ape, which, exposed to ever-changing climatic conditions and thrown into ever-changing ecological contexts, has always saved itself by inventing new tools, techniques, and ways of life, and by pushing other groups (and organisms) to the margins. Ultimately, ecological dominance led to the agricultural revolution, the marginalisation of numerous other populations and species, the anthropocentric illusion, and the current climatic and ecological crisis (the 'Anthropocene').

*Problem: Does ecological dominance ultimately lead to ecological and climatic disasters?*
How likely is it that such semi-artificial 'techno-beasts' will arise on other planets, even in our universe? In general, the idea of 'moral evolution' through arms races or self-domestication seems compatible with the idea of convergent evolution. However, it does not become more likely when we consider the bizarre coincidence of extinction waves and climatic oscillations that seem to have contributed greatly to human evolution, especially human cognition. How likely is it that there are other planets that have episodes of such climatic fluctuations and tectonic shifts?

Right now, our technological-agricultural success story seems to present us with major problems. This could mean that our success is short-lived on an evolutionary time scale. Our arms race and propensity for self-destruction have produced not an angel but a hyper-technological beast, increasingly controlling nature but not yet itself, and often still obsessed with tribal myths. Our taste for speed and meat has led to bizarre industries that could endanger the biosphere. We may even become extinct as a result of the same opportunistic use of technology that has made us successful, and even as a result of weapons designed to increase our security.

Convergent evolution elsewhere in the universe, it follows, would similarly make ecologically dominant species with enhanced technological capabilities highly susceptible to self-destruction, thus reducing the likelihood that such species will ever encounter each other.

### What is rationality, morality, civilization? Bottleneck 6: The one we are in

We have already seen that new emergent properties cannot violate the laws of underlying or previous levels of organisation. Life does not violate the physical laws of nature. Sensitivity and consciousness are both functional and allow learning through trial and error. Consciousness is based on emotions, which allow organisms to weigh their options. We have seen that moral emotions could evolve in the context of kin selection and cooperation. This immediately implies that morality is always limited because it must be 'evolutionarily stable': its results cannot be guaranteed. In fact, the evolutionary process will sometimes lead to trade-offs between, for example, traits that favour physical competition and sexual selection, and traits that enable cooperation and indirect reciprocity. In many cases, moral talents perish in the competition for resources, status, and reproductive opportunities.

Similarly, cumulative culture owes its emergence and existence to the flexibility it provides. It remains dependent on the cooperation and social exchange necessary for the transmission of relevant information. Moreover, culture is not only used to promote common interests, but is also an arena in which struggles for status and reproductive opportunities take place (Slurink 2002). As we already noted, processes of sexual selection lead to a messy and complicated coupling of cultural success and reproductive success. One might wonder whether the pursuit of status and money in contemporary Western culture is so strongly rewarded that it thwarts much of the potential for moral evolution. Do the conditions that Boehm said drove moral evolution still apply in the present, now that the biggest egoists and graspers are gaining unprecedented influence and power? Is it possible that the domestication process could backfire at some point?

Outside the realm of science, rationality is a somewhat obscure concept. It is acting on the basis of reason – acting on the basis of facts and honest cost-benefit analysis. But it remains unclear for whom these costs and benefits are calculated and matter. So reason itself remains ultimately a perspectival, evolutionary product, calculating desirability partly on the basis of interests. In the end, what Kant calls 'practical reason' (Kant 1788) is still based on feelings and human values. This system of values and feelings is fine-tuned by a variety of selection pressures that can lead to conflicting outcomes: *e.g.*, sexual selection, kin selection, and direct and indirect reciprocal altruism. Depending on, for example, gender/age categories, each 'rational' person will reach a different balance between self-interest, family interest, and the common good. From an evolutionary point of view, it is to be expected that practical reason will in the end serve a compromise between group-interests and the genes of those who embody it.

Ideally, a 'civilization' should be a society based on reason and compassion, but its bearers on planet Earth are locked in competition (*e.g.* between the USA and China), and within societies there is a conflict between morality and power, status and shorttime interests. The conclusion here is that, unfortunately, we seem to be stuck in bottleneck 6. To some extent, 'rationality' and 'civilization' may be too high a goal for biological beings in general. In particular, the term 'civilization' seems to be partly a social construct that obscures the underlying arm races and competition. Humanity seems like an experiment in 'civilization' that is constantly in danger of failing.

Everyone will agree that civilization presupposes at least some form of morality, but even the term 'morality' refers to a rather paradoxical reality involving aggression and competition towards supposedly 'anti-social' parties (Slurink 1994; Wrangham 2020). It is unclear how to define 'the good', but at least it includes a component of 'devotion to the common good'. But then you might ask, are we good enough for this planet? Are we capable of keeping it habitable for future generations and the ecosystems on which we depend? Are we not already caught in a technotrap that could, in principle, spell the end of humanity or usher in a kind of 'New Dark Age'?

The problems we are currently experiencing on our planet are probably not unique. Elsewhere, similar bottlenecks and filters are at work, shaping the opportunities for life to evolve. Elsewhere, but probably not in many other places in the cosmos, evolution is likely to provide opportunities for ecologically dominant predators to develop intelligence and technology. There they are likely to experience the same tension between cooperative imperatives and selfish genes. If we ever encounter aliens, we should also be aware of their intentions in seeking and encountering us. They are likely to be driven by the same mix of curiosity, inquisitiveness, and selfishness as we are.

Let us not forget that our own civilization was forged from the predatory tendencies of the Yamnas, Vikings, colonisers, industrialists, and today's hyper-capitalists – our cultural achievements are the result of a series of historical arms races. Our colonial history and the Western industrial revolution reflect the behaviour of an invasive exotic species rather than an organism well adapted to specific local ecologies. The very idea of four types of Kardashev super-civilizations (using the available energy of a planet, a star, a galaxy or the whole universe) and of 'monons' or super-civilizations lined up to form 'world patterns' (Bresch 1977) smacks, in my view, of elitist dreaming and bears the stamp of post-war optimism. Such a cosmic civilization is not very attractive either – it would almost certainly degenerate into a huge bureaucracy or some kind of technological dictatorship. In such a world, we philosophers might even be reduced to rubbish collectors, since recycling would probably be the biggest job creator in such a 'civilization'. And would there still be birds?

For the time being, our civilization is not sustainable and climate-neutral. This is because short-term profit and growth are often still perceived as more important than solutions for sustainable development, at the corporate level, at the state level, as well as in the minds of citizens. In both dictatorships and democracies, leaders and citizens do not want to risk losing out in the quest for sustainability. As our ecological problems and climate catastrophes progress, hopefully there will come more political will to bring our society into balance with the ecological systems around this planet. We are already in the first stages of an interesting protein transition with a mix of old technology and smart, new techniques, which may finally give us some control over our past as predators. Now finally the realisation must sink in that we have mostly evolved during the Ice Ages and are completely dependent on terrestrial ecosystems, highly dependent on the current sea level and even higher on the human climate niche (Xu *et al.* 2020).

Elsewhere in the cosmos there may already be intelligent and wise beings who have overcome their conquering urges and are also dedicated to the preservation of their planet. In a way, we have much to learn from these silent aliens. If we were really visited by extraterrestrials, they would probably be very different types who have long since destroyed their local flora and fauna and are looking for new resources and territories. I don't know if you want those types in your yard. We can actually learn a lot more from those who don't visit us.

So let us concentrate on this planet and look up to the birds, not to theoretical aliens. Just as Neanderthals and various European Ice Age hunter-gatherers did (Finlayson 2019; Hussain 2023). The richness of human life is not just in the future: countless human-like creatures have enjoyed the richness of life on this planet, despite all the horrors and miseries they too have experienced. Above all, let us celebrate what we already have and what we have already achieved on this planet, instead of pursuing the impossible. Everything we need is already here, and we should be careful not to lose it.

*Fermi's paradox*
The Italian-born physicist Fermi wondered over lunch in 1940 why we had not yet encountered extraterrestrial intelligence if it was indeed everywhere in the universe. It is possible, of course, that such life already exists, and that Ezekiel does indeed describe extraterrestrial life in his first chapter. Besides, there are a lot of strange people walking the streets...

However, I personally suggest that we take a closer look at our 'civilization'. Is it not a deadly technotrap, irrevocably leading to a shortage of resources and an excess of waste – if not of people? Are we not irrevocably doomed by our own supposed 'success', now that we appear to be responding far too slowly to the climate and biodiversity emergencies? It now looks as if the next century will be one of heat, famine, refugees, and probably war.

Perhaps Fermi's paradox stems from the fact that, from a cosmological perspective, technologically advanced, 'civilised' beings have only one basic choice: to perish from their own excessive reproduction, luxury, and expansionism, or to find an ecological balance at a much lower but more sustainable level of wealth and technological development. Such a lower level of prosperity probably does not involve a vast space programme, but rather a general knowledge of everything that lives on the planet in question, what can be eaten, grown, cultivated, domesticated, and lived with, or what simply must be enjoyed. Whatever these aliens have chosen to do – we will never hear about it. That is why the universe is so astonishingly silent.

ACKNOWLEDGEMENTS
Dear Raymond, thank you for the many trips, excursions and conversations we have had over the decades (and millennia). I also thank Shumon Hussain and Gerrit Dusseldorp for their corrections, suggestions and good help in writing this piece.

REFERENCES
Alexander, R. 1987. *The Biology of Moral Systems.* New York: Aldine de Gruyter.

Alexander, R. 1990. *How did Humans Evolve? Reflections on the uniquely unique Species.* Ann Arbor: University of Michigan.

Bainbridge, D. 2012. "Middle Age: A Triumph of Human Evolution." *New Scientist,* March 7, 2012.

Berman, R. 2021 "Every 27.5 Million Years, the Earth's Heart Beats Catastrophically". *Big Think.* June 22, 2021.

Bertrand, O.C., S.L. Shelley, T.E. Williamson, J.R. Wible, S.G. Chester, J.J. Flynn, L.T. Holbrook, T.R. Lyson, J. Meng, I.M., Miller, H.P. Püschel, T. Smith, M. Spaulding, Z.J. Tseng, and S.L. Brusatte 2022. "Brawn before Brains in placental Mammals after the end-Cretaceous Extinction". *Science.* 376 (6588), 80-85.

Bickerton, D. 2009. *Adam's Tongue: How Humans Made Language, How Language Made Humans.* New York: Hill and Wang.

Binford, L.R. 1962. "Archaeology as anthropology". *American Antiquity* 28, 217-225.

Boehm, C. 2012. *Moral Origins: The Evolution of Virtue, Altruism, and Shame.* New York: Basic Books.

Böhme, M. 2020. *Wie wir Menschen wurden.* München: Wilhelm Heyne.

Bonner, J. 1980. *The Evolution of Culture in Animals.* Princeton: Princeton University Press.

Bramble, D., and D. Lieberman. 2004. "Endurance Running and the Evolution of Homo". *Nature* 432 (7015), 345-352. DOI:10.1038/nature03052

Brenan, P. 2020. "Discovery Alert: 2 Planets Orbit a Sun-like Star". *Exoplanet Exploration,* News, July 23, 2020.

Bresch, C. 1977. *Zwischenstufe Leben: Evolution ohne Ziel?* München: Piper.

Carrigan, M.A., O. Uryasev, C.B. Frye, B.L. Eckman, C.R. Myers, T.D. Hurley, and S.A. Benner. 2014. "Hominids adapted to metabolize ethanol long before human-directed fermentation". *PNAS Early Edition* 112 (2): 458-463.

Churchland, P. 1995. *The Engine of Reason, The Seat of the Soul: A Philosophical Journey into the Brain.* Cambridge, MA: MIT Press.

Comins, N. 1993. *What if the Moon didn't Exist?* New York: Harper Collins.

Conway Morris, S. 2003. *Life's Solution: Inevitable Humans in a Lonely Universe.* Cambridge: Cambridge University Press.

Corbey, R.H.A., A. Jagich, K. Vaesen and M. Collard. 2016. "The Acheulean Handaxe: More like a Bird's Song than a Beatles' Tune?" *Evolutionary Anthropology* 25 (1), 6-19. DOI:10.1002/evan.21467

Dunbar, R. 1998. *Grooming, Gossip, and the Evolution of Language.* Cambridge: Harvard.

Dunbar, R. 2015. *Human Evolution.* London: Penquin Books.

Dunbar, R. 2020. *Evolution. What Everyone Needs to Know.* Oxford: Oxford University Press.

Feinberg, T., and J. Mallatt. 2018. *Consciousness Demystified.* Cambridge: MIT Press.

Finlayson, C. 2019. *The Smart Neanderthal.* Oxford: Oxford University Press.

Foote, A.D., N. Vijay, M.C. Ávila-Arcos, R.W. Baird, J.W. Durban, M. Fumagalli, R.A. Gibbs, M.B. Hanson, T.S. Korneliussen, M.D. Martin, K.M. Robertson, V.C. Sousa, F.G. Vieira, T. Vinař, P. Wade, K.C. Worley, L. Excoffier, P.A. Morin, M.T.P. Gilbert, and J.B.W. Wolf 2016. "Genome-culture coevolution promotes rapid divergence of killer whale ecotypes." *Nature Communications* 7 (11693), DOI:10.1038/ncomms11693.

Gallup, G. Jr. 1970. "Chimpanzees: Self recognition." *Science* 167 (3914), 86-87.

Gamillo, E. 2022. "A Star-Producing, Cosmic Bubble Shrouds Our Solar System." *Smithsonian Magazine,* January14, 2022.

Gardner, A., B. Chiarelli, and F.C. Plooij, eds. 1994. *The Ethological Roots of Culture.* Dordrecht: Kluwer Academic Publishers.

Guthrie, D. 2007. "Haak en Steek: The Tool that Allowed Hominins to Colonize the African Savanna and to Flourish There." In *Guts and Brains: An Integrative Approach to the Hominin Record,* edited by W. Roebroeks, 133-161. Leiden: Leiden University Press.

Hopcroft, R. 2006. "Sex, status, and reproductive success in the contemporary United States". *Evolution and Human Behavior* 27 (2), 104-120.

Hussain, S.T. 2023. "Did Upper Palaeolithic People Provision Food for their Raven Neighbours?". *Nature Ecology and Evolution, Behind the Paper.* June 22, 2023. https://go.nature.com/440sYEw

Kant, I. 1788. *Critic der practischen Vernunft.* Riga: Johann Friedrich Hartknoch.

Leslie, A., and U. Frith. 1987. "Metarepresentation and autism: How not to lose one's marbles". *Cognition* 27 (3), 291-294.

Lorenz, K. 1954. "Psychologie und Stammesgeschichte". In *Vom Weltbild des Verhaltensforschers,* edited by K. Lorenz, 35-95. München: Deutscher Taschenbuch Verlag.

Maslin, M. 2017. *The Cradle of Humanity: How the changing landscape of Africa made us so smart.* Oxford: Oxford University Press.

Mayr, E. 1988. "The Multiple Meanings of Teleological." In *Toward a New Philosophy of Biology,* edited by E. Mayr, 38-66. Cambridge, MA: Harvard University Press.

McMillan, P.J., J. Petersson, T. Tepper-Garcia, J. Bland-Hawthorn, T. Antoja, L. Chemin, F. Figueras, S. Khanna, G. Kordopatis, P. Ramos, M. Romero-Gómez, and G. Seabroke 2022. "The Disturbed Outer Milky Way Disc." *Monthly Notices of the Royal Astronomical Society* 516 (4), 4988-5002.

Muller, R. 1989. *Nemesis: the Death Star – The Story of a Scientific Revolution.* London: Weidenfeld and Nicolson.

Ortega y Gasset, J. 1960 [1940]. "Betrachtungen über die Liebe" ["Estudios sobre el Amor"]. In *Triumph des Augenblicks, Glanz der Dauer,* edited by K.A. Horst. Stuttgart: Deutsche Verlags-Anstalt.

Ortega y Gasset, J. 1975. *An Interpretation of Universal History.* [Courses of 1948-49, translated by M. Adams.] New York: Norton.

Potts, R. 1996. "Evolution and Climate Variability." *Science* 273 (5277), 922-923.

Preston, L. 2016. *Goldilocks and the Water Bears: The Search for Life in the Universe.* London: Bloomsbury.

Pugh, G. 1978. *The Biological Origins of Human Values.* London: Routledge & Kegan Paul.

Rampino, M., K. Caldeira, and Y. Zhu. 2021. "A Pulse of the Earth: A 27.5-Myr underlying cycle in coordinated geological events over the last 260 Myr." *Geoscience Frontiers* 12 (6), 101245.

Shipman, P., and A. Walker. 1989. "The Costs of Becoming a Predator". *Journal of Human Evolution* 18, 373-392.

Siraj, A. and A. Loeb. 2020. "The Case for an Early Solar Binary Companion". *The Astrophysical Journal Letters* 899 (2), L24.

Slurink, P. 1992. "De dierlijke Rede, of Kennen om te Overleven". *Algemeen Nederlands Tijdschrift voor Wijsbegeerte* 84 (2), 121-142.

Slurink, P. 1993. "Ecological Dominance and the Final Sprint in Hominid Evolution". *Human Evolution* 8 (4), 265-273.

Slurink, P. 1994a. "Paradox and Tragedy in Human Morality". *International Political Science Review* 15 (4), 347-378.

Slurink, P. 1994b. "Causes of our Complete Dependence on Culture". In *The Ethological Roots of Culture,* edited by A. Gardner, B. Chiarelli, and F.C. Plooij, 461-474. Dordrecht: Kluwer Academic Publishers.

Slurink, P. 2002. "Culture: the Human Arena". In *Why some apes became humans: Competition, Consciousness, and Culture,* 171-229. Doctoral Dissertation. Nijmegen University, P.S. Press.

Taylor, T. 2010. *The Artificial Ape: How Technology Changed the Course of Human Evolution.* New York: Palgrave Macmillan.

Trivers, R. 1985. *Social Evolution.* Menlo Park, California: Benjamin/Cummings.

Vining, D. 1981. "Group Selection via Genocide". *The Mankind Quarterly.* 22, 27-41.

Wetzel, C. 2023. "Wild African elephants may have domesticated themselves". *New Scientist,* April 3, 2023.

Whyte, C. 2017. "Chimps Beat up, Murder and then Cannibalise their former Tyrant". *New Scientist,* January 30, 2017.

Wilkinson, G. 2003. "Social and Vocal Complexity in Bats." In *Animal Social Complexity,* edited by F. de Waal, and P. Tyack, 322-341. Cambridge: Harvard University Press.

Wrangham, R..2019. *The Goodness Paradox: The Strange Relationship Between Virtue and Violence in Human Evolution.* New York: Pantheon Books.

Xu, C., T. Kohler, and T. Lenton. 2020. "Future of the Human Climate Niche". *PNAS* 117 (21), 11350-11355. DOI:10.1073/pnas.1910114117

In Hussain, S.T. and G.L. Dusseldorp (eds) 2025. Sitting on the fence: Negotiating archaeology, anthropology and philosophy. Festschrift for Prof. Dr Raymond H.A. Corbey in celebration of his 70th birthday. *Analecta Praehistorica Leidensia* 54. Leiden: Sidestone Press, pp. 69-74.

# Psychic plants: A critique on Helmut Plessner's plant-animal boundary

## Norbert N.G.J Peeters

### Abstract

The animal-human boundary is a central and re-occurring theme in Raymond Corbey's corpus, from his dissertation in philosophy *De mens een dier?* (1988) to his seminal book *The Metaphysics of Apes: Negotiating the Animal-Human Boundary* (2005). On the one hand he is an advocate for minding the gap between animals and humans, influenced by philosophical anthropologists and sociologists such as Emile Durkheim, Marcel Mauss, and Helmuth Plessner. On the other hand he is a proponent of bridging the gap between the two. Old demarcations between humans and animals have become derelict, *e.g.*, tool making/use, reciprocity, cooperation, and language. But what about the other boundary? The one between animals and plants? As it turns out, here too, the old boundary stones that kept the two kingdoms apart have become dilapidated. Plant physiologists from the nineteenth century, such as Charles Darwin, have showed through painstaking experimentation that plants show (autonomous) movement, sensory perception, and sexuality (cross fertilization). There was even a hypothesis that plant showed a form of intelligence, bridging not just the boundary with animals, but also with humans. And as it turns out, Plessner, again, is one of the first philosophers that jogs our memory to also mind the gap between plants and animals.

*Keywords: plant-animal boundary, plant movement and behaviour, biopsychic*

### Introduction

In his last essay *Walking* (1862), Henry David Thoreau, in the midst of an era of novel and revolutionary modes of transportation, wrote an ode to the ancient art of sauntering. In this essay, he proclaims to have encountered only a few people who have mastered this art. An odd statement for a bipedal hominid, but one that nevertheless rings true to my ears. Not to boast about my own walking skills, but I have, throughout the years, had the joy of running into a few excellent walkers. Raymond Corbey, is one such wayfarer. Our first encounters bookended my academic training. During my first year in Archaeology at Leiden University, Corbey piqued my interest for cultural and philosophical anthropology, and during my last year, he guided me in writing my master thesis in Philosophy. But it was after my studies that I encountered his acquaintance as a fellow walker. Similar to our walks, our talks tended to meander. Roaming through the outskirts of Leiden, or zigzagging through the alleyways of the inner city, we discussed wide ranging topics, from reciprocity to urban evolution, and from birding to Palaeolithic cave art. And on these promenades, we often were accompanied by philosophers of old, such as Thomas Hobbes, Ludwig Wittgenstein, but also Max Scheler and Helmuth Plessner. Especially the last two names popped up time and again, notably during

**Norbert N.G.J. Peeters**

Institute of Philosophy, Leiden University, The Netherlands and owner of Philosophia Botanica
norbert_peeters@hotmail.com

some heated debates on plant intelligence. Corbey's first perambulation into academia was a dissertation focusing on these two thinkers. On several occasions, he urged me to study their work on philosophical botany, and I am grateful for the opportunity to take him up on this here.

## DAS BLUMENWUNDER

In his dissertation *De mens een dier? Scheler, Plessner en de crisis van het traditionele mensbeeld* (*The Human an Animal? Scheler, Plessner and the Crisis of the traditional Image of Man*, 1988), Corbey quotes a curious letter from Max Scheler to his second wife Märit Furtwängler, on the 3rd of March 1927 (Corbey 1988, 27). Scheler wrote to her right after watching time-lapse images of growing plants in the film *Das Blumenwunder*. "24 hours of plant life were compressed into one second", he declares, and in that very instant: "The natural impression that the plant is inanimate disappears completely." He was particularly enthralled with footage of a climbing member of the cucumber family (*Cucurbitaceae*). He watched the tendrils in a frantic "search" for support, and the "satisfaction" when they finally found a pole to twine around. After the tentacles had reached to the fourth, and final pole, they "desperately" probed into the void, searching and searching until the tendrils seized their pursuit and secured themselves to the fourth pole. Scheler concludes: "Oh how "life" overall is the similarly delightful, twitching and suffering... so everything is, all life is one." (Corbey 1988, 27) Time-lapse recordings showed that the sessile nature of plants was but a limitation of our own perception. And Scheler was not just struck by the autonomous movement. These plants showed signs of sensory perception, and even goal-oriented behavior. Corbey claims that these time-lapse images corroborated Scheler's assumption that both plants, animal, and in fact all lifeforms, share a certain drive, or urge (*Drang*) (Corbey 1988, 27).

Corbey himself is somewhat hesitant to share Scheler's excitement. He even admits that the very idea that plants show *Drang*, even in the minutest sense, seems quite absurd (Corbey 1988, 27). And he warns his readers that Scheler is edging too close to anthropomorphism. Corbey's critical stance is backed up by Plessner. In *Die Stufen der Organischen und der Mensch* (1928), Plessner wholeheartedly disagrees with Scheler's assessment on plant life: "[A]ny level-headed person must time and again oppose the tendency to imbue a still plant with a soul"

(Plessner 1928, 131). Yet he agrees with Scheler that the tendrils of *Cucurbitaceae* vines are impressive sped up "ten thousand times on film." (Plessner 1928, 224-225) But he argues:

> "[T]*here is not the least reason to assume that sensation-based or even only centrally mediated processes underlie these phenomena," Plessner (1928, 225).*

He likens Scheler's reaction to that of a child who is inclined to give animate or human physiognomic qualities to inanimate objects, such as chairs, tables, and spoons (Plessner 1928, 131). Plessner quotes Hedwig Conrad-Martius asserting that: "All of the plant's movements happen *to* it but never originate *from* it" (Plessner 1928, 223). Or, in other words, plant movement is aitionomic, not autonomous. And Plessner further argues that: "The vast majority of plants are sessile, in accordance with a maximum degree of integration into the surrounding medium" (Plessner 1928, 223). This statement, especially the latter part, needs some clarification.

## VERDURE DIVIDUALS

In the fifth chapter of *Die Stufen*, Plessner discusses the main difference between plants and animals. In opposition to Scheler, he argues that life is not one and the same, claiming there to be an important difference in organizational form. In general, plants are characterized by an open form, as opposed to the closed or centric form of an animal. The form is "open" since a plant lacks a center, or central organs, that tie the whole body together (Plessner 1928, 121-120). The plant is characterized by a border where there is nobody or nothing on either side, neither subject nor object. So, in this sense it does not stand apart from its environment, and therefore plants lack what Plessner calls "positionality" (Plessner 1928, 237-245). This positionality arises from the closed or centric organizational form of the animal. Thus, it differs from plants in that it not only *has* a body, but it is also *in* its body. For the animal, border traffic is mediated by a center physically located in the nervous system, which enables animals to be aware of their surroundings.

Plessner confesses that he was not the first to draw attention to the distinction between the open and closed organizational form. This distinction was introduced by the German biologist and philosopher Hans Driesch. But Plessner places a lot more emphasis on it, and he even uses the distinction to dismiss

Scheler's claim, arguing that "[s]ensation and action contradict the nature of the open form" (Plessner 1928, 225). Plessner was well aware that plant physiology had proved the existence of plant movement induced by sensory perception. He familiarized himself with plant physiological research, such as the work of Austrian botanist Gottlieb Haberlandt. Haberlandt garnered experimental proof of plant movement induced by several sensory signals: "[P]hototropism, thigmotropism, chemotropism, and geotropism" (Plessner 1928, 223-224). Tropism comes from the Greek *trepein* (τρέπειν), meaning "to turn", and the adjectives signify what sensory perception is in play: light, touch, chemicals, or gravity. Plessner even goes so far as to admit that "such perception zones play a supportive role in the progress of stimulated movements oriented toward light, gravity, or elsewhere [...]" (Plessner 1928, 224).

However, he rejects any analogy between plant and animal perception. For an animal has specialized organs of perception that "mediate the stimulus *object*" (original emphasis) (Plessner 1928, 224). Equally incomparable are "stimulus conduction" in plants and "nervous processes" in animals (Plessner 1928, 224). Plessner argues that these faulty analogies come to prominence because plant physiology took shape in response to the functional schematic of animal physiology. But plant physiology should not forget that the centric or closed form is a prerequisite for autonomous movement, sensory perception and goal-oriented behavior:

> "*Flowers opening and closing, the day- and nighttime positions of leaves, the growth of stems and roots towards gravity or the light are in no way centrally mediated movements that can be attributed to instinctual or even volitional impulses,*" Plessner (1928, 223).

The fundamental difference in organizational form is, so Plessner argues, best seen in the ontogeny of plants and animals. This still rings true today. A related difference between plants and animals is the fact that virtually all plants are indeterminate or modular in growth. This means they maintain clusters or layers of embryonic cells or stem cells, that are always capable of changing into roots, stems, leaves, or any other specialized tissues. Animals, by contrast, convert all stem cells into specialized tissues and largely lose the ability to grow or replace damaged areas. Animal ontogeny in a certain sense led to a more or less finished form, whereas the plant remains plastic and open-ended in its development. The different parts of the plant are highly self-sufficient, so much so that we can propagate them by grafting or cuttings. A plant, according to Plessner, is therefore not an individual but a *dividual* (Plessner 1928, 220). A plant is not a unified entity, such as most animals, but fundamentally fragmented.

## CIRCUMNUTATIONS

Max Scheler finds a compatriot in Charles Darwin. Darwin's first venture into the topic of plant movement occurred in the early 1860s. The subject of plant movement was brought to his attention by Harvard professor of Botany and friend Asa Gray, who had sent him his article on the movements of the tendrils of some *Cucurbitaceous* plants. This led Darwin to study climbing plants on a far grander scale. In his greenhouse, he carefully observed how these plants scaled to great heights, publishing his findings in the *Journal of the Linnaean Society* under the title *On the movements and habits of climbing plants* (1865).

Later on, Francis Darwin, who was trained as plant physiologist with a doctoral degree from the University of Würzburg, assisted his father with his *magnum opus* on plant movement: *The Power of Movement in Plants* (1880). A treasure trove of revolutionary experimental data, it contains numerous odd illustrations with spiraling, and squiggly lines. These, it turns out, are two-dimensional time-lapse images of plants. Since Charles Darwin and his son Francis did not have the adequate technology at their disposal, they fabricated an ingenious setup to record plant movements over longer stretches of time. They would glue small glass tubes to some young shoots or leaf tips of a plant. At the end of the tubes, they placed a blow of black beeswax. Then they placed a stick in the soil slightly below with a round piece of cardboard attached, with a black dot in the middle, as a fixed point. Above the setup or to the side the placed a large glass plate, where the two points met, they drew a dot on the glass plate. They did this in various time intervals at day and night (the staff helped with the nightly measurements). When the dots were connected, the spiraling lines emerged. These traces revealed the most common form of spontaneous plant movement, which they called "circumnutation", a term they borrowed from the German botanist Julius Sachs. In his *Lehrbuch der Botanik nach dem gegenwärtigen Stand der Wissenschaft* (1874), Sachs uses the word *nutation* (derived from the Latin word *nutare*, meaning "to nod" or "bend") for the movement of individual leaves and shoots in their upward or lateral growth. Strictly speaking, the plant does not merely bend back and forth, but "bends successively to all points of the compass" Darwin notes (C. Darwin 1880, 1). This, according to Sachs, results in either a rotating (*rotierende*) or a revolving (*revolutive*) movement (Sachs 1874, 452).

## ROOT-BRAIN HYPOTHESIS

In the plant nursery and laboratory at Down House, Charles Darwin and his son Francis discovered far more than the capacity of autonomous movement in plants. They also laid bare the different ways in which leaves, shoots, and roots react to various external environmental stimuli, directing their up- and downward growth and development. One third of *The Power of Movement in Plants* is dedicated to the root tip and their navigation through the underground. Father and son discover that root tips, whilst circumnutating like little antennae through the underground, are capable of sensing the direction of gravity, but also moisture, obstacles, and other underground stimuli. And based on these impressions, the root determines its course through the soil. These curious findings led them to conclude their 573-page book with a bold analogy, later dubbed the "root-brain hypothesis":

*"It is hardly an exaggeration to say that the tip of the radicle thus endowed, and having the power of directing the movements of the adjoining parts, acts like the brain of one of the lower animals; the brain being seated within the anterior end of the body, receiving impressions from the sense-organs, and directing the several movements," Darwin (1880, 573).*

From several letters we can ascertain that Charles Darwin took this analogy seriously. He corresponded with numerous trusted friends on the topic, for example speculating about the evolutionary origin of the nervous system with British biologist Francis Maitland Balfour (Darwin Correspondence Project, "Letter no. 12706"). And he (Darwin Correspondence Project, "Letter no. 12841") jokingly wrote to his close friend Joseph Hooker:

*"The case, however, of radicles bending after exposure for an hour to geotropism, with their tips (or brains) cut off is, I think, worth your reading (bottom of p. 525); it astounded me."*

At the meeting of the *British Association for the Advance of Science* (BAAS) on September 2, 1902, Francis Darwin gave a lecture on plant psychology. He argues that animals and plants both show extreme sensitivity to certain external stimuli and transmit these from one part of the body to another. He also detects a certain form of memory and forming of habits in plants – *behavior* so to speak. Remaining cautious about imbuing plants with intelligence, he nonetheless concludes: "It is impossible to know whether plants are sentient or not; but [...] in all living beings there is something psychic" (F. Darwin 1908, 11). Corbey has shown that Scheler reaches a similar conclusion when he equates being "alive" with the term "biopsychic" (another term he uses is "psychovital") (Corbey 1988, 26). According to Plessner's view, this is a grave error. By appealing to "psychological or psychoid forces", one betrays "the essence of the plant" and even "the essence of nature" (Plessner 1928, 226) because you pretend that the secrets of nature lie behind it.

In his book *Rustic Sounds* (1917), Francis Darwin reminisces about the root experiments he undertook with his father and writes: "Gravitation is nothing more than a signpost or signal to the plant – a signal which the plant interprets in the way best suited to its success in the struggle for life, just as what we see or hear gives us signals of changes in the exterior world by which we regulate our conduct." (F. Darwin 1917, 42) This conclusion undermines Plessner's reasoning, by presenting experimental prove of the extreme sensitivity of plant cells to stimuli from its surrounds, and the power of transmitting this influence to adjoining parts of the plant, and all of this in the absence of a central nervous system, or centric form. Plessner seems blind-sighted by his own categorical logic, maintaining that a centric or closed form is a necessary prerequisite of sensation and action. Daniel Dennett labels this fallacy "cerebrocentrism" (Pollan 2013). Plessner, accordingly, fails to entertain the idea that sensation, action, and even goal-oriented behavior is achieved by open forms of life as well. Or, perhaps the whole distinction between open and closed forms is misguided. Curiously, Plessner seems well-aware of this. He writes how Driesch himself, for example, studied animals with an open organizational form, such as corals, hydrozoans (polyps and medusae), bryozoans (moss animals), and ascidians (tunicates and sea squirts) (Scheler 1928, 219).

Let me conclude my perambulation on plant movement and sensation with a possible way to read and understand the notion of "psychic", both employed by Scheler and Charles Darwin's son Francis, without going down the path of metaphysics. My namesake Norbert Wiener provides an important clue in this context. Working as an engineer in guiding missile technology during World War II, he quickly realized that all sophisticated machinery follows the feedback principle. To hit a moving target, a missile must constantly adjust and re-adjust its flight path, which is impossible without the aid of feedback mechanisms. Wiener surmised that this was not only true of sophisticated technology, the feedback principle must be a key feature of life as well. For example, both animals and plants have an inbuilt biological clock that follows a circadian rhythm. In both cases, this clock can run autonomously for a while, but to keep running properly the clock is regulated by the perception of blue light. It is curious that this biological clock, and in fact every feedback mechanism, combines an open and a closed organizational form *sensu* Plessner. Perhaps the feedback principle will thus enable us to clarify the cryptic word "psychic" in relation to animal and plant life!

And, *perhaps*, this could be a topic for a future walk!

## Acknowledgements

Let me express my gratitude to Raymond Corbey for the advice, discussions and guidance provided over the years as a teacher, a friend and a philosopher. Your sincere and persistent enthusiasm for science, art and philosophy are exemplary! And a word of praise is also in order towards plants, may our distant green cousins and fellow verdure travelers continue to provide inspiration and bewilderment.

## Primary sources

Darwin Correspondence Project:
"Letter no. 12706," accessed on 4 February 2023
"Letter no. 12841," accessed on 4 February 2023

## References

Anonymous. 1908. "What Darwin Thinks of the Thoughts of Plants". *The New York Times*, Section M, p. 11.

Corbey, R..H.A.. 1988. *De mens een dier?: Scheler, Plessner en de crisis van het traditionele mensbeeld*, Proefschrift Nijmegen.

Darwin, C.R. 1875. *On the Movement and Habits of Climbing Plants*. London: John Murray.

Darwin, C.R. 1880. *The Power of Movement in Plants*. London, London: John Murray.

Darwin, F. 1908. "The Address of the President of the British Association for the Advancement of Science I, Science 28 (716), 353-362.

Darwin, F. 1917. *Rustic Sounds, and other Studies in Literature and Natural History*. London: John Murray.

Keller, D. 2011. *The Restless Plant*. Harvard: Harvard University Press.

Plessner, H. 1928. *Die Stufen des Organischen und der Mensch: Einleitung in die philosophische Antropologie*. Berlin: De Gruyter.

Pollan, M. 2013. "The Intelligent Plant". *The New Yorker*, https://www.newyorker.com/magazine/2013/12/23/the-intelligent-plant [accessed on 4 February 2023].

Rensberger, B. 1982. "To Land, to Seed, to Flower". *Mosaic* 13 (4), 30-35.

Sachs, J. 1874. *Lehrbuch der Botanik nach dem gegenwärtigen Stand der Wissenschaft*, Vierte Auflage. Leipzig: W. Engelmann.

Wiener, N. 1948. *Cybernetics: Or Control and Communication in the Animal and the Machine*, Paris: Hermann & Cie, Cambridge (Mass.): MIT Press.

In Hussain, S.T. and G.L. Dusseldorp (eds) 2025. Sitting on the fence: Negotiating archaeology, anthropology and philosophy. Festschrift for Prof. Dr Raymond H.A. Corbey in celebration of his 70th birthday. *Analecta Praehistorica Leidensia* 54. Leiden: Sidestone Press, pp. 75-84.

# Challenging the human-nonhuman boundary: Biological and cultural diversity

Annette Lanjouw

## ABSTRACT

Traditional framings of biological diversity focus on genetic variation and evolutionary adaptations between and within species. As a consequence, the conservation and protection of biodiversity is primarily aimed at safeguarding the diversity of species and subspecies in perpetuity. This definition is not applied to human diversity, however, where ethnic and cultural as well as other behavioural forms of diversity are both recognized and valued. The cultural diversity of nonhuman animals, defined as transgenerational social learning within a social group, has intrinsic and, at least in some cases, significant adaptive value to groups or individuals. These culturally acquired capacities can potentially impact a species' ability to survive in a world shaped by rapidly mounting anthropogenic pressures. Recognizing cultural diversity in nonhuman species can then form a bridge between the acknowledgement of an individual's intrinsic value and that of the group or the species. Conservation efforts in the present must therefore consider the cultural dimensions of biodiversity and work towards new ways of recognizing the value of nonhuman cultures.

*Keywords: Culture, speciesism, compassionate conservation, biocultural diversity.*

## INTRODUCTION

In many parts of the world, and particularly in the Global North, humans consider themselves to be exceptional, a separate biological category from all other animals. As our understanding of animal biology and their varied behaviours and abilities increases, it has become apparent that in many abilities traditionally defined as uniquely human, the differences between humans and non-human animals are more a matter of degree than absolute. Acknowledging the continuity and similarity between all animal species challenges speciesist concepts that attribute moral and intellectual superiority to humans, thereby enabling human exploitation of non-human lives. Culture is a case in point, when defined as socially transmitted learning that is shared between members of a group. Culture is present in countless animal species and provides rich diversity of life experiences, adaptations, and behaviours. For meaningful and compassionate conservation of biodiversity, it is important to shift attention from focusing exclusively on the protection of an archetypical phenotype to including the safeguarding of cultural diversity among non-human animals as well. This does not mean prioritizing culture over biological diversity, but including all aspects of diversity in the conservation paradigm. Indigenous knowledge systems in many parts of the world recognize the

**Annette Lanjouw**
Arcus Foundation, Cambridge, United Kingdom
alanjouw@arcusfoundation.org
ORCID: 0000-0001-8354-4115

connection between the animal and human worlds and provide examples of how humans can be better integrated as part of broader ecosystems where every creature and their experiences form part of an interdependent whole.

## THE HUMAN–NONHUMAN BOUNDARY

Humans have historically tended to grant themselves a level of privilege within the living world, distinguishing themselves from all other living creatures. The roots of this long-held belief can be traced back to Judaeo-Christian ideas about the soul, and the image of God in humanity, with man holding dominion over all the other earthly creatures (Peterson 2001; Corbey 2005). The notion of human exceptionalism is also influenced by Descartes' foregrounding of the rational mind, and the "unique mental capacities" that humans purportedly possess (Anderson 2018). This perspective on the boundary between human and animal neatly differentiates humans from other animals and declares that only humans, with symbolizing minds and as moral persons, can transcend nature.

The discourse on human exceptionalism has involved the deployment of what Derrida termed 'zoopolitical logic' (Vaughan-Williams 2015a; 2015b), wherein perceived fundamental differences in certain capacities, traits, or behaviours between humans and non-human animals are used as criteria to define the human/animal divide, and for making ethical and political distinctions between human and nonhuman life (Agamben 1998; Derrida 2008; 2009). Examples of such benchmark capacities include reason and intelligence, morality and associated technological achievements, or sophistication (Garner 2004; Srinivasan 2010; Tomasello 2014). Yet Charles Darwin (1982) already forcefully argued for evolutionary continuity, stressing that variations among species amount to differences in degree rather than in kind.

Historically, it has often been of great value to humans to cultivate this paradigm of exceptionalism, as it has divorced the question of how we treat nonhuman animals from moral considerations, and therefore frequently helped justifying animal exploitation, leading to unnecessary suffering or negative impacts on wild animal populations (Livingstone Smith 2013; Nussbaum 2023). The paradigm has similarly been used to exploit and abuse other groups of humans, through their dehumanization and comparison to animals, and ascribing to them characteristics that are less than human (Livingstone Smith 2013; Machery 2013). Negotiating the human-animal boundary has historically been (mis)used as a colonial approach, with marginalisation and suppression of the 'Other' fuelled by animal metaphors and trait ascriptions used to legitimize the power and supremacy of the Western colonizer (Aderinto 2022; Corbey 2005). Speciesism, or the discrimination against or exploitation of certain animal species to the sole benefit of human beings, involves assigning different values and rights to other species (Bekoff 2013). The cultivation and development of human wellbeing, in the form of increasing consumption aimed at enhancing health, comfort and pleasure, is only rendered possible by the use, exploitation, and re-design of nonhuman nature including animals (Srinivasan and Kasturirangan 2016).

Much research has focused on assessing the capacities of nonhuman animals in those domains where humans have considered their own abilities to be unique (de Waal 1999). In a range of different species including cetaceans, primates, canids, birds, cephalopod molluscs, and arthropods, scientists have started to challenge this supposed uniqueness with regard to the intellectual, sensory, emotional, and behavioural abilities of these animals. Language, or the ability to communicate thoughts through complex and compositional communication was traditionally considered the unique domain of humans, but evidence has mounted for varied species able to communicate through language or language-like forms of vocalisation, so that the emphasis has now shifted on syntactical language supposedly being the exclusionary domain of humans (Leroux et al. 2023). The latter, however, is also increasingly challenged as researchers begin to understand the uncharted communicative ecologies of nonhuman animals (Suzuki et al. 2016).

The mental representation of symbols – characters that arbitrarily represent another object, function or process – is traditionally regarded to have underpinned the development of language and as such to be instrumental in the evolution of language in our hominid ancestors and cousins. In part also because of this framing, psychologists, anthropologists, and philosophers have often questioned the ability of nonhuman animals to comprehend and employ symbols, yet numerous studies have now demonstrated the ability of animals to engage in symbolic communication (Mejdell et al. 2016). Tool use, culture, theory of mind, and a concept of self, altruism, and empathy (de Waal 2016) have all been attested to different degrees in diverse species. Morality is sometimes still seen as being unique to humans, yet existing evidence points to a sense of justice and 'fairness' in some nonhuman animals, sensibilities which are frequently viewed as cornerstones of morality and justice (Brosan 2013). Less positive, 'darker' qualities often considered uniquely human have also been found in non-human species, including warfare (chimpanzees, ants), coercive sex (ducks, geese, dolphins, chimpanzees), torture (orca, cats), infanticide (lions, gorillas, dolphins) and cannibalism in more than 1500 species (Polis 1981). Even the feeling of pain, anxiety, and distress has long been denied to creatures with no brain or spinal cord. Yet, ongoing research shows that many invertebrates consciously feel pain and act on it, in a voluntary and rational manner (Fossat *et al.* 2014; Birch 2021).

Scientific evidence collected over the years has therefore dismantled many of the myths of human exceptionalism and has clearly demonstrated that many of the firmly held beliefs of what sets humans apart from nonhuman animals are often misleading, and that the human-animal boundary is in reality only a matter of degree rather than an absolute gulf.

## HUMAN RIGHTS AND SPECIESISM
The 1948 *Universal Declaration on Human Rights*, including input from biologists and anthropologists, makes reference to evolutionary and population-genetic findings that there is an overarching biological and genetic unity in humankind (UN 1948). The major locus of variation between different groups of humans is behavioural and cultural. The 1964 *Proposals on the Biological Aspects of Race* by UNESCO (the United Nations Educational Scientific and Cultural Organisation) similarly states that all people living today belong to a single species, *Homo sapiens*, and that neither in the field of hereditary potentialities concerning intelligence and the capacity for cultural development, nor in that of the physical traits, is there any justification for the concept of 'inferior' vs. 'superior' races (Selcer 2011). The variations between the different groups of humans are rooted in their culture, their adaptations to environmental conditions, and in learned behaviours.

Yet the emphasis on all humans as being more similar than different, while at the same time being distinct from all other nonhumans, ignores the many similarities between humans and nonhumans. Many of the traits that we share as humans are also shared by other creatures, whether mammal, fish, bird, or

reptile. There are differences of scale and degree, of course, but many of the fundamental characteristics that make us human are common to countless other species. It is much easier to perceive those similarities in our closest relatives, the great apes, and much more challenging to observe them in cetaceans, fish, or birds, yet the similarities exist. Cleaner wrasse, a fish found in tropical coral reefs, for example, have demonstrated a clear sense of self through the mark test (also called mirror test), a capacity previously believed to be lacking in fish (Kohda *et al.* 2022). Speciesism is founded on the belief that humans are cognitively and morally superior to other animals, and are thus afforded greater rights, as well as the implicit permission to exploit, consume, and destroy other species and the habitats they depend on. This belief is the very foundation of our social democracies and legal systems worldwide and has enabled humanity to colonize, develop thriving economies, and alter natural ecosystems and landscapes around the world, to the detriment of the many other species that live there.

## CULTURE
UNESCO (2001) defines culture as a "set of distinctive spiritual, material, intellectual, and emotional features of society or a social group, and that it encompasses, in addition to art and literature, lifestyles, ways of living together, value systems, traditions and beliefs". In 2005, UNESCO adopted an international treaty, the *Convention on the Protection and Promotion of the Diversity of Cultural Expressions*, which built on the 2001 *Universal Declaration on Cultural Diversity*, calling on nations and institutions to work together for the preservation of culture in all of its forms, and for policies that help to share ideas across cultures and inspire new forms of creativity. The declaration connects the preservation of culture with central issues in human rights.

Although the offered definition of culture is not necessarily human-specific, it has been broadly understood to be unique to humans and one of the factors that sets human populations apart from each other and from nonhuman species. Most definitions of culture adopted by anthropologists explicitly reference humans alone. Based on Edward Taylor's widely cited concept of culture from 1871, culture is often defined as including knowledge, belief, art, morals, law, custom, and any other capabilities and habits acquired by man [sic] as a member of society (Welsh *et al.* 2020).

To be useful, a concept of culture must be concerned with observables – phenomena – without

the necessity of prior knowledge of internal states
or constructs (such as beliefs or values) in beings
with whom we share no common language. As Kevin
Laland and his colleagues (2009) state: rather than
benchmarking culture at one's favourite species
or orienting it according to academic interest, it is
important to look for "the most useful way to define
culture". A definition must thus at least allow for the
*theoretical possibility* of nonhuman culture and should,
at the same time, not a priori exclude phenomena in
animals commonly considered cultural in humans,
such as language, music, and ritual. Culture can then
perhaps more inclusively be defined as "[b]ehaviour
patterns shared by members of a community that
rely on socially learned and transmitted information"
(Whitehead and Rendell 2014, 19).

Cultural heritage is often divided into the
'tangible' and 'intangible' assets of a group or society
inherited from past generations. Tangible, or material
culture, can include monuments, books, works
of art, and artifacts, and intangible heritage may
include traditions, stories, language, and knowledge –
phenomena that are less easily graspable. Human
culture is extraordinarily diverse and includes
languages, cuisines, religions, technologies, political
systems, literature, art, music, dance, social
conventions, etc. One of the reasons often provided by
people who believe culture to be unique to humans,
is that humans have cumulative culture building
up over time in a manner that no single individual
could reasonably achieve in a lifetime. This notion
of culture encompasses morality as well as culturally
transmitted and symbolic ethnic markers. There is
no doubt that human culture has some extraordinary
attributes and qualities, but the common
understanding of culture has been shaped by the
implicit desire to set humans apart, and to specify
the distinctiveness of humans vis-à-vis nonhuman
animals. Culture has therefore been traditionally
defined in a way that underscores our inherited
sense of exceptionalism. However, as philosopher
Thomas White (2009) argues, evaluating whales or
dolphins according to human features is profoundly
one-sided and thus ultimately biased. It would be
much more objective and balanced to assess how
humans compare to other animals by mobilising a
concept of culture that is designed to be inclusive and
non-speciesist from the onset. Such a concept cannot
be grounded or take its point of departure in *Homo
sapiens* alone, but instead needs to be developed
based on comparative insights drawn together from
across all of the living world.

## NONHUMAN CULTURE

Culture can be understood as an extension of biology,
as it is an inheritance system (social inheritance)
in turn building on the foundation of a genetic
inheritance system (genetically acquired traits). But
culture is also a strong directing force that exerts
significant influence on the development of individual
and group behaviours, thereby contributing to
evolutionary processes and dynamics, cumulative or
not (Boyd and Richerson 1985; Whiten *et al.* 2017).

By mapping socially learned and transmitted
behaviours in nonhuman animals, behavioural
ecologists and ethologists have since the
mid-20th century started to reveal the breadth of
cultural diversity found in the animal kingdom
(Whiten 2021). Regional birdsong dialects, washing
of food by Japanese macaques, perforating milk
bottle tops to extract the cream by British passerines,
and nut cracking and termite fishing by different
chimpanzee groups are but some of the better-known
examples. These cultural expressions range from
tool use to food-processing, and from social to sexual
behaviours. Culture in this sense has been discovered
and described across a large range of taxa as
diverse as whales, primates, fish, bees, and fruit flies
(Brakes 2020). Although its scope and distribution
across the tree of life is subject to ongoing research
and much speculation, culture must therefore be
treated as a significant component of the living world
as a whole, especially within metazoans (animals),
and not the sole domain of humans. This realisation
leaves open, of course, how human and nonhuman
cultures precisely compare.

## CULTURE AND CONSERVATION

The general definition of biological diversity, or
biodiversity, encompasses the variety of all life on
earth, at all levels of organization, from the genetic
architecture of organisms to the species diversity of
biomes (Swingland, 2000; Lovejoy and Hannah 2006).
Different species and organisms are interconnected
and bound up in ecosystems, dependant on a network
of relationships that supports life in all its forms,
and the notion of biological diversity thus entails
complex interactions among species. Diversity
within ecosystems can be discussed in relation to
four broad levels of organization and scale: genetic
diversity (between individuals), population diversity
(between same-species populations), species
diversity (between species), and ecosystem diversity
(between ecosystems), and all the interactions and

interdependencies between these levels. All of these diversity-levels are fundamentally based on the genetic diversity of each form of life, whether at the individual or group level. But the concept of *biodiversity* rarely encompasses the diversity that exists outside of genetic diversity, such as experience, personality, age/life stage, knowledge, taste, and, ultimately, culture. Given the mounting evidence for widespread nonhuman cultures, considerations of ecosystem diversity must take stock of culture as yet another source of considerable within-ecosystem variation.

The conservation of biological diversity is both a moral philosophy and a sociopolitical movement, focused on protecting species from extinction, safeguarding natural resources, maintaining and restoring habitats and ecosystems, and enhancing valued ecosystem services. As a result, conservation tends to focus on the genetic and phenotypic diversity of life and seeks to ensure that the latter are protected and continue to function as a living, intricate web. Standard conservation approaches thus typically identify discrete population units and try to identify, evaluate and mitigate the threats posed to those units, for example by anthropogenic change.

*But what do we lose by focusing exclusively on biological (genetic) diversity?*

a.  Individual differences: for example personality, experience, life stage, and how they influence each other as well as higher-level interactions
b.  Differences between social groups: for example, ecological adaptations, learning, and shared knowledge

When we orient conservation policies primarily towards the protection of the genetic diversity of life on this planet, we lose sight of much of the richness that is found in the diverse societies of social animals. To some extent, such a loss would be comparable to focusing on the human species without taking into account the rich diversity *within* that species. We are all part of the same species, *Homo sapiens*, but nobody can deny that within that category, there is incredible behavioural diversity.

In many parts of the world, humans and non-human animals have developed behaviours derived from interactions and cohabitation with each other, often evolved over hundreds of years. Humans and non-human animals can collaborate or have sometimes developed symbiotic relationships that are mutually beneficial, such as honey-guides and hunter-gatherers in Tanzania, dolphins and fishers in Brazil

(Cantor *et al.* 2023), and many others. Protected areas have traditionally been defined by the exclusion of humans. In most cases, however, Indigenous Peoples and local communities are part of those ecosystems and shape them in ways that are often vital for their livelihoods. Protected areas that have been established without the free, prior, and informed consent of local communities, or that are legally gazetted for the protection of wildlife and exploitation for tourism/research without consideration of the interests and needs of the local communities that are part of those landscapes, are a perpetuation of capitalist conservation's cumulative negative impacts, and ultimately unsustainable. The focus on 'conservation' of wildlife can be seen to prioritize the concern to retain the status quo or some form of perceived 'natural state/condition' even though ecosystems are inherently dynamic and subjected to continual change and species-reconfigurations, especially in the face of the Anthropocene.

By integrating behaviour and social learning into concepts of biological diversity, conservation approaches can include behavioural diversity into their conceptual framework. Social learning and culture influence the transmission of behaviours that can impact the reproductive success or survival of different species. In that manner, they have an enormous influence on demographic processes. The resulting approach to conservation would cultivate a new focus on *biocultural diversity*. Culture and sociality were already built into the 2017 *Convention of Migratory Species of Wild Animals* (Brakes *et al.* 2019; Convention on the Conservation of Migratory Species of Wild Animals 2017), and cultural nonhuman data now inform the conservation management of eastern tropical Pacific sperm whales (*Physeter macrocephalus)*, Western chimpanzees (*Pan troglodytes verus*), and numerous other species (Whiten 2021).

Understanding how behaviour and social learning can influence survival is a critical factor for conservation and the management of wild animal populations, as well as larger multispecies habitats and ecosystems. Learning about where to forage during times of shortage, how to avoid predators, or when to migrate, or how to extract nutrition or medicinal properties from difficult to process food items, is critical for individuals and groups, and many of these processes are now recognised as being fundamentally subjected to cultural evolution not just in humans (Aikens *et al.* 2022).

For example, among two distinct populations of orcas coexisting in the coastal waters of the North Pacific, one relies primarily on chinook salmon for 90% of its diet, while the other eats primarily sea mammals such as seals. The populations are not reproductively isolated, although they very rarely interbreed (Kardos *et al.* 2023). The chinook salmon are declining throughout their range and are highly threatened. These cultural differences in food choice have led to physiological differences in the whales' digestive enzymes and jaw strength and make each population vulnerable to changes affecting their prey. Crashes in chinook salmon populations have led to starvation and malnutrition in the salmon-eating population of orcas. Conservation interventions to protect the populations of orca must thus also focus on the populations of salmon, for example strengthening fishery policies and preventing the construction of dams that negatively affect the breeding success of the salmon (Brakes 2020).

Cultural adaptations, finally, also offer important insight into how different nonhuman animal species adjust to changing climatic conditions, or the environmental impacts of those changes. For instance, chimpanzees in Senegal, Tanzania and the Democratic Republic of Congo have culturally learned strategies for finding water during droughts, making them more resilient during times of climatic stress (Lanjouw 2002; Péter *et al.* 2022; Wessling *et al.* 2018). Cultural adaptations are therefore not merely an add-on to biological adaptations, they are a key locus of population, species, and ecosystem diversity and also co-shape the diversity patterns found where they occur. Nonhuman culture, for this reason, forms part of the important foci of conservation efforts and needs to be protected accordingly. Doing so is not trivial and requires broad-scale concern with cultural variation among nonhuman animals.

Due to the emphasis on protecting biological diversity, conservation tends to focus on large, intact areas with as many different species and large populations as possible, such as protected areas (Büscher *et al.* 2020). However, we know that many species and populations of species exist in small fragments or isolated areas. To survive in those smaller, often marginal areas, the animals within have often had to learn and adapt in order to survive. They have had to develop unique strategies and cultural adaptations that have set them apart from groups in other patches of habitat, despite being genetically similar. By focusing only on large intact areas, some of the adaptations to such habitats can easily be lost.

## INDIGENOUS BELIEFS ABOUT NONHUMAN CULTURE

Attention to nonhuman animal culture is relatively recent within zoology and animal behaviour research and predominantly shaped by Western (European and North American) scholarship and its attendant conceptual frameworks. Indigenous belief and knowledge systems have long held that humans are to be included into the world of animals, and that many, if not most, of these animals have agency and culture (Brightman and Lewis 2017). These understandings of nonhuman nature, and the values that underpin them continue to influence how many Indigenous peoples live alongside and interact with other species and the ecosystems (Fa *et al.* 2020). Integrating indigenous knowledge more effectively into Western scientific approaches and literature can provide valuable insights and understanding of the interdependence of human and nonhuman lives.

Biodiversity and cultural diversity, both animal and human, are deeply intertwined. Throughout history, humans have interacted with nature, and as part of ecosystems, to meet their needs. This has included the acquisition of food, shelter, and medicine to ensure their mental and spiritual well-being. Nature is part of people's belief systems, tradition, and culture and defines multiple aspects of their lives, including language and spirituality. Through these interactions humans have shaped landscapes and, at the same time, been shaped *by* nature, holding a wealth of information about plants, animals, ecosystems, ecological processes, and the relationships and interdependencies between them. Most Indigenous peoples have a deep understanding of and respect for nature, both as part of nature and in terms of the importance of maintaining a balance within and between them. How to live "well" with nature is, to various extents, deeply build into their culture (Lewis 2019). Such links between human cultural practices and biodiversity are not coincidental. The two can be mutually sustaining (Pretty *et al.* 2009) and this is arguably the reason why an estimated 80% of the planet's terrestrial biodiversity is found on land governed or managed by Indigenous peoples and local communities (Sobrevila 2008). A growing number of studies indicate that where Indigenous peoples and local communities have strong ties to their territories, are able to remain on them and sustain them and their cultures from external threats and infringement, ecosystems remain intact and 'healthy' (Fa *et al.* 2020; Garnett 2018) and populations of otherwise threatened species often thrive (O'Brien *et al.* 2019; Schuster *et al.* 2019). The biodiversity crisis is therefore also, and perhaps primarily, a crisis of how most humans, as cultural beings, have come to inhabit the planet. Patterns of biodiversity and cultural practices are inherently linked and biodiversity conservation therefore needs to pay more attention to this linkage and its consequences.

Incorporating biocultural diversity into the broader conservation narrative can advance conservation efforts and make them more just and effective. Such a perspective on conservation also provides a strong basis for thinking more holistically about a rights-based approach to conservation that considers the rights of all beings, and the survival of humans and nonhumans (Nussbaum 2023; Bekoff and Pierce 2010). This being said, the emphasis on the value of culture and social learning purely as adaptations to a changing world, can also be limiting in this regard. For example, it begs the question of whether culture needs to have outcome-related 'value' that is obvious to a human observer. It is not necessarily clear that all human traditions of food acquisition and management, language, or music have obvious value to our survival as a species. It may be possible that culture, from the songs of sperm whales to the different tools used by chimpanzees, can have intrinsic value to the group or population, and perhaps this is enough.

## Conclusions

The conservation of biological diversity has mainly concentrated on the safeguarding in perpetuity of genetic diversity in the natural world, from the level of organisms to that of biomes. This is of vital importance for the survival of our planet, and the human and nonhuman life it sustains. Yet, by focusing exclusively on genetic architecture, there is a danger of losing sight of another domain of diversity that is both surprisingly rich, interesting, and potentially important for animal survival: behavioural diversity, related to culture and the social transmission of information from one generation to the next, is a factor that often significantly impacts the survival of individuals, groups, and populations. Culturally mediated learning that enables species, groups, and individuals to adapt to a changing world can therefore make an important contribution to emerging conservation paradigms and needs to be both understood and seriously considered. Although culture can have significant adaptive value, it needs not only be considered from this perspective. Social and cultural behaviours that have intrinsic value for the group or the individual may be sufficient to motivate protection and conservation.

## Acknowledgements

Raymond Corbey was my "thought-partner" and co-conspirator, pulling together a conference at the Desmond Tutu Center in New York in 2011, entitled *Humans and other apes: rethinking the species interface.* The conference resulted in the co-edited book "The Politics of Species: Reshaping our relationship with other animals". This experience, and the input of the many contributing authors, has substantially shaped my thinking, and also in many ways elevated the support of conservation efforts focusing on apes and other animals ever since. Intellectually challenging the assumptions and limitations of a human-centric perspective is symptomatic for Raymond Corbey's influence and will hopefully continue to impact human and other lives in the future.

## References

Addessi, E., A. Mancini, L. Crescimbene, C. Padoa-Schioppa, and E. Visalberghi. 2008. "Preference Transitivity and Symbolic Representation in Capuchin Monkeys (Cebus apella)". *PLOS ONE* 3 (6), e2414. DOI: 10.1371/journal.pone.0002414

Aderinto, S. 2022. *People and Animals in Nigerian History – Animality and Colonial Subjecthood in Africa: The Human and Nonhuman Creatures of Nigeria.* Athens: Ohio University Press.

Agamben, G. 1998. *Homo Sacer: Sovereign Power and Bare Life.* Stanford: Stanford University Press.

Aikens, E.O., I.D. Bontekoe, L. Blumenstiel, A. Schlicksupp and A. Flack. 2022. "Viewing animal migration through a social lens". *Trends in Ecology & Evolution* 37 (11), DOI: 10.1016/j.tree.2022.06.008.

Anderson, K., and C. Perrin 2018. "Removed from Nature: the Modern Idea of Human Exceptionality." *Environmental Humanities* 10 (2), 447-472.

Bekoff, M. 2013. "Who lives, who dies and why? How speciesism undermines compassionate conservation and social justice". In *Politics of Species*, edited by R.H.A. Corbey and A. Lanjouw, 15-27. Cambridge: Cambridge University Press.

Bekoff, M., and J. Pierce. 2010. *Wild Justice: The Moral Lives of Animals.* Chicago: University of Chicago Press.

Birch, J., C. Burn, A. Schnell, H. Browning, and A. Crump. 2021. "Review of *Evidence of sentience in cephalopod molluscs and decapod crustaceans.*", LSE Consulting. LSE Enterprise Ltd. The London School of Economics and Political Science. Available at: https://www.lse.ac.uk/News/News-Assets/PDFs/2021/Sentience-in-Cephalopod-Molluscs-and-Decapod-Crustaceans-Final-Report-November-2021.pdf

Boyd, R. and P. Richerson. 1985. *Culture and the Evolutionary Process*. Chicago: University of Chicago Press.

Brakes, P., S.R.X. Dall, L. Aplin, S. Bearhop, E.L. Carroll, P. Ciucci, V. Fishlock, J.K.B. Ford, E.C. Garland, S.A. Keith, P.K. McGregor, S.L. Mesnick, M.J. Noad, G. Nortobartolo di Sciara, M.M. Robbins, M.P. Simmonds, F. Spina, A. Thornton, P.R. Wade, M.J. Whiting, J. Williams, L. Rendell, H. Whitehead, A. Whiten and C. Rutz. 2019. "Animal cultures matter for conservation". *Science* 363, 1032-1034.

Brosnan S.F. 2013. "Justice- and fairness-related behaviors in nonhuman primates". *Proceedings of the National Academy of Sciences* 110 (Suppl 2), 10416-23.

Brosnan, S.F., and F.B.M. de Waal. 2003. "Monkeys reject unequal pay". *Nature* 425, 297-99.

Büscher, B. and R. Fletcher. 2020. *The Conservation Revolution: Radical Ideas for Saving Nature Beyond the Anthropocene*. New York: Verso.

Cantor, M., R. Farine, and F.G. Daura-Jorge. 2023. "Foraging synchrony drives resilience in human – dolphin mutualism". *Proceedings of the National Academy of Sciences* 120 (6), e2207739120. DOI:10.1073/pnas.2207739120

Convention on the Conservation of Migratory Species of Wild Animals. 2017. "Decisions 12.75 to 12.77 – Conservation Implications of Animal Culture and Social Complexity." *Convention on the Conservation of Migratory Species of Wild Animals.* Accessed 8 April 2024. https://www.cms.int/en/page/decisions-1275-1277-conservation-implications-animal-culture-and-social-complexity.

Corbey, R.H.A. 2005. *The Metaphysics of Apes: Negotiating the Animal-Human Boundary*. Cambridge: Cambridge University Press.

Darwin, Charles, 1982 [1871]. *The Descent of Man, and Selection in Relation to Sex*. Princeton, NJ: Princeton University Press.

De Waal, F.B.M. 1999. "Anthropomorphism and anthropodenial: Consistency in our thinking about humans and other animals". *Philosophical Topics* 27, 255-80.

De Waal, F.B.M. 2014. *Are we smart enough to know how smart animals are?* New York: W.W. Norton & Company.

Derrida, J. 2008. *The Animal That therefore I Am.* New York: Fordham University Press.

Derrida, J. 2009. *The Beast & the Sovereign Volume I.* Chicago: University of Chicago Press.

Fa, J.E., J.E.M. Watson, I. Leiper, P. Potapov, T.D. Evans, N.D. Burgess, Z. Molnár, A. Fernández-Llamazares, T. Duncan, S. Wang, B.J. Austin, H. Jonas, C.J. Robinson, P. Malmer, K.K. Zander, M.V. Jackson, E. Ellis, E.S. Brondizio, and S.T. Garnett. 2020. "Importance of Indigenous Peoples' lands for the conservation of Intact Forest Landscapes". *Frontiers in Ecology and the Environment* 18 (3), 135-140. DOI:10.1002/fee.2148

Fossat, P., J. Bacqué-Cazenave, P. De Deurwaerdère, J.P. Delbecque, and D. Cattaert. 2014. "Anxiety-like behavior in crayfish is controlled by serotonin". *Science* 344 (6189), 1293-1297. DOI:10.1126/science.1248811

Garner, R. 2004. *Animals, Politics and Morality 2nd ed.* Manchester: Manchester University Press.

Garnett, S.T., N.D. Burgess, J.E. Fa, A. Fernández-Llamazares, Z. Molnár, C.J. Robinson, J.E.K. Watson, K.K. Zander, B. Austin, E.S. Brondizio, N.F. Collier, T. Duncan, E. Ellis, H. Geyle, M.V. Jackson, H. Jonas, P. Malmer, B. McGowan, A. Sivongxay and I. Leiper. 2018. "A spatial overview of the global importance of Indigenous lands for conservation." *Nature Sustainability* 1, 369-374. DOI:10.1038/s41893-018-0100-6

Kardos, M., Y. Zhang, K.M. Parsons, Y. A, H. Kang, X. Xu, C.O. Matkin, P. Zhang, E.J. Ward, M.B. Hanson, C. Emmons, M.J. Ford, G. Fan and S. Li. 2023. "Inbreeding depression explains killer whale population dynamics". *Nature Ecology & Evolution* 7, 675-686. DOI:10.1038/s41559-023-01995-0

Kohda M, S. Sogawa, A.L. Jordan, N. Kubo, S. Awata, S. Satoh, T. Kobayashi, A. Fujita and R. Bshary. 2022. "Further evidence for the capacity of mirror self-recognition in cleaner fish and the significance of ecologically relevant marks". *PLoS Biology* 20 (2), e3001529. DOI:10.1371/journal.pbio.3001529

Laland, K.N. and B.G. Galef, eds. 2009. *The Question of Animal Culture*. Boston: Harvard University Press.

Laland, K.N. and W. Hoppitt. 2003. "Do animals have culture?". *Evolutionary Anthropology* 12 (3), 150-159.

Lanjouw, A. 2002. "Behavioural adaptations to water scarcity in Tongo Chimpanzees." In *Behavioural Diversity in Chimpanzees and Bonobos* edited by C. Boesch, G. Hohman, and L. Marchant, 52-60. Cambridge: Cambridge University Press.

Leroux, M., A.M. Schel, C. Wilke, B. Chandia, K. Zuberbühler, K.E. Slocombe and S.W. Townsend. 2023. "Call combinations and compositional processing in wild chimpanzees." *Nature Communications* 14, 2225. DOI: 10.1038/s41467-023-37816-y

Lewis, J. 2019. *Flourishing Diversity: Learning from Indigenous Wisdom Traditions*. London: Flourishing diversity. DOI: 10.13140/RG.2.2.22467.96802

Livingstone Smith, D. 2013. "Indexically yours: why being human is more like being here than like being water." In *Politics of Species* edited by R.H.A. Corbey and A. Lanjouw, 40-53. Cambridge: Cambridge University Press.

Lovejoy, T.E. and L. Hann. Editors. 2006. *"Climate Change and Biodiversity."* Yale: Yale University Press.

Machery, E. 2013. "Apeism and racism: reasons and remedies." In *The politics of species: Reshaping our relationships with other animals* edited by R.H.A. Corbey and A. Lanjouw, 53-66. Cambridge: Cambridge University Press.

Mejdell, C.M., T. Buvik, G.H.M. Jørgensen, and K.E. Bøe. 2016. "Horses can learn to use symbols to communicate their preferences." *Applied Animal Behaviour Science* 184, 66-73.

Nussbaum, M. 2023. *Justice for animals: Our collective responsibility*. New York: Simon & Schuster.

O'Bryan, C.J., S.T. Garnett, J.E. Fa, I. Leiper, J. Rehbein, Á. Fernández-Llamazares, M.V. Jackson, H.D. Jonas, E.S. Brondizio, N.D. Burgess, C.J. Robinson, K.K. Zander, O. Venter, and J.E.M. Watson. 2019. "The importance of Indigenous Peoples' lands for the conservation of terrestrial vertebrates" *bioRxiv* 2019.12.11.873695. DOI: 10.1101/2019.12.11.873695

Péter, H., K. Zuberbühler and C. Hobaiter. 2022. "Well-digging in a community of forest-living wild East African chimpanzees (*Pan troglodytes schweinfurthii*)." *Primates* 63, 355-364. DOI: 10.1007/s10329-022-00992-4

Peterson, A.L. 2001. *Being Human: Ethics, Environment, and Our Place in the World*. Berkeley: University of California Press.

Polis, G. A. 1981. "The Evolution and Dynamics of Intraspecific Predation". *Annual Review of Ecology and Systematics.* 12, 225-251.

Pretty, J., B. Adams, F. Berkes, S. Ferreira de Athayde, N. Dudley, E. Hunn, L Maffi, K. Milton, D. Rapport, P. Robbins, E. Sterling, S. Stolton, A. Tsing, E. Vintinner and S. Pilgrim. 2009. "The Intersections of Biological Diversity and Cultural Diversity: Towards Integration." *Conservation and Society* 7 (2), 100-112.

Schuster, R., R.R. Germain, J.R. Bennett, N.J. Reo and P. Arcese. 2019. "Vertebrate biodiversity on indigenous-managed lands in Australia, Brazil, and Canada equals that in protected areas." *Environmental Science & Policy* 101, 1-6.

Selcer, P. 2012. "Beyond the Cephalic Index: Negotiating Politics to Produce UNESCO's Scientific Statements on Race." *Current Anthropology* 53, S173-S184.

Sobrevila, Claudia. 2008. *The role of indigenous peoples in biodiversity conservation: the natural but often forgotten partners. Report No. 44300, Vol.1*. Washington D.C.: World Bank Group.

Srinivasan, K. 2010. "The Social Science Imagination in India: Deconstructing Boundaries and Redefining Limits." *Sociological Bulletin* 59 (1), 22-45.

Srinivasan, K., and R. Kasturirangan. 2016. "Political Ecology, Development, and Human Exceptionalism." *Geoforum* 75, 125-128. DOI: 10.1016/j.geoforum.2016.07.011

Suzuki, T., D. Wheatcroft, and M. Griesser. 2016. "Experimental evidence for compositional syntax in bird calls." *Nature Communications* 7, 10986.

Swingland, I. 2000. "Biodiversity, Definition of." In *Encyclopedia of* Biodiversity, edited by S.M. Scheiner, 377-391. New York: Elsevier.

Tomasello, M. 1999. *The Cultural Origins of Human Cognition*. Boston: Harvard University Press.

Tomasello, M. 2014. *A Natural History of Human Thinking*. Boston: Harvard University Press.

United Nations 1948. *Universal Declaration of Human Rights*. New York: United Nations. https://www.un.org/en/about-us/universal-declaration-of-human-rights

United Nations 1998. *UN Universal Declaration on the Human Genome and Human Rights*. Paris: UNESCO. https://www.ohchr.org/en/instruments-mechanisms/instruments/universal-declaration-human-genome-and-human-rights

United Nations 2001. *UNESCO Universal Declaration on Cultural Diversity*. Paris: UNESCO

Vaugham-Williams, N. 2015. ""We Are Not animals!" Humanitarian Border Security and Geopolitical Spaces in Europe." *Political Geography* 45, 1-10.

Vaughan-Williams, N. 2015. *Europe's Border Crisis: Biopolitical Security and Beyond*. Oxford: Oxford University Press.

Welsh, R.L., and L.A. Vivanco. 2020. *Cultural Anthropology: Asking questions about humanity 3rd Edition*. Oxford: Oxford University Press.

Wessling, E.G., H.S. Kühl, R. Mundry, T. Deschner,
      and J.D. Pruetz. 2018. "The costs of living at the
      edge: Seasonal stress in wild savanna-dwelling
      chimpanzees." *Journal of Human Evolution* 121,
      1-11. DOI:10.1016/j.jhevol.2018.03.001
White, L. 1967. "The Historical Roots of our Ecological
      Crisis." *Science* 155, 1205.
White, T. 2009. *In Defense of Dolphins: The New Moral
      Frontier*. Hoboken: Wiley-Blackwell.
Whitehead, H., and L. Rendell. 2014. *The Cultural Lives
      of Whales and Dolphins.* Chicago: University of
      Chicago Press.
Whiten, A. 2021. "The burgeoning reach of animal
      culture." *Science* 372, 46.
Whiten, A., F.J. Ayala, M.W. Feldman, and K.N. Laland.
      2017. "The extension of biology through culture".
      *Proceedings of the National Academy of Sciences.*
      114, 7775-7781.

In Hussain, S.T. and G.L. Dusseldorp (eds) 2025. Sitting on the fence: Negotiating archaeology, anthropology and philosophy. Festschrift for Prof. Dr Raymond H.A. Corbey in celebration of his 70th birthday. *Analecta Praehistorica Leidensia* 54. Leiden: Sidestone Press, pp. 85-94.

# Epistemology on Acid: Is Darwinism really such a dangerous idea?

Angus A.A. Mol

## ABSTRACT

This paper builds upon Raymond Corbey's approach to epistemology as it emerged from his course 'Epistemology for Archaeologists', referred to here as 'grounded epistemology.' How this epistemology works in practice is shown through an encounter the author had with the challenging evolutionary theory of costly signalling during this course. This serves as a springboard to examine Daniel Dennett's (1995) idea that Darwinism is a 'universal acid': an epistemological version of the alkahest, an alchemical substance that dissolves everything without undergoing change. The paper takes Dennett's notion seriously, experimenting with it through a previous study in which Corbey and I conducted a Darwinian analysis of the Old English epic poem, Beowulf (2012). This study reinterpreted the epic's portrayal of gift-giving and warrior culture, framing it within the context of costly signalling. While it uncovered a complex interplay between cultural practices and evolutionary strategies, this also exposes the limitations of Darwinian theory as a universal corrosive. Before abandoning the idea of an acidic epistemology altogether, the paper also tests it against another theory: Huizinga's notion of play (1949). While this brief ludic analysis of the Beowulf suggests one could see it fully through the lens of play, it also underlines that potential universal acids tend to 'stick' to other theories rather than dissolve them. In short, this experiment shows that Dennett's informal epistemology, based on the theory that any idea, most notably evolutionary theory, can be a universal acid is self-defeating by definition and in practice. Instead, it suggests that theories interact, adhere, and transform in response to one another, a 'sticky' process that gives rise to more comprehensive and intricate forms of knowledge. This conclusion aligns with the principles of grounded epistemology, as championed by Raymond, which promote the dynamic interplay of ideas, encourage critical examination by peers, and welcome adaptability.

*Keywords: Universal acid, epistemology, Beowulf, Darwinian theory, play theory, gift theory*

## INTRODUCTION

This chapter builds on Raymond Corbey's work on and with evolutionary theory as a (de)structuring epistemology for science and society at large. In his teaching and writing, Raymond has frequently referenced, explored, and scrutinized Daniel Dennett's (1995) idea of Darwinism as 'universal acid'. Dennett's idea in his most famous work, *Darwin's Dangerous Idea*, is that Darwinism presented, and still presents, such an epistemologically 'dangerous' theory that it transforms and even dissolves almost all other ideas it is applied to. As will be outlined below, I

**Angus A. A. Mol**
Centre for the Arts in Society and
Centre for Digital Humanities,
Leiden University, The Netherlands
a.a.a.mol@hum.leidenuniv.nl
ORCID: 0000-0001-5448-3712

encountered these dangerous qualities of Darwinian theory in the context of a course on archaeological epistemology taught by Raymond. As a result of this, I began actively incorporating evolutionary theory in my own thinking and became intrigued by how an acidic theory could be used as an epistemological base. This *Festschrift* in honour of the self-described trickster philosopher seems to be the right place to examine the tricky question of whether, in fact, an idea can be a universal acid? I will probe this question by first providing a reflection on my encounter with evolutionary theory. Subsequently, I will distil the properties of universal acid from the original formulation by Dennett. This is followed by a re-appraisal of previous work by Raymond and me in which we applied (post-)Darwinian theory to interpret the *Beowulf* (Corbey and Mol 2012). To round out this appraisal of an acidic epistemology, I will briefly trace the corrosive qualities of other ideas, most notably Huizinga's theory of play as formulated in *Homo ludens* (1949).

## GETTING DOWN AND DIRTY WITH EPISTEMOLOGY

During my studies, I embraced the idea that there were few reasons to rise early, especially on Fridays. Yet, 'Epistemology for Archaeologists', a staple of Raymond's course offerings at Leiden University's Faculty of Archaeology, was the exception to prove this rule. The fact that the class was enthusiastically attended on Fridays at 9:15 AM by 20 or more graduate students is even more of a feat if we consider that many archaeologists, especially in the Netherlands, have little taste for theory, let alone fundamental questions in epistemology and the nature of what we know. Normally, archaeologists prefer to get down and dirty to study the past, instead of waxing philosophically about the construction of knowledge. What worked so well is that this is exactly what Raymond asked of us: to get down and dirty with our own epistemology and with that of our fellow students. We had a diverse and fat stack of reading to do, from French classical sociology to the then newest publications in biological anthropology (*e.g.*, Mauss 1924/1925, Smith *et al.* 2003). Lively debates between peers, rather than the recitation of academic 'book knowledge', were the heart of Raymond's 'grounded epistemology'. In every class, a couple of us took the lead by introducing a specific case study, which became a testing ground for an open exploration of young archaeologists' ideas concerning all sorts of aspects of human culture and society and most importantly how these are reflected archaeologically.

As Raymond had told us at the start of the course, he would be 'sitting on the fence' in these debates, watching us spin out and contest old and new theories. He seemed to be interested by, and open to, our wild wordplay wherever it led, but it was nonetheless clear that this epistemological playground was drawn with quite specific boundaries. Whether we discussed the *Kula* ring (Malinowski 1922), Lévi-Strauss' structuralism (1955), Yanomami kinship and conflict (Chagnon 1968), or Charles P. Snow's 'The Two Cultures' (1958), our discussions almost always revolved around the perceived (in)compatibility – or (in)commensurability, as Raymond preferred to call it – of cultural (anthropological) theory with evolutionary theory. The latter was, perhaps counterintuitively, not a large part of the archaeology curriculum at Leiden for most students (at least outside of Palaeolithic Archaeology). I suspect none of our professors doubted the basic tenets of evolutionary theory, but most paid practically little to no attention to it, and some even vociferously held the view that evolutionary theories were largely useless for understanding human cultures and societies. In other words, the emphasis on evolutionary theory for this graduate course appeared to be an unconventional choice to most of its participants. Some of us, including me, entertained semi-serious speculation that Raymond was in fact a clandestine evolutionary evangelist, strategically positioned atop his perch to steer us towards Darwinism and evolutionary inquiry.

A fellow student and I once formulated a plan to try and lure Raymond off the fence and to force him to fess up to his evolutionary principles. We had been asked to introduce a discussion on the legendary epic *Beowulf* (see *e.g.*, Kiernan 2016). Specifically, the task was to do so based on an interpretation of the classic text by the archaeologist Jos Bazelmans (1999), who saw the *Beowulf* as an anthropological reflection of the cultural world of seventh to tenth century Northwestern Europe. In Bazelmans' reading, by way of the gift theories introduced by Marcel Mauss (1924/1925) and Louis Dumont (1970), the plot and overall cosmology of *Beowulf* was regarded as driven by a set of highly hierarchical, structured, and symbolic, as well as fully reciprocal, society-making relationships. Yet instead of focusing on these ideas by Bazelmans, we decided to add a perspective from a biological anthropological paper we had recently read in class. It discussed turtle hunts undertaken by the Meriam of the Torres Strait Islands (Smith *et al.* 2003). This turtle hunt offered suboptimal caloric returns compared to other available subsistence options and was also quite dangerous. In short, it seemed to be evolutionarily maladaptive. At the same time, the practice was a highly social and therefore visible undertaking, which led the authors of the respective paper to conclude that the hunt could be explained as 'costly signalling'. Costly signalling is a (sexual) selection theory that posits that certain qualities, which are otherwise unobservable, are made visible by exaggerating and elaborating them in a maladaptive manner, with the peacock's tail as the standout example (Zahavi 1975).

Our plan was to concoct and present costly signalling as a universal theory: that all of human culture could be understood as a giant peacock's tail. This evolutionary theory could then be inserted into cherished, canonical stories such as the *Beowulf*. However, we believed it would miss its mark in actually producing new knowledge about such texts. Our plan had two weaknesses, however. First of all, we thought that costly signalling was a niche, even a discredited, component of evolutionary theory. I later learned this was not at all the case. Costly signalling or 'the handicap principle' had been put to the fore by Amotz Zahavi in 1975 but wrongfully debunked as nonsense in Richard Dawkins' enormously influential *The Selfish Gene* (1976). Subsequent theoretical and empirical work had shown its explanatory value and potential within evolutionary theory – to such an extent that even Dawkins later changed his mind about it in the second edition of *The Selfish Gene* (*cf.* Brockman 2009, 335-339). A further aspect of our plan was that we thought costly signalling theory would be ridiculously reductive when applied to the *Beowulf*. This should prompt Raymond to step into the fray, and salvage what was left of a more modest and specific evolutionary theory. Needless to say, our plan backfired.

Costly signalling turned out to be a pretty powerful theorical lens. It did a pretty good job in explaining the goings-on in a diversity of canonical texts and, in particular, was commensurable with many elements of the story of *Beowulf*, including its focus on the exchange of gifts in the form of highly visible warrior accoutrements. Costly signalling seemed to make more sense than Bazelmans' (1999) original reading of the text, which provided a view of the societies in the *Beowulf* as harmonious, fixed, and hierarchically stratified. This did not align either with the legendary world presented in the text or what was archaeologically and historically known about the period. As a result, my views shifted and I found myself defending what I initially considered to be a ridiculous idea to my fellow students.

Afterwards, I had considerable trouble getting rid of this idea. I started seeing costly signals in classes, at birthday parties, in celebrity culture, in museums, and many other places – basically everywhere around me. Costly signalling could also be inserted, with relatively little friction or apparent resistance, into all sorts of empirical and theoretical scholarly work. This was helped by the fact that there were quite some evolutionary, social, and cultural theories with notable synergies with costly signalling, including but not limited to Wilson's (1975) sociobiology and the idea of conspicuous consumption in Veblen's classic *The Theory of the Leisure Class* (1899). Furthermore, the idea of reading canonical texts as evolution was not original either: at the time, literary Darwinism, a subfield of literature studies that uses evolutionary theory as a heuristic lens, had just kicked off (*e.g.*, Carroll 2004). Eventually, in a Master thesis on social exchange in the pre-colonial Caribbean, I connected costly signalling thinking with Maussian theories of the gift (Mol 2006). By that time, I had also started to work together with Raymond on an expanded evolutionary reading of the *Beowulf* (2012), to which I will return further below.

## THE THEORY OF IDEAS AS A UNIVERSAL ACID

I offer the above account partly as a testament to the effectiveness of the 'grounded epistemology' employed by Raymond. His qualities as a teacher notwithstanding, the foregoing is also a good example of the persuasive nature of evolutionary theories in general. This persuasiveness is simultaneously investigated and propagated as a positive virtue by the philosopher Daniel Dennett, notably in *Darwin's Dangerous Idea: Evolution and the Meanings of Life* (1995). In this book, Dennett probes the profound implications of Darwin's idea that evolution, as a form of algorithmic process, births intricate designs from simplicity, all without any guiding hand (anti-teleology). By bridging disciplines like biology, computer science, religion, and philosophy, Dennett underlines the unsettling nature of this perspective, how it challenges deep-seated notions of divine design, purpose, directionality, and the exceptionalism of human culture. Despite these 'dangerous' implications, Dennett asserts that the lens of evolution as an algorithmic process not only provides a coherent scientific explanation for the complexity of life, but also a source of profound wonder and a transformed understanding of our place in the world. It is here that Dennett offers the theory that Darwin's idea is a 'universal acid', which becomes a tagline for the book and is worth quoting in full:

> "Did you ever hear of universal acid? This fantasy used to amuse me and some of my schoolboy friends – I have no idea whether we invented or inherited it, along with Spanish fly and saltpeter, as a part of underground youth culture. Universal acid is a liquid so corrosive that it will eat through anything! The problem is: what do you keep it in? It dissolves glass bottles and stainless-steel canisters as readily as paper bags. What would happen if you somehow came upon or created a dollop of universal acid? Would the whole planet eventually be destroyed? What would it leave in its wake? After everything had been transformed by its encounter with universal acid, what would the world look like? Little did I realize that in a few years, I would encounter an idea – Darwin's idea – bearing an unmistakable likeness to universal acid: it eats through just about every traditional concept, and leaves in its wake a revolutionized world-view, with most of the old landmarks still recognizable, but transformed in fundamental ways," Dennett (1995, 23).

When I read Dennett's book, about half a year after the failed experiment to goad Raymond off the fence, I understood what was described here and began to understand what had happened to me. There was no way of stopping the encroachment of evolutionary thinking. So, seeing its potential effectiveness, how does an acidic epistemology actually work?

Contrary to Dennett's claims, the idea of a universal acid has quite clear roots. Paracelsus, whose work is an important link between older forms of alchemy and its later incarnation as proto-science, first discussed the existence of such a universal acid, called alkahest (1572, Chapter X). The particular idea of alkahest as an infinitely reusable, universal solvent became prominent through the work of Jan Baptist van Helmont (1580-1644) and Robert Boyle (1627-1691). These philosopher-scientists worked from the theory of Corpuscularianism, a post-Aristotelian mechanical theory that posits matter consists of particles. It was believed that the alkahest, in contrast to known substances, would be infinitely corrosive due to the extremely small size of its particles. These would insert and separate the particles of any other matter, but not transmute its own structure. Of course, the alkahest was never found – according to van Helmont, its secret was

given only to a select few by God – and it can safely be called a chemical myth (Alfonso-Goldfarb et al. 2010). Still, it is understandable that the promise of a universal acid must have been tantalizing: an insoluble substance capable of dissolving all other substances.

This, then, is also the promise of evolutionary theory as espoused in *Darwin's Dangerous Idea*: it is an insoluble idea with which to dissolve all other ideas. Taking apart its separate components, it is possible to distil Dennett's acidic epistemology as describing a theory that is boundless, a powerful solvent, elementary, transformative, revolutionary, and immutable. So, in Dennett's thinking, why is evolutionary theory *boundless*? Clearly evolutionary thinking is not limited to biology, where the concept of natural selection originates. Instead, it seeps into different domains of knowledge and belief. The latter constitutes an especially important touchstone in *Darwin's Dangerous Idea*, serving as an argument to shore up evolutionary theory in the face of anti-evolutionary, notably religious, views of the world. Evolutionary theory then also needs to be a *powerful solvent*. The universal acid metaphorically stands for an idea that can 'digest' and explain complex phenomena, like evolutionary theory can according to Dennet. Dennett thereby moves from traditional metaphysical hierarchies where divine beings structure a basic chaos to a hierarchy of complex design based on evolutionary principles. These principles are also *elementary* at its base: in relation to the complex phenomena it seeks to explain, the elements of evolutionary theory are (comparatively) small and easily explained. For example, Dennett outlines the broader workings of evolutionary theory in the first part of the book in such a way that a curious but previously uninformed reader can understand what kind of much wider knowledge of the world it affords.

This incisive, 'elementary' theory allows Dennett to tackle complex matters in the second half of the book where he shows evolutionary theory to be an idea of great *revolutionary* and *transformative* capacity. The theoretical evolutionary alkahest, he posits, will continue to react until all reactive ideas are transformed. In the final sections of the book, Dennett then lays out his ideas about what it means to live in a scientific, social, cultural, and moral world that is completely transformed by the universal acid of evolutionary theory. Yet to provide this solid ground, evolutionary theory as a universal acid must be *adaptive but immutable*. In contrast to natural selection, which relies on constant change as an effect of the algorithmic replication of variation, the theory of an epistemological universal acid concerns a self-replicating idea that adapts its contexts to itself yet in its basic form does not materially change in the process. It cannot do so as this elementary form, its basic theoretical constituents, are both the base foundation and the transformative acid at the same time.

This is curious, as it makes it highly unlikely that a universally acidic idea can exist. Ideas change in interaction with each other, which eventually also changes them, even at their most basic level. This is where we may find Dennett's epistemology on acid tripping, so to speak. To check if the idea of an universal acid is just a flight of fancy, let us consider how the universal acid of evolutionary thought fared in the case of the Darwinian perspective on *Beowulf*, which I developed together with Raymond.

## BEOWULF'S COSTLY SIGNALS

*Beowulf*, an Old English epic poem, delineates the heroics of the eponymous protagonist in the face of formidable adversaries, thereby intertwining themes of bravery, loyalty, and honour. Beowulf – the Geatish warrior – engages in mortal combat, defeating the monster Grendel, which has terrorized the mead hall of the Danish king Hrothgar. Beowulf then needs to defeat Grendel's mother, thereby garnering honour in the eyes of the Danish and Geatish people and receiving many gifts. His subsequent encounter with a dragon, albeit fatal, further underscores his unwavering heroism. As a narrative of daring exploits, the *Beowulf* epic illuminates the complex power dynamics, social exchanges, and costly behaviours in an early medieval Northwestern European world. This is reflected in, and enhanced by the central role of material culture in the text, particularly of weaponry and armour. Weapons and armour in the *Beowulf* are not merely tools of warfare, they are potent symbols of prowess, power, status, and social connections. In a traditional reading, they serve as tokens of honour in reciprocal exchanges, aiding in the establishment of hierarchical relationships and alliances, hence reflecting a broader preoccupation with power negotiation and status assertion among early medieval elites.

In our work on the *Beowulf*, Raymond and I contended that the poem's long tradition of culturalist readings, including those of Bazelmans (1999), failed to account for the evolutionary underpinnings of the often-violent human actions it portrays (Corbey and Mol 2012). We therefore combined evolutionary and cultural anthropological reasoning to interpret the epic. In particular, we sought to understand human behaviour by contrasting the level of cultural meaning-making to the level of biological causality. We especially suggested that the weapons and other warrior accoutrements cannot just be understood as reflections of cultural practices, but also as representations of costly power negotiations, and as such an evolutionary strategy employed by (male) elites in their jockeying for status. This also meant that these objects were not just symbols in the traditional sense of the concept, they played a role as costly signals within the wider evolutionary dynamics that underpinned the society depicted in *Beowulf*. While the proximal historical motivations for men to fight may be based on received ideas and enculturated benefits, we argued that the ultimate biological causes are tied to (genetic) replication (Tinbergen 1963). In concluding, we admitted that our interpretation might be criticized as 'adaptationist storytelling', and conceded that alternative or complementary explanations could also be offered. Nonetheless, we argued that our approach, incorporating both evolutionary and cultural perspectives, provided a more nuanced and realistic understanding of the social dynamics in the *Beowulf* poem. In line with other recent work in literary Darwinism (*e.g.*, Boyd 2009), we argued that the *Beowulf* provides a blueprint report for a historically situated, successful evolutionary strategy of societal reproduction and adaptation. Even so, it can hardly be argued that evolutionary theory dissolved 'all culture' from this interpretation.

Our reading is somewhat congruent with the idea of evolutionary theory as a powerful acid. One can of course insist on the reciprocal, pacific, symbolic, and cosmological nature of the *Beowulf*, as Bazelmans had done. Yet, as soon as we let the acid seep in and stared through the holes it left in that theory, we could see that what was going on under the surface was, to quote a perennial phrase of Raymond, 'not any different from the snapping jaws of the crocodile'. This led us, among other things, to answer another question that had long hounded interpretations of the *Beowulf*: why is the successful hero such a bad leader (Gwara 2008)? After his untimely demise at the hands of the dragon, the Geats fall on hard times, and never recover from the costly heroism of their now dead king. Our solution to the conundrum of how a good hero can be a bad king was the following: while costly signalling may be an attractive strategy for heroes, it is a terrible long-term strategy for political leaders. Costly behaviour often undermines socio-political and economic stability.

In this way, our Darwinian reading offered previously untapped explanatory potential. It did so because it broke free from traditional literary and anthropological readings of the text. It fared less well, however, in being elementary, transformative, revolutionary, and immutable. It was not elementary and immutable because our reading heavily relied on a complex and contextual understanding of medieval Northwestern European material culture and social practices. By combining it with Maussian gift theory, we also added more nuance to the *Beowulf*, rather than reducing it to a basal evolutionary explanation of ultimate causes. Additionally, our reading was not fully transformative in two important ways. First, we were stuck with a very tricky situation for a Darwinian literary approach. Beowulf, the main character, did not have any identifiable heirs or even genetically related family members.

The story is quite specific about this: after his death, Beowulf is succeeded by Wiglaf, who is identified as a member of the same clan and can at best be referred to as a very distant cousin. This is a strong indication that, in the context of the story, Beowulf did not father any children or have any other direct family members fit to lead. In other words, Beowulf may have been heroically fit and certainly frames a legendary meme, but his fictional genetic makeup may not have survived the battle of the fittest. From the narrow perspective of genetic evolution and the sexual selection theory of costly signalling, his efforts were literally not noteworthy. Even from a more inclusively framed understanding of fitness such as group selection, canonically the story ends in a costly, ignominious end for Beowulf's companions and the Geats overall.

The second issue with the transformative quality of our perspective is that it is certainly not widely quoted and discussed – straightforward criteria for impact and transformation. It is thus only fair to say that, even if it changed my own thinking, our application of evolutionary theory has not (yet) revolutionized the field of Beowulf studies. The same can be said, to a lesser extent, for the subfield of literary Darwinism as a whole.

The only weakly acidic nature of our Darwinian reading of the *Beowulf* thus points to some general issues with an epistemology of acid associated with evolutionary theory. Dennett seems to have overplayed the hand Darwin dealt him, obfuscating the complexities of interacting epistemologies and theories in his dreams of a universal acid. Even so, the 'failure' of evolutionary theory to live up to this standard, does not necessarily entail that the theory that an idea exists that can be a universal acid is wrong. For example, it may be possible to substitute evolutionary theory with another theory that has similar claims to universal acidity. There are many potential candidates, but here I will stick to a theory I have become even more familiar with than evolutionary thinking: the theory of play by Johan Huizinga.

## PLAYING WITH ACID

In *Homo ludens*, cultural historian Johan Huizinga (1949, ix) famously argues that "civilization arises and unfolds in and as play," and asserts that play is the cornerstone of human experience, development and culture. Play is an integral component of our interaction with and understanding of the world, and it serves as a fundamental mechanism for creating and re-enacting new worlds. Play is and always has been a ubiquitous human activity, often carried out in solitude but also shared with others, harbouring the potential for infectious enjoyment. Play is thus deeply woven into the fabric of humanity, but in Huizinga's view of play, it manifests far beyond human culture:

> *"Since the reality of play extends beyond the sphere of human life it cannot have its foundations in any rational nexus, because this would limit it to mankind. The incidence of play is not associated with any particular stage of civilization or view of the universe. Any thinking person can see at a glance that play is a thing on its own, even if his language possesses no general concept to express it. Play cannot be denied," Huizinga (1949, 3).*

Without delving into the specifics of this account (see Politopoulos *et al.* 2023 for an introduction geared to archaeologists), it should be clear that Huizinga outlines a far-reaching, fairly comprehensive theory of play. Like evolutionary theory, play endeavours to explain and is even argued to give rise to culture and morality. It is thereby located *outside* of the latter two, explicitly eluding human ratio (Huizinga 1949, 213). But even so, like Darwinian theory, Huizinga's view of play is as an elementary aspect of reality – which is, in the final pages of *Homo ludens*, placed under the purview of the Christian God. Although difficult to put into words, explaining play is even simpler than explaining evolutionary theory: you know it when you do it (Sutton-Smith 2001). Play reaches far beyond gaming and gamification, however, and following game developer and philosopher Ian Bogost (2016), it is possible to transform anything into play. According to some notions, even life and particle physics may be viewed as a form of play (*e.g.,* Graeber 2014). Doing so can be a transformative epistemological activity (Politopoulos *et al.* 2023), and play, in its incarnation as video gaming, has certainly revolutionized 21st century society (Zimmerman 2015). In Huizinga's view of play, it is also elementary, it is impossible to transform into anything else, as doing so would change the autotelic nature of play. While many play and game scholars have an ambivalent relation to the figure of the *Homo ludens* (see *e.g.,* Zimmerman 2012), the point here is not whether Huizinga's theory of play is uncontested, but if it can be in principle the basis of a universally acidic theoretical perspective, an elementary way of knowing the world. So, what happens when we apply this playful acid to the *Beowulf*?

Huizinga himself refers to the *Beowulf* on several occasions in *Homo ludens*, for example highlighting the boasting between Beowulf and other warriors in his chapter on 'play and contests as a civilizing function', invoking the swimming contest between Beowulf and Brecca as an example of the dead seriousness of play (1949, 70, 196). Generally, fighting is playful in the *Beowulf*. The pivotal fight between Beowulf and Grendel for instance is described as a wrestling match, and one of the metaphors for combat in the poem is 'sword-play' (*e.g.,* line 1040, *sweorda gelac*). Huizinga also outlines the playful role of courtly poets, lorekeepers, and jesters (1949, 121). In the *Beowulf* epic, this position is taken by Unferth, an adversary blocking Beowulf's access to the Danish king. It would have also been these types of poetic merrymakers that would have told and played the story of Beowulf and many others in the mead halls of medieval Europe. Nowadays the *Beowulf* has become a much more static text. Even so, it still invites all sorts of playful reimagining, such as the excellent comic *Bea Wolf*, about a troupe of troublemaking kids who need to defend their tree house from the fun-hating old man next door (Weinersmith 2023). In this version, toys and candy, rather than warrior accoutrements, become a big focus of the story.

The latter highlights what is perhaps the most noticeable play element in *Beowulf*: the joyful extravagance with which its material culture and associated practices are described and how these things become, quite literally, larger than life for the characters. It would be easy to describe, analyse, and theorize material culture and its associated practices

in the *Beowulf* as play phenomena *sui generis*. Warriors playing with their things for play's sake. At the same time, such a focused play perspective would ignore an important contextual element. In the world of the *Beowulf*, playing with things and play more generally also provide a costly means of signalling 'worth' (*wyrd*), thereby negotiating and instigating potential conflicts between characters. To be more specific: swords, horns, shields, armrings, and other things are all part of one big 'tournament of value', similar in dynamic and delight to *Kula* or *Potlatch* exchanges (Mauss 1924/1925).

It is noteworthy, then, that analysing the *Beowulf* as play quickly ends up in the same place as where Bazelmans and our own reading departed: gift giving. This shows that theories of the gift can similarly be deployed in boundless contexts, thereby explaining, giving rise, and transforming our understanding of human social practice, often in revolutionary ways. Does this then suggest that gift theory is also or even more universally acidic? No. Rather than continuing to distil acids from acids, I suggest that the strong associations between costly signalling, play, and gift theory indicate that these ideas are not that acidic at all. Instead, they are highly *adhesive*.

## THE STICKINESS OF RAYMOND CORBEY'S GROUNDED EPISTEMOLOGY

The foregoing can be described as a rather wild epistemological experiment, which is bound to happen when an archaeologist learns epistemology in the playpen of a trickster philosopher. Still, it has taken us to a specific conclusion: an epistemology based on universal acid is bound to be as fanciful as the quest for the alchemic alkahest referred to above. This does not principally preclude the possibility that a theory can have universal application, but I would contend there are no scientific theories which are quite as dangerously and universally acidic as Dennett suggested evolutionary theory to be.

To be fair, Dennett likely did not mean to deploy the notion of a universal acid as a fully-fledged theory of knowledge. As Dennett (1995, 12) explains in the preface of *Darwin's Dangerous Idea*, the book refrains from technicalities in its argumentation, because it intends to convince people of evolutionary theory by telling a good story. Charitably, the idea of a universal acid is good rhetoric, it is a pertinent metaphor to build a story with which to wither away opposition. Yet, as any philosopher – or the poets of the *Beowulf* – will insist, metaphors do matter: the best of their kind are memorable and meaningful guides for the complex ways through which we come to know the world. The theory of a universal acid certainly is memorable, but it seemingly lacks meaningful and practical epistemological handholds. As shown by our not-so acidic Darwinian reading of the *Beowulf*, there are plenty of problems with this metaphor in practice.

To give another example. While costly signalling theory stuck with me for a while, frankly, the theory – alongside other evolutionary theories – has increasingly taken a backseat in my thinking. This is not to say that I believe it or the theory of evolution is fundamentally flawed, let alone wrong. Certainly not. It simply means that the tendency for ideas to get unstuck – or indeed to not really stick at all, as was the case with evolutionary thinking for many other students in Raymond's epistemology course – is a major strike against the theory that *any* idea *can* be a universal acid. This should already have become clear from the paragraph in which Dennett shares his schoolboy amazement about the existence of a universal acid. He wonders how a universal acid can be stopped from burning through everything? This idea for an epistemology on acid then becomes the main ingredient for quite a trip: in his book Dennett shows how Darwinian theory can shine a new light on our beliefs about humanity and the world we live in. When the trip is over, we are all the richer for this insight. Nevertheless, it certainly seems the world and our multiple ways of knowing it have largely survived 'Darwin's acid attack.'

Indeed, as alchemists similarly found out as they turned into chemists, the answer is that there is no such insoluble, unstoppable acid. Evolutionary theory, or Huizinga's theory of play, or the Maussian theory of the gift, or any other scientific idea can and indeed should *not* be able to continuously advance in its elementary form. One basic reason for this is that an idea, if it aspires to be scientific knowledge, at minimum needs to be open to critique, reconfiguration, and other amendments, especially if these target some of its core elements. An epistemological theory of science that is rooted in one insoluble solution – one elementary, immutable idea – is unscientific and, therefore, self-defeating. Not unimportantly, it is also rather boring, which is in direct contrast to the excitement that can come from doing theoretical work.

Rather than hunting for one universal idea to rule them all, it is much more interesting to see what happens when an idea confronts another idea that it sticks to and then 'hangs out' with, becoming a more powerful solution in the process. Seeing what ideas stick and understanding how they do so may seem dangerously complex to those who like their epistemologies to be as straightforward as possible, but it produces more comprehensive, and intricate theories. Just look at the example of the *Beowulf*. Gifts and other things can be seen as costly signals, which can be understood as a dangerous evolutionary play, while playing in the *Beowulf* is importantly done through things and their exchanges. In short, costly signalling theory adheres to gift giving, which adheres to play theory, which in turn adheres to costly signalling theory. This sticky and messy process engenders a more cohesive and comprehensive interpretation of the text than any acidic idea alone. This is the adhesiveness of knowing.

While both can be vested in evolutionary thinking, I would argue this is the essential difference between an epistemology on acid and the grounded approach to epistemology taught by Raymond. One epistemology fantasizes about finding an idea that will bite through all others, the other lets ideas, and the people that inhabit them, interact. In their pure forms, one easily leads to dogma and just-so stories, while the other aspires to consilience of knowledge and, as a result, often arrives at unexpected, new places. Granted, such a grounded epistemology is premised on tricky and complicated work: it involves getting others to play along with alternative ways of thinking, and throwing many competing ideas around to see which ultimately *stick*. One cannot avoid getting down and dirty with some dangerously good and bad ideas along the way. Unless, of course, you are really clever and find a bunch of archaeology students to do some of the dirty work for you.

## Acknowledgements

I would like to thank the editors of this volume for their thoughtful comments and their many clarifying edits. This chapter was supported by the Dutch Research Council (NWO projects "Playful Time Machines: Experiencing The Past in Video Games", grant number VI.Vidi.211.249). I warmly thank Raymond Corbey for all our thought-provoking interactions and for having been and remaining one of my guiding lights in academia.

## REFERENCES

Alfonso-Goldfarb, A.M., M.H. Mendes Ferraz, and P.M. Rattansi. 2010. "Lost Royal Society documents on 'alkahest' (universal solvent) rediscovered." *Notes and Records of the Royal Society* 64 (4), 435-456.

Bazelmans, J. 1999. *By Weapons Made Worthy: Lords, retainers and their relationship in Beowulf.* Amsterdam: Amsterdam University Press.

Bogost, I. 2016. *Play anything. The pleasure of limits, the uses of boredom, and the secret of games.* New York: Bloomsbury.

Boyd, B. 2009. *On the origin of stories: Evolution, cognition, and fiction.* Harvard: Harvard University Press.

Brockman, J. ed. 2009. *What have you changed your mind about? Today's leading minds rethink everything.* New York: Harper Perennial.

Carroll, J. 2004. *Literary Darwinism: Evolution, human nature, and literature.* London: Routledge.

Chagnon, N.A. 1968. *Yąnomamö, The Fierce People.* San Diego: Harcourt Brace Jovanovich.

Corbey, R., and A. Mol. 2012. ""By weapons made worthy": a Darwinian Perspective on Beowulf." In *Creating consilience: Integrating the sciences and the humanities,* edited by E. Slingerland and M. Collard, 342-367. Oxford: Oxford University Press.

Dawkins, R. 1976. *The Selfish Gene.* Oxford: Oxford University Press.

Dennett, D.C. 1995. *Darwin's Dangerous Idea.* New York: Simon & Schuster.

Dumont, L. 1970. *Homo Hierarchicus: An Essay on the Caste System.* Chicago: University of Chicago Press.

Graeber, D. 2014. "What's the Point If We Can't Have Fun?." *The Baffler* 24, 50-58.

Gwara, S. 2008. *Heroic Identity in the World of Beowulf.* Medieval and Renaissance Authors and Texts 2. Leiden: Brill.

Huizinga, J. 1949. *Homo ludens: A study of the play-element in our culture.* London: Routledge & Kegan Paul.

Kiernan, K.S. 2015. *Electronic Beowulf – Fourth Edition.* https://ebeowulf.uky.edu/ebeo4.0/CD/main.html.

Lévi-Strauss, C. 1955. "The structural study of myth." *The Journal of American folklore* 68 (270), 428-444.

Malinowski, B. 1922. *Argonauts of the Western Pacific: An Account of Native Enterprise and Adventure in the Archipelagoes of Melanesian New Guinea.* London: Routledge & Kegan Paul.

Mauss, M. 1924/25. "Essai sur le don, forme archaïque de l'échange." *Année sociologique* 1, 30-186.

Mol, A.A.A. 2006. *Costly Giving, Giving Guaizas: towards an organic model of the exchange of social valuables in the Late Ceramic Age Caribbean.* Leiden: Sidestone Press.

Paracelsus. 1572. *De Viribus Membrorum Spiritualium.* Strassbourg: Bernard Jobin.

Politopoulos, A., A.A.A. Mol, and S. Lammes. 2023. "Finding the fun: Towards a playful archaeology." *Archaeological Dialogues* 30 (1), 1-15.

Smith, E.A., R. Bliege Bird, and D.W. Bird. 2003. "The benefits of costly signalling: Meriam turtle hunters." *Behavioral Ecology* 14 (1), 116-126.

Snow, C.P. 1959. "Two cultures." *Science* 130 (3373), 419-419.

Sutton-Smith, B. 2001. *The Ambiguity of Play.* Cambridge, MA: Cambridge University Press.

Tinbergen, N. 1963 "On Aims and Methods of Ethology." *Zeitschrift für Tierpsychologie* 20, 410-433.

Veblen, T. 1899. *The Theory of the Leisure Class: An Economic Study of Institutions.* New York: Macmillan.

Weinersmith, Z. 2023. *Bea Wolf.* New York: Macmillan.

Wilson, E.O. 1975. *Sociobiology: The New Synthesis.* Cambridge, MA: Belknap Press.

Zahavi, A. 1975. "Mate selection – a selection for a handicap." *Journal of Theoretical Biology* 53, 205-214.

Zimmerman, E. 2012 "Jerked around by the magic circle – clearing the air ten years later." *Gamasutra. com* 7, 7 February 2012.

Zimmerman, E. 2015. "Manifesto for a ludic century." In *The gameful world: Approaches, issues, applications,* edited by S.P. Walz and S. Deterding, 19-22. Massachusetts: The MIT Press.

In Hussain, S.T. and G.L. Dusseldorp (eds) 2025. Sitting on the fence: Negotiating archaeology, anthropology and philosophy. Festschrift for Prof. Dr Raymond H.A. Corbey in celebration of his 70th birthday. *Analecta Praehistorica Leidensia* 54. Leiden: Sidestone Press, pp. 95-102.

# *Homo sapiens*, the four elements and the Anthropocene

Corrie Bakels

ABSTRACT

The 'Anthropocene' is a concept which has led, and still leads, to much debate. It is meant to define a geological epoch that is characterised by human dominance on the planet Earth. An internationally agreed upon reference point which defines its lower boundary, a so-called Global boundary Stratotype Section and Point (GSSP) or 'golden spike', is looked for. In this paper I present my personal opinion that the search for a golden spike is futile, unless the arrival of Homo sapiens on Earth is to be considered as such. My overview of the relation *Homo sapiens* – Earth shows that the influence of human beings is a gradual one. This overview is based on *Homo sapiens*' dealings with the four classical elements: fire, earth, water, and air.

Keywords: Anthropocene; the four elements; golden spike; geo-engineering

*To Raymond Corbey, who is interested in all that people do.*

## INTRODUCTION

*Homo sapiens* as a being does not stand alone. People are part of an ecosystem: a complex of four elements. Three elements are inanimate. They comprise the lithosphere, the hydrosphere, and the atmosphere. The fourth is the living element, known as the biosphere. The lithosphere is the Earth's crust beneath people's feet. The hydrosphere encompasses all kinds of water, from oceans to rivers. The atmosphere is the air above land and water. All three have interactions with each other and with the fourth (figure 1). *Homo sapiens* is part of the biosphere. This is the ecological way of approaching the study of people in relation to their environment. However, it is not the only possible approach.

In Classical Antiquity another set of elements was minted, also consisting of four constituents. These are fire, earth, water, and air (figure 2). They were introduced by the Greek philosopher Empedocles who lived in the middle of the fifth century BCE (Inwood 1992). As far as can be deduced from the fragments of his work that survive, he saw them as physical elements of the outside world. In later times the four elements were transferred to the inside of the human body and became known as humours: yellow bile, black bile, phlegm, and blood (Lindemann 2010), but it is the intention of this paper to discuss the originals. I will look at fire, earth, water, and air as part of the physical world and consider the ways *Homo sapiens* made use of those four.

## FIRE

I start with fire, because the oldest direct trace of the relationship of *Homo sapiens* with any of the four elements is the relation to fire. Natural fire has its origin in

**Corrie Bakels**

Faculty of Archaeology, Leiden University, The Netherlands
c.c.bakels@arch.leidenuniv.nl

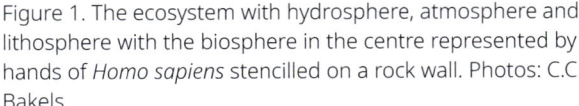

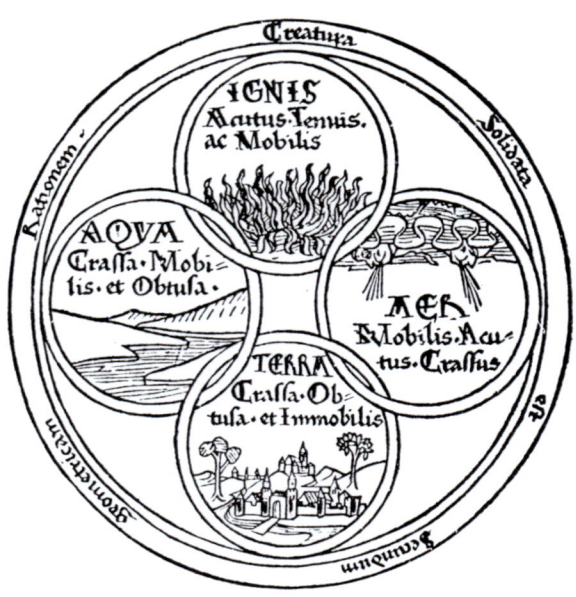

Figure 1. The ecosystem with hydrosphere, atmosphere and lithosphere with the biosphere in the centre represented by hands of *Homo sapiens* stencilled on a rock wall. Photos: C.C. Bakels.

Figure 2. The four elements, from Lucretius: De Rerum Natura.

lightning or volcanic activity. Humans recognised its usefulness at an early stage. When and where is open to debate, see for instance Roebroeks and Villa 2011. Fire is thought to have been caught from natural fire events, to be nurtured and kept alive, but this was only the beginning. At a certain point in the distant past, the practice developed into true control when the actual making of fire was discovered. This point seems to have been reached c. 50,000 years ago, in the Middle Palaeolithic. Neanderthals were able to produce fire at will (Sorensen *et al.* 2018). Since then the use of fire has assumed enormous proportions. Fire provides warmth in cold environments and light beyond daylight. It allows cooking, a process that broadens the range of eatable items, especially plant foods. Many plants only become edible after some treatment with fire, first and foremost by cooking. This way of processing food has influenced human life to a considerable extent (see for instance Goudsblom 1992, Perlès 1979 and Wrangham *et al.* 1999 on this subject).

Another important aspect is the use of fire in altering the landscape. Hunter-gatherers use fire to create open space and lush herbal vegetation in order to attract animals and lure them to predictable places, but also to enhance the availability of food plants for themselves (Scherjon *et al.* 2015). Such off-site use of

fire was possibly already practiced by Neanderthals (Roebroeks and Bakels 2015). With the introduction of the production of food, opening up landscapes became necessary for crop cultivation. Fire was and still is used to remove tree growth. Deforestation is for a considerable part achieved through setting fire.

But there is more. Without fire, the smelting of ores would have been impossible. Without fire, there would be no bronze or iron, and foundries and smithies need fire as well.

All uses require control of fire, but now and then control is lost. The outcome may be that a dwelling, a complete town, or even a vast stretch of landscape catches fire and burns down. Such disasters are as old as fire use. The oldest written law known, the Codex of Hammurabi, c. 1780 BCE, issued in the city of Babylon, deals with houses on fire in paragraph 25 (Harper 1904).

## Earth

Earth stands for the solid part of the planet's surface. It is the surface *Homo sapiens*, a land dweller, lives on. The interaction of people with the element earth has many aspects. Humans continuously modify the surface and all what is to be found there to meet their requirements. Many animals and even plants do the same (Jones *et al.* 1994), but *Homo sapiens* outdoes them all.

Removing tree growth to create open space for the erection of dwellings or, to a greater extent, for the creation of hunting grounds and arable fields, is ubiquitous in human history. Disappearance of forest can be the result of climate change. Glaciations, for instance, reduce the surface on which tree growth is possible. But when climate is not the steering actor, most deforestation is to be ascribed to human agency. The adoption of food production, at first alongside, and later superseding hunting-gathering, accelerated the process. Most of the staple crops are herbs which require light, and that is open space. Domestic animals need grazing grounds. The shift to food production took place everywhere on earth, though not at the same time. But between 10,000 and 8000 years ago people on almost all continents adopted the practice (see for instance Denham *et al.* 2003; Lu *et al.* 2009; Molina *et al.* 2011; Piperno *et al.* 2009; Stahl and Norton 1987; Vigne 2011; Weiss and Zohary 2011; Willcox 2007).

Agriculture further depletes the soil of plant nutrients and in response, people invented the practice of manuring. The history of this interference with soil is the subject of recent research and not completely known, but in Europe it goes back to at least the Bronze Age or even the Late Neolithic, c. 2000 BCE (Bakels 2018; Kanstrup 2014). Another measure to enhance food production was, and still is, to create suitable surface in addition to that created by the removal of trees and shrubs. One technique is terracing. In this way slopes are converted into level surfaces. The practice is documented world-wide (Arnaéz *et al.* 2015). Although terraces are difficult to date, it seems to be an old practice. Asins-Veles (2006) writes that terrace construction in West Asia and the Mediterranean dates back to the second millennium BCE and comparable ages are reported from the Andes in South America (Brooks in Denevan 2001). A second approach is land (re)clamation. It is a subject hardly studied, but it is, for example, clear that already before 1900 BCE people made an effort to drain the Pontine Marshes south of Rome, Italy (Sevink *et al.* 2023). People in Central and South America created islands in large lakes, for example the inhabitants of Tenochtitlán, the precursor of Mexico City, who constructed islands in Lake Texcoco as early as the 14th century CE (Calnek 1972). The Dutch reclaimed parts of the sea from the Middle Ages onwards (Hacquebord and Hempenius 1990).

Nevertheless, land reclamation is a very minor action in comparison with terracing.

Earth as a source of food is one thing, but the element provides non-food resources as well, for instance stone and metal. If such materials are not available on the immediate surface, they are quarried or mined. Quarrying and mining stone for the provisioning of tools with cutting edges is a very old practice and became a technically highly developed activity, especially during the Neolithic. But the search for stone was not restricted to materials for making tools. In Eswatini (formerly Swaziland, Southern Africa), the procurement of red ochre for colouring is reported as one of the oldest mining activities in the world (Matsebula 1988). Quarrying and mining for gems is another example, and mining for salt resulted in impressive underground galleries. But, following the mastering of metal working, the mining of metal ores surpassed it all.

Food as well as other resources are both indispensable for *Homo sapiens*, but their procurement has its drawbacks. The removal of vegetation can lead, and has led in the past, to soil erosion. The (pre)history of this process remains rather unexplored. Nevertheless, the activities of hunter-gatherers already led to sand drift in the Netherlands (Sevink *et al.* 2023). In Greece substantial human-induced erosion seems to have occurred from the mid-fourth to mid-third millennium BCE onwards (Van Andel *et al.* 1990). According to He *et al.* (2014), soil erosion in the loess-covered regions of northwest China started around 3000 years ago. And Jenny *et al.* (2019) have demonstrated that a significant portion of the Earth's surface was already subjected to human-driven erosion 4000 years ago.

Quarrying, but especially mining, causes damage as well. Prehistoric activities of this sort left holes, shafts, galleries, and dumps. In many regions these are still visible, even if they are thousands of years old. Prehistoric copper mining and smelting in Austria, for instance, left distinct traces in the mountains and not only in the form of scars in the rock. As copper salts are toxic to plants, even today prehistoric smelting places can be recognised by the complete absence of or very sparse vegetation (Pittioni 1951). Environmental pollution is also reported from other localities, for instance in China and North America (Lee *et al.* 2008; Pompeani *et al.* 2014). Another kind of impact is provided by the well-known copper industry of Timna (Israel). The exploitation of copper started there in the fifth millennium BCE and was at its height in the late eleventh to tenth centuries BCE, leaving behind thousands of tons of slag. The smelting required all of the fuel available in the surroundings and caused environmental degradation and desertification in the entire region (Cavanagh *et al.* 2022).

## WATER

*Homo sapiens* cannot survive without drinking water. Yet, the oldest major example of human dealings with the element water is the crossing of surface water by boat or otherwise. The best example is the arrival of humans on the Australian continent, which is set at 45,000-42,000 years ago (O'Connell and Allen 2004), if not at 65,000 years ago (Clarkson *et al.* 2017). Even during periods characterised by low sea level, not a single land bridge existed between Australia and the landmasses north of the continent. Thus, people had to cross the sea in some, as yet unknown, way. In later periods traffic by water was, wherever possible, important to the land-dweller *Homo sapiens*.

Nevertheless, access to fresh water for drinking must have been a main issue. Digging holes to obtain access to the subsoil water table must have been common practice in absence of suitable streams, lakes and ponds, but such holes are hardly described in archaeological records. However, deeper holes, called wells, are recognised as such. In West Asia wells are known from the Neolithic onwards. The oldest accurately dated well is reported from Cyprus, is eight metres deep and was dug around 8700-8200 BCE (Peltenburg 2003). Early wells have also been detected in other parts of the world.

Agriculture called for yet another kind of action related to water. In regions lacking in sufficient amounts of rainwater, irrigation was applied to ensure a reliable harvest. Impressive systems of irrigation canals are reported from West Asia, where in the region known as Mesopotamia ancient river channels were intentionally modified into canals (Gibson 1974; Jacobsen and Adams 1958). The oldest system dates to 3000-2400 BCE (Jacobsen and Adams 1958), and stable isotope analysis of crop remains shows that the practice began even earlier (Wallace *et al.* 2015 and the literature cited therein). Canal irrigation was not restricted to West Asia, but was practiced in many other parts of the world: China, the Indus region, Mesoamerica, and Peru (Denevan 2001; Schjellerup 2016; Spooner *et al.* 1974). The construction and maintenance of irrigation systems was certainly not a minor activity. For instance, a feeder canal from the river Tigris, part of the irrigation system in Mesopotamia and constructed in mid-first

century CE, had a length of 300 kilometres (Jacobsen and Adams 1958). Irrigation on the north coast of Peru may have started as early as in Mesopotamia (Denevan 2001, 143) and large irrigation systems were laid out around 1000 CE. In the Cañete valley such works led to an increase in cultivated land from an initial 1500 to 150,000 hectares (Engel 1976).

A fourth item connected with the element water is the use of water power. The energy provided by falling water was and is used for several purposes, ranging from the lifting of water linked to irrigation or the drainage of underground mines to water-powered mills. Water wheel technology was developed in China as well in the classical Grecian world. In both cases the beginning is set in the first centuries BCE (Wikander 2000). To provide a maximum power, several wheels could be installed one after another.

Use of water can, as much as in the case of the elements discussed above, lead to problems. A serious problem, for example, is salinisation as a result of irrigation. Uncontrolled irrigation in combination with deficient drainage ends in the accumulation of salt in the soil, a process that impedes plant growth and causes decline in agricultural yields. Early examples of this are reported for Mesopotamia, where the problem was already recognised around 2400 BCE (Jacobsen and Adams 1958). Another case is mentioned for a valley system in Peru where around 1200 CE, after more than a 1000 years of crop irrigation, people moved to settle elsewhere, a fact that is partly ascribed to salinisation of their fields (Willey 1953). Shahid *et al.* (2018) write that today some ten million hectares of irrigated land is given up because of salinisation and related problems.

## AIR

The first meddling with air must have been heating. Raising temperature by fire is presumably as old as the use of fire. Cooling air is also possible and in this respect the catching of wind has to be mentioned. This activity may have been common practice in all kinds of structures including tents and that from early times onwards. Impressive architectural creations are, for example, the wind catchers in Iran. These turrets provide cool space in areas with a hot climate.

Another kind of use made of wind is the use of its power. One application is sailing. It is not yet clear when people started to equip boats with sails. A picture on a pottery disc found in Kuwait and dated to the sixth-fifth millennium BCE might represent a boat with a mast (Carter 2002). Better records are provided by images and models left by the Egyptians.

Boats on the river Nile became equipped with a sail around 3500 BCE, and a fleet equipped with sails was sent across the Mediterranean to the Levant around 2475 BCE (Casson 1994). According to Horridge (2006) traffic across Asian seas and the Pacific involved the use of sailing boats from c. 2000 BCE onwards. The sail was also used off the coast of South America and this before the arrival of the Spanish (Ruiz 1526 mentioned in De Xerez s.a.).

Wind power forms also the basis of windmill technology. According to Shepherd (1990) the earliest mentions of the use of this kind of power harnessing are from the region India-Tibet, Afghanistan and Persia. Almost all records dating from the first to the twelfth century CE come from West and Central Asia.

Applications, or better manipulations, other than the use of airflow, are much more recent and are today known as part of geo-engineering. An example is the conditional raining out in order to have clear skies whenever desired. And, beyond geo-engineering, further upwards, distant parts of 'air' or sky are being used for satellites.

Just as in the case of the three elements mentioned before, air is affected by the actions of *Homo sapiens*, but not so much by its actual use, unless the use of air as dump area, unconscious or conscious, is considered as such. Smoke from fires, dust connected with erosion, and other pollutions have adverse effects on the air's quality. And at present, the emission of gases alters the global climate.

## THE ANTHROPOCENE

The use *Homo sapiens* made, and still makes, of the four elements, had and has an impact on the surface of the planet and its envelope of air (figure 3). The impact is such that is has led to the coinage of the concept 'Anthropocene', a name for a geological epoch, characterised by human dominance on the planet Earth (Crutzen and Stoermer 2000). A debate is ongoing concerning its beginning and relation to the Holocene. Crutzen (2002) proposed a beginning in the last decades of the 18th century when global concentrations of carbon dioxide and methane started to rise. Smith and Zeder (2013, 12) proposed the onset of agriculture as a beginning: "In practical terms, it seems more useful to begin the Anthropocene when there is clear evidence on a global scale for human societies first developing the tools, in this case domesticates, that will be employed in reshaping the earth's terrestrial ecosystems [...]", These authors have set the boundary at 9000-11,000 years ago. Steffen *et al.* (2015) argue that

the fundamental human induced shifts in the Earth's system start only in the mid-twentieth century. Lewis and Maslin (2015) looked for a sharp boundary, a so-called golden spike, and proposed the year 1964 CE on the basis of atmospheric $^{14}$C measurements, or, as an alternative, the year 1610 CE based on a significant dip in carbon dioxide value. They express a slight preference for 1610. Foley *et al.* (2013) plea for 1780 CE, a date that marks important rises in human populations and carbon emission, but, interestingly, admit that people were active before that year. They propose the term Paleoanthropocene for the epoch preceding the Anthropocene. This Paleoanthropocene started with the first effects on the environment, presumably coupled with the use of fire. According to them the epoch encompasses the entire Holocene and much of the Pleistocene. Glikson (2013) coins an Early Anthropocene starting with the mastering of fire, a Middle Anthropocene starting with the development of agriculture and a Late Anthropocene, which is the industrial age. Malhi (2017, figure 3) depicts a timeline of human influence on the planet. In this picture several points are indicated which can provide possible start dates of the Anthropocene, the oldest being related to

Figure 3. The four elements, as manipulated and employed by *Homo sapiens* (represented by human hand stencils). Photos of the elements earth (terracing) and water (irrigation) C.C. Bakels; photo of the element fire (cooking): Sunilla02; photo of the element air (wind turbines): Wikimedia, photographer unknown.

the use of fire. Nevertheless, the timeline is smooth, without 'steps'.

In view of the dealings *Homo sapiens* had, and has, with the four elements described above, I consider it useless to pinpoint a start date for the Anthropocene, unless the arrival of *Homo sapiens* is considered as such. This 'golden spike' does not exist. And what about the end of the Anthropocene? Every epoch has an end as well. With rising numbers of *Homo sapiens* and accompanying activities, their impact also rises. Malhi (2017) depicts three possible futures linked to such human impacts: a safe Anthropocene, a good Anthropocene and an Anthropocene rupture, but he does not look into a more distant future. In the end every species becomes extinct at some point. That will be the end of the Anthropocene and that end may be as diffuse as its beginning.

## Conclusion

The search for a golden spike defining the lower boundary of an 'Anthropocene' is futile.

## Acknowledgements

I would like to express my gratitude to Sasja van der Vaart-Verschoof for improving my English and Joanne Porck for help with the figures.

## References

Arnáez J., N. Lana-Renault, T. Lasanta, P. Ruiz-Flaño and J. Castroviejo. 2015. "Effects of farming terraces on hydrological and geomorphological processes, a review." *Catena* 12, 122-134.

Asins-Veles S. 2006. "Linking historical terrace with water catchment, harvesting and distribution structures." In *The archaeology of crop fields and gardens*, edited by J.-P. Morel, J. Tresseras Juan, and J.C. Matamala, 21-40. Bari: Edipuglia.

Bakels, C. 2018. "Maintaining fertility of Bronze Age arable land in the northwest Netherlands." *Analecta Praehistorica Leidensia* 49, 65-76.

Calnek, E.E. 1972. "Settlement pattern and chinampa agriculture at Tenochtitlán." *American Antiquity* 37, 104-115.

Carter, R. 2002. "The Neolithic origins of seafaring in the Arabian Gulf." *Archaeology International* 6 (1), 40-47.

Casson, L. 1994. *"Ships and seafaring in ancient times."* London: British Museum Press.

Cavanagh, M., E. Ben-Yosef, and D. Langgut. 2022. "Fuel exploitation and environmental degradation at the Iron Age copper industry of the Timna Valley, southern Israel." *Scientific Reports* 12, 15434.

Clarkson, C., Z. Jacobs, B. Marwick, R. Fullagar, L. Wallis, M. Smith, R.G. Roberts, E. Hayes, K. Lowe, X. Carah, S.A. Florin, J. McNeil, D. Cox, L.J. Arnold, Q. Hua, J. Huntley, H E.A. Brand, T. Manne, A. Fairbairn, J. Shulmeister, L. Lyle, M. Salinas, M. Page, K. Connell, G. Park, K. Norman, T. Murphy, and C. Pardoe. 2017. "Human occupation of northern Australia by 65,000 years ago." *Nature* 547 (7663), 306-310.

Crutzen, P.J. 2002. "Geology of Mankind." *Nature* 415 (3), 23

Crutzen, P.J. and E.F. Stoermer. 2000. "The 'Anthropocene'." *IGBP Newsletter* 41 (May), 17-18.

Denevan, W.M. 2001. *Cultivated landscapes of native Amazonia and the Andes.* Oxford: Oxford Geographical and Environmental Studies.

Denham, T.P., S.G. Haberle, C. Lentfer, R. Fullagar, J. Field, M. Therin, N. Porch, and B. Winsborough. 2003. "Origins of Agriculture at Kuk Swamp in the Highlands of New Guinea." *Science* 301 (5630), 189-193.

De Xerez, F. s.a. *Verdadera relación de la conquista del Perú.* Madrid, published 1891.

Engel, F.A. 1976. *An Ancient World preserved: relics and records of prehistory in the Andes.* New York: Crown Publishers.

Foley, S.F., D. Gronenborn, M.O. Andreae, J.W. Kadereit, J. Esper, D. Scholz, U. Pöschl, D.E. Jacob, B.R. Schöne, R. Schreg, A. Vött, D. Jordan, J. Lelieveld, C.G. Weller, K.W. Alt, S. Gaudzinski-Windheuser, K.-C. Bruhn, H. Tost, F. Sirocko, and P.J. Crutzen. 2013. "The Palaeoanthropocene – The beginnings of anthropogenic environmental change". *Anthropocene* 3, 81-88.

Gibson, M. 1974. "Violation of fallow and engineered disaster in Mesopotamian civilization." In *Irrigation's impact*, edited by T.E. Downing and M. Gibson, 7-19. Tucson, Arizona: The University of Arizona Press.

Glikson, A. 2013. "Fire and human evolution: The deep-time blueprints of the Anthropocene." *Anthropocene* 3, 89-92.

Goudsblom, J. 1992. *Fire and civilization.* Hammondsworth: Penguin.

Hacquebord L. and A.L. Hempenius. 1990. *Groninger dijken op deltahoogte.* Groningen: Wolters-Noordhoff/Egbert Forsten.

Harper, R.F. 1904. *The Code of Hammurabi King of Babylon about 2250 B.C. Autographed Text Transliteration Translation Glossary Index of Subjects Lists of Proper Names Signs Numerals*

*Corrections and Erasures.* Chicago: University of Chicago Press.

He, X., K. Tang and X. Zhang. 2004. "Soil erosion dynamics on the Chinese loess plateau in the last 10,000 years." *Mountain research and development* 24 (4), 342-347.

Horridge, A. 2006. "The Austronesian Conquest of the Sea – Upwind." In: *The Austronesians*, edited by P. Bellwood, J.J. Fox and D. Tryon, 143-160 (Chapter 7). Canberra: ANU Press.

Inwood, B. 1992. *The poem of Empedocles, a text and translation with an introduction.* Toronto/Buffalo/London: University of Toronto Press.

Jacobsen, T and R.M. Adams. 1958. "Salt and silt in ancient Mesopotamian agriculture." *Science* 128 (3334), 1251-1258.

Jenny, J.-P., S. Koirala, I. Gregory-Eaves, P. Francus, C. Niemann, B. Ahrens, V. Brovkin, A. Baud, A.E.K. Ojala, A. Normandeau, B. Zolitschka and N. Carvalhais. 2019. "Human and climate global-scale imprint on sediment transfer during the Holocene." *PNAS* 116 (46), 22972-22976.

Jones, C.G., J.H. Lawton and M. Shachak. 1994. "Organisms as ecosystem engineers." *Oikos* 69, 373-386.

Kanstrup, M., M.K. Holst, P.M. Jensen, I.K. Thomsen and B.T. Christensen. 2014. "Searching for long-term trends in prehistoric manuring practice; $\delta^{15}$N analyses of charred cereal grains from the 4th to the 1st millennium BC." *Journal of Archaeological Science* 51, 115-125.

Lee, C.S.L., S-h. Qi, G. Zang, C-l. Luo, L.Y.L. Zhao and X-d. Li. 2008. "Seven Thousand Years of Records on the Mining and Utilization of Metals from Lake Sediments in Central China." *Environmental Science & Technology* 42 (13), 4732-4738.

Lewis, S.L. and M.A. Maslin. 2015. "Defining the Anthropocene." *Nature* 519 (7542), 171-180.

Lindemann, M. 2010. *Medicine and Society in Early Modern Europe, second edition.* Cambridge: Cambridge University Press.

Lu, H., J. Zhang, K-b Liu, N. Wu, Y. Li, K. Zhou, M. Ye, T. Zhang, H. Zhang, X. Yang, L. Shen, D. Xu and Q. Li. 2009. "Earliest domestication of common millet (*Panicum mileaceum*) in East Asia extended to 10,000 years ago." *PNAS* 106 (18), 7367-7372.

Lucretius, edition 1472. *De Rerum Natura*, published by T. Ferrando, Brescia.

Malhi, Y. 2017. "The Concept of the Anthropocene." *Annual Review of Environment and Resources* 42, 77-104.

Matsebula, J.S.M. 1988. *A history of Swaziland.* Cape Town: Longmans.

Molina, J., M. Sikora, N. Garud, J.M. Flowers, S. Rubinstein, A. Reynolds, P. Huang, S. Jackson, B.A. Schaaf, C.D. Bustamante, A.R. Boyko, and M. D. Purugganan. 2011. "Molecular evidence for a single evolutionary origin of domesticated rice." *PNAS* 108 (20), 8351-8356.

O'Connell, J.F. and J. Allen. 2004. "Dating the colonization of Sahul (Pleistocene Australia – New Guinea): a review of recent research." *Journal of Archaeological Science* 3, 835-853.

Peltenburg, E. 2003. *The Colonisation and Settlement of Cyprus. Investigations at Kissonerga-Mylouthkia. Lemba Archaeological project III.1.* Göteborg: Paul Aström.

Perlès, C. 1979. Les origines de la cuisine. In *Communications. 31, La nourriture. Pour une anthropologie bioculturelle de l'alimentation* edited by C. Fischler, 4-14. Paris: Seuil.

Piperno, D.R., A.J. Ranere, I. Holst, J. Iriarte and R. Dickau. 2009. "Starch grain and phytolith evidence for early ninth millennium B.P. from the Central Balsas river valley, Mexico." *PNAS* 106 (13), 5019-5024.

Pittioni, R. 1951. "Prehistoric copper mining in Austria: Problems and facts." *Institute of Archaeology Seventh Annual Report*, 16-43.

Pompeani, D.P., M.B. Abbott, D. Bain, S. DePaqual and M.S. Finkenbinder. 2014. "Copper mining pollution detected on Isle Royale in Lake Superior between 6500 and 5400 years ago using sediment geochemical studies." Poster American Geophysical Union Fall Meeting.

Roebroeks, W. and C. Bakels. 2015. "'Forest Furniture' or 'Forest Managers'? On Neanderthal presence in last interglacial environments." In *Settlement, Society and Cognition in Human Evolution, landscapes in mind,* edited by F. Coward, R. Hosfield, M. Pope and F. Wenban-Smith, 174-188. Cambridge: Cambridge University Press.

Roebroeks R. and P. Villa. 2011. "On the earliest evidence for habitual use of fire in Europe." *PNAS* 108 (13), 5209-5214.

Scherjon, F., C. Bakels, K. MacDonald and W. Roebroeks. 2015. "Burning the land." *Current Anthropology* 56 (3), 299-326.

Schjellerup, I. 2016. "Landscape change and agricultural terraces in the Peruvian Andes." In *Earth 3, Agricultural and pastoral landscapes in pre-industrial society*, edited by F. Retamero, I. Schjellerup and A Davies, 187-200. Oxford: Oxbow Books.

Sevink, J., T.C.A. de Haas, L. Alessandri, C.C. Bakels, and F. Di Mario. 2023. "The Pontine Marshes: An integrated study of the origin, history, and future of a famous coastal wetland in Central Italy." *The Holocene* 33 (9), 1087-1106. DOI:10.1177/09596836231176495.

Sevink, J., J. Wallinga, T. Reimann, B. van Geel, O. Brinkkemper, B. Jansen, M. Romar and C.C. Bakels. 2023. "A multi-staged drift sand geo-archive from the Netherlands: New evidence for the impact of prehistoric land use on the geomorphic stability, soils, and vegetation of aeolian sand landscapes." *Catena* 224, 106969.

Shahid, S.A., M. Zaman and L. Heng. 2018. "Soil salinity: historical perspectives and a world overview of the problem." In: *Guideline for salinity assessment, mitigation and adaptation using nuclear and related techniques*, edited by M. Zaman, S. Shahid and L. Heng, 43-53. Cham: Springer.

Shepherd, D.G. 1990. "Development of the Windmill. *NASA Contractor Report* 4337." Ithaca/New York: Cornell University.

Smith, B.D. and M.A. Zeder. 2013. "The onset of the Anthropocene." *Anthropocene* 4: 8-13.

Sorensen, A.C., E. Claud, and M. Soressi. 2018. "Neandertal fire-making technology inferred from microwear analysis." *Scientific Reports* 8, 10065.

Spooner, D.M., K. McLean, G. Ramsay, R. Waugh and G.J. Bryan. 2005. "A single domestication for potato based on multilocus amplified fragment length polymorphism genotyping." *PNAS* 102 (41): 14694-14699.

Stahl, P.W. and P. Norton. 1987. "Precolumbian animal domesticates from Salango, Ecuador." *American Antiquity* 52 (2), 382-391.

Steffen, W., W. Broadgate, L. Deutsch, O. and C. Ludwig. 2015. "The trajectory of the Anthropocene: The Great Acceleration." *The Anthropocene Review* 2 (1), 81-98.

Van Andel, T.H., E. Zangger and A. Demitrack. 1990. "Land use and soil erosion in prehistoric and historical Greece." *Journal of Field Archaeology* 17, 379-396.

Vigne, J.-D. 2011. "The origins of animal domestication and husbandry: a major change in the history of humanity and the biosphere." *Comptes Rendus Biologies* 334, 171-181.

Wallace, M.P., G. Jones, M. Charles, R. Fraser, T.H.E. Heaton and A. Bogaard. 2015. "Stable carbon isotope evidence for Neolithic and Bronze Age crop water management in the eastern Mediterranean and Southwest Asia." *PlOS ONE* 10 (6), e0127085.

Weiss, E. and D. Zohary. 2011. "The Neolithic southwest Asian founder crops, their biology and archaeobotany." *Current Anthropology* 52, Supp. 4, 137-254.

Wikander, Ö. 2000. *Handbook of ancient water technology.* Leiden/Boston/Köln: Brill.

Willcox, G. 2007. "The adoption of farming and the beginnings of the Neolithic in the Euphrates valley: cereal exploitation between the 12th and 8th millennia cal BC." In *The origins and spread of domestic plants in southwest Asia and Europe*, edited by S. Colledge and J. Connolly, 21-36. Walnut Creek CA: University College of London Institute of Archaeology Publications.

Willey, G.R. 1953. "Prehistoric settlement patterns in the Virú valley, Peru." *Bureau of American Ethnology Bulletin* 155, Smithsonian Institute.

Wrangham, R.W., J. Holland Jones, G. Laden, D. Pilbeam and N-L. Conklin-Brittain 1999. "The raw and the stolen, cooking and the ecology of human origins." *Current Anthropology* 40 (5), 567-593.

In Hussain, S.T. and G.L. Dusseldorp (eds) 2025. Sitting on the fence: Negotiating archaeology, anthropology and philosophy. Festschrift for Prof. Dr Raymond H.A. Corbey in celebration of his 70th birthday. *Analecta Praehistorica Leidensia* 54. Leiden: Sidestone Press, pp. 103-114.

# 'Intentions do not fossilize' – Unpacking persistent domain assumptions in Pleistocene lithic studies

Shumon T. Hussain

## ABSTRACT

It is often stated that 'intentions do not fossilize' and the study of intentionality in the lithic record is therefore virtually impossible. I argue this view is fed by strong but problematic domain assumptions about the nature of the record, lithic data, and the structure of intentionality. I first show that, indeed, intentions do not fossilize but that nothing of relevance follows from this conclusion as intentions always need to be inferred. I then show that the dominant and mostly Anglophone critique of recovering intentions through the study of lithic technology relies on a misleading and far too intuitive understanding of intentions and intentionality that lacks precision and differentiation. From this stems an analytical focus that is too narrow and simultaneously demands too much from the available lithic evidence. I ultimately argue that understanding intentionality in the lithic record requires to overcome one-sided artefact-centric approaches to the problem and to embrace a relational, context-dependent conception of intention and intentionality. My contribution thereby illustrates the importance and often underestimated productivity of deconstructing the basic epistemological premises of archaeological analysis, debate, and critique.

*Keywords: Lithic technology, intentionality, fallacies, epistemology, cognitive archaeology, mind-body problem*

*Für Raymond – seine Wertschätzung, Unterstützung und seinen erfrischend kritischen Blick*

**Shumon T. Hussain**
Center for Multidisciplinary
Environmental Studies in the
Humanities (MESH) & Institute for
Prehistoric Archaeology,
University of Cologne, Germany
s.t.hussain@uni-koeln.de
ORCID: 0000-0002-6215-393X

## DOMAIN ASSUMPTIONS

A recurrent focus of Raymond's scholarship as an 'embedded philosopher' working in the tradition of the history and philosophy of science is the critical analysis of so-called 'domain assumptions' across a range of academic fields including paleoanthropology and Pleistocene archaeology. Domain assumptions, broadly speaking, are unreflected ideas and concepts which guide what questions we ask, how we ask these questions, how we seek to answer them, and what theories we formulate and/or draw on in particular discursive contexts, typically in academic disciplines or research fields, but also in more closely-knit scholarly communities. According to sociologist Alvin Gouldner (1970), domain assumptions act as 'master conceptual frames of reference' which affect the kinds of models and hypotheses that are imaginable – and therefore possible – in a given time or social milieu. As Raymond often put it, commanding domain assumptions therefore shed light on the foundations or basic principles (*Grundlagen*) of scholarly endeavours and draw attention to the 'implicit ontology' of scientific research and its fruits of knowledge. They are, in other words, the 'metaphysical' precondition of scholarly inquiry and as such come with both an enabling and a constraining face. Domain assumptions *enable* insight and knowledge production precisely because they remain implicit and withdrawn from scrutiny, while supplying the required conceptual resources to frame and investigate target phenomena. They coevally *constrain* such investigations, however, because they limit the range of conceptual resources that can be brought to bear and thus block considerations as to the adequacy of the so employed frames of reference.

Because domain assumptions are rarely discussed themselves and are typically shaped by research history, academic upbringing and socialization, they can easily lead astray. As Imre Lakatos (1970) has shown, broader research programmes are normally defined by a shared canon of such 'metaphysical core assumptions' and the whole point is that these are not available for critique from within because they lend collective identity and scholarly productivity. Yet, because there can in principle be no 'God's eye point of view' (Putnam 1981) or 'view from nowhere' (Wylie 2015; 2002), as Raymond's work keeps reminding us (Corbey 1998; 2005; Corbey and Roebroeks 2001), the limitations, biases, and blind spots of such productivity must similarly be examined. This is where the lens of the 'embedded philosopher' can fruitfully be deployed. By making use of the toolkit of conceptual and critical analysis as developed in historical epistemology and the philosophy of science, we can examine otherwise unexamined domain assumptions, and in this way make room for re-considerations of the very foundations of inquiry. This is particularly important when scholarly discourses become static and somewhat sterile, or have apparently reached an impasse that cannot be overcome by simply gathering more and/or better data.

This paper comes as a provocation. It aims to intervene with a perennial problem in Pleistocene archaeology – how to study and reconstruct 'intentions' and 'intentionality' in stone artefact technology – to excavate and lay bare rarely questioned domain assumptions that fuel associated debates and which may lead us astray in our quest for better understanding of the past. The resulting paradox is thorny: even though the involved domain assumptions have, from the perspective of disciplinary history, made possible a range of key methodological developments and insights, they are most likely misleading and as such need to be critiqued, belaboured, and ultimately supplanted. My exploration is deliberately exaggerated but hopes to showcase the critical importance of radical foundational reflexivity vis-à-vis taken-for-granted conceptual frameworks in Pleistocene archaeology and beyond. With Gouldner (1970), such conceptual groundwork is required to shift increasingly unproductive domain assumptions to help new models, hypotheses, and interpretations emerge from the pressure of the accumulating evidence.

## INTENTIONS DO NOT FOSSILIZE

### Approximating the problem

French-style *chaîne opératoire* studies in Palaeolithic archaeology are regularly criticised for their 'over-intentionalist' reading of the stone artefact record (see esp. Hussain 2019 and references therein), and such an approach, fuelled by Lewis Binford's (1967) seminal attack on what he called 'palaeo-psychology', is often readily dismissed by the supposedly self-evident assertion that 'intentions do not fossilize'. By juxtaposing the search for intentional structure to recent developments in processual-behavioural thinking, Turq and colleagues (2013, 642) give voice to similar concerns by contending that "there still exists a strong research tradition that assumes that [lithic] assemblages are to some degree fossilised examples of former intentionality", and add that "[s]ome scholars focus on inferring the goals of ancient knappers by constructing the 'conceptual schemes' of reduction, more or less implicitly assuming that lithic artefacts represent desired and 'cognitively real' end products", committing what they term the 'complete reduction sequence fallacy'. Complementarily, the 'finished artefact fallacy' has been evoked to question the ability of lithic analysts to advance to the proximate aims of past hominin stone knapping (Davidson and Noble 1993), and to conflate intentionality with processual outcome and adaptive value. Dibble and colleagues (2017, 828) take the now largely paradigmatic and majoritarian stance within the Anglophone lithic research community that "categories such as end products, by-products, and waste reflect the archaeologists' perspective more than past reality." They link their critique of intentional reading to an argument about the 'unattainability of the goal to study emic realities' in stone artefact research (Dibble *et al.* 2017, 838). But what precisely do these authors mean with their objection that 'intentions do not fossilize'? What concept of 'intent(ion)' or 'intentionality' do they rely on and mobilise to make such claims? How are these concepts motivated, on what kind of domain assumptions do they draw? And do they provide a robust basis of critique?

My intervention is that the complicit concepts of intentionality are 1) extremely *narrow* and *demand* too much from the lithic data, 2) and this *arbitrarily* so, 3) are now largely *outdated*, 4) do not serve the legitimate ambition to learn about the *hominin design of lithic technical systems*, and thus 5) ultimately undermine meaningful talk of stone artefact *technology*. I also do not think that emic access to the past is a necessary precondition for studying intentionality. The fact that the distinction between 'emic' and 'etic' is brought to bear rather informs us about the kinds of conceptualisation that underpin the intentionality debate in much archaeological scholarship.

*Some further background*
The statement that intentions do not fossilize primarily suggests that they cannot directly be retrieved from the archaeological record, that is, excavated as they are. This statement is less spectacular than some might think as it only states that intentions always need to be *inferred*. This seems trivial as the archaeological record is a material entity and intentions are normally considered immaterial. The contention that 'intentions do not fossilize', from this perspective, has therefore much less bearing than often assumed, as it seems descriptive (a truism) more than implicative. Inferences of this sort, it can be argued, are and should indeed be the core business of archaeology – archaeology, at least to some extent, simply *is* an inferential endeavour. Moreover, as Carlo Ginzburg (2013: 103) has poignantly stated, "historical knowledge is indirect, presumptive, conjectural."

It is certainly ironic, then, that Binford's influential critique of 'palaeo-psychology' was initially motivated by Christopher Hawkes (1954) 'ladder of inference', but Hawkes' argument did never imply the impossibility of inferring immaterial dimensions of the archaeological past, it only pointed to the serious challenges involved. Importantly, Hawkes (1954: 162) original account was very clear about the fact that in order to truly learn about the *human qualities* of the past, one must face and overcome these challenges rather than to hide behind the supposedly 'lower' rungs of his proposed ladder. Hawkes is often misunderstood in this point. The ladder of inference in fact *incentivises* us to

develop better means to capture and describe past immaterial qualities like intentions and motivations.

In addition, Ian Hodder (1989) has convincingly argued that Binford's scepticism must be regarded as a consequence of his behaviourist inclinations, viewing the archaeological record primarily as an outcome of stimuli-driven behaviour, thus effectively black-boxing internal mental states. Just like in psychological behaviourism, this position entailed a rejection of introspective methods and a commitment to understand past behaviours only through measuring observable outcomes and events and discovering their ultimate causes. Notably, Hodder (1989, 253) showed that Binford's position was fuelled by an implicit language model of human cognition, and by implication that intentionality takes propositional form, which "encouraged the conclusion that archaeologists without access to verbal accounts would have difficulty understanding the arbitrary meanings of symbolic practices." There is broad consensus today that this model of human cognition is not only fundamentally misleading but also that intentionality is a widely shared quality of organic life, not limited to humans or linguistic beings, and that it *can* be studied comparatively and without necessitating privileged introspective access (*e.g.*, Rosenberg 2022; Walsh 2015; Walsh and Rupik 2023; Godfrey-Smith 2020). Although intentionality is by definition 'directed' and in addition implies some sort of 'content', such content does not necessarily need to take propositional form (Grzankowski and Montague 2018). This point is important because propositional, language-based understandings of intentionality typically subscribe to 'representationalism' – the influential notion that minds being directed to the world produce and draw exclusively on mental images (representations). Representationalist understandings of intentionality, therefore, easily commit to the idea that so represented entities are represented as *properties*. In relation to intentionality, this view is called 'adverbialism' (D'Ambrosio 2019). I will come back to this point below as it arguably feeds into some of the dominant renderings of intentionality in Pleistocene lithic studies and archaeology at large. Note also, more generally, that the widespread intuition that access to past intentions presupposes a privileged emic perspective seems to be equally based on the premise that intentional content takes propositional form, and to adequately characterising it thus requires access to the internal representations of past minds which are private. If one argues that a representational view of intentionality is limited, as I do, the emic argument simply dissolves. The basic realisation, however, is of course that intentionality comes in many faces and that it is neither intuitive nor trivial to talk about 'intentions' or 'intentionality' in archaeology. We thus need to take a step back and briefly address this plurality of relevant concepts of intentionality.

### Entering the fray: intentionality and the 'mark of the mental'

There are many definitions and theories of intentionality (*e.g.*, Dennett 1998, Chapter 10); this alone should make us sceptical about absolutist positions on the subject such as those cited above. Broadly speaking, intentionality describes a mind that is directed *towards* something else (attends to a target) and has some content (*e.g.*, Crane 2016; Pierre 2023). Intentionality is thus the mind's capacity to direct itself to the world and to structure behaviour in this world; it is typically examined in relation to mental states such as beliefs and desires – often as a consequence of the latter. Intentionality, accordingly, has been referred to as the 'mark of the mental' (Crane 1998). As we have seen before, some scholars think that human intentionality primarily references properties in the world (adverbialism), and, when paired with naturalistic epistemologies, identify them with properties of the external world as studied by the natural sciences. The problem of intentionality then becomes mainly a problem of how internal mental states are directed at the world to bring forth particular external properties (and how these properties 'refer back' to the respective mental states). This formulation re-tables the classic mind-body problem. The alternative view is phenomenological and holds that intentionality is grounded in consciousness (Gallagher and Zahavi 2021, Chapter 5). This understanding of intentionality is not so much concerned with external properties, but with how consciousness is structured and how this structure intersects with and co-constructs observable phenomena in the world. Consciousness is thereby considered dynamic, ongoing, and multi-layered, and as such inaugurates a complex topology of intentional states, structures, and relationships (directedness, content). Phenomenological theories of consciousness consequently tend to reject Cartesian mind-body dualisms and can defend radically anti-representationalist viewpoints (Schlicht

and Starzak 2021). In the classic formulation of intentionality, we can further distinguish between an 'intender' (whatever entity holds the intention) and an 'intendum' (what the intention is about; *e.g.*, Le Morvan 2005), but even there the precise meaning and significance of these concepts depend on the broader flavour of intentionality adopted. The intender is typically a human subject but can in principle also be a social group or community as we will see below, and the intendum may refer to properties but also relationships, structures and even systems.

Archaeologists rarely engage with these discussions, however, and tend to adopt pragmatic, common-sense notions of intention and intentionality. Some of these conceptions are close to what Malle and Knobe (1997) have termed the 'folk concept of intentionality', at the core of which is a basic distinction between intentional and unintentional action (and outcome). Typically, such common-sense understandings foreground the idea that intentionality is simply about enacting a desired outcome in the world. Because 'intentions do not fossilize', archaeologists who wish to identify the original intentions primarily need to pinpoint the 'desired outcomes'. But this simplified rationale can be highly misleading and, when tied to strong domain assumptions infusing further scepticism about cognitive inferences as such, greatly impedes our capacity to examine intentionality in the archaeological record. With all of this in mind, we can investigate the conceptual underpinnings of the intentionality debate in Pleistocene lithic studies introduced above.

### Concepts of lithic intentionality: arbitrary, narrow, and pretentious?

Coming back to the initial discussion in lithic studies, we can now examine a few implications of the critiques outlined above. Dibble and colleagues (2017) for example seem to think that in order to get to the intentions involved in lithic knapping, one needs to mindread past knappers (which is evidently impossible) or at least objectively demonstrate that certain artefactual outcomes were sought after while others were not. The criteria for doing so also need to pertain to physical traces found on the stone artefacts themselves. The authors draw attention especially to the disconnect between production and selection (ibid., 825-828) and argue that in most cases only demonstrably utilised (use-wear traces) or secondarily modified artefacts (formal tools) can be regarded as 'intentional' in a relevant sense (ibid., 816-822), and even this typically proves difficult. They further point out that some of these objects do not belong to the same kinds of artefacts as those that intention-oriented lithic analyses have identified as technological goals, an example being unretouched preferential Levallois products. In addition, Dibble and colleagues (2017) maintain that in many ethnographically documented cases the production of lithic blanks and the selection of such blanks for future use is not necessarily linked to the behaviour of the same person. They therefore conclude that selection and use do not necessarily 'reflect back' on the original knapping intentions, especially if different minds are involved. Yet this, in my view, mainly shows three things: 1) a stable, complete, and fully transparent relationship between a pre-action intention and a post-action outcome is thought to be required for attesting intentionality; 2) intentionality is defined as a property of individuals; and 3) intentionality is fundamentally conceptualised as an either-or-question, behavioural outcomes are intentional or not. All three propositions are problematic and can be challenged. (A fourth point may be added, namely that intentional outcomes are exclusively identified with discrete, monadic artefacts.)

The first proposition assumes that knapping goals are fully formed, and must therefore be cognitively available, to any given knapper *before* the knapping process is initiated. This is for instance reflected in the notion of the 'mental template' (Chase 2016), or at least in how the latter is overwhelmingly understood in the literature. It also assumes that the knapper is fully aware, at almost all times, of the precise consequences and outcomes of individual knapping actions and behaves accordingly (assumption of perfect knowledge and full access to intentional dispositions). This effectively delivers a static and inflexible view of lithic knapping that is theoretically and empirically untenable. The idea is that intentionality effectively needs to be analysed as a cause-and-effect relationship, in which the original intention is the 'cause' and artefactual outcomes are candidate 'effects' of the respective intention. One may wish to add a third component: a potential interference (or constraint), for example in the form of time and energy budgets and/ or stone raw material qualities. In order to retrieve intentionality, we thus need to demonstrate the correspondence or unambiguous linkage between the two by taking possible interferences into account (or discounting for them). I have previously termed this the 'machine view' of lithic technology (Hussain 2019). The question of intention, through this optic, becomes a quest for the original cognitive input(s) *required* to

successfully run the knapping machinery and *explain* the utilization of its outputs.

But lithic knapping is an irreducibly *dynamic* process where actions and outcomes are constantly cross-adjusted and where the goals of specific actions can change along the way. Knapping is also embodied and not every intention is cognitively available to the knapper – intentions can be actualized through encultured action schemes, learned conventions, and updated by exploited, situational affordances. In other words, a lithic knapper may know what to do and how to do it given shifting circumstances to achieve a broadly defined set of desired outcomes, without possessing a fully fleshed-out propositional understanding of all the details of that output or the detailed process and procedures how to arrive at the target output. To question the intentionality of such fluid processes would be equally foolish. This being said, we nonetheless do not need to accept that all of the documented artefactual outcomes are *equally* intentional, and we can still retain a useful notion of non-intentional 'accidental' outcomes, for example. The main problem is the overly intellectual or cognitivist understanding of intentionality that is increasingly confronted with more practice-oriented – or praxeological – understandings of (technical) action and cognition (Schatzki, Knorr-Cetina, and Savigny 2001). What Schatzki (2002) and Thévenot (2001) call 'pragmatic regimes' of action or 'regimes of engagement' are not less intentional just because they are contingent on situational configurations. At any rate, a key problem, and this is linked to the third proposition, therefore also seems to be the non-differentiated or monothetic concept of intentionality typically adopted, and which only recognises intentional and non-intentional outcomes (coded as 1s or 0s). But outcomes may be *more-or-less* intentional and, importantly, there may be *hierarchies* of knapping intentions, and these are likely context-specific. This is one of the reasons why some French *chaîne opératoire* proponents have come to distinguish between 'primary', 'secondary' and 'tertiary' technical intentions (Pelegrin 2011; Valentin, Weber, and Bodu 2014; Pelegrin 1995).

The issue is even more complicated. Not every intention is necessarily of the same *kind*. To properly analyse knapping intentions, we therefore need to introduce the possibility of different *types* of intentions. This is not merely a theoretical problem but has strong bearing on what can count as 'intentional' in the record and what criteria are used to base such claims on. It also bears directly on the second proposition that intentions have their source in individuals. My critique is not that this proposition is generally problematic but rather what is made of it. The potential disconnect between production and selection which Dibble and colleagues (2017) draw attention to is a great example. Yet the example may not so much call into question our ability to isolate intentions, it may rather show that the notion of intentionality mobilised by many authors is unproductive. The reason is that, generally speaking, we do not need to assume that an 'unbroken stream of intentionality' unifies the lithic operational sequence as a whole, so that a segmentation of the latter becomes a problem for intentional inferences or the capacity to meaningfully speak about intentions.

This problem is in fact well-recognised by technological approaches – chiefly by techno-economic research – and, among other things, pertains to the spatiotemporal *fragmentation* of lithic operational sequences (Geneste 2010; Perlès 1980). Lithic production goals may simply not always align with blank selection goals and the latter may not always align with modification goals, and so forth. This suggests it is important to be able to distinguish between such goals, and to arrive at a position where lithic analysts can empirically investigate their content, relevance and interrelationship (convergence, divergence, independence, etc.). This is long acknowledged in the literature, at least implicitly, and clearly cannot be solved on universal theoretical grounds, at least not without establishing an inventory of relevant intentions. Investigating the structure of intentionality with regard to these questions demands a flexible concept of intentionality that allows us to do so.

To make things even worse, not all relevant intentionality may play out on the level of individuals, and there is a substantial literature now on higher-level 'collective intentionality' (*e.g.*, Schmid and Schweikard 2009; Tuomela 2013; Janković and Ludwig 2017). Collective intentionality may be implicated when two or more individuals undertake a task together, often involving coordinated division of labour. My suspicion is that much talk about intentions in archaeological debates on lithic technology makes reference to such forms of intentionality. Rather than demonstrating the limits of intentional inference, the disconnect between blank production and the selection of blanks for lithic tool production may then provide evidence of how individuals differentially contribute to intended collective outcomes (action patterns). From

the perspective of Tuomela and Miller's (1988) famous analysis of 'we-intentions', individuals only need to hold the intention to fulfil their part within a given group action, believe that the intended group task is possible and achievable, and hold the belief that all other possibly partaking individuals believe so too and similarly intend to do their part. There are of course many different accounts of collective intentionality and scholars sometimes fiercely disagree on the details of reconstructing such higher-level intentional structures (Schweikard and Schmid 2021) but this makes it even more pressing to not oversimplify how we analyse and discuss intentionality with reference to the archaeological record. From this perspective, more generally speaking, many of the knapping intentions we intuitively locate in past individuals may actually reflect collective structures of decision-making, as recurrent knapping patterns arguably also carry, at least to some extent, the 'mental mark' of larger communities of practice. These patterns *also* result from the coordination of learned behaviours and needs, and they arise from the dynamic adjustment of lived intersubjective expectations, and even basic intentional structures may thus to some extent be *shared*. These structures need to be analysed differently and it would be important to clarify these differences. It is for example possible, but needs to be carefully examined, that applications of cultural evolutionary theory in lithic studies (Liu and Stout 2023; Lycett and von Cramon-Taubadel 2015) rely and build on a strong concept of collection action and joint intentionality.

## The relationality of intentionality

The discussion has so far shown that the dominant critique of recovering intentionality from the archaeological record is probably based on an overly narrow conception of the intended and simultaneously demands too much from the lithic evidence. It does so arbitrarily because of its conceptual ignorance of the complexity of potentially relevant degrees, forms, and types of intentionality, placing the emphasis exclusively on individual artefactual outcomes. It is not even clear what artefactual outcomes are candidate targets and why. The result, in any case, is an *artefact-centric view* of intentionality, often tied to the search for intentional properties (adverbialism), and I suggest that this logic is part of the basic problem rather than offering any attractive solutions. What if the kind of intentionality lithic analysts are mostly interested in amounts to a distributed, system-level property, and is as such fundamentally a *relational phenomenon*? What if technical intentions are located in processes more than in artefacts? What if, in other words, lithic technological intentionality is more processual and practice-oriented than concerned with outcomes? The statement 'intentions do not fossilize' may then be misleading in a double sense: 1) as a tautology with unclear implications (see above); and 2) as bewilderingly placing the burden on self-contained lithic artefacts, thereby clouding the view for lithic technical systems as potential key loci of intentional structures. The shift away from individual lithic artefacts to their participation in knapping systems implies a shift to the *design* of such systems. The basic intentionality of such systems cannot be disputed, they represent *purposed systems* supplying functionality – in the lithic case varying configurations of cutting-edge. The intentional structure of such systems can then be analysed by determining the position of individual artefacts in the reduction process and by analysing the relationship between technical behaviours (raw material selection, preparation, blank production, blank selection, modification, use, etc.). Intentionality then becomes a question of *ordered relations*, for example of what kind of blanks (what properties do they have and when do they arise during knapping) are transformed into what kind of tools and how, what kind of blanks are simply discarded, and what kind of blanks are used in plain state, how strong these associations and patterns are or whether such relationships are mostly absent (*e.g.*, Hussain 2015; Pelegrin 2011; Pesesse 2018). The field has developed a range of formal, sophisticated methods to investigate these technical relationships but to meaningfully speak of intentionality likely requires interrelating them all. Moreover, to formulate an effective critique of studying the intentionality of past stone working practices requires to attack or refute the fruits of such relational investigations, which are already a core component of *chaîne opératoire*-based lithic studies, rather than continue to discuss artefact-centred straw men. What is seemingly often conflated, simply put, is the intentionality of the organisation of lithic production systems and the intentionality of individual artefact forms, configurations, and morphologies.

A brief consideration of so-called 'knapping accidents' can clarify this important point. What is a knapping accident? And what is convincing evidence for it being an accident? The traditional answer within Palaeolithic archaeology has been artefact-centric. Classic examples are 'hinged' products or 'overshot' blanks and these reflect adverbialism (a stable relationship between intentions and material properties). In the first case, the underlying assumption is that intentional products should include a feather termination, in the second case it is presumed that target blanks should bear evidence for the control of distal shape and termination and an overshot by definition violates this expectation. The problem is not that this reasoning may generally be flawed – it is indeed often accurate – the problem is rather that it is not *always* useful or reasonable and this is because intentions themselves are *not* stable. For example, given particular core configurations, overshot products may be deliberately – in a controlled and planned manner – deployed in order to rejuvenate the reduction surface and to correct for relevant surface convexities, often distally and within unidirectional reduction systems. In such contexts, we may reasonably speak of intentional overshots. How is this possible? The answer is that an artefact-centric view of intentionality paired with a universalist-leaning epistemology is unable to detect such intentionality and in fact excludes its very possibility *a priori*. To put it even more provocatively: why should have hominins always, under all possible circumstances, intended to obtain feathered products? There is no doubt that certain properties make certain objects more likely candidates of intentional outcome but no property can by itself guarantee it.

The absurdity of all of this is for example illustrated by an overshot blank with distal endscraper modification. Suddenly the 'accident' counts as a formal tool which, by definition, is an intentional outcome. Or is it suddenly not? The dilemma should at least be clear and has to do with the unreflected, privileged role of certain artefact-level traits, and not others, in the analysis and determination of lithic intentionality – a situation that severely limits the possibilities of insight for the lithic analyst and tends to create much interpretive confusion. Notably, Jacques Tixier (2012), the founding figure of French-style technological lithic research, has already discussed similar issues in his agenda-setting work in 1978. So what about hinged products for example? Can such artefacts count as prototypical unintended outcomes? What if such products are sometimes sought after because of their robust matrix and supremely rectilinear edge-profiles? They may in some cases even be used as blanks for transversal bladelet extraction on their distal-ventral hinge protrusion (I have seen examples of this myself in a stratified lithic assemblage from Kammern-Grubgraben, Lower Austria). Hinged products may at the very least not always adequately be described as 'accidents', and thus as strictly 'unintended' artefacts. The reason, again, is contextual. Some core configurations for instance simply supply elevated risks of hinging. Relatively flat, wide core surface configurations with low transversal and longitudinal convexity can yield significant numbers of short, hinged products, but this is not because of technical errors or knapping mistakes but rather because flat, straight products are often searched for in such systems and diverse hinged forms arise *in the process*. Even if we maintain that these products are maximally tolerated rather than intended, situations like this considerably complicate lithic debates on the relevant 'mark of the mental' and the requirements of identifying intentional structures. We may for instance conclude that such hinged products may not be the intended products vis-à-vis retouching goals, which we may wish, depending on the specific knapping preferences identified, to qualify as primary intentions, but that they nonetheless represent *anticipated* or *expected* products and as such can be said to be sought-for, for example vis-à-vis expedient plain blank utilization goals (secondary/tertiary intentions).

This again recalls the potential multiplicity of co-occurring intentions with their associated sets of specific knapping and transformation goals as well as the resulting populations of lithic artefacts. It is therefore of key importance to remember that, realistically, the study of lithic intentionality can rarely be reduced to the quest for a single 'desired' outcome but in most cases pertains to complex *configurations of intentions* (varying intentions which interact in specific ways and possibly relate to different elements of operational sequences). In many ways, this view provides another definition of named lithic technical systems such as Levallois, Quina and Discoid. The latter's defining *schemas opératoires* (*e.g.*, Inizan *et al.* 1999; Perlès 1987; Boëda 1994; Pelegrin 1995) can then be understood simply as a specification of such generalised webs of intentionality. The more general point is that any talk of 'final products' may be misleading precisely because it is unclear what 'final' really means. Does it refer to products that only arise at the final stages of the knapping sequence? Or does it instead refer to blanks that enter the modification/ tool confection stage? And does it include blanks that are utilised without being modified? The former by definition excludes intentionality in early knapping products, which seems minimally problematic and maximally arbitrary. The latter point further showcases this arbitrariness, as what precisely renders

a given product 'final' remains ambiguous. Because in many cases core volumes are subjected to change in exploitation patterns as they enter the near-discard stages of their life history, the resulting 'final' products do often not reflect the intentions that guide organised knapping before this stage (the majority of knapping), again pointing to basic issues in assuming a narrow set of well-defined and overall stable intentions. Such intentional structure is likely a very special case and the exception rather than the norm.

The presented thought experiment on the possible relevance of hinged products within larger knapping processes also exemplifies why lithic analysts such as Richter (1997) sometimes speak of a 'sortiment' character of knapping: intentionality is said to reside not in a single type of lithic product but precisely in the *organised diversification of a specified range of products*, typically procured at different moments in the core exploitation process. Another instructive example from the praxis of lithic research is the so-called 'ramification' of operational sequences, argued to be a diagnostic organisational principle especially of some Middle Palaeolithic stone artefact technologies (*e.g.*, Bourguignon 2004; Mathias and Bourguignon 2020). Ramified reduction trajectories are characterised, broadly speaking, by the ongoing co-optation of knapping products as new core matrices for the next generation of downstream lithic products, with the Kombewa technique (Tixier and Turq 1999) being a textbook symptom of such an approach to raw material exploitation. But what, then, is the locus of intentionality in cases of structural ramification? Are the 'intentional' products only these that are not subjected to further exploitation? Or is the hallmark of intentionality rather that some products are withdrawn from further transformation? To me at least, there seems to be no straightforward way to decide between these options, adding up to the above-outlined ambiguity. The ramification example, I suggest, instead highlights that such questioning may in many cases be fundamentally misleading and indeed typically misses the point. First-generation knapping intentions can become the source of second-generation knapping intentions for example, and we may thus again be better served to dissect the overall intentional structure of technological ramification. As such, we may be forced to shift the attention from the parts (artefacts) to the whole (reduction structures), and thus possibly from questions of intended artefactual outcomes to *intended opportunities of use and transformation*. The latter is an issue of lithic technological organisation as a whole and therefore cannot be discussed based on artefact-level properties alone. Intellectualist and overly cognitivist understandings of intentional action again lead us astray.

Lithic artefacts, then, are perhaps not the only possible targets of lithic intentionality. What becomes obvious from this discussion at the very least, I hope, is that it rarely makes sense to frame intentionality as an either-or-question. We need to attend to the potential multiplicity and heterogeneity of knapping intentionalities and the possibility that such intentionality comes in degrees, pertains to different levels of organisation, and may change in the course of the exploitation, use, and re-use of lithic raw materials. What matters greatly are always *differences*, even though subtle, in the relationships between actions and material outcomes and these can rarely be conceptualised as a linear equation. Our concept(s) of intentionality, it follows, need to be sensitive to such *differences* in the organisation of knapping behaviours, and levels and differentiations of knapping intentionality and its contexts thus matter greatly for lithic analysts. Such sensitivity and contextual openness arguably cannot be achieved if we limit ourselves to the study of individual artefact-level properties which are inherently *equifinal* with regards to questions of intended outcomes and processes, the degree thereof, how individual intentions mediate other intentions, or the intentional organisation of stone artefact technologies as a whole.

## Some implications and qualifications

These interventions, I hope, demonstrate the need to insist on differentiations and to pay more attention to how we conceptualise intentionality for the study of the lithic record. If such matters are not reflected upon and critically discussed, the underlying domain assumption may impede meaningful scholarly exchange and undermine any progress. It simply is not enough to draw on a common-sense understanding of intention or intentionality, or to start with a deeply sceptical stance. We of course always have to consider why we are interested in the study of intentionality to begin with. If the answer is to better characterise and understand lithic technology, and not merely self-contained lithic artefacts, and thereby hope to learn about the varying intersections of hominin minds and material worlds, our concept of intentionality needs to serve this analytical purpose. We cannot draw on, in other words, notions of intention and

intentionality that are unable to inform a substantial concept of *technology*, no matter how implicit the latter may be. Because I argue that such a substantial concept of technology must achieve more than simply recast technology as the aggregate sum of all individual artefacts within a relevant archaeological context, questions of intentionality cannot simply be negotiated vis-à-vis artefact-level data. It is likely that a phenomenological conception of intentionality highlighting the heterogeneity, structure and complexity of constitutive intentions is more useful in such a context. In any case, whether and how intentionality can and should be studied in the lithic record greatly depends on how the archaeological record and key concepts such as technology are constructed and theorised – and we thus need to critically attend to implicit domain assumptions that feed into our basic understanding of the same.

Some may interject that the 'complete reduction sequence fallacy' introduced in the beginning makes it generally impossible to identify and describe lithic technology as a relational configuration, or even individual lithic technical systems, as we can never be certain about the contemporaneity and completeness of the lithic assemblage context under scrutiny. Yet, this riposte is superfluous as it often comes with the assumption that, again, *all* assemblages represent time-averaged products of millennial-scale hominin behaviour, even though there is good sedimentological and extensive refitting evidence that show that this need not always be the case. Indeed, careful technological analysis is arguably capable to productively engage with the question of missing artefacts and provides a rarely considered means to sort heterogeneous and mixed assemblages into relevant analytical units. This capacity, however, can only be fully harnessed if we remain conceptually vigilant and do not fall back into supposedly 'self-evident' assertions that cannot withstand critical interrogation. Another reason is that many intentional structures that archaeologist can recover from the lithic record may be tied to patterns of collective action and as such to group and perhaps even population-level processes. Because of all of this, it is imperative, and without alternative, I would argue, to finally emancipate ourselves from the urge to frame lithic debates in terms of catholicity and to finally acknowledge that almost everything *depends*, in turn calling for a more flexible conceptual apparatus, perhaps especially with regard to questions of intentionality.

## BRIEF CONCLUSION

Yes, intentions do not fossilize but nothing spectacular follows from this realisation. Intentions always need to be inferred and this undertaking is far from futile, at least if we pay critical attention to both the empirical details and the respectively employed research concepts. I have attempted to show that the dominant critique of what may be called the intentional analysis of lithic technology stands on a surprisingly weak conceptual footing. I have pointed out that the critique often relies on a very narrow and often misleading conceptualisation of intentionality and therefore cannot live up to the challenges posed by the lithic record. I have tried to show that this has to do with the domain assumptions at play and that an artefact-centric, too often universalist proclivity of analysis, deeply rooted in the respective research epistemologies, is frequently more of an obstacle than an asset in productively discussing knapping intentions. These approaches merely show that *they* are ill equipped to deal with the problem rather than that we cannot deal with and say something meaningful about it. My contribution is thus intended – pun intended – to showcase the need to more seriously engage in conceptual groundwork in order to break up one-sided debates and to draw attention to currently overlooked difficulties and prospects of inquiry.

## ACKNOWLEDGEMENTS

I dedicate these critical reflections to Raymond Corbey and his persistent occupation with the cognitive status of stone artefacts. Raymond often invoked the apparently self-evident assertion referred to in the title in our conversations, but he never really examined its conceptual basis 'from the fence' as I have tried to (somewhat polemically) do here. As Raymond used to emphasise, no certainties are certain, at best they are statements we can agree upon based on particular standpoints and from a shared epistemological perspective. Critique of such certainties is therefore essential to a truly non-dogmatic stance and amounts to basic research (*Grundlagenforschung*). I hope that this paper takes up this impetus and thereby celebrates Raymond's scholarly legacy.

## REFERENCES

Binford, L.R. 1967. "Comment on Chang". *Current Anthropology* 8, 234-35.

Boëda, E. 1994. *Le Concept Levallois: Variabilité Des Méthodes.* Paris: CNRS Éditions.

Bourguignon, L., J.-Ph. Faivre, and A. Turq. 2004. "Ramification Des Chaînes Opératoires : Spécificité Du Moustérien ?" *Paléo* 16, 37-48.

Chase, P.G. 2016. "Form, Function, and Mental Templates in Paleolithic Archaeology". In *Archaeological Variability and Interpretation in Global Perspective*, edited by A.P. Sullivan, and D.I. Olszewski, 291-306. Boulder: University of Colorado Press.

Corbey, R.H.A. 1998. "Theoretische Probleme Zur Kognition, Sprache Und Gesellschaft Bei Frühen Hominiden". *EAZ – Ethnographisch-Archäologische Zeitschrif* 39, 321-33.

Corbey, R.H.A. 2005. *The Metaphysics of Apes: Negotiating the Animal-Human Boundary.* Cambridge/New York: Cambridge University Press.

Corbey, R.H.A., and W. Roebroeks. 2001. "Biases and Double Standards in Palaeoanthropology". In *Studying Human Origins: Disciplinary History and Epistemology*, 67-76. Amsterdam: Amsterdam University Press.

Crane, T. 1998. "Intentionality as the Mark of the Mental". *Royal Institute of Philosophy Supplements* 43 (March), 229-51. DOI:10.1017/S1358246100004380.

Crane, T. 2016. "Intentionality". In *Routledge Encyclopedia of Philosophy*, 1st ed. London: Routledge. DOI:10.4324/9780415249126-V019-1.

D'Ambrosio, J. 2019. "A New Perceptual Adverbialism". *The Journal of Philosophy* 116 (8), 413-46. DOI:10.5840/jphil2019116826.

Davidson, I, and W. Noble. 1993. "Tools and Language in Human Evolution". In *Tools, Language and Cognition in Human Evolution*, edited by K.R. Gibson and T. Ingold, 363-88. Cambridge: Cambridge University Press.

Dennett, D.C. 1998. *The Intentional Stance.* Cambridge, Mass.: MIT Press.

Dibble, H. L., S.J. Holdaway, S.C. Lin, D.R. Braun, M.J. Douglass, R. Iovita, S.P. McPherron, D.I. Olszewski, and D. Sandgathe. 2017. "Major Fallacies Surrounding Stone Artifacts and Assemblages". *Journal of Archaeological Method and Theory* 24 (3), 813-51. DOI:10.1007/s10816-016-9297-8.

Gallagher, S., and D. Zahavi. 2021. *The Phenomenological Mind*. Third edition. London/New York, NY: Routledge/Taylor & Francis.

Geneste, J.-M. 2010. "Systèmes techniques de production lithique". *Techniques & Culture. Revue semestrielle d'anthropologie des techniques* 54-55, 419-49. DOI:10.4000/tc.5013.

Ginzburg, C. 2013. *Clues, Myths, and the Historical Method*. Baltimore: JHU Press.

Godfrey-Smith, P. 2020. *Metazoa: Animal Life and the Birth of the Mind*. First edition. New York: Farrar, Straus and Giroux.

Gouldner, A.W. 1970. *The Coming Crisis of Western Sociology*. New York: Basic Books.

Grzankowski, A., and M. Montague, eds. 2018. *Non-Propositional Intentionality*. Oxford/New York: Oxford University Press.

Hawkes, C. 1954. "Archeological Theory and Method: Some Suggestions from the Old World". *American Anthropologist* 56 (2), 155-68.

Hodder, I. 1989. "This Is Not an Article about Material Culture as Text". *Journal of Anthropological Archaeology* 8 (3), 250-69. DOI:10.1016/0278-4165(89)90015-9

Hussain, S.T. 2015. 'Betwixt Seriality and Sortiment: Rethinking Early Ahmarian Blade Technology in Al-Ansab 1'. In *Pleistocene Archaeology of the Petra Area in Jordan*, edited by J. Richter and D. Schyle, 131-47. Rahden/Westf.: Marie Leidorf.

Hussain, S.T. 2019. *The French-Anglophone Divide in Lithic Research: A Plea for Pluralism in Palaeolithic Archaeology*. Leiden: Open Access Leiden Dissertations. https://hdl.handle.net/1887/69812.

Inizan, M.-L., M Reduron-Ballinger, H. Roche, and J. Tixier. 1999. *Technology and Terminology of Knapped Stone*. Paris: Cercle de Recherches et d'Etudes Préhistoriques.

Janković, M., and K. Ludwig, eds. 2017. *The Routledge Handbook of Collective Intentionality*. 1 [edition]. Routledge Handbooks in Philosophy. New York: Routledge/Taylor & Francis.

Lakatos, I. 1970. "History of Science and Its Rational Reconstructions". *PSA: Proceedings of the Biennial Meeting of the Philosophy of Science Association* 1970, 91-136. DOI:10.1086/psaprocbienmeetp.1970.495757.

Le Morvan, P. 2005. "Intentionality: Transparent, Translucent, and Opaque". *Journal of Philosophical Research* 30, 283-302.

Liu, C., and D. Stout. 2023. "Inferring Cultural Reproduction from Lithic Data: A Critical Review". *Evolutionary Anthropology: Issues, News, and Reviews* 32 (2), 83-99. DOI:10.1002/evan.21964.

Lycett, S.J., and N. von Cramon-Taubadel. 2015. "Toward a "Quantitative Genetic" Approach to Lithic Variation". *Journal of Archaeological Method and Theory* 22 (2), 646-75. DOI:10.1007/s10816-013-9200-9.

Malle, B.F., and J. Knobe. 1997. "The Folk Concept of Intentionality". *Journal of Experimental Social Psychology* 33 (2), 101-21. DOI:10.1006/jesp.1996.1314

Mathias, C., and L. Bourguignon. 2020. "Cores-on-Flakes and Ramification during the Middle Palaeolithic in Southern France: A Gradual Process from the Early to Late Middle Palaeolithic?" *Journal of Archaeological Science: Reports* 31, 102336. DOI:10.1016/j.jasrep.2020.102336

Pelegrin, J. 1995. *Technologie Lithique: Le Châtelperronien de Roc-de-Combe (Lot) et de La Côte (Dordogne)*. Paris: Éditions de CNRS.

Pelegrin, J. 2011. "Sur Les Débitages Laminaires Du Paléolithique Supérieur". In *François Bordes et La Préhistoire*, edited by. F. Delpech and J. Jaubert, 142-52. Paris: Éditions du C.T.H.S.

Perlès, C. 1980. "Économie de La Matière Première et Économie Du Débitage: Deux Exemples Grecs". In *Préhistoire et Technologie Lithique*, edited by J. Tixier, 37-41. Paris: Centre régional de publication de Sophia Antipolis.

Perlès, C. 1987. *Les Industries Lithiques Taillées de Franchthi (Argolide, Grece), Tome I : Présentation Générale et Industries Paléolithiques*. Bloomington/Indianapolis: Indiana University Press.

Pesesse, D. 2018. "Segmentation Technique, Segmentation Sociale ? Tester l'hypothèse Au Paléolithique Supérieur". *Bulletin de La Société Préhistorique Française* 115 (3), 439-54.

Pierre, J. 2023. "Intentionality". In *The Stanford Encyclopedia of Philosophy*, https://plato.stanford.edu/archives/spr2023/entries/intentionality/.

Putnam, H. 1981. *Reason, Truth and History*. Cambridge: Cambridge University Press. DOI:10.1017/CBO9780511625398.

Richter, J. 1997. *Sesselfelsgrotte III: Der G-Schichten-Komplex der Sesselfelsgrotte. Zum Verständnis des Micoquien*. Suttgart: Franz Steiner Verlag.

Rosenberg, M. 2022. *The Dynamics of Cultural Evolution: The Central Role of Purposive Behaviors*. Vol. 12. Studies in Human Ecology and Adaptation. Cham: Springer. DOI:10.1007/978-3-031-04863-0

Schatzki, T.R. 2002. *The Site of the Social: A Philosophical Account of the Constitution of Social Life and Change*. University Park, PA: Pennsylvania State University Press.

Schatzki, T.R., K. Knorr-Cetina, and E. von Savigny, eds. 2001. *The Practice Turn in Contemporary Theory*. New York: Routledge.

Schlicht, T., and T. Starzak. 2021. "Prospects of Enactivist Approaches to Intentionality and Cognition". *Synthese* 198 (1), 89-113. DOI: 10.1007/s11229-019-02361-z

Schmid, H.B., and D.P. Schweikard. 2009. *Kollektive Intentionalität: eine Debatte über die Grundlagen des Sozialen*. Suhrkamp-Taschenbuch Wissenschaft 1898. Frankfurt am Main: Suhrkamp.

Schweikard, D.P., and H.B. Schmid. 2021. "Collective Intentionality". In *The Stanford Encyclopedia of Philosophy*, https://plato.stanford.edu/archives/fall2021/entries/collective-intentionality/.

Thévenot, L. 2001. "Pragmatic Regimes Governing the Engagement with the World". In *The Practice Turn in Contemporary Theory*, edited by T.R. Schatzki, K. Knorr-Cetina, and E. von Savigny, 56-73. London: Routledge.

Tixier, J. 2012. *A Method for the Study of Stone Tools/ Méthode Pour l'Étude Des Outillages Lithiques*. Luxemburg: ArchéoLogique 4.

Tixier, J., and A. Turq. 1999. "Kombewa et alii". *Paléo, Revue d'Archéologie Préhistorique* 11 (1), 135-43. DOI: 10.3406/pal.1999.1174

Tuomela, R. 2013. *Social Ontology: Collective Intentionality and Group Agents*. Oxford: Oxford University Press.

Tuomela, R, and K. Miller. 1988. "We-Intentions". *Philosophical Studies* 53 (3), 367-89. DOI: 10.1007/BF00353512

Turq, A., W. Roebroeks, L. Bourguignon, and J.-Ph. Faivre. 2013. "The Fragmented Character of Middle Palaeolithic Stone Tool Technology". *Journal of Human Evolution* 65 (5), 641-55. DOI: 10.1016/j.jhevol.2013.07.014

Valentin, B., M.-J. Weber, and P. Bodu. 2014. "Initialisation and Progression of the Core Reduction Process at Donnemarie-Dontilly (Seine-et-Marne, France), Site of the Belloisian Tradition: New Interpretative Key for Comparisons with Contemporaneous Industries and "Federmesser-Gruppen" Assemblages". *Bulletin de La Société Préhistorique Française* 111 (4), 659-78.

Walsh, D. M. 2015. *Organisms, Agency, and Evolution*. Cambridge: Cambridge University Press.

Walsh, D. M., and G. Rupik. 2023. "The Agential Perspective: Countermapping the Modern Synthesis". *Evolution & Development*, ede.12448. DOI: 10.1111/ede.12448

Wylie, A. 2002. *Thinking from Things: Essays in the Philosophy of Archaeology*. Berkeley: University of California Press.

Wylie, A. 2015. "A Plurality of Pluralisms: Collaborative Practice in Archaeology". In *Objectivity in Science: New Perspectives from Science and Technology Studies*, edited by F. Padovani, A. Richardson, and J.Y. Tsou, 189-210. Cham: Springer. DOI: 10.1007/978-3-319-14349-1_10

In Hussain, S.T. and G.L. Dusseldorp (eds) 2025. Sitting on the fence: Negotiating archaeology, anthropology and philosophy. Festschrift for Prof. Dr Raymond H.A. Corbey in celebration of his 70th birthday. *Analecta Praehistorica Leidensia* 54. Leiden: Sidestone Press, pp. 115-126.

# Hand Axes as Hyena Jaws

Jan Kolen

ABSTRACT

This article is dedicated to Raymond and meant as a provocative hypothesis, consisting of elements that have been put forward earlier by others as well as some new ideas that I have developed myself. In just a few pages, and therefore a bit (too) ambitious, I will argue: that (a) the phenomenon of the hand axe has been approached one-sidedly from the perspective of cognition, social learning and genetics (like the Baldwin Effect), and that environmental affordances have been overlooked (or are simply considered to be no longer "fashionable"); and (b) that early hominins in Europe – specifically the "Acheuleans" – successfully emulated natural competitors in their technologies and that the hand axe might have been an outcome of this. I will selectively refer to specific Paleolithic sites but I do not intend to suggest that these sites are representative (as systematic research is needed). However, neither should it be taken as baseless "reasoning by example". Hopefully, the examples do show that the hypothesis is evidence-based to a certain extent.

*Keywords: Hand axes, Acheulean, Baldwin Effect, affordance theory, environmental learning, the human mirror mind*

## INTRODUCTION: RAYMOND AND HAND AXES

Raymond has a special interest in hand axes. It is not so much that he has a desire to collect them. However, his background in anthropology, philosophy and psychology makes him fond of reflecting on interdisciplinary topics from different angles and the hand axe phenomenon lends itself to just doing that in many ways. During a visit to Raymond's home, the discussion often turns to hand axes and their role in the harsh survival-world and cognitive evolution of early hominins. Discussions also quickly result in an election of the most impressive hand axe, in which we often appear to have different opinions. Is it the well-known giant hand axe from Furze Platt (Wymer 1982, Pl.XIII), an even larger (and perhaps more beautiful) biface from Vailly-sur-Aisne (figure 1; Joullie and Kelley 1961), a hand axe of modest dimensions with a remarkable fossil that has been recognized and saved by the maker (?) or a perfectly symmetrical triangulate? In such sessions we wonder why, when we see Paleolithic hand axes, we are so strongly guided by our own aesthetic experience, especially our sense of symmetry (Hodgson 2011), and whether this really distinguishes us from earlier hominins. Or whether there may be some truth in the old hypothesis that typological differences in stone tools expressed the stylistic values and identity of different ethnic groups. Ultimately, however, for Raymond, reflection on their evolutionary significance wins out.

Recently, Raymond (from now on: Corbey) published a highly original hypothesis in *Evolutionary Anthropology* aligning well with recent insights from evolutionary biology and potentially explaining the longstanding "success" of

**Jan Kolen**
Faculty of Archaeology,
Leiden University, The Netherlands
j.c.a.kolen@arch.leidenuniv.nl

Figure 1. Lower and Middle Palaeolithic hand axes in the Metropolitan Museum of Art, New York. In the middle: the giant hand axe from Vailly-sur-Aisne. Courtesy: Metropolitan Museum of Art, New York.

the hand axe in the early history of humankind: *The Acheulean hand axe: More like a bird's song than a Beatle's tune?* (Corbey *et al.* 2017), and, later, *Baldwin effects in early stone tools* (2020), a response to his critiques. In these articles, Corbey and colleagues point out the possibility that the production of Acheulean hand axes was under genetic control, at least in part, and more specifically conforming to the so-called "Baldwin Effect":

> *"If phenotypically plastic individuals grow up time and again, over hundreds if not thousands of generations, in a technological niche while manipulating stone, and provided that the cost-benefit ratio is right: would not selection in the long run favor features of the organism befitting their technological capacities, so crucial for survival? This is a Baldwin Effect, a progressive encoding in the genome of initially non-genetic, plastic responses, acquired by learning, to changing environmental conditions. In the long run, phenotypic plasticity for a particular trait is reduced in favor of stereotyped, experience-independent, innate routines which mimic the initial plastic response," Corbey (2020, 1-2).*

Various experts responded critically yet constructively to Corbey's Baldwinian account. McNabb (see also Hosfield *et al.* 2018) turns to Occam's Razor and argues that the proposition of genetic control is redundant, because principles of cultural transmission and social learning already sufficiently explain the "hand axe phenomenon" (McNabb 2019). Wynn and Gowlett (2018) respond to the issue from a different perspective. While Wynn, in his early paleo-psychological work on hand axes, mainly drew attention to the role of mental templates and cognitive schemes in the early hominin mind (*e.g.*, Wynn 1995), Wynn and Gowlett refer in their response to a decisive constellation of no fewer than six ergonomic constraints on the shaping of hand-held tools. Corbey, however, answers to his critics suggesting that these accounts are not necessarily mutually exclusive, but should be seen in relation to each other, although McNabb seems to reject dual cultural-genetic inheritance altogether.

What actually limits all these arguments is that they locate the "hand axe phenomenon" one-sidedly (sometimes exclusively) in the early hominin itself – in the early mind, the skills and ergonomic constraints, the innate capacity for cultural transmission and learning, sexual dimorphism, the genes, etc. This gives the impression that hand axe technologies were created and evolved in an environmental vacuum. This is surprising because in Paleolithic archeology and human origins research more generally special interest has, at the same time, arisen in the importance of human niche construction for biological and cultural evolution (*e.g.,* Iovita *et al.* 2021).

Also, a one-sided emphasis is often placed on the hand axe as an "involuntary" *product* or *outcome* of cognitive drivers, styles, raw material constraints, cultural transmission, Baldwin effects, etc. (Hussain and Will 2020). However, the hand axe was not simply a *product* or *type*, but a *tool*, and phenomenologically speaking the tool always mediates between the mind and body of its maker/user and the social and natural environment (Ingold 1999).

In this contribution I want to correct this one-sidedness in the development of theories about hand axes, by drawing attention to the relationships between early hominins and their niche. In this framework I will discuss the (underestimated) role of environmental preferences, affordances, and emulation in the Acheulean. I use the term "affordances" here deliberately because the concept is widely associated with the work of the psychologist James Gibson (1979, 119-137). Instead of an environment that determines the existence and behavior of animals (and therefore also people), he speaks of niches and affordances that animals offer something: "affordances of the environment are what it *provides* or *furnishes* [...]. It implies the complementarity of the animal and the environment" (Gibson 1979, 127). Whether something in the environment is seen as affordance can differ per species, group or even per individual, and can also change over time. Responding to affordances can also be at the expense of another species, group or individual. The second part of the definition emphasizes the non-deterministic nature of the relationship and the fact that by using affordances animals simultaneously change their environment and "give something back". A good example of this is the use of fire by hunters and gatherers, and possibly even by early hominins (MacDonald *et al.* 2021), as a "landscaping tool" (Scherjon *et al.* 2015), deliberately changing the environment and creating new affordances in the process. In these reciprocal relationships, which we generally call "niche construction", the tool plays an important manipulative role. It is neither separate from the individual nor from the environment, but mediates between the two and so unlocks particular affordances. In what follows I will apply this concept to the Acheulean niche.

## THE ACHEULEAN IN 500 WORDS

The Acheulean is a notoriously complex and heavily debated archaeological and cultural concept, and it is therefore dangerous to deal with it in 500 or so words, especially since it has attracted colleagues who became experts in this early hominin "industry" only after decades of intensive study and research. Here I will define the Acheulean in a rather pragmatic way as an Early and early Middle Pleistocene technological complex, associated with *Homo erectus* s.l. and (in Europe) *Homo heidelbergensis*, with a wide but consistent distribution in time and space, characterised by lithic assemblages with large proportions of mostly bifacially worked tools including enigmatic "hand axes" (see *e.g.,* Clark 1994; Lycett and Gowlett 2008; Lycett and Bae 2010; Moncel *et al.* 2020). The hand axe therefore is a key element in the tool-making repertoire, although there are other characteristic components, like cleavers, picks and various core reduction technologies (McNabb 2017, 2019). Acheulean complexes occur in vast and contiguous areas across Africa, West and South Asia, and Europe. Chronologically, the Acheulean fills a time window of hundreds of thousands of years, roughly between c. 1.8 and 0.15 ma, depending on the region. Regional technological and typological variation is fairly extensive. In some areas, hand axes are more frequent than in other areas, and some regions seem to be characterized by the regular co-occurrence of chopping tools or cleavers (which in fact would deserve the term "hand axe" more so than classic hand axes themselves). Also, accompanying core reduction technologies may differ from one region to another, although there are also some striking similarities that are explained as the result of convergent evolution (Sharon 2019).

It should be emphasised that the large proportions of hand axes that characterize Acheulean assemblages may have resulted from very different processes and combinations thereof. In well-preserved archaeological sites that have formed in low energy sedimentary environments, like at Boxgrove (Roberts and Parfitt 1999), *behavioral* drivers must have been mainly responsible for their accumulation. But even in those cases (exception: the so-called "Horse Butchery Site" at Boxgrove, see Pope *et al.* 2020), we most probably will not be able to ever find out whether this happened within 15 minutes or, say, 15 years, even within a single specific scatter of flint, however well that scatter is defined and delineated. In the large river valleys of Western Europe that are considered "type-locations" of the Acheulean, however, such as the Somme valley (Antoine *et al.* 2010), the large number of hand axes will at least partly (in some cases predominantly) reflect selective fluvial activity. High currents resulted in thick gravel deposits in which hand axes were simply sedimentary "particles", although early hominin activities must have focused on these valleys as well. In arid regions, accumulations of hand axes may have resulted also from longstanding erosional processes resulting in so-called "desert pavements" (Knight and Zerboni 2018; Hussain and Will 2020). Whatever the case, the high frequency of hand axes in Acheulean assemblages is a core element and must be explained.

The apparently universal utility and especially the exceptional long-term success of the hand axe in the Early and Middle Pleistocene cannot be explained exclusively by social learning principles and Baldwin Effects. These hypotheses mainly refer to the "input side" of the phenomenon and ignore the fact that hand axes – as tools – effectively mediated between early hominins and their environments during their active life histories. Therefore, there is a need for accounting for long-term environmental preferences and the importance of environmental affordances therein. We can find a basis and first approximation for this in the remarkably sustainable geographical pattern "behind" the Acheulean phenomenon.

## THE ACHEULEAN NICHE

In Europe, the region I will focus on here, the Acheulean appears to have been a predominantly Mediterranean-Atlantic and coastal-fluvial phenomenon (*cf.* Roebroeks and van Kolfschoten eds. 1995; Moncel *et al.* 2020). The distribution of the Acheulean industries – and thus the occurrence of early sites with large numbers of hand axes – is mainly tied to Mediterranean and Atlantic regions. Within those regions, "Acheuleans" preferred coastal plains, including their beaches and tidal zones, lagoons, deltas and estuaries, and connected (Atlantic) river systems. We find Acheulean sites in long-stretched zones along the Mediterranean coasts from Northern Africa and the Levant (Ubeidyia; Gesher Benot Ya'aqov) to Italy (Notarchirico), France (Tautavel) and Spain (La Boella; Cueva Negra; Atapuerca), and along the Atlantic coasts of Western Europe and in the main river systems that connected to it, from Portugal (Douro and Tagus) and France (Loire, Seine and Somme) to England (Thames; the Pleistocene Midlands/Bytham River) and the Pleistocene river systems of "Doggerland" (figure 2).

Although ecologically varied, the natural habitats in these geographical zones always had at least the following four characteristics, which may have acted as landscape attractors for early hominins: they are (1) very rich and diverse in food and other resources, (2) with a high probability of encountering these resources, and good accessibility, (3) a relatively high degree of predictability of the landscape conditions and (4) a temperate climate. It is therefore not a bold assumption that the Early Pleistocene pioneers of Europe could have spread relatively quickly from the Levant along the coastal areas of the Mediterranean and Atlantic Europe by simply following the coastlines and estuaries and thereby familiar environmental characteristics (*cf.* Langbroek 2004).

The universal wealth and diversity of resources in coastal areas and Atlantic fluvial systems through time is well-known and well-documented based on palaeo-environmental studies (*e.g.,* Hosfield 2020 for the European Pleistocene), historical-ecological studies (*e.g.,* Sanderson 2009 for Northeast America), and research in modern ecosystem services (*e.g.,* Barbier *et al.* 2011). The opportunities for early hominins to get food and other resources in coastal and riverine landscapes must have been endless, even in competitive situations. All kinds of resources could be found along the coasts themselves, on the beaches and in tidal areas: washed up marine mammals, birds, fish, shellfish and crustaceans, edible seaweed, etc. In leftover pools and between rocks it was possible to fish with simple means. Along the banks of the estuaries and rivers (further inland) there was always a chance to find carcasses of large grazers and browsers, or to isolate and kill animals. The deciduous and coniferous forests along the coasts and rivers harbored countless fruit- and nut-bearing plant and tree species, edible tubers and plants, mushrooms, small mammals that could be smoked out with fire, etc. Bird eggs of different species could be collected in all these habitats. In dry parts of the riverbed, stony beach deposits and outcrops along the edges of the river valleys, suitable raw materials could be collected for making tools. On the beaches wood and sometimes pyrite could be found for making fire. Along steep edges and in the caves and abris there were sufficient locations available where sleeping places and home bases could be arranged. The affordances were therefore exceptional, and the options for shelter were numerous.

All coastal areas covered by early hominins contained suitable habitats for what archaeologists

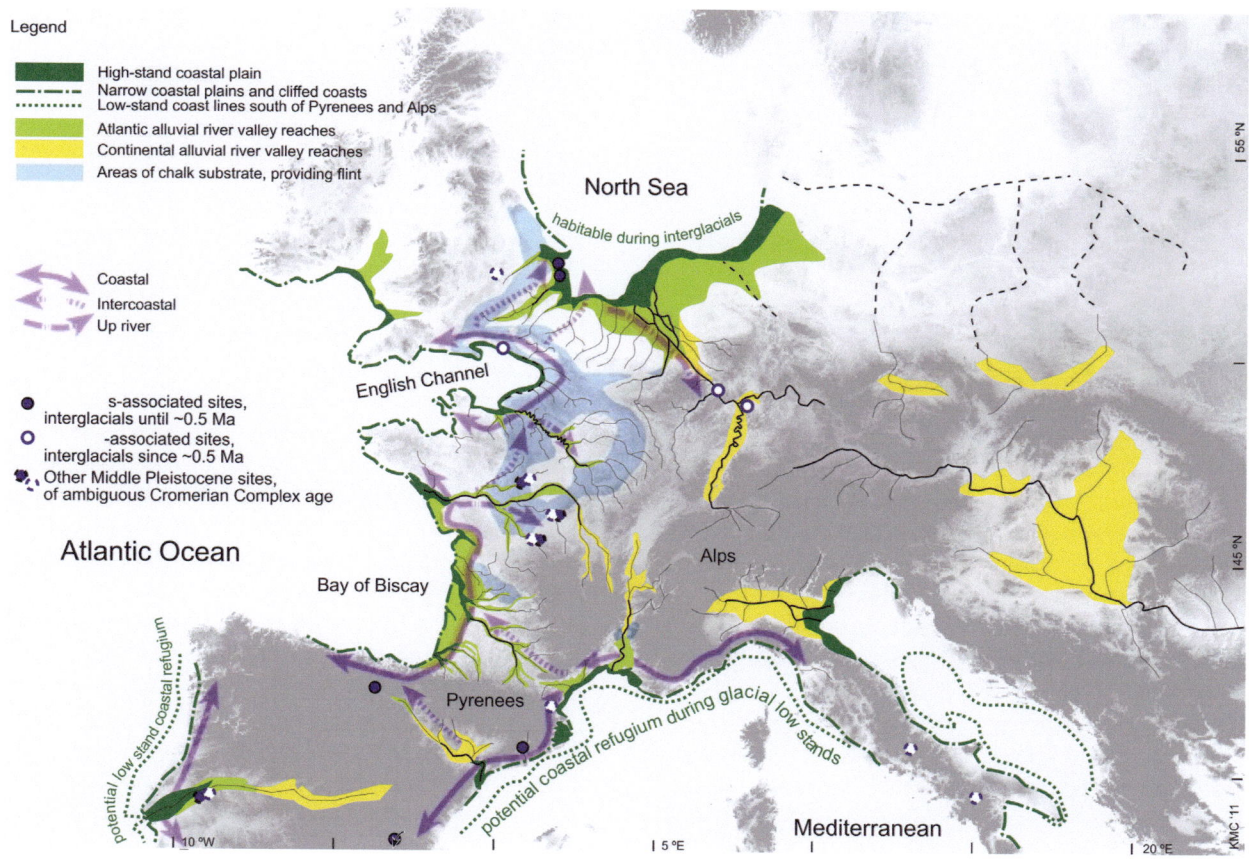

Paleogeographical reconstruction of coastlines (dark green), Atlantic river systems (light green), continental river systems (yellow), flint-bearing chalk formations (blue), and possible hominin migration routes (arrows) in Europe during the Lower Palaeolithic. After: Cohen *et al.*2012, with permission.

call a "broad-spectrum economy" when dealing with later periods such as the Mesolithic (Stiner 2001; Weiss *et al.* 2004). Although the proportion of meat in the diet of early hominins in Europe will have been high at least seasonally, and many of the above sources have not (yet?) been shown to have been actually exploited, the importance of hunting early hominin subsistence strategies are probably currently overestimated. While the role of scavenging was emphasized too one-sidedly in the "Binford era" (Binford 1985), a small number of iconic discoveries, such as the "throwing javelins" from Schoningen (Thieme 1997), some detailed faunal studies (*e.g.,* Pope *et al.* 2020) and perhaps our own consumption preferences may have tilted the picture too far back again towards the organized hunt. A recent ethnohistorical survey by Speth (2022) shows that in historical and recent hunter-gatherer-fisher communities, the rotting and fermented meat of animals and rotten fish, apart from being nutritious,

was generally considered a delicacy. In addition, the organs, the brain and bone marrow often appeared to be preferred, whether from scavenged or hunted animals. This would have been no different for early hominins, especially in the nutrient-rich and diverse habitats described above. Our modern addiction to large portions of fresh red meat can therefore not be used as a model for the dietary volition of historical hunters and gatherers, nor for early hominins.

The attractiveness of coastal landscapes and Atlantic rivers to early hominids would have been further enhanced by the temperate climate conditions in these habitats and the high degree of predictability of environmental opportunities. Coastal and river landscapes, in contrast to vast plateaus in continental regions and, for example, the late Pleistocene mammoth steppe (sensu Guthrie 1990), are distinguished by a well-recognizable spatial zoning, with many lateral and longitudinal gradients and associated marine, fluvial and terrestrial ecologies (Calow and Petts 1992). The chances within it for scavenging, gathering, fishing and hunting were high, irrespective of climate and biome. Moreover, the geomorphological and hydrological structure of these landscapes provided a natural infrastructure in which early hominins could move well and migrate easily (Hussain and Floss 2016). The necessity of seasonal migration will have been low due to the averaging effect of the sea on the Atlantic climate. On the other hand, explorations into "new land" and territorial shifts could easily take place along the coasts due to the absence of significant climatic barriers.

## Hand axes as hyena jaws

In the foregoing we have seen that, on a basic level, the coastal areas and Atlantic river systems of Pleistocene Europe were full of potent environmental affordances to be recognised and exploited by early hominins. In a sense, their landscapes and habitats "invited" early hominins to do things in particular ways and to shape and organize their technologies accordingly. The opportunities were plenty and varied, which welcomed generalized strategies as there was always something to get or find in a specific landscape zone. These more-or-less opportunistic strategies demanded transportable tools that could be used for different tasks, like cutting and scraping, butchering and breaking, hammering and crushing, throwing and digging: the *hand axes* (Keeley 1993).

"Expeditions" using hand axes would have been targeted in this generalized sense, but within small home ranges that covered several zones and gradients, from coastline to forest and river to valley edge. There is no reliable evidence for the regular transportation of Acheulean hand axes over large distances for specialized use beyond immediate needs. Hand axes were taken from one location to another over short distances and sometimes even finished on the spot (Pope *et al.* 2020). At Boxgrove, the flint used for hand axes was collected in the collapsed chalk cliff nearby (Wenban Smith 1989). Most hand axes found at Cagny-la Garenne were also made from flint collected in the local chalk outcrops along the riverbank (Lamotte 1991).

It is because of their multifunctionality that hand axes have been compared to Swiss army knives (Calvin 2002). Use-wear analysis (including macroscopic traces) of hand axes from European, Asian and African sites indeed show that they were handy multi-purpose tools, used on various materials (meat, bone, wood, plants) and for a wide range of activities, like cutting, scraping, butchering, hammering, drilling and wedging (Keeley 1980, 1993; Echegaray *et al.* 1998; Dominguez-Rodrigo *et al.* 2001; Murray 2017). The latter activities unambiguously point to the use of hand axes, like is generally inferred for cleavers, in heavy duty tasks. At the recently excavated Acheulean site of Porto Maior (Galicia, Spain), situated on a terrace of the Mino River and dating to c. 0.2-0.3 ma, early hominins left behind a dense scatter of giant hand axes and cleavers that were used in the processing of hard materials, in activities like the breaking up of carcasses (Mendez-Quintas *et al.* 2020). At Notarchirico (Venosa, Italy), the skull of a juvenile elephant was found upside down, with the mandible detached and broken, and surrounded by some dozens of hand axes and choppers (Mussi 1995). For Hoxne, the use of hand axes in butchering and the dismembering of large carcasses was already suggested by Keeley (1993, 129-149), based on micro-wear studies. At the previously mentioned "Horse Butchery Site" at Boxgrove, hand axes were made and used by a tight-knit group of collaborating "Heidelbergs" in the slaughtering and processing of a female horse in a tidal area (Pope *et al.* 2020). The frequent association of hand axe technologies with intense bone fragmentation, such as at Boxgrove and Hoxne, is a further indication of the deployment of hand axes as heavy-duty tools aimed at marrow extraction.

These are only a few examples of the many indications that the "Acheuleans" settled at the top of the food pyramid among the large carnivores and carcass destroyers in their environments: hyenas, bears, cave lions, sabretooth cats and wolves (Turner 1992). Their strategies appear to have been targeted at the "quick and dirty" butchery of hunted and scavenged animals and probably the transportation of body parts to safe areas to fully exploit their resource potential: the meat, organs, brains, bones and bone marrow (*cf.* Langbroek 2004). Carcass destroyers like hyenas exploit their victims optimally, including the bones, tendons and marrow, by literally crushing all body parts. Early hominins in Europe now did the same by using hand axes at Acheulean sites, particularly under selective pressure from key competitors.

This shows that the Acheulean niche was not only full of affordances but also full of competitors. Yet, these competitors offered affordances as well as they may have induced early hominines to innovate through emulation. There is no doubt that the hand axe using hominins in coastal and Atlantic environments were armed with sharp observational powers and a highly developed environmental sensibility (*cf.* Hussain and Floss 2015; Hussain *et al.* 2022). They will have learned rapidly about – and *from* – the anatomy and behavior of their prey animals and competitors. It is therefore not a bold assumption that their technology also "copied" the successful behavior and effective "tools" that early hominins observed in the large flesh eaters and carcass destroyers in their environment. In the long process of environmental learning, covering hundreds or thousands of generations, hand axes and cleavers selectively proved to be the best alternatives for saber teeth and hyena jaws, enabling early hominins to be as successful as their competitors and to execute some of the same tasks. The additional use of fire (Gowlett 2006; Roebroeks and Villa 2011) may have then given them a significant advantage.

## DISCUSSION: ENVIRONMENTAL AFFORDANCES, MIMETIC TECHNOLOGY AND CONVERGENT EVOLUTION

The hand axe is the undisputed archetype of early human cultural evolution. As a multifunctional tool, it is one of the most groundbreaking, successful and "sustainable" (long-lived) technological solutions in the deep history of humankind. This is also evident from the widespread distribution of Acheulean industries across Africa, Asia and Europe. It is therefore not surprising that researchers go to all possible theoretical and empirical lengths to understand the Acheulean phenomenon and the issue remains far from resolved. In the introduction, I have argued that most accounts locate the long-term success of the hand axe in the early hominin *itself*, that is, in the early hominin mind and body – *e.g.*, with regard to skills and genes. It so seems as if this smart tool survived hundreds of thousands of years in an environmental vacuum, while the hand axe-using *erectus* and *heidelbergensis* populations showed long-standing environmental preferences for coastal regions and Atlantic river systems. It is well-known that these types of environments, globally, are very rich and varied in terms of habitats, animal species and thus potential (food) resources for hominin populations – irrespective of their diets and economies. From this perspective, coastal and Atlantic fluvial habitats were in a general sense also reliable and predictable for hunters, gatherers and fishers, as there was always something to extract, and climatic

and seasonal differences tended to be averaged out. I concluded that these environments were thus ripe of affordances, and that early hominins were attracted to these affordances and dealt with them in flexible ways. I also suggested that the competitors of early hominins, the large flesh eaters and carcass destroyers, similarly acted as another layer of environmental affordances. They provided hominins with models for exploitation and the invention and success of the hand axe might well be based on this creatively engaging with this nonhuman model.

It is here that the early human mind and body come into the picture again, but now as environmentally embedded perception (*cf.* Ingold 2000) rather than as related sets of pregiven cognitive schemata, social learning capacities or Baldwin effects. The human "mirror mind" is perhaps key in this respect. It is well-known that humans show a deeply rooted tendency to unconsciously or semi-consciously copy the gestures, body movements and behaviors of others easily (Heyes 2009). Even to such an extent that imitation is considered "at the heart of social cognitive neuroscience" because it "provides a channel of evolutionary, cultural inheritance that makes us distinctively human" (Heyes 2009, 2293). Nonetheless, it is observed in other primates as well. Particularly important is the discovery of "mirror neurons" in the primate brain that respond when an action is executed but also when that same or a similar action is observed in the environment (Gallese *et al.* 1996). This indicates that action perception and action production are closely related, creating "common codes" or "bimodal structures".

It is agreed that imitation can have systematic and far-reaching effects on cultural evolution:

*"imitation provides a non-genetic route for the inheritance of phenotypic attributes, and has the potential to support the cumulative properties of human culture – the conservation and dissemination of innovations in ways that allow technologies and practices to improve over time,"* Heyes (2009, 2295).

At the neurocognitive level, imitation in humans is also considered to be strongly related to the development of empathy (Heyes 2009, 2295: "bridging the gap between minds"; Bastiaansen *et al.* 2009) and the early development of a *theory of mind* in human infancy (Corbey 2010). However, human mimetic behavior is not exclusively characteristic of personal development and small-scale social situations, but also extends to the "wider" environment and the human interaction with non-human animals. Through time, human societies have shown to be successful in forcing innovations and finding adaptive solutions in part based on "environmental emulation", often exploring animal anatomy and behavior to this end. Well-known modern examples – amongst many – are human flight (based on studies of the bird wing), earthquake resistant bridge architecture (inspired by the functioning of animal limbs) and the development of less painful needles (*mosquito proboscis*).

As a basic cognitive and behavioral principle, the copying of other animals seems to be the outcome of a long evolutionary history that is also well-attested by paleoanthropological and archaeological research. Neanderthals, Denisovans and Anatomically Moderns in Europe adopted animal body parts like teeth, bones, feathers and claws as body ornaments and "transformed" their own bodies accordingly, in this way mimicking "the other", for whatever functional and/or ritual (symbolic) reason (Wragg Sykes 2020). Recent discoveries indicate that *H. heidelbergensis* already copied successful adaptations from animals and introduced them within their own social domain or even in their own embodied behavior. Fine cutmarks on metatarsal bones from cave bears at Schöningen provide evidence for the exploitation of bear skins, suggesting that hominins from this site protected their bodies against the cold like cave bears did (Verheijen *et al.* 2023). Comparable behavior was suggested earlier for early hominins at Biache-Saint-Vaast and Taubach (Dusseldorp 2009, 153). Another good candidate for animal-emulated behavior is nest-building. Early hominins could have copied or reused the dens of hyenas, bears and lions in caves or could have created similar structures after their example in open-air locations (*cf.* Kolen 1999). Given the long-term stability of Acheulean hand axe technologies, surviving for hundreds of thousands of years, it is likely that these reflected strongly developed mimetic cultures (Donald 1991). It is therefore not a bold proposal that these technologies emerged from behaviorally embedded principles of environmental emulation, copying the successful tactics and "tools" of competitors with which they shared long co-evolutionary histories (Baynes-Rock 2015; Hussain *et al.* 2022). The combination with increasingly controlled fire use may have ultimately given early hominins and adaptive advantage (Roebroeks and Villa 2011).

One of the challenges for scholars of the Acheulean is, the great stability of the hand axe. In this paper, I have focused on the role of environmental affordances and environmental learning and their potential to elucidate some of these long-noted yet still puzzling patterns. I concluded that the success of hand axe technologies may have been based on long-term environmental preferences, selectively exploiting coastal and fluvial environments, in combination with a strongly developed "mirror mind" that both informed social learning principles and successfully co-opted elements from nonhuman nature.

I close with a message for Raymond. Despite the hypothesis I presented here, I am a fan of Baldwin effects! But perhaps Raymond's answer, as in his response to McNabb, Wynn and Gowlett, would be that the alternative account presented here and his Baldwin Effect-based perspective would actually merge well and so cross-pollinate each other....

## Acknowledgements

I thank Shumon Hussain and Gerrit Dusseldorp for their excellent feedback and valuable suggestions for literature, concepts, examples, etc.

## References

Antoine, P., P. Auguste, J.-J. Bahain, C. Chaussé, C. Falguères, B. Ghaleb, L. Lozouet, J.L. Locht, P. Voinchet. 2010. "Chronostratigraphy and palaeoenvironments of Acheulean occupations in Northern France (Somme, Seine and Yonne valleys)." *Quaternary International* 223-224, 456-461.

Barbier, E.B., S.D. Hacker, C. Kennedy, E.W. Koch, A.C. Stier, B.R. Silliman. 2011. "The value of estuarine and coastal ecosystem services." *Ecological Monographs* 81 (2), 169-193.

Bastiaansen J.A.C.J., M. Thioux, and C. Keysers. 2009. "Evidence for mirror systems in emotions." *Phil. Trans. R. Soc. B* 364, 2391-2404.

Baynes-Rock, M. 2015. "Converging on Ancient Bones: A Review of the Evidence for the Close Relatedness of Humans (Homo Sapiens) and Spotted Hyenas (Crocuta Crocuta)." *Humanimalia* 7 (1), 1-22.

Binford, L.R. 1985. "Human ancestors: Changing views of their behavior." *Journal of Anthropological Archaeology* 4 (4), 292-327.

Calow, P. and G.E. Petts. 1992. *The rivers handbook: hydrological and ecological principles.* Vol. 1-2. New York: Blackwell Science.

Calvin, W.H. 2002. "Rediscovery and the cognitive aspects of toolmaking: Lessons from the handaxe." *Behavioral and Brain Sciences* 25 (3), 403-404.

Clark, J.D. 1994. "The Acheulian Industrial Complex in Africa and elsewhere." In *Integrative Paths to the Past – Paleoanthropological Advances in Honor of F. Clark Howell*, edited by R.S. Corruccini and R.L. Ciochon, 451-469. Englewood Cliff, New Jersey: Prentice Hall.

Cohen, K.M., K. MacDonald, J.C.A. Joordens, W. Roebroeks, P. L. Gibbard. 2012. "The earliest occupation of north-west Europe: a coastal perspective." *Quaternary International* 271, 70-83.

Corbey, R.H.A. 2010. "De mens blijft verborgen. Helmuth Plessner laveerde tussen Kant en Darwin." *De Academische Boekengids* 79, 9-11.

Corbey, R.H.A. 2020. "Baldwin effects in early stone tools." *Evolutionary Anthropology* 29 (5), 1-8. DOI:10.1002/evan.21864

Corbey, R.H.A., A. Jagich, and K. Vaesen. 2016. "The Acheulean hand axe: More like a bird's song than a Beatle's tune?" *Evolutionary Anthropology* 25 (1), 6-19. DOI:10.1002/evan.21467

Dominguez-Rodrigo, M., J. Serrallonga, J. Juan-Tresserras, L. Alcala, and L. Luque. 2001. "Woodworking activities by early humans: a plant residue analysis on Acheulian stone tools from Peninj (Tanzania)." *Journal of Human Evolution* 40 (4), 289-299.

Donald, M. 1991. *Origins of the modern mind: Three stages in the evolution of culture and cognition.* Harvard: Harvard University Press.

Dusseldorp, G.L. 2009. *A view to a kill: Investigating Middle Palaeolithic subsistence using an optimal foraging perspective.* Leiden: Sidestone Press.

Echegaray, G., J. Freeman, and L. Gordon. 1998. *Le Paléolithique inférieur et moyen en Espagne. Collection L'homme des origines.* Série Préhistoire d'Europe 6.

Gallese V., L. Fadiga, L. Fogassi, and G. Rizzolatti. 1996. "Action recognition in the premotor cortex." *Brain* 119, 593-609.

Gibson, J.J. 1979. *The ecological approach to visual perception.* London: Houghton Mifflin & Co.

Gowlett J.A.J. 2006. "The elements of design form in Acheulian bifaces: Modes, modalities, rules and language." In *Axe age: Acheulian tool-making from quarry to discard*, edited by N. Goren-Inbar and G. Sharon, 203-221. London: Equinox.

Guthrie, R.D. 1990. *Frozen Fauna of the Mammoth Steppe: The story of Blue Babe.* Chicago and London: The University of Chicago Press.

Heyes, C. 2009. "Evolution, development and intentional control of imitation." *Philosophical Transactions of the Royal Society of London Series B* 364 (1528), 2293-2298.

Hodgson D. 2011. "The first appearance of symmetry in the human lineage: Where perception meets art." *Symmetry* 3 (1), 337-353.

Hosfield R. 2020. *The earliest Europeans, a year in the life: seasonal survival strategies in the Lower Palaeolithic.* Oxford: Oxbow.

Hosfield, R., J. Cole, and J. McNabb. 2018. "Less of a bird's song than a hard rock ensemble." *Evolutionary Anthropology* 27 (1), 9-20. https//:doi.org/10.1002/evan.21551

Hussain, S.T., and H. Floss. 2015. "Sharing the World with Mammoths, Cave Lions and Other Beings: Linking Animal-Human Interactions and the Aurignacian "Belief World"." *Quartär* 62, 85-120.

Hussain, S.T., and H. Floss. 2016. "Streams as Entanglement of Nature and Culture: European Upper Paleolithic River Systems and Their Role as Features of Spatial Organization." *Journal of Archaeological Method and Theory* 23 (4), 1162-1218.

Hussain, S.T., M. Weiss, and T. Kellberg Nielsen. 2022. "Being-with Other Predators: Cultural Negotiations of Neanderthal-Carnivore Relationships in Late Pleistocene Europe." *Journal of Anthropological Archaeology* 66, 101409. DOI:10.1016/j.jaa.2022.101409

Hussain, S.T., and M. Will. 2020. "Materiality, Agency and Evolution of Lithic Technology: An Integrated Perspective for Palaeolithic Archaeology." *Journal of Archaeological Method and Theory* 28 (2), 617-670.

Ingold, T. 1999: ""Tools for the Hand, Language for the Face": An Appreciation of Leroi-Gourhan's Gesture and Speech." *Studies in History and Philosophy of Science Part C: Studies in History and Philosophy of Biological and Biomedical Sciences* 30 (4), 411-453

Ingold, T. 2000. *The Perception of the Environment.Essays on Livelihood, Dwelling and Skill.* London: Routledge.

Iovita, R., D. R. Braun, M.J. Douglass, S.J. Holdaway, S.C. Lin, D.I. Olszewski, and Z. Rezek. 2021. "Operationalizing niche construction theory with stone tools." *Evolutionary Anthropology* 30 (1), 28-39.

Joullie, H., and L.H. Kelley. 1961. "Recherches recentes sur le paleolithique de la region de Vailly-sur-Aisne." *Bulletin de Societé Prehistorique Française* 58 (7), 440-449.

Keeley, L.H. 1993. *Microwear Analysis of Lithics. The Lower Palaeolithic site at Hoxne, England*. London: University of Chicago Press.

Knight, J., and A. Zerboni. 2018. "Formation of desert pavements and the interpretation of lithic-strewn landscapes of the central Sahara." *Journal of Arid Environments* 153, 39-51.

Kolen, J. 1999. "Hominids without homes. On the nature of Middle Palaeolithic settlement in Europe." In *The Middle Palaeolithic Occupation of Europe*, edited by C. Gamble and W. Roebroeks, 139-175. Leiden: Leiden University Press.

Lamotte, A. 1991. *Etude des vestiges lithiques des niveaux du gisement de Cagny-la-Garenne (Somme) et de niveau A du gisement de Gouzeaucourt*. Memoire de D.E.A. Lille: Universite des Sciences et Techniques de Lille.

Langbroek, M. 2004. *Out of Africa: an investigation into the earliest occupation of the Old World*. Oxford: Archaeopress.

Lycett, S.J., and C.J. Bae. 2010. "The Movius Line controversy: the state of the debate." *World Archaeology* 42 (4), 521-544.

Lycett, S.J., and J.A.J. Gowlett. 2008. "On questions surrounding the Acheulean 'tradition'." *World Archaeology* 40 (3), 295-315.

MacDonald, K., F. Scherjon, E. van Veen, K. Vaesen, and W. Roebroeks, 2021. "Middle Pleistocene fire use: The first signal of widespread cultural diffusion in human evolution." *Proceedings of the National Academy of Sciences* 118 (31), e2101108118. DOI:10.1073/pnas.2101108118

McNabb, J. 2017. "Journeys in space and time: Assessing the link between Acheulean hand axes and genetic explanations." *Journal of Archaeological Science* 13, 403-414.

McNabb, J. 2019. "Further thoughts and the genetic argument for hand axes." *Evolutionary Anthropology* 29, 1-17. DOI:10.1002/evan.21809

Méndez-Quintas, E., M. Santonja, A. Pérez-González, M. Duval, M. Demuro, and L.J. Arnold. 2018. "First evidence of an extensive Acheulean large cutting tool accumulation in Europe from Porto Maior (Galicia, Spain)." *Scientific Reports* 8, 3082. DOI:10.1038/s41598-018-21320-1

Moncel, M.-H., C. Santagata, A. Pereira, S. Nomade, P. Voinchet, J.-J. Bahain, C. Daujeard, A. Curci, C. Lemorini, B. Hardy, G. Eramo, C. Berto, J.-P. Raynal, M. Arzarello, B. Mecozzi, A. Iannucci, R. Sardella, I. Allegretta, E. Dell'università, R. Terzano, P. Dugas, G. Jouanic, A. Queffelec, A. d'Andrea, R. Valentini,

E. Minucci, L. Carpentiero, and M. Piperno. 2020. "The origin of early Acheulean expansion in Europe 700 ka ago: new findings at Notarchirico (Italy)." *Scientific Reports* 10, 13802. DOI:10.1038/s41598-020-68617-8

Murray, J. K., 2017. *Exploring handaxe function at Shishan Marsh – 1: combining qualitative and quantitative approaches using the edge damage distribution method*. Victoria: University of Victoria Library.

Mussi, M. 1995. "The earliest occupation of Europe: Italy". In *The earliest occupation of Europe, Proceedings of the European Science Foundation Workshop at Tautavel (France), 1993* edited by W. Roebroeks and T. van Kolfschoten, 27-49. Leiden: Leiden University Press.

Pope, M., M. Roberts, and S. Parfitt. 2020. *The Horse Butchery Site GTP17: A high-resolution record of Lower Palaeolithic hominin behaviour at Boxgrove*. London: SpoilHeap Publications

Roberts, M., and S. Parfitt. 1999. *Boxgrove: A Middle Pleistocene Hominid Site at Eartham Quarry, Boxgrove, West Sussex*. London: English Heritage.

Roebroeks, W., and T. van Kolfschoten, eds. 1995. *The earliest occupation of Europe, Proceedings of the European Science Foundation Workshop at Tautavel (France), 1993*. Leiden: Leiden University Press.

Roebroeks, W., and P. Villa. 2011. "On the earliest evidence for habitual use of fire in Europe." *Proceedings of the National Academy of Sciences* 108 (13), 5209-5214. DOI:10.1073/pnas.1018116108

Sanderson, E.W. 2009. *Mannahatta. A Natural History of New York City*. New York: Abrams.

Scherjon, F., C. Bakels, K. MacDonald, and W. Roebroeks. 2015. "Burning the Land: An Ethnographic Study of Off-Site Fire Use by Current and Historically Documented Foragers and Implications for the Interpretation of Past Fire Practices in the Landscape." *Current Anthropology* 56, 299-326.

Sharon, G. 2019. "Early convergent cultural evolution: Acheulean giant core methods of Africa." In *Sqeezing minds from stones: Cognitive archaeology and the evolution of the human mind*, edited by K. A. Overmann and F. Coolidge, 237-250. New York: Oxford University Press.

Speth, J. 2022. *Archaeology, ethnohistory, early hominins, and some cherished scientific myths*. Vierenveertigste Kroon-Voordracht. Amsterdam: KNAW.

Stiner, M. 2001. "Thirty Years on the 'Broad Spectrum Revolution' and Paleolithic Demography." *Proceedings of the National Academy of Sciences* 98 (13), 6993-6996.

Thieme, H. 1997. "Lower Palaeolithic hunting spears from Germany." *Nature* 385, 807-810.

Turner, A. 1992. "Large carnivores and earliest European hominids: changing determinants of resource availability during the Lower and Middle Pleistocene." *Journal of Human Evolution* 22, 109-126.

Verheijen, I., B. M. Starkovich, J. Serangeli, T. van Kolfschoten, and N. J. Conard. 2023. "Early evidence for bear exploitation during MIS 9 from the site of Schöningen 12 (Germany)." *Journal of Human Evolution* 177, 103294. DOI: 10.1016/j. jhevol.2022.103294

Weiss, E., W. Wetterstrom, D. Nadel, and O. Bar-Yosef. 2004. "The Broad Spectrum Revisited: Evidence from Plant Remains." *Proceedings of the National Academy of Sciences* 101 (26), 9551-9555.

Wenban-Smith, F.F. 1989. "The use of canonical variates for determination of biface manufacturing technology at Boxgrove Lower Palaeolithic site and the behavioural implications of this technology." *Journal of Archaeological Science* 16 (1), 17-26.

Wragg Sykes, R. 2020. *Kindred: Neanderthal Life, Love, Death and Art.* London: Bloomsbury Sigma.

Wymer, J. 1982. *The Palaeolithic Age.* Beckenham: Croom Helm Ltd.

Wynn, T., and J. Gowlett. 2018. "The hand axe reconsidered." *Evolutionary Anthropology* 27, 21-29.

In Hussain, S.T. and G.L. Dusseldorp (eds) 2025. Sitting on the fence: Negotiating archaeology, anthropology and philosophy. Festschrift for Prof. Dr Raymond H.A. Corbey in celebration of his 70th birthday. *Analecta Praehistorica Leidensia* 54. Leiden: Sidestone Press, pp. 127-136.

# Bone hammers: Efficient but rare

## Thijs van Kolfschoten

**Thijs van Kolfschoten**

Faculty of Archaeology, Leiden University, The Netherlands & Joint International Research Laboratory of Environmental and Social Archaeology and Institute of Cultural Heritage, Shandong University, People's Republic of China

t.van.kolfschoten@arch.leidenuniv.nl

ORCID: 0000-0003-1716-3394

### ABSTRACT

The Lower Palaeolithic site of Schöningen 13 II-4, known as the spear horizon, yielded many bone tools, including bone hammers. Experiments have indicated that these hammers are efficient in fragmenting long bones to exploit the bone marrow. However, these types of bone tools are generally rare in the Palaeolithic record. The only other site with a large amount of bone hammers is Xuchang-Lingjing (China). This study explores the usage of metapodial bone hammers for marrow extraction, shedding light on their rarity in the archaeological record. While hammerstones were traditionally thought to be the primary tools for bone fracturing, experiments and archaeological findings from sites like Schöningen and Xuchang-Lingjing now suggest the utilization of metapodial bone hammers for these tasks by early hominins. Experiments involving horse and bovid bones confirm these tools' efficacy in accessing bone marrow. Despite evidence of successful use, the scarcity of metapodial hammers across various sites remains enigmatic, challenging their use as stone working tools and demanding further investigation.

*Keywords: Palaeolithic bone tools, marrow exploitation, bone fragmentation, Schöningen, Xuchang-Lingjing*

### INTRODUCTION

In his 2010 book entitled *The Paleoanthropology and Archaeology of Big-Game Hunting: Protein, Fat, or Politics*, John Speth raises thought-provoking questions as to the role of meat in the diets of prehistoric societies and earlier hominins in particular. Speth (2010) suggests that a shift in perspective has occurred among paleoanthropologists, challenging the traditional notion that meat, due to its high protein content, was a primary source of calories and nutrition in human evolution. The focus has considerably expanded to consider the potential significance of fat, particularly from large animals, in the diets of early hominins. This concept is notably emphasised in the context of brain and marrow fat, which might have been a key nutritional resource (Speth 2010, xiii).

The value of brain and marrow fat is mirrored in the archaeological record, where numerous fragmented long bones have been discovered at Palaeolithic sites (*e.g.*, Boxgrove and Swanscombe (U.K.): Smith 2013; Salzgitter-Lebenstedt (Germany): Gaudzinski and Roebroeks 2000). These bone fragments, while often interpreted as evidence of hominin marrow exploitation, are potentially subject to a range of factors that can lead to bone fracturing. These factors include trampling, carnivore bone gnawing (with hyenas being particularly effective bone crackers), weathering, and other post-burial influences. Distinguishing between natural and hominin-induced fractures, as well as discerning the role of hominins in the bone fragmentation process, has been a central focus of studies investigating the taphonomic agents responsible for the fractured bones (Behrensmeyer 1978; Lyman 1994). Researchers have tried identifying specific features on archaeological bone fragments that might indicate the agent responsible for their fragmentation (*e.g.*, Orłowska et al. 2023). Notably, studies have highlighted that certain features (*e.g.*, green bone fractures, dry bone fractures, the presence or absence of impact notches and scores) or combinations of features on bone fragments can provide clues about the agents responsible for their fracture (Lyman 1994), thereby contributing to a more comprehensive understanding of prehistoric dietary practices and bone utilization.

Bones consist of a composite material with both mineral and organic components, rendering them mechanically robust when fresh. The cortical layer of long bones, holding the sought-after bone marrow, boasts a considerable thickness. The task of breaking solid long bones, such as those from a horse, to access the marrow thus presents a challenge. Information about fracturing long bones is, however, limited. Binford (1978, 153), reports on a series of marrow-cracking experiments conducted by two Nunamiut Eskimos. They successfully cracked 23 caribou long bones, encompassing two front and six rear legs. Before this process, thorough bone cleaning was undertaken, involving the removal of all tendon and connective tissue from the bone. Additionally, the shank of the bone was meticulously scraped, leading to the removal of most of the periosteum (Binford 1978, 153). The bone-cracking procedure further involved the employment of three distinct types of tools. Johnny Rulland utilized the back of a hunting knife, while Johnny's sister, Jane, employed stones and intact long bones (specifically, a caribou humerus and a femur). In this context, the proximal head of the humerus served as the percussion point. In contrast, the femur was gripped at its proximal end, with the distal condyles serving as the designated percussion area. Binford (1978) observed that significant and recognisable impact marks were evident despite each hammer bone being used to crack only two additional marrow bones. Using bones as hammers was suggested to offer enhanced control and result in fewer, well-defined impact chips penetrating the marrow (Binford 1978, 154).

The utilization of bone hammers for the purpose of marrow cracking presents an intriguing possibility also for early hominins. Conventionally, it is hypothesized that hammerstones were employed to achieve bone fracture (Voormolen 2008). However, Binford's (1978) ethnoarchaeological observations suggest that Palaeolithic hominins might have employed traditional hammerstones and bone hammers to fracture long bones and access the marrow. Yet despite this possibility, concrete evidence from the Palaeolithic record remained scarce until the discovery of several metapodial hammers at Schöningen in northern Germany. A significant milestone in this regard is the Schö 13 II-4 site at Schöningen, which yielded an archaeological assemblage featuring multiple metacarpal and metatarsal bones exhibiting flaking and crushing damage. These traces of use have been attributed to the deployment of metapodial hammers specifically for marrow cracking (van Kolfschoten *et al.* 2015a). Xuchang-Lingjing (China) (van Kolfschoten *et al.* 2020; van Kolfschoten *et al.* in prep.) is a second Palaeolithic site, investigated by the author, that yielded an archaeological assemblage with metapodial bones with similar flaking and crushing damage.

This study reviews published experimental evidence (Hutson *et al.* 2015; Bonhof and van Kolfschoten 2021) to validate the hypothesis that bone hammers, such as those found at the Schö 13 II-4 and the Xuchang-Lingjing sites in China, were used to fracture other animal long bones, while also comparing the resulting battering damage to traces observed on the fossil bone hammers. The paper provides an overview of bone hammers from these two archaeological sites and a summary of the published experimental record, followed by concluding remarks and a discussion.

## THE SCHÖNINGEN RECORD

Situated in northern Germany, Schöningen (52°08'N/10°57'E) lies north of the Harz mountains and at the fringes of a region with (remnants of) huge open-cast lignite quarries. Pleistocene lacustrine deposits on top of the lignite-bearing sediments have yielded a notable array of dispersed archaeological sites featuring Palaeolithic artefacts, as well as botanical and faunal remains. Most of these sites originate from the late Middle Pleistocene Reinsdorf Interglacial, a period correlated with Marine Isotope Stage (MIS) 9, dating back approximately 320,000 to 300,000 years (Serangeli *et al.* 2018).

Within this complex of Middle Pleistocene hominin occupations, the Lower Palaeolithic site known as Schö 13 II-4 (also recognized as the 'Spear Horizon' in the literature) holds a pivotal place due to the discovery of wooden spears and a wooden throwing stick (Thieme 1997; Thieme 2007). Beyond these exceptional findings, the site yielded around 1,500 stone artefacts, and an expansive, highly diverse collection of large mammal remains, comprising roughly 15,000 bones and bone fragments. Notably, the assemblage is dominated by remains of the Middle Pleistocene horse species *Equus mosbachensis*. The exceptional preservation of a substantial portion of vertebrate remains at Schö 13 II-4 is related to a depositional environment characterised by anaerobic, waterlogged sediments enriched with calcium carbonate-rich groundwater (van Kolfschoten *et al.* 2015b).

Schö 13 II-4 is located at the periphery of a former lake, in a mosaic landscape with a mixture of forested areas and open grasslands (Urban *et al.* 2023). The bulk of the archaeological discoveries is notably clustered, exhibiting densities of up to 150 specimens per square meter. The finds are concentrated within a distinct 10-meter-wide strip, aligned in a north-south orientation that follows the contours of the former lake shoreline (Serangeli *et al.* 2015).

Within this assemblage, the presence of disarticulated but nearly complete skeletal remains of at least 20 horses is remarkable. These specimens exhibit clear indications of butchering by hominins. Nonetheless, it is important to highlight that not all the discovered items were necessarily accumulated through hominin activity. For instance, bones displaying more advanced stages of weathering probably reflect part of the natural background fauna, underscoring the complexity of discerning human-driven accumulation from natural site formation processes (van Kolfschoten *et al.* 2015b). That being said, a significant collection of larger mammal remains, with a notable emphasis on horse bones, exhibits well-preserved features indicative of direct hominin involvement.

Among these discoveries are distinct anthropic marks on the bones, providing insights into various butchering activities encompassing skinning, defleshing, and marrow extraction. The marks are particularly pronounced on skeletal elements rich in marrow, such as the humerus, radius, femur, and tibia (Voormolen 2008; van Kolfschoten *et al.* 2015b).

An intriguing aspect of the assemblage is the pronounced fragmentation of long bones, coupled with many impact notches, pointing towards unusually intensive marrow extraction. Many bone fragments further bear the characteristic scars of conchoidal flakes, indicative of the tools involved in these activities. Furthermore, some bones even exhibit evidence of impact depressions on their cortical surfaces, underscoring the nature of hominin interaction with these remains.

Another distinct set of deliberately induced characteristics is associated with bones that apparently served as both stone knapping tools and bone hammers. This remarkable ensemble comprises 143 bone tools, encompassing both intact bones and bone fragments. These were probably employed as percussive instruments to retouch flint tools. The bone tools show scraping marks and bear visible indications of this kind of use, manifested as discernible diagnostic traces, including well-developed pits and scores, left behind during the process of knapping lithic tools (van Kolfschoten *et al.* 2015a; Hutson *et al.* 2018). A noteworthy aspect distinguishing these organic stone working tools from Schöningen is the relatively frequent occurrence of knapping surfaces with embedded flint chips, demonstrating the physical interaction of bone and stone.

The Schöningen Lower Palaeolithic record is unique because of the additional occurrence of the so-called 'metapodial hammers' qualified as such and presented by the author in earlier work (van Kolfschoten et al. 2015a). This remarkable category of bone tools encompasses fourteen horse metapodials and a single bovid metacarpal, each bearing epiphyses marked by flaking and evident battering. The telltale signs of crushing, chipping, and flaking damage predominantly manifest along the medial and/or lateral margins of the distal condyles of these metapodia (see Fig. 1).

Strikingly, the extent of battering damage observed on a majority of the metapodials suggests the application of substantial force against rigid objects. Van Kolfschoten and colleagues (2015a) have previously argued that, given the lack of stone particles or associated marks on the respective bones and the absence of sizeable stones suitable for use as hammers or anvils within the Schö 13 II-4 deposits, the battered metapodia unearthed from Schöningen most likely served the purpose of breaking larger limb bones for marrow extraction.

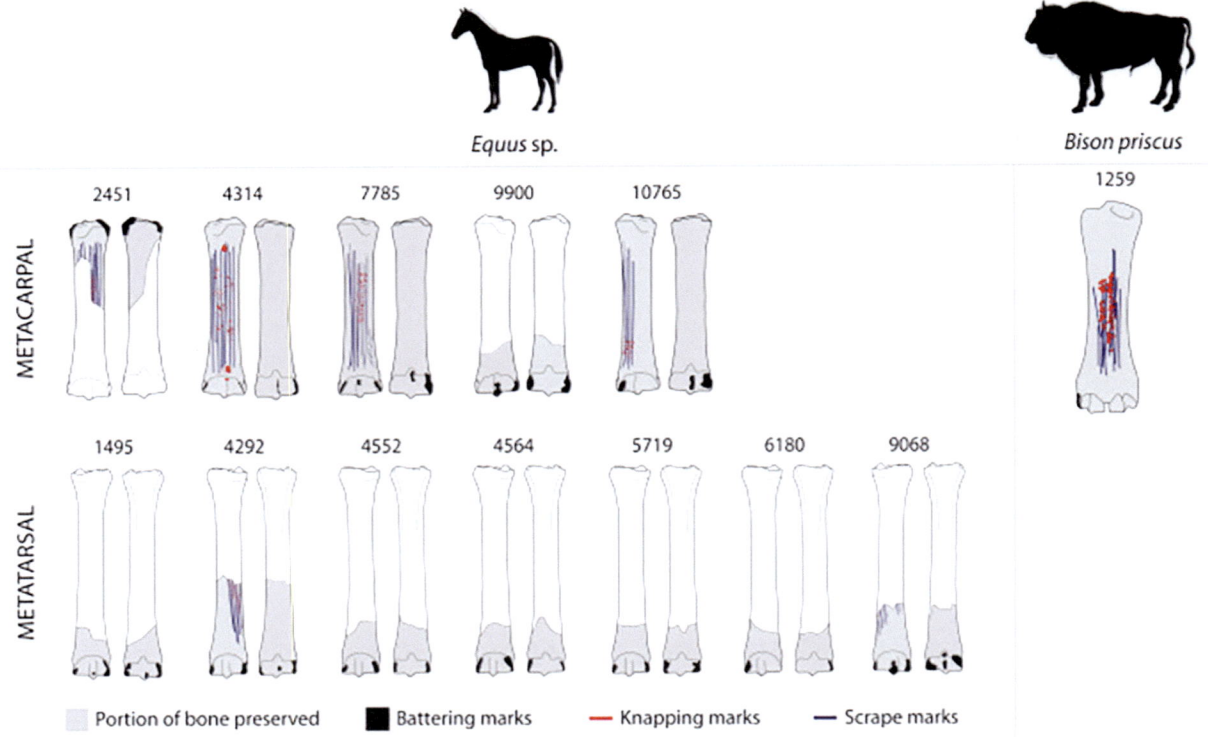

Figure 1. Metapodial hammers by taxon and anatomical element (not to scale). From: van Kolfschoten *et al.* (2015).

## THE LINGJING RECORD

The Chinese site of Xuchang-Lingjing (34⁰04'N, 113⁰41'E), c.750 km south-south-east of Beijing, provides a possible parallel to Schö 13 II-4. The site is located in modern-day Henan Province at the southern edge of the North China Plain, east of the Qinling Mountains. Layers 10 and 11 of the exposed section, dated by Optical Stimulated Luminescence (OSL) to between ~96 ± 6 ka and ~102 ± 2 ka (Layer 10) and between ≈105 ka and ≈125 ka (Layer 11) respectively, have yielded important assemblages of Middle Palaeolithic lithic artefacts and animal remains. Among the most spectacular finds from Lingjing Layer 11 are two incomplete human skulls (Xuchang 1 and Xuchang 2: Li *et al.* 2017). Considering the stratigraphical age of the skulls and the geographical position of the site, they might be Denisovan skulls as suggested by Martinón-Torres *et al.* (2017).

The more than 40,000 faunal remains from the lower part of Level 10 and from Level 11 together represent at least 20 mammalian species characteristic of a grassland-dominated palaeo-environment, with a mosaic of scattered forest and mixed forest vegetation (Wang *et al.* 2021). Xuchang-Lingjing is interpreted as an open-air kill-butchery site located at the edge of a former lake.

Hominins played a pivotal role in shaping the composition of the Xuchang-Lingjing faunal assemblage, which notably features an abundance of prime-adult specimens from two predominant prey species: onager (*Equus hemionus*) and aurochs (*Bos primigenius*). Evident cut marks, indicative of disarticulation and meat retrieval, are preserved on the upper and lower limb bones. Notably, the number of complete bones within the Xuchang-Lingjing assemblage is very low. The 2017 Lingjing excavation of layers 10 and 11 yielded 976 and 1260 finds respectively: 85% of the zooarchaeological finds from Layer 10 and 70% from Layer 11 are less than 5 cm long (Doyon *et al.* 2019). This high degree of fragmentation is consistent with hominin exploitation of marrow.

Three different types of bone tools have been discovered in the archaeological assemblages of Xuchang-Lingjing Layer 10 and 11: 1) deliberately knapped long-bone fragments with a high number of flake scares (Doyon *et al.* 2021), 2) a few dozen bone retouchers used in passive and active pressure flaking activities (Doyon *et al.* 2019), and 3) metapodial bone hammers (see Fig. 2).

Figure 2. Metatarsal bone (10L3152) of an Aurochs *Bos primigenius* with obvious battering damage from Xuchang-Lingjing. The outer edge of the medial epiphyse shows chipping and crushing damage and the lateral epiphyse is broken off. Left: anterior view; right: distal view.

Numerous metapodial bones and metapodial bone fragments exhibit modification patterns indicative of battering damage, strongly suggesting their use as bone hammers. The observed patterns of crushing, chipping, and flaking damage are primarily localized along the medial and/or lateral margins of the distal condyles of metapodials of large herbivore bones, including those of equids (approximately 20 specimens), cervids (2 specimens), and bovids (>150 specimens). The most severe form of damage documented on the metapodial hammers are diaphyseal and/or distal fractures. All the distal epiphyses and the diaphysis of the metacarpal and metatarsal bones identified as being used as hammer are fused, which indicates that only bones of adult individuals are used.

The distal metacarpal and metatarsal bones from both equid species, *Equus* cf. *przewalskii* and *Equus hemionus*, display a range of damage types. These span from initial stages of crushing damage along the lateral and/or medial sides and the medial ridge to the absence of big flakes and major crushing and chipping damage at the lateral and medial edges of the epiphyses. In the case of aurochs metapodials, their abundance is striking. Given the extensive size variation observed, it is evident that both male and female aurochs are well-represented within the bone tool assemblage.

The collection of aurochs bone hammers presents a spectrum of battering damage, encompassing a range from no discernible damage to incipient, minor, and major damage variants. Within the context of major damage, this extends beyond mere crushing encompassing chipping and flaking damage, in addition to instances of transverse breaks positioned just above the distal epiphyses. These fractures frequently result in the absence of one, and in several cases, both distal epiphyses (cf. Fig. 2). This phenomenon helps elucidate the presence of a considerable quantity (approximately 70) of isolated epicondyles, many of which exhibit signs of both crushing and chipping damage.

## THE EXPERIMENTAL RECORD

To test the potential utilization of archaeological bone hammers for fracturing long bones to access bone marrow by early hominins, a series of experiments were conducted using both horse and bovid bones.

The first set of experiments was devised and executed by Wouter Bonhof and André Ramcharan from the Faculty of Archaeology, Leiden University (the Netherlands) (Bonhof and van Kolfschoten 2021). Fresh horse (*Equus caballus)* bones, comprising 14 metapodia and 13 designated target long bones, were used for this study. Following the removal of horse meat, the metapodia and target bones for marrow extraction (humerus, radius, femur, tibia) underwent careful disarticulation and cleaning.

In this experimental setup, the target bones were hit at both the proximal and distal ends of the diaphysis at areas that showcase the highest percentage of impact marks in the archaeological assemblage from

Schöningen 13 II-4 (Voormolen 2008). The diaphyseal cortex is relatively thin in these regions (Sisson and Daniels Grossman 1938), and the bone mineral density of the cortex is notably lower at the proximal and distal ends of the diaphyseal shaft (Lam *et al.* 1999).

The target bones were struck with the metapodia until either the target bone was broken and access to the bone marrow was achieved (n=8) or until the metapodium became unusable (n=5). One experiment was terminated because after 102 impacts, the cortical bone of the respective femur only had a crushed area remaining, and no distinct fracture line, indicative of an impending break, was visible.

Only one remained undamaged out of the fourteen metapodia subjected to the experiments (Fig. 3). Three specimens experienced complete fractures, while the remaining twelve exhibited evident flaking, chipping, and crushing damage, affecting either one or both sides (lateral and medial) of the epicondyle. Battering damage on the distal epicondyles spanned a spectrum from minimal impact to severe crushing and flaking. Notably, the articular surfaces of the distal epiphyses of these metapodia exhibited cortical material loss in the range of 5 to 10 mm in the form of flakes. The experimental metapodia all yielded varying degrees of crushing and flaking damage, a variation that is also observed in the metapodial assemblage from Schöningen (Van Kolfschoten *et al.* 2015a; Hutson *et al.* 2018) as well as from Xuchang-Lingjing (van Kolfschoten *et al.* in prep.).

Among the thirteen successful horse bone experiments, eight yielded outcomes comparable to the archaeological patterns observed, thereby affirming the hypothesis posited by Van Kolfschoten *et al.* (2015a): horse metapodia were most likely used to fracture other long bones at Schö 13 II-4. These experimental results offer compelling comparative evidence of the high efficacy of horse metapodial hammers in effectively fragmenting long bones for bone marrow exploitation.

But what about the bovid bone hammers? What does experimental evidence reveal about the possible use context of archaeological bovid metapodia? Hutson *et al.* (2015) have previously undertaken a series of experiments involving young adult bovid bones (*Bos taurus*) to explore the feasibility of breaking limb bones from the same species. Their findings similarly corroborated the effectiveness of metapodials as tools for fracturing other limb bones. In their experimental setup, they used a set of five metatarsal bones as bone hammers, alongside six designated target bones comprising two humeri, two ulnae/radii, one femur, and a single tibia. Across seven trials in their experiment, Hutson and his team utilized the distal ends of bovid metatarsi to break other limb bones. In these trials, they succeeded in fracturing three target bones (humerus, femur, and tibia) after a respective tally of 8, 5, and 53 impacts. The experiments were terminated in the remaining four trials due to the metatarsal breaking before reaching the target bone. The successful trials resulted in minimal damage to the distal condyles, manifesting as slight crushing marks. In contrast, the metatarsal bones used in the unsuccessful trials exhibited evident signs of crushing, flaking, and fractures spanning both the shaft and the condyle. These results show the range of damages one may expect in the fossil record. However, the picture is most probably incomplete due to the low number of experiments executed by Hutson and colleagues (2015).

## DISCUSSION AND CONCLUSION

The experiments that were conducted can be interpreted as evidence that even individuals without specialized expertise can effectively fracture the limb bones of horses or bovids using metapodial bone hammers, thereby facilitating access to valuable bone marrow. Furthermore, the battering damage patterns observed on the bone hammers utilized in these experiments exhibit a striking resemblance to those on metapodial bones found in the Lower Palaeolithic assemblages from Schöningen and the Middle Palaeolithic assemblage from Xuchang-Lingjing. This pronounced similarity substantiates the assumption that metapodial bones can be used to fracture long bones. It validates the hypotheses formulated by van Kolfschoten *et al.* (2015a), affirming the role of bone hammers in the practice of marrow exploitation.

Boudewijn Voormolen (Leiden University, the Netherlands) initially recognized the battering damage on horse metapodials from Schöningen 13 II-4, proposing that such damage could have stemmed from stone working activities (Voormolen, 2008). Hutson *et al.* (2018) later put this hypothesis to the test, suggesting that stone working might offer an alternative explanation for the observed battering damage. However, this notion has now been largely refuted, as outlined by arguments presented by Bonhof and van Kolfschoten (2021). A central counterargument is the absence of stone chips embedded in the bone-knapping tools and the lack of accompanying scars on the metapodia.

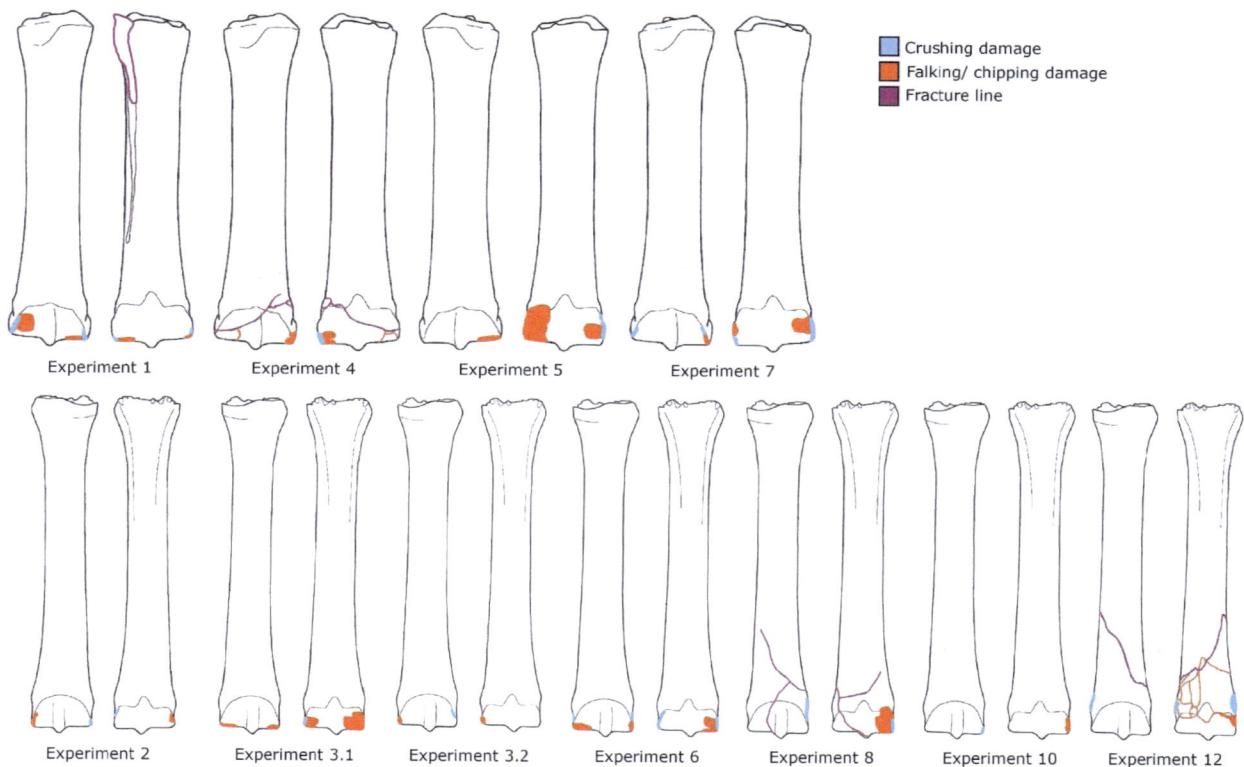

Figure 3. Schematic overview of the distribution and type of damage present on the horse metapodia used in the experimental setup. The metapodia from Experiments 9, 11, and 13 are not depicted, as they did not yield enough visual damage to determine damage type and location. Top row: metacarpals. Bottom row: metatarsals. From: Bonhof and van Kolfschoten (2021).

The utilization of horse and large bovid metapodia as bone tools to fracture limb bones and access bone marrow is remarkably effective. These tools are characterized by their simplicity, practicality, and efficacy, and the distinctive pattern of battering damage observed on the metapodia further reinforces their identification as bone hammers.

Numerous Middle and Late Palaeolithic sites indicate extensive marrow exploitation (Gaudzinski-Windheuser and Niven 2009) which supports Speth's assumption that marrow fat was a key nutritional resource (Speth 2010). Despite the co-occurrence of fractured limb bones and horse and/or large bovid metapodials, the presence of bone hammers is, however, surprisingly rare. Notably, only the two aforementioned sites, Schöningen 13 II-4 and Xuchang-Lingjing, have yielded a significant number of metapodial bone hammers. This being said, Parfitt et al. (2022) have recently reported three similar bone hammers at the Lower Palaeolithic site of Clacton-on-

Sea (UK), which include a Bison metatarsal used for knapping flint.

The limited documentation of metapodial hammers in Palaeolithic contexts presents an intriguing puzzle. It seems improbable that they have consistently been overlooked, but this is possible. Notably, both the here-described experiments (Bonhof and van Kolfschoten 2021) and earlier experimental trials (Hutson et al. 2018) produced instances where bone hammers sustained no discernible battering damage, even after tallies of 102 and 53 blows, respectively. This underscores the potential importance of bone hammers even when diagnostic traces are lacking, which may render their use invisible in some contexts.

Another point should be considered. The conventional role of hammer stones in bone-breaking during the Palaeolithic (e.g., Pickering and Egeland 2006) raises the possibility that bone hammers were used in the absence of such tools, as the case for example at Schöningen 13 II-4. However, this explanation falls short when considering the substantial number of hammer stones represented at Xuchang-Lingjing. The latter site yielded a significant assemblage of mineral hammer tools, thus leaving the question of why bone hammers used for bone fracturing have so far been observed only at two distinct locations, both geographically and chronologically.

This enigmatic pattern poses a compelling challenge for further investigation and understanding but may point to considerable situational flexibility of behaviour and tool use in the Middle Pleistocene.

## Acknowledgements

This paper is a tribute to commemorate the 70th birthday of Raymond Corbey. Throughout the years, Raymond has consistently remained a source of inspiration and a valued colleague. Raymond, thank you for contextualizing my research within a broader historical framework. I also extend my appreciation to the editors of the *Festschrift*, Gerrit Dusseldorp and Shumon Hussain, for the invitation to contribute and Shumon Hussain for his valuable suggestions to improve the original manuscript. Lastly, I thank André Ramcharan from Leiden University for his invaluable contribution to the bone hammer experiments.

## References

Behrensmeyer, A.K. 1978. "Taphonomic and ecologic information from bone weathering." *Paleobiology* 4, 150-162.

Binford, L.R. 1978. *Nunamiut Ethnoarchaeology*. New York: Academic Press.

Bonhof, W.J., and T. van Kolfschoten. 2021. "The metapodial hammers from the Lower Palaeolithic site of Schöningen 13 II-4 (Germany): The results of experimental research." *Journal of Archaeological Science: Reports* 35, 13. DOI: 10.1016/j.jasrep.2020.102685

Doyon, L., H. Li, Z.Y. Li, H. Wang, and Q. Zhao. 2019. "Further evidence of organic soft hammer percussion and pressure retouch from Lingjing (Xuchang, Henan, China)." *Lithic Technology* 44, 100-117.

Doyon, L., Z.Y. Li, H. Wang, L. Geis, and F. d'Errico. 2021. "A 115,000-year-old expedient bone technology at Lingjing, Henan, China." PLoS ONE 16 (5), e0250156. DOI: 10.1371/journal.pone.0250156

Gaudzinski-Windheuser, S., and L. Niven. 2009. "Hominin Subsistence Patterns During the Middle and Late Paleolithic in Northwestern Europe." In *The Evolution of Hominin Diets*, edited by J.-J. Hublin, and M.P. Richards, 99-111. Dordrecht: Springer.

Gaudzinski-Windheuser, S., and W. Roebroeks. 2000. "Adults only. Reindeer hunting at the Middle Palaeolithic site Salzgitter-Lebenstedt, Northern Germany." *Journal of Human Evolution* 38 (4), 497-521.

Hutson, J.M., A. Villaluenga, A. García-Moreno, E. Turner, and S. Gaudzinski-Windheuser. 2018. "On the use of metapodials as tools at Schöningen 13II-4." In *The Origins of Bone Tool Technologies: Retouching the Palaeolithic: Becoming Human and the Origins of Bone Tool Technology*, edited by J.M. Hutson, A. García-Moreno, E.S. Noack, E. Turner, A. Villaluenga Martínez, and S. Gaudzinski, 53-91. Mainz: Verlag des Römisch-Germanischen Zentralmuseums.

Lam, Y., X. Chen, and O. Pearson. 1999. "Intertaxonomic variability in patterns of bone density and the differential representation of Bovid, Cervid, and Equid Elements in the Archaeological Record." *American Antiquity* 64 (2), 343-362.

Li, Z.Y., X.-J. Wu, L.-P. Zhou, W. Liu, X. Gao, X.-M. Nian, and E. Trinkaus. 2017. "Late Pleistocene archaic human crania from Xuchang, China." *Science* 355, 969-972.

Lyman, R.L. 1994. *Vertebrate Taphonomy*. Cambridge: Cambridge University Press.

Martinón-Torres, M., X. Wu, J. María Bermúdez de Castro, S. Xing, and W. Liu. 2027. "*Homo sapiens* in the Eastern Asian Late Pleistocene." *Current Anthropology* 58, 434-448.

Orłowska, J., K. Cyrek, G.P. Kaczmarczyk, W. Migal, and G. Osipowicz. 2023. "Rediscovery of the Palaeolithic antler hammer from Biśnik Cave, Poland: New insights into its chronology, raw material, technology of production and function." *Quaternary International* 665-666, 48-64.

Pickering, T., and C. Egeland. 2006. "Experimental zooarchaeology and its role in defining the investigative parameters of the behavior of Early Stone Age hominids." *Journal of Archaeological Science* 33, 459-469.

Serangeli, J., U. Böhner, T. van Kolfschoten, and N.J. Conard. 2015. "New results from large-scale excavations in Schöningen," *Journal of Human Evolution* 89, 27-45.

Serangeli, J., B. Rodríguez-Álvarez, M. Tucci, I. Verheijen, G. Bigga, U. Böhner, B. Urban, T. van Kolfschoten, and N.J. Conard. 2018. "The Project Schöningen from an ecological and cultural perspective." *Quaternary Science Reviews* 198, 140-155.

Sisson, S., and J.D. Grossman. 1938. *Anatomy of the Domesticated Animals.* Philadelphia: W.B. Saunders Company.

Speth, J.D. 2010. *The Paleoanthropology and Archaeology of Big-Game Hunting: Protein, Fat or Politics?* New York: Springer.

Thieme, H. 1997. "Lower Palaeolithic hunting spears from Germany." *Nature* 385, 807-810.

Thieme, H. 2007. *Die Schöninger Speere – Mensch und Jagd vor 400 000 Jahren.* Stuttgart: Theiss Verlag.

Urban, B., T. Kasper, K.J. Krahn, T. van Kolfschoten, B. Rech, M. Holzheu, M. Tucci, and A. Schwalb. 2023. "Landscape dynamics and chronological refinement of the Middle Pleistocene Reinsdorf Sequence of Schöningen, NW Germany." *Quaternary Research* 114, 148-177.

van Kolfschoten, T., E. Buhrs, and I. Verheijen. 2015b. "The larger mammal fauna from the Lower Paleolithic Schöningen Spear site and its contribution to hominin subsistence." *Journal of Human Evolution* 89, 138 -153.

van Kolfschoten, T., Z. Li, H. Wang, and L. Doyon. 2020. "The Middle Palaeolithic site Lingjing (Xuchang, Henan, China): preliminary new results." *Analecta Praehistorica Leidensia* 50, 21-28.

van Kolfschoten, T., S.A. Parfitt, J. Serangeli, and S.M. Bello. 2015a. "Lower Paleolithic bone tools from the "Spear Horizon" at Schöningen (Germany)." *Journal of Human Evolution* 89, 226-263.

Voormolen, B. 2008. *Ancient hunters – modern butchers: Schöningen 13 II-4, a kill-butchery site dating from the northwest European Lower Palaeolithic.* Unpublished Doctoral Dissertation, Leiden University.

Wang, H., Z. Li, H. Tong, and T. van Kolfschoten. 2021. "Hominin paleoenvironment in East Asia: The Middle Paleolithic Xuchang-Lingjing (China) mammalian evidence." *Quaternary International* 633, 118-133.

In Hussain, S.T. and G.L. Dusseldorp (eds) 2025. Sitting on the fence: Negotiating archaeology, anthropology and philosophy. Festschrift for Prof. Dr Raymond H.A. Corbey in celebration of his 70th birthday. *Analecta Praehistorica Leidensia* 54. Leiden: Sidestone Press, pp. 137-150.

# Diamonds are an early 20th century archaeologist's best friend – On the interactions between diamond mining and Acheulean archaeology

Gerrit L. Dusseldorp

## ABSTRACT

A review of the interaction of South African diamond-mining with Stone Age archaeology shows that the occurrence of rich Acheulean stone tool assemblages in diamond-bearing river gravels has been instrumental in shaping the early understanding of the South African archaeological chrono-cultural sequence. Current relations between the heritage sector and diamond mining are more ambiguous and sometimes adversarial, focused on the mitigation of destruction of cultural heritage. However, the co-occurrence of handaxes and diamonds in river gravels appears to be an artefact of taphonomy, rather than rooted in early hominin behaviours focused on diamond-bearing gravels.

*Keywords: Archaeological classification, Earlier Stone Age, Acheulean, South Africa, Vaal River, Diamond mining*

## INTRODUCTION

One exhibit in The *African Peoples Hall* in the American Museum of Natural History in New York showcases an important archaeological by-product of South African diamond extraction in the late 19th and 20th century (figure 1). Among ethnographic dioramas, currently themselves of great epistemological interest (Schildkrout and Lacey 2017), and material culture from human societies from across the continent one encounters a geological cross-section of the Vaal River deposits, illustrating the types of archaeological artefacts, occurring in the differently-aged river terraces.

Exhibitions in this section of the museum are gradually being upgraded, so this fascinating window into the southern African Stone Age sequence may not be on display for much longer. From a museological point of view, this is undoubtedly the right choice. After all, the depicted typological sequence is now considered outdated (Underhill 2011), and modern-day museum visitors expect much more slickly styled, interactive displays, with touchscreens, moving images and sound effects. Yet, there is a niche audience for which this display is of huge interest, among which I count Raymond Corbey, as well as myself. The fluvial terraces of the Vaal and Gariep (previously Orange) rivers played a seminal role in the establishment of a chronocultural sequence of the African Stone Age (Goodwin and Van Riet Lowe 1929; also see Underhill 2011). These insights were afforded by countless diamond diggings opening windows into the archaeological contents of the fluvial gravels of southern Africa's main river system.

**Gerrit L. Dusseldorp**
Faculty of Archaeology, Leiden University, The Netherlands
g.l.dusseldorp@arch.leidenuniv.nl
ORCID 0000-0001-6147-710X

Figure 1. Schematic cross-section of the Vaal river valley and its terraces with representative examples of stone artefacts found in the different deposits. This geological understanding of the landscape was based in great part on the study of artefacts exposed in diamond diggings.

The association of Acheulean bifaces and diamonds is clearly a source of fascination for Raymond Corbey, who has throughout the years frequently brought this up time and again in our conversations. And while his teaching always emphasises the importance of understanding the research history of a topic. This encounter in a New York museum led me to explore the changing relationship between diamond extraction and Stone Age archaeology in southern Africa, from the formulation of the chronocultural sequence in the early 20th century to recent, more adversarial

relationships. I end by reviewing the possible causes of the co-occurrence of lithic artefacts and diamonds and on the role of "bling" in the Pleistocene archaeology of southern Africa.

## Overcoming "the failings of Geology"

The first attempts to formulate a typology of southern African Stone Age materials were based on a comparison of South African materials with European stone tools. This led to the adoption of European naming conventions for chronological divisions. Peringuey (1911), director of the South African Museum in Cape Town, proposed the Chellean, Acheulean, Mousterian, Solutrean, Magdalenian and Azilian assemblage-sequence in South Africa, yet remarked "that these South African implements do not fit in with the classification that answers to the requirements of, and is founded upon, the evidence obtained in Europe." (Peringuey 1911, 8).

Early classifications of stone artefacts in South Africa, largely based on surface finds, focused mainly on the comparisons of artefact shape coupled with assumptions on technological development or (cognitive) progress (*e.g.*, Gooch 1882). The degree of weathering was proposed to be a marker of the artefacts' antiquity (Penning 1887). This was increasingly recognised to be unsatisfactory and materials from stratified contexts were sought after. Some excavations were conducted in caves. The main objective appears to have been the search for human skeletal remains as few stratigraphic observations were made, and many finds were assumed to belong to relatively recent Khoe and San populations (Peringuey 1911, 143-174). Peringuey (1911, 5-6) observes that types that "might be assimilated perhaps to the Aurignacian or Magdalenian, they are exposed on the surface, or occur in shell mounds or in rock-shelters", but that presumably older materials which he classified as Chellean-Mousterian "are bedded in alluvial deposits, often very deeply." (Peringuey 1911, 6).

Here the increasing interest in human prehistory fortuitously coincided with the increasing importance of diamond mining. Diamonds were first discovered in South Africa in secondary position in fluvial sediments deposited by the Gariep River, but soon after also in primary position in pipes of volcanic rock, Kimberlite.[1]

The Vaal and Gariep have eroded various diamond-bearing sediments and redeposited them along their course and offshore of South Africa's West Coast. The diamond discoveries in the second half of the 19th century precipitated intensive prospection and mining activities (Underhill 2011). Large-scale prospection of alluvial sediments in the interior of South Africa thus led to numerous exposures of river gravels found also to contain Stone Age artefacts.

Diamond mining thus provided opportunities to describe the stratigraphic succession of different types of archaeological artefacts. The Vaal and Gariep valleys

present a complex succession of river terraces, and interpreting these deposits and their archaeological and palaeontological contents proved challenging at first. Early exploration of diamond cuttings, for example, sometimes reveals the co-occurrence of Pleistocene artefacts and more recent material such as ceramics, said to be comparable to those produced by contemporary KhoeSan people. Some of the lithics show traces of aeolian weathering, suggesting that they were incorporated as surface materials into the respective fluvial sediments only much later (Peringuey 1911, 58). Peringuey summarised the problem as follows:

*"Great, almost unsurmountable, therefore are the difficulties fronting the Antiquarian in South Africa: first, because geology and palaeontology fail him in affording precise indications of an old period from which deductions other than speculative might be drawn," Peringuey (1911, 8).*

This "failing" of geology was blamed on the absence of clear Ice Age markers in southern Africa, which would have resulted in faunal turnovers and provided clear stratigraphic evidence for a sediment's antiquity (Peringuey 1911; 1915).

## YES, THE RIVER KNOWS: A STONE AGE SEQUENCE TAKES SHAPE

Working with river terrace successions is nevertheless a staple of early prehistory. The early decades of the 20th century continued to bring to light archaeological and palaeontological materials in diamond cuttings. The study of these materials increasingly provided a relative temporal framework for archaeological chronologies and the faunal succession (biostratigraphy) in the region (*e.g.*, Haugton 1921; Hodgkinson 1926).

The Vaal and Gariep diamond cuttings were also studied at this time by Robert Broom and Raymond Dart, who would go on to be among South Africa's great palaeoanthropologists. Just like Boucher de Perthes in 18th century France, the South Africans gave much attention to the recurrent association between certain stone tools and the remains of Pleistocene animals. Broom, who would later describe *Paranthropus robustus*, published a paper (1913) *Man contemporaneous with extinct animals in South Africa*, where he observed that extinct mammal species co-occur with stone tools in the river gravels, but that due to the problematic geological context it is difficult to be certain that they were contemporaneous. He

---

1   https://www.capetowndiamondmuseum.org/about-diamonds/south-african-diamond-history/

established contemporaneity at a nearby spring, however, now known as the site of Florisbad (Broom 1913). Dart, who in 1925 described the famous Taung child (*Australopithecus africanus*) from a nearby limestone quarry (Dart 1925), reported mammoth teeth found together with stone tools in a former riverbed of the Vaal. He stated:

*"There is no lithic problem of greater urgency than that of the separation of the different age strata and there is every likelihood that the Vaal river in this respect will be of premier value,"* Dart (1927, 44).

The lithic problem alluded to by Dart was ultimately solved by (one of) South Africa's "father(s) of archaeology", John Goodwin (South African Archaeological Society 1972). He also worked on the terrace sequences of the Vaal and Gariep rivers, which in places are extremely rich in stone artefacts. Goodwin proposed that a South African naming system should emancipate itself from European terminology (Underhill 2011). He devised such a system with his colleague John Van Riet Lowe, published as the seminal work, *The Stone Age cultures of South Africa* (Goodwin and Van Riet Lowe 1929). In subsequent years, the sequence was refined numerous times (*e.g.*, Van Riet Lowe 1952) for the Earlier Stone Age – almost solely based on the study of diamond cuttings.

Goodwin and Van Riet Lowe (1929) introduced the tripartite division of the southern African Stone Age into an Earlier, Middle and Later Stone Age, which is still in use across the African continent today (see Lombard *et al.* 2012; 2022). The main periods were further subdivided into specific stone artefact industries, whose relative position was informed by diamond exposures providing information on their stratigraphic succession and thus relative chronology. The Earlier Stone Age, for example, contains the Stellenbosch, Victoria West and Fauresmith industries. The first two are now grouped as Acheulean, while the Fauresmith is thought to represent a transitional phenomenon between the Acheulean and the Middle Stone Age, characterised by prepared core technology (Lombard *et al.* 2012; 2022).

The potential of so-called eoliths was also discussed in this early work, but Goodwin and Van Riet Lowe (1929) recognised that some "crude" tools may have that appearance because of lower quality raw materials and they realised that other processes could also produce tool-like forms in stone. Up to now, Oldowan assemblages (which might have appeared to early workers as eoliths) have been reported

at limestone caves near Johannesburg (notably Sterkfontein and Swartkrans), but also at Wonderwerk Cave, in the Northern Cape province, located only about 50 km Northeast of the Vaal River Valley (Lombard 2012; 2022). In this regard, the report of reworked Oldowan artefacts in Van Riet Lowe's (1952) update on the Vaal River chronology is intriguing, they may represent similar objects to what earlier workers termed eoliths. The current consensus is that no bona fide Oldowan assemblages are known from the Vaal and Gariep river gravels, and that Oldowan assemblages are only known from limestone cave sites.

Overall, the developing understanding of the chronocultural sequence of southern Africa's Stone Age can be cast as a by-product of diamond mining activities, but the relation between archaeology and early diamond mining may have been even more reciprocal, as already outlined by Goodwin and Van Riet Lowe:

*"In other words, if an experienced digger discovers Stellenbosch-type remains in a gravel, he immediately feels that the chances are a thousand to one that he will also discover diamonds,"* Goodwin and Van Riet Lowe (1929, 39).

## Diamond diggers – Handaxes as industrial nuisance

Archaeological practice is no longer closely tied to diamond extraction. Whereas Goodwin and Van Riet Lowe constructed their 1929 chronocultural framework in large part by "travelling widely and observing diamond diggings" (Underhill 2011, 6), this is no longer practically possible. Both the character of diamond exploitation and of archaeological research have fundamentally changed, resulting in the structural decoupling of both activities.

In the early 20th century, the high value of diamonds led to large-scale investment in manual and lightly mechanised labour, providing archaeologists with insight into deposits that would otherwise be inaccessible. With the increasing mechanisation and the consolidation of diamond mining into progressively larger-scale companies and operations not only in the primary deposits, but also of alluvial deposits, the high value of diamonds now had adverse effects. Diamond mining can be profitable even if as little as one carat (0,2 gram) of diamond is recovered per 100 tons of gravel (Leader 2016)! This calculation is predicated on quick and efficient sediment removal and makes diamond quarries no longer suitable for detailed geological and archaeological observations, if only from a health and safety point of view (figure 2). Much of the destruction of the archaeological record therefore happens "out of sight", as large-scale mining operations may not aid the recognition of important deposits and finds and so the exact destructive impact of mining on archaeological research is difficult to evaluate.

At the same time, archaeologists now require far more detailed information to address their research questions. Collections of selected (often striking) stone artefacts are no longer sufficient, as most archaeologists aim to analyse complete and context-secure assemblages of such artefacts. Indeed, the sedimentary context is considered crucial to understand the formation and character of lithic assemblages and their technological background. Unfortunately, the documentation of the provenance of early Acheulean stone artefact material recovered from diamond digs is often poor (Leader 2009), and recent archaeological work in the course of diamond mining has been hampered by difficult circumstances of collection, with materials for example collected *ex situ* from conveyor belts and spoil heaps (figure 3; Leader 2009; Kuman and Gibbon 2018).

Figure 2. Exposure of the Rietputs formation in a diamond quarry. Archaeologist George Leader examines the lower exposures. Photo courtesy of George Leader.

Figure 3. Archaeologist Justin du Piesanie scanning a conveyor belt at a diamond quarry for stone artefacts. Photograph: courtesy of George Leader.

Counteracting the potential destruction of archaeological sites by large-scale mining throughout the 20th century, the legal protection of archaeological remains has gradually been strengthened in South Africa. Deacon (1993) described how the *Bushman Relics Act* of 1911 proscribed the export of archaeological materials and rock art. With the *National Monuments Act* of 1969, archaeological remains in the ground gained some protection, but mining operations, inter alia, are exempted from the obligation to protect archaeological sites (Humphreys 1973; Deacon 1993). Yet, there are some exceptions: caves, rockshelters and shell middens are protected from such extractive activities (Deacon 1993). As seems to be the case in other regions of the world, archaeology was subsumed under legislation managing the environmental impact of large building projects. In South Africa, this is signalled by the *Environment Conservation Act* of 1989 (Deacon 1993; Chirikure 2014). Destruction of archaeological sites under this legal framework is "mitigated" by allowing for the documentation and (partial) excavation of sites.

In 1994, for example, the removal of dune sand along the coast in the extreme north-west of South Africa to exploit diamond-bearing beach gravels, revealed two rockshelter sites – Boegoeberg 1 and 2 (Klein *et al.* 1999). When they were initially recognised, unfortunately only after one of them was largely destroyed, they were systematically excavated. The destroyed rockshelter appears to have contained a Middle Stone Age shell midden, while the other subsequently excavated rockshelter revealed mainly hyena activities (Klein and Cruz-Uribe 1996; Klein *et al.* 1999).

With the advent of civic democracy in South Africa, a new legal framework to deal with cultural heritage was needed that remedied the imbalance of Apartheid-era legislation, which prioritised the preservation of colonial heritage over African people's heritage (Deacon 1993, 2015). This ultimately led to the *National Heritage Resources Act* of 1999 (Deacon 2015). Any development now had to consider the archaeological values of the target terrain and take steps for appropriate management (Fourie 2008). As a result, in the current system much effort is expended in such mitigation before any mining activities can take place. However, the kind of mitigation generally depends upon the results of surface surveys and oral histories, and more recent archaeological remains may thus be better protected than ancient, buried sites.

Mitigation may also be conducted on a wider scale through sponsoring. The De Beers Diamond mining company for example has been an important driving force in the (ultimately successful) nomination for World Heritage status of the Mapungubwe Cultural Landscape (Chirikure and Mathoho n.d.). The company has donated land and sponsored archaeological research in the area around its Venetia Diamond mine, located in the World Heritage site's buffer zone. The company also includes archaeological impacts in its environmental incident reporting (De Beers Group 2013).

### Canteen Kopje

Although legal frameworks and policies are now in place to balance the demands of mining with the management of heritage sites, conflict still arises, not only in southern Africa but worldwide. This is especially the case if heritage sites are assessed as important enough to warrant preservation, as this takes off the table the option to continue extractive activities after "mitigation" (generally the mapping and archaeological excavation of (part of) the site). A few years ago, such a conflict played out at the important Early and Middle Stone Age site of Canteen Kopje.

After the discovery of diamonds, a "diamond rush" centred on the town of Klipdrift (now called Barkly West) on the Vaal river. A hill (*kopje* or *koppie* in Afrikaans), with gravel deposits on its northwestern side flanked by the current Vaal river to the south and by a now dry palaeo-channel to the north saw early alluvial diamond exploitation from the 1860s onwards (De Wit 2008; Chazan *et al.* 2020). Both open pits and underground mines into the diamond-bearing gravels were exploited (Chazan *et al.* 2020). After an initial rush, the intensity of diamond exploitation at the location diminished from 1871, as attention shifted to more profitable primary diamond-bearing sediments at Kimberley, but the exploitation continued well into the 20th century (De Wit 2008; Chazan *et al.* 2020). As the location of South Africa's first diamond mine, the historic archaeology of the site of Canteen Kopje is of considerable scientific interest. It documents the material culture of a mining society composed of people of many different social groups and backgrounds, before centralised governmental control severely restricted access to the industry. The site documents intensive exploitation of the now-extinct quagga, and a mixed material culture with elements of Tswana and European ceramics, and fragments of retouched glass bottles, presumably produced by KhoeSan people (Chazan *et al.* 2020).

The site was declared a national monument for a different reason though. In the gravel deposits, not only diamonds were recovered, but also great quantities of stone tools. The site is indeed so rich in bifaces that the *eminence grise* of Stone Age archaeology, Abbé Breuil, said of it: "Not only are there enough specimens to fill a museum to overflowing, but to build it of them also" (Clark 1959, 127). In 1929, a human skull, said by Broom (1929) to be heavily fossilised, was discovered at the location, further adding to the site's archaeological and societal significance. A recent re-investigation demonstrated the skull to be of very recent in age, however, representing historic populations from the area rather than an early Stone Age person (Smith *et al.* 2012). The site has been listed as a national monument since 1948 (Jones 2016a), and at this time diamond mining stopped (Chazan *et al.* 2020).

Canteen Kopje is of great archaeological importance as the site documents a long succession of different stone tool technologies, with a sequence of multiple Acheulean assemblages, showing changes in core organisation (described as "simple" and "organized" cores), followed by Acheulean assemblages with Victoria West cores, overlain by Fauresmith assemblages, as well as Middle and Later Stone Age assemblages (*e.g.,* Forssman *et al.* 2010; Li *et al.* 2017; Kuman, Lotter and Leader 2020). Assemblage integrity varies, but the presence of small flaking debris throughout the sequence suggests it represents one of the very few deeply stratified sequences where a good impression of the entire *chaîne opératoire* can be obtained (Lotter *et al.* 2016).

The occurrence of Victoria West technology at the site has been interpreted as an early development of prepared core technology (Li *et al.* 2017). Victoria West cores can be seen as a modification of handaxe technology, with the cores having a shape that is similar to handaxes. The large predetermined flakes that are produced then often serve as blanks to produce actual bifaces but also notably cleavers (Li *et al.* 2017). The occurrence of the Victoria West assemblage within the Acheulean at Canteen Kopje is estimated to date to around 1 Ma (Lotter *et al.* 2017). This very early age estimate and the clear roots of Victoria West in the Acheulean may serve to support the idea that prepared core technology developed independently at multiple locations (*cf.* Adler *et al.* 2014; Li *et al.* 2017) and may be a relatively

"natural" development for people producing so-called Mode 2 technology (*e.g.,* White, Ashton and Scott 2011).

Despite the listing of the Canteen Kopje site as a national monument, illegal small-scale artisanal mining still takes place at the site (Leader pers. comm. 2022). This small-scale activity can be considered a minor threat to the site. Recent years, however, have seen larger threats. Despite the decades-long listing as a national monument, a permit for diamond mining at the site was issued in 2014 by the Department of Minerals and Energy, but the South African Heritage Resources Agency (SAHRA) took legal action to prevent the mining taking place. In 2016, the order not to mine at the site was suddenly lifted, perhaps due to the exercise of political influence (Leader 2016). This happened without the archaeological permit-holder and other stakeholders being informed (Ryan 2016). Over a long weekend due to a public holiday, mining commenced and a large trench was dug across the site (Leader 2016). Dr. David Morris of the Kimberley Museum, finally managed to obtain a police interdict to halt operations. The protected status of the site was upheld by the court and the site was thus safeguarded from further destruction afterwards (Jones 2016b). The case illustrates how different branches of government may be working at cross-purposes and how the impression to politicians that mining brings large rewards while preserving heritage does not, can result in severe damage to heritage sites.

## Causal co-occurrence, or coincidence?

An obvious reason for the juxtaposition of archaeological finds and diamond digging activities, as well as other mining sites, is the removal of staggering amounts of overburden. I focus on the co-occurrence of diamonds and Acheulean artefacts, but other forms of mining have also led to significant archaeological discoveries in roughly the same period from the late 19th century through the first half of the 20th century. An important example in South Africa is the discovery of gold in the Witwatersrand. With the discovery of cyanidation procedures in the late 19th century to treat the relatively impure South African ore, a supply of lime was required. This supply was mined, inter alia, in dolomitic limestone areas in South Africa (Esterhuysen 2019). These fossil-bearing deposits yielded hominin remains, first at Taung in the Northern Cape (Dart 1925) and then also near Johannesburg, at Sterkfontein and similar sites (Broom 1938). These sites now form the UNESCO World Heritage complex "the Cradle of Humankind", and they have yielded countless *Australopithecus* and *Paranthropus* fossils as well as important Oldowan and Acheulean artefacts and some of the rare fossils of early representatives of the genus *Homo*.

In the case of lime mining, the juxtaposition of hominin fossils and limestone caves appears an artefact of taphonomy (see Brain 1981). The caves were not hominin living sites and they represent delimited spots in the landscape with good or exceptional preservation conditions, while the respective hominins likely ranged far more widely in areas where fossil-bearing deposits are not preserved.

As to the co-occurrence of Acheulean archaeological finds and diamonds, their accumulation in the same deposits due to suitable taphonomic conditions is also the 0-hypothesis to be examined. Nevertheless, two other possibilities could play a role: 1) hominins were after the diamonds themselves, or 2) the diamond-bearing sediments were somehow an attractive resource (or indexed other resources) for hominins. In the former case, we would expect to encounter diamonds in archaeological sites outside of the main diamond-bearing river deposits. In the latter case, we would at least expect to find Acheulean artefacts in diamond-bearing deposits at greater than expected quantities. I will briefly examine the 0-hypothesis and discuss these two cases in what follows.

*Diamonds and handaxes: a match made in riverine geology and the efficient removal of overburden?*
The geographic distribution of sediment deposits of Lower and Middle Pleistocene age in South Africa is generally limited. Southern Africa has been tectonically stable, and as such, large parts of the South African landscape have been erosional landscapes throughout the Pleistocene (Klein 2000). Hence, river gravels and terraces represent one of the few opportunities to document Pleistocene lithic assemblages with some form of stratigraphic control. The co-occurrence of diamonds and Acheulean artefacts in the same deposits has consequently been attributed to taphonomic processes from early in the history of southern African archaeology. Peringuey (1915) for example asserts:

> "So numerous are these relics in parts of Swaziland, as also in the valley of the Vaal River, where diamond 'dry diggings' obtain, that one might be superficially' led to the conclusion that they are the tools of early miners, whereas both artefacts and minerals have gradually found

> their way to these deposits through extensive denudation of the higher levels of the country round the deposits," Peringuey (1915, 231).

Current understanding of the development of the river valleys is that the Vaal and Gariep traverse an old erosion surface across much of the "Highveld", the interior plateau of South Africa. The rivers have removed or reworked older gravels. At some distance from the river, older gravel terraces grouped as the "Windsorton formation" are documented. They are generally dated as Miocene to Pliocene and thus pre-date the Acheulean. These gravel beds have also occasionally been preserved in depressions in the bedrock of the valley floor (Botha 2021). Although diamonds are present in these deposits, only some intrusive stone artefacts have been reported in these deposits (Helgren 1978). Diamonds also occur in reworked lag deposits called "Rooikoppies gravels", comprising the remains of even older gravels (Botha 2021).

After the deposition of the Windsorton formation, an erosional phase is documented. This younger "Rietputs formation" is deposited some time after and contains large numbers of stone artefacts associated with diamonds. Regarding the chronology the Rietputs formation, assays have been obtained using cosmogenic nucleide dating, suggesting a formation of the sedimentary package after 1.8 ma. An early Acheulean assemblage has been recovered from the basal gravels of the formation and is estimated to date to c. 1.7 ma based on lithic typological comparisons with material from Canteen Kopje, which has been placed to 1.51 ma (Kuman and Gibbon 2018).

The erosional character of the South African landscape also means that many older diamond-bearing deposits have probably been cleaned up or reworked. As such, the most ubiquitous "remaining" deposits belong to the temporal window in which Acheulean artefacts were also deposited in the landscape. Hence, taphonomic factors play an important role in the apparent regular co-occurrence of handaxes and diamonds.

*Prehistoric bling*
Are stone artefacts also present in these deposits because people in the Early and Middle Stone Age were after the diamonds themselves? In southern Africa, this hypothesis has never been very popular. One early proposal comes from a Major Feilden (1884). He collected stone artefacts during the first Anglo-

Boer war while on the march and near his camp in Newcastle (KwaZulu-Natal Province, South Africa). In his time in South Africa, he already observed that in Zulu society quartz crystals are sometimes collected and worn on necklaces with other elements, such as crocodile and leopard teeth.

While collecting stone artefacts, Feilden also observed that alluvial lithics sometimes occur with quartz crystals showing wear. He surmised that the materials are likely in secondary position, deposited by the stream, but assumed the artefacts and crystals have a shared provenance and the stream eroded tools and crystals together (Feilden 1884, p.169). He accordingly predicted:

*"In connection with this wearing of crystals by the stone-age people, I have a suggestion to make which perhaps may some day bear fruit. As these stone-using tribes of hunters appear to have been interested in rock-crystals as objects of adornments, or as charms, it is probable that the more beautiful and striking crystallisation of the diamond would attract their attention; consequently I should not be surprised to hear that searchers for stone implements among the alluviums of the diamond-producing districts of South Africa were rewarded by finding diamonds that had been used as ornaments by the stone-age people," Feilden (1884, 169-170).*

This hypothesis can be dismissed for a duck – to my knowledge, no diamond worked into either ornament or lithic artefact has hitherto been recovered from Stone Age contexts in southern Africa since 1884. Yet, the use of quartz crystals noted by Feilden is clearly in evidence during the Stone Age, at least from Fauresmith onwards. The collection and use of quartz crystals is ethnographically also well-documented. Quartz crystals are used by shamans and consequently are regarded to be powerful objects among the San in southern Africa (Hampson, 2013). In the Later Stone Age of the Holocene, quartz was observed as an archaeological assemblage component already by early excavations. Goodwin (1938), for example, published the likely mid-Holocene burial of two young children, thought to be twins, containing a quartz crystal placed into the socket of the left eye of one of the children. At the same site, quartz crystals are sometimes worked into stone tools, such as a scraper (Goodwin 1938, 251).

Recently, some notable attention has been given to the collection of non-utilitarian objects by Late

Figure 4. Quartz crystal from the terminal Pleistocene level III at Shongweni South Cave. Scale bar 1cm. Photograph: Gerrit Dusseldorp.

Pleistocene societies in southern Africa. Some sites from the terminal Pleistocene and earlier in KwaZulu-Natal contain hexagonal quartz crystals (Pargeter and Hampson 2019). Middle Stone Age sites also illustrate the collection of calcite crystals by *Homo sapiens* in the African interior (Wilkins *et al.* 2022). At Wonderwerk Cave, quartz crystals are associated with the Fauresmith (Chazan and Horwitz 2009), currently regarded as a lithic industry transitional between the Earlier and Middle Stone Age (Lombard *et al.* 2012; 2022). Some of these quartz crystals may have been modified and reduced using bipolar knapping (Chazan and Horwitz 2009), a phenomenon also observed in terminal Pleistocene stone artefact assemblages (Pargeter and Hampson 2019). Recent excavations at Umhlatuzana have shown that quartz crystals occur in both Holocene and Pleistocene contexts, and we have documented similar examples in the lithic collections from the nearby site Shongweni South (figure 4). From the Fauresmith period onwards, people thus clearly collected ready-made natural crystals, but not the rough diamonds in the river gravels and there is consequently little reason to believe that this has anything to do with archaeological visibility but represents "evidence of absence".

### Diamond-bearing gravels are a sought-after resource

Based on current knowledge, the occurrence of "gravel-sized" artefacts in river gravels that also contain diamonds may not be overly surprising. Both can simply be deposited as components of a river's sediment load. But there are other factors that can further reinforce their co-occurrence. The gravels were also a source of suitable raw materials. The lithic assemblages recovered from the Vaal and Gariep river terraces are generally made on cobbles. Lithic raw materials common in the local gravels are generally also well-represented in stone artefact assemblages at the respective archaeological sites (*e.g.*, Kuman and Gibbon 2018; Lotter and Kuman 2018). At some sites, selection for specific raw materials is in evidence, leading to a difference in frequency between raw material types present in the local gravels and raw material configurations exploited for the production of archaeological artefacts (Leader *et al.* 2018). The exploitation and/or frequentation of the diamond-bearing deposits as valuable raw material sources may thus have led to the overrepresentation of handaxes in these geological contexts. This link is notoriously difficult to evaluate, however, as these geological contexts have historically become a magnet location for archaeologists searching for Stone Age artefacts, so this impression may be an artefact of research history too.

Acheulean settlement in southern Africa has been suggested to be closely tied to water availability (Helgren 1978; Deacon and Deacon 1999), at least much more so than in subsequent periods. The attraction to water would have similarly reinforced the association of Acheulean artefacts with diamond-bearing river sediments. The presence of Acheulean artefacts in active (at the time) fluvial contexts and their absence from older terrace surfaces highlights the importance of water availability. If diamond-bearing gravels themselves were attracting Acheulean hominins, they would have also left abundant implements on older diamond-bearing deposits. This is not apparent, although "Kafuan" or pebble tools (now generally

regarded as geofacts) have been reported from older terrace surfaces (e.g. Smuts 1937; Breuil 1943).

That being said, some authors strongly dispute the reliance of Acheulean hominins on the availability of standing water (Kandel and Conard 2012). Here too, research history may thus play a role in shaping our perception of the Acheulean and hominin behaviour therein, as river valleys represent privileged locations with suitable sediment traps preserving archaeological assemblages largely *in situ*. They are in turn a focus of archaeological attention.

## CONCLUSION: DIAMOND-BASED LITHIC CLASSIFICATION SYSTEMS ARE FOREVER

The co-occurrence of handaxes and diamonds has proved to be a serendipitous situation that led to important archaeological insights. Why did it work out that way (but no longer)? The short answer that may be given is: the market economy. The high market value of this translucent variety of carbon drove the manual removal of stupendous volumes of overburden during the late 19th and early 20th century, at a time when fascination with human prehistory was similarly growing. The wealth of archaeological artefacts surfacing as a product of these fortuitous developments proved to be astounding, particularly for visiting European scholars such as Abbé Breuil.

The inversed suggestion that "Stellenbosch-type" artefacts can function as an indicator for diamond-bearing gravels by Goodwin and Van Riet Lowe (1929) is intriguing here. The presence of such artefacts may thus have been a useful heuristic for pre-industrial artisanal diamond miners. Yet again, this does not inform us on hominin involvement or any meaningful behavioural connection between stone artefacts and diamonds. As the discussion has shown, the curious co-occurrence of archaeological remains and diamonds likely has taphonomic reasons alone, no archaeological evidence for early use of diamonds exists and insufficient evidence is available to test if the gravel deposits were preferentially used by people during the Earlier Stone Age, or if the archaeological attention to these deposits results in the impression of a higher density of Acheulean materials.

Nevertheless, the study of the stone artefact material in the Vaal and Gariep River gravels contributed greatly to the early formulation of archaeological systematics in southern Africa. Goodwin and Van Riet Lowe (1929) based the formulation of their local division of the Stone Age to a large extent on discoveries and stratigraphic considerations derived from diamond digging activities, largely dropping typological labels developed in European archaeology. The subdivision of the Acheulean into different phases has now been superseded by the consideration of factors such as raw material influence (*e.g.*, Humphreys 1970) as well as the advent of radiometric dating, showing that the occurrence of different assemblage types is less clearly sequential than initially thought (Underhill 2011). Yet the tripartite division originally proposed by Goodwin and Van Riet Lowe (1929) is still in use in southern African archaeology today and terms such as Fauresmith and Victoria West similarly retain their heuristic value.

## ACKNOWLEDGEMENTS

First and foremost, thank you Raymond Corbey, for the many stimulating discussions we had over the years and for time and again disrupting my thinking. Diamonds are just one of the topics I would never have reflected on without your bringing them up frequently. This paper is based in part on a contribution to a very stimulating workshop on multi-species ethnographies of mining, for which Jan-Bart Gewald kindly invited me. Thanks Jan-Bart for the fascinating discussions! George Leader supplied photos and provided important context on the Canteen Kopje situation. Scott Williams provided a better-quality photograph of the American Museum of Natural History display than I had managed to take during my visit. Matt Caruana, Marlize Lombard, Matt Lotter and Sarah Wurz hosted me at their field site of Wonderboom and their showcase of some of the site's lithics was instrumental to my understanding of some archaeological classification issues. This work was funded by NWO Vidi-grant 276-60-004, awarded to Gerrit Dusseldorp.

## REFERENCES

Botha, G.A. 2021. "Cenozoic stratigraphy of South Africa: current challenges and future possibilities." *South African Journal of Geology* 124 (4), 817-842. DOI:10.25131/sajg.124.0054

Brain, C.K. 1981. *The hunters or the hunted? An introduction to African cave taphonomy*. Chicago: University of Chicago Press.

Breuil, H. 1943. "Archaic chipped pebble and flake industries from the older gravels of various sections of the Vaal valley." *South African Journal of Science* 40, 282-284.

Broom, R. 1913. "Man contemporaneous with extinct animals in South Africa." *Annals of the South African Museum* 12, 13-16.

Broom, R. 1928. "Mammoths and Man in the Transvaal." *Nature* 121 (3044), 324-324.

Broom, R. 1929. "Australoid Element in the Korannas." *Nature* 124 (3127), 507-507.

Broom, R. 1938. "The Pleistocene Anthropoid Apes of South Africa." *Nature* 142 (3591), 377-379.

Chazan, M., and L.K. Horwitz. 2009. "Milestones in the development of symbolic behaviour: a case study from Wonderwerk Cave, South Africa." *World Archaeology* 41 (4), 521-539.

Chazan, M., A. Sumner, L.K. Horwitz, and D. Morris. 2022. "Mining on the frontier: Archaeological excavation of the historical component at Canteen Kopje, Northern Cape Province, South Africa." *Quaternary International* 614, 146-163.

Chirikure, S. 2014. "'Where angels fear to tread': ethics, commercial archaeology, and extractive industries in southern Africa." *Azania: Archaeological Research in Africa* 49 (2), 218-231.

Chirikure, S., and E.N. Mathoho n.d. *Replacement of electricity poles as part of maintenance of the bundle conductor and transformer structures inside Mapungubwe National Park and World Heritage Site Limpopo Province, South Africa* (Vol. Millennium Heritage group for De Beers, Venetia Mine). South Dale.

Clark, J.D. 1959. *The prehistory of southern Africa: The latest discoveries about the origins and cultural history of primitive man in southern Africa*. Harmondsworth: Pelican Books.

Dart, R.A. 1925. "The Taungs Skull." *Nature* 116 (2917), 462-462. DOI:10.1038/116462a0

Dart, R.A. 1927. "Mammoths and Man in the Transvaal." *Nature* 120 (3032), 41-48. DOI:10.1038/120041a0x

Deacon, J. 1993. "The Cinderella Metaphor: The Maturing of Archaeology as a Profession in South Africa." *The South African Archaeological Bulletin* 48 (158), 77-81. DOI:10.2307/3888945

Deacon, J. 2015. "Great expectations: Archaeological sites and the National Heritage Resources Act (Act 25 of 1999)." *The South African Archaeological Bulletin* 70 (202), 220-223.

Deacon, H.J., and J. Deacon. 1999. *Human beginnings in South Africa: Uncovering the secrets of the Stone Age*. Cape Town: David Philip Publishers.

De Beers Group. (2013). *How are we performing: Living up to diamonds report to society 2013*. London: De Beers Group of Companies.

De Wit, M.C.J. 2008. "Canteen Koppie at Barkly West: South Africa's first diamond mine." *South African Journal of Geology* 111 (1), 53-66.

Esterhuysen, A. 2019. "If we are all African, then I am nothing." In *Interrogating Human Origins: Decolonisation and the Deep Human Past*, edited by M. Porr and M. Matthews, Ch. 13. London: Taylor & Francis.

Feilden, H.W. 1884. "Notes on Stone Implements from South Africa." *The Journal of the Anthropological Institute of Great Britain and Ireland* 13, 162-174. DOI: 10.2307/2841721

Forssman, T.R., K. Kuman, G.M. Leader, and R.J. Gibbon. 2010. "A Later Stone Age assemblage from Canteen Kopje, Northern Cape." *The South African Archaeological Bulletin* 65 (192), 204-214.

Fourie, W. 2008. "Archaeological Impact Assessments within South African Legislation: Paper Presented at the Archaeological Resources Management Workshop, 17 May 2007." *The South African Archaeological Bulletin* 63 (187), 77-79.

Gibbon, R. J. 2009. *The fluvial history of the lower Vaal River catchment*. Johannesburg: PhD thesis, University of the Witwatersrand.

Gibbon, R.J., D.E. Granger, K. Kuman, and T.C. Partridge. 2009. "Early Acheulean technology in the Rietputs Formation, South Africa, dated with cosmogenic nuclides." *Journal of Human Evolution* 56 (2), 152-160. DOI: 10.1016/j.jhevol.2008.09.006

Gooch, W.D. 1882. "The Stone Age of South Africa." *The Journal of the Anthropological Institute of Great Britain and Ireland* 11, 124-183. DOI: 10.2307/2841509

Goodwin, A.J.H. 1937. "Archaeology of the Oakhurst shelter, George, Part II Disposition of the skeletal remains." *Transactions of the Royal Society of South Africa* 25 (3), 247-257. DOI: 10.1080/00359193709519752

Goodwin, A.J.H., and C. Van Riet Lowe. 1929. "The Stone Age cultures of South Africa." *Annals of the South African Museum* 27, 1-289.

Hampson, J. 2013. "The Materiality of Rock Art and Quartz: a Case Study from Mpumalanga Province, South Africa." *Cambridge Archaeological Journal* 23 (3), 363-372. DOI: 10.1017/S0959774313000498

Helgren, D.M. 1978. "Acheulian settlement along the Lower Vaal river, South Africa." *Journal of Archaeological Science* 5 (1), 39-60. DOI: 10.1016/0305-4403(78)90017-1

Hodgkinson, E.T. 1926. "The stone cultures of the Vaal River diggings." *South African Journal of Science* 23, 876-886.

Humphreys, A.J.B. 1970. "The Role of Raw Material and the Concept of the Fauresmith." *The South African Archaeological Bulletin* 25 (99/100), 139-144. DOI: 10.2307/3888138

Humphreys, A.J.B. 1973. "Museum Collecting in Archaeology." *The South African Archaeological Bulletin* 28 (111/112), 67-72. DOI: 10.2307/3888562

Jones, N. 2016a. "Diamond mine threatens Stone Age artefacts." *Sapiens*. https://www.sapiens.org/archaeology/canteen-kopje-under-threat/ (last access: 01.11.2023).

Jones, N. 2016b. "Stone Age site saved." *Sapiens*. https://www.sapiens.org/archaeology/canteen-kopje-saved/ (last access: 01.11.2023).

Kandel, A.W., and N. J. Conard. 2012. "Settlement patterns during the Earlier and Middle Stone Age around Langebaan Lagoon, Western Cape (South Africa)." *Quaternary International* 270, 15-29.

Klein, R.G. 2000. "The Earlier Stone Age of Southern Africa." *The South African Archaeological Bulletin* 55 (172), 107-122. DOI: 10.2307/3888960

Klein, R.G., and K. Cruz-Uribe. 1996. "Exploitation of large bovids and seals at Middle and Later Stone Age sites in South Africa." *Journal of Human Evolution* 31, 315-334.

Klein, R.G., K. Cruz-Uribe, D. Halkett, T. Hart, and J.E. Parkington. 1999. "Paleoenvironmental and Human Behavioral Implications of the Boegoeberg 1 Late Pleistocene Hyena Den, Northern Cape Province, South Africa." *Quaternary Research* 52 (3), 393-403. DOI: 10.1006/qres.1999.2068

Kuman, K., and R.J. Gibbon. 2018. "The Rietputs 15 site and Early Acheulean in South Africa." *Quaternary International* 480, 4-15. DOI: 10.1016/j.quaint.2016.12.031.

Kuman, K., M.G. Lotter, and G.M. Leader. 2020. "The Fauresmith of South Africa: A new assemblage from Canteen Kopje and significance of the technology in human and cultural evolution." *Journal of Human Evolution* 148, 102884.

Kuman, K., M.B. Sutton, T.R. Pickering, and J.L. Heaton. 2018. "The Oldowan industry from Swartkrans cave, South Africa, and its relevance for the African Oldowan." *Journal of Human Evolution* 123, 52-69.

Leader, G.M. 2016. "World Heritage gone: South African diamond mining destroys archaeological sites daily." *Leakey Foundation Blog*, accessed 29 June 2023. https://leakeyfoundation. org/world-heritage-gone-south-african-diamond-mining-destroys-archaeological-sites-daily/

Leader, G.M., K. Kuman, R.J. Gibbon, and D.E. Granger. 2018. "Early Acheulean organised core knapping strategies ca. 1.3 Ma at Rietputs 15, Northern Cape Province, South Africa." *Quaternary International* 480, 16-28. DOI:10.1016/j. quaint.2016.08.046

Li, H., K. Kuman, M.G. Lotter, G.M. Leader, and R.J. Gibbon. 2017. "The Victoria West: earliest prepared core technology in the Acheulean at Canteen Kopje and implications for the cognitive evolution of early hominids." *Royal Society Open Science* 4 (6), 170288.

Lombard, M., J. Bradfield, M.V. Caruana, T.V. Makhubela, G.L. Dusseldorp, J.D. Kramers, and S. Wurz. 2022. "The Southern African stone age sequence updated (II)." *South African Archaeological Bulletin* 77 (217), 172-212.

Lombard, M., L. Wadley, J. Deacon, S. Wurz, I. Parsons, M. Mohapi, J. Swart, and P. Mitchell. 2012. "South African and Lesotho Stone age sequence updated (I)." *South African Archaeological Bulletin* 67 (195), 123-144.

Lotter, M.G., R.J. Gibbon, K. Kuman, G.M. Leader, T. Forssman, and D.E. Granger. 2016. "A Geoarchaeological Study of the Middle and Upper Pleistocene Levels at Canteen Kopje, Northern Cape Province, South Africa." *Geoarchaeology* 31 (4), 304-323. DOI:10.1002/gea.21541.

Lotter, M.G., and K. Kuman. 2018. "The Acheulean in South Africa, with announcement of a new site (Penhill Farm) in the lower Sundays River Valley, Eastern Cape Province, South Africa." *Quaternary International* 480, 43-65.

Pargeter, J., and J. Hampson. 2019. "Quartz crystal materiality in Terminal Pleistocene Lesotho." *Antiquity* 93 (367), 11-27. DOI:10.15184/aqy.2018.167

Penning, W.H. 1887. "Notes Upon a Few Stone Implements Found in South Africa." *The Journal of the Anthropological Institute of Great Britain and Ireland* 16, 68-70. DOI:10.2307/2841741

Peringuey, L. 1911. "The Stone Ages of South Africa as represented in the collection of the South African Museum." *Annals of the South African Museum* 8, 1-177.

Peringuey, L. 1915. "The Bushman as Palaeolithic Man." *Transactions of the Royal Society of South Africa* 5 (1), 225-236. DOI:10.1080/00359191509519720

Ryan, B. 2016. "Kimberley Museum 'enraged' as miner threatens Stone Age site." *Miningmx*. https://www. miningmx.com/news/diamonds/26958-kimberley-museum-enraged-as-miner-threatens-stone-age-site/_(last access: 01.11.2023).

Schildkrout, E., and J. Grace Lacey. 2017. "Shifting Perspectives: The Man in Africa Hall at the American Museum of Natural History at 50." *Anthropology Now* 9 (2), 14-26.

Smith, P., L. K. Horwitz, R. Nshimirimana, F. De Beer, D. Morris, L. Jacobson, and M. Chazan. 2012. "Canteen Kopje: a new look at an old skull." *South African Journal of Science* 108 (1), 1-9.

Smuts, J.C., Jun. 1937. "The climate and stone implements of Rooikop," *Transactions of the Royal Society of South Africa* 25 (4), 343-365.

South African Archaeological Society. 1972. "Introduction." *Goodwin Series* 1, 1-2.

Underhill, D. 2011. "A history of stone age archaeological study in South Africa." *South African Archaeological Bulletin* 66 (193), 3-14.

Van Riet Lowe, C. 1952. "The Vaal River Chronology: An Up-to-Date Summary." *The South African Archaeological Bulletin* 7 (28), 135-149. DOI:10.2307/3887341

White, M., N. Ashton, and B. Scott. 2011. "The Emergence, Diversity and Significance of Mode 3 (Prepared Core) Technologies." In *Developments in Quaternary Sciences*, edited by N. Ashton, S. G. Lewis, and C. Stringer, 53-65. London: Elsevier.

Wilkins, J., B.J. Schoville, R. Pickering, L. Gliganic, B. Collins, K.S. Brown, J. Von der Meden, W. Khumalo, M.C. Meyer, S. Maape, A.F. Blackwood, and A. Hatton. 2021. "Innovative *Homo sapiens* behaviours 105,000 years ago in a wetter Kalahari." *Nature* 592 (7853), 248-252. DOI:10.1038/s41586-021-03419-0

In Hussain, S.T. and G.L. Dusseldorp (eds) 2025. Sitting on the fence: Negotiating archaeology, anthropology and philosophy. Festschrift for Prof. Dr Raymond H.A. Corbey in celebration of his 70th birthday. *Analecta Praehistorica Leidensia* 54. Leiden: Sidestone Press, pp. 151-162.

# On Mousterian, Micoquian, and the origin of new Neanderthals in Western Europe ~70,000 years ago

Philip Van Peer

## ABSTRACT

Many narratives of the Upper Pleistocene Middle Palaeolithic of Western Europe oppose two cultural spheres of influence, derived from the apparent co-presence of two overarching technocomplexes: the Mousterian in the south and the Micoquian in the north. As formal taxonomic concepts they have been intensively discussed. In this contribution, I wish to take up the issue from two angles which have been rarely explored. First, I will consider the existence of two Middle Palaeolithic technocomplexes in Western Europe from an ethno-demographic perspective, based on the chronospatial layout of the archaeological record. Second, I look into variability structures as revealed by the systematics used to describe the Mousterian and the Micoquian. This consideration leads me to propose a new significant threshold ~70 ka in the European archaeological timescale.

*Keywords: Mousterian, Micoquian, variability, Middle Palaeolithic, taxonomy*

## INTRODUCTION

I have a vague recollection of a cursory discussion with Raymond Corbey in which we were exchanging ideas on how to teach students on the issue of Middle Palaeolithic lithic variability. I remember him pointing out that just bringing them at level with regard to the history of the Micoquian as a taxonomic concept, would in itself consume a significant amount of class time. Even if this must have happened a long time ago, that phrase has been laying dormant in the back of my mind. Now seems an appropriate time to dust it off and to write down of few thoughts on the matter.

Throughout the history of European Palaeolithic archaeology, the question of geographic overlap between the Mousterian and Micoquian 'worlds apart' has been much debated (Otte 2017; see Frick 2020 for a historiographic account). The concepts originated in the 19th century as products of regional research communities and gained momentum when formal typologies were devised in the 1960s as analytical instruments by scholars like François Bordes (1961) and Gerhard Bosinki (1967). It is not my intention here to review this utterly complex taxonomic history of the Western European Middle Palaeolithic: this has been beautifully done in an extensive review by J.A. Frick (2020). As other authors before (*e.g.*, Richter 2016), Frick points out that the Mousterian and Micoquian are to an extent just artefacts of the archaeological 'grammar' used. In that sense they are an excellent example of how archaeological systematics often tend to create difference where there is

**Philip Van Peer**

Centre for Archaeological Research of Landscapes, University of Leuven, Belgium

Philip.vanpeer@kuleuven.be

ORCID: 0000-0002-7745-9528

sameness and vice versa. They thus often do exactly
the opposite of what they are supposed to do, *i.e.*, to
measure and qualify real observed variation in the
archaeological record (O'Brien and Lyman 2000), and
accordingly to put us on the trail of living people of
the past. No reminder is needed to emphasise that the
'anthropological turn' in archaeological theory building
has been concerned with the creation of Middle Range
Theory to provide precisely the principles for walking
that trail (Binford 1962).

In this short contribution, I will examine the
way we have structured the Upper Pleistocene
Middle Palaeolithic of Western Europe from such
an anthropological angle. First, I shall confront
its spatial patterning with the deep-time scale of
the archaeological record. How does the observed
patterning match with the proposed Mousterian and
Micoquian spheres of influence? Secondly, it appears
that the different 'grammars' imposed on the record
have resulted in very different apparent patterns of
variability. For the Mousterian, the significance of
its interstratified, supposedly 'timeless' variability
structure as revealed by Bordean systematics has
generated sixty years of heated discussion. The
Micoquian, by contrast, has mostly been explored in
terms of its diachronic change over tens of millennia
from Middle Pleistocene through late Upper Pleistocene
times (Frick 2020; Jöris 2003). Do these different
orientations expose real differences in spatio-temporal
structures or are the latter mostly products of the
formal filters applied, masking behavioural sameness?

I am aware that some of the ideas I will propose
may, in good Corbey style, sound overly provocative at
first. Yet they are rooted in robust empirical evidence
and therefore they are legitimate research hypotheses
to consider at the very least. I shall argue that the
early Micoquian and the Mousterian are stages in a
phylogenetic trajectory of cultural change in early
Upper Pleistocene Neanderthals as they displace their
territories on a geographic gradient. Western Europe
during these times is sparsely occupied, with many
regions almost empty. Only in MIS 3 the entire region
of Western Europe is occupied as a consequence
of re-colonisation and demographic growth. All
throughout this region we find the archaeological
residus of exactly the same behavioural system even
though they are labeled late Micoquian in the north
and Mousterian in the south. They both exhibit an
identical pattern of cyclic, directional change in lithic
assemblage-types. This feature in particular makes this

late Middle Palaeolithic record profoundly different
from what existed until the Pleniglacial.

## TEMPORAL AND SPATIAL SCALES

Looking at the overall geographic distribution
of Upper Pleistocene Middle Palaeolithic sites in
Western Europe, we observe that sites are more
or less continuously distributed in an area bound
by the 52° parallel in the north, the Hercynian
mountains of Bohemia in the east, and the mountain
ranges of the Alps and Pyrenees in the south but
with some archaeological sites extending along
the Cantabrian coast. The total surface area of this
distribution amounts to ~850,000 km². Interestingly,
this area is easily matched by ethnographic territories
such as those of mobile Athapaskan populations
of the northwest American coast (Suttles 1968) or
the Labrador Inuit (Damas 1968). The territory
covered by the Dogrib of northwest Canada (total
population size: ~1000 individuals) over a period
of 70 years of ethnographic documentation amounts
to ~160,000 km² (Helm 1968).

From an ethnographic, or more precisely a
palaeoethnographic perspective, which is almost
by definition concerned with deep-time patterning,
it can be questioned if archaeological regional
systematics leading to the recognition of Micoquian
and Mousterian 'worlds apart' have grasped anything
real as to the behaviour and history of the groups
responsible for such patterning of sites. It can be easily
imagined, for example, that over the course of a few
centuries, let alone a few millennia, an archaeological
record across the entire Western European area
could have been left by just a few viable social
units even when only shifting their catchments at
slow pace (Pedersen *et al.* 2018; see also Hublin
and Roebroeks 2009). This being said, the empirical
support for territorial displacement as a mechanism
behind this continuous distributional pattern would
need to come from chronological evidence. Can any
chronological gradients be recognized?

### Eemian sites

There has been quite some controversy on the question
of Neanderthal occupation of Eemian environments –
of the forests and wetlands of the European north in
particular. Although the number of securely dated
Eemian sites has notably increased in recent years,
the fact remains that comparatively speaking such
sites are very thin on the ground. Defleur *et al.* (2020)
have for example persistently argued for demographic

collapse – and occasionally ensuing consumption cannibalism – during the Last Interglacial. In further support of their claims, they quote the presence of just a handful of Eemian sites in the whole of France. In the Low Countries there is not even a single site that can confidently be dated to the Eemian, nor are there any in Great Britain (Ashton and Scott 2016).

Sites of that age, on the other hand, are quite well represented in central and east Germany, at the southern fringes of the north European plain. If not for demographic collapse, the evidence at least pleads for a significant contraction of Neanderthal occupations at high latitudes in the continental ecozone of present-day central Germany. The site of Neumark Nord 2/2 is an extraordinary flagship site, throwing the spotlight on a high-density occupation at a lake shore (Laurat and Brühl 2021). The lithic industry here as well as in other Eemian sites is remarkable with regard to the small size of its products and the near-absence of retouched tools. These technological features will be further considered below.

### The early Last Glacial in the Scheldt Basin

Until now the archaeological record in this part of northwest Europe at the edge of the Pleistocene habitable world is extremely sparse, but new archaeostratigraphical evidence is forthcoming from a drilling project in the Flemish Valley in the northern part of the Scheldt Basin (Van Peer et al. 2017). So far, slightly under 500 mechanical drillings reaching the base of the Quaternary were carried out in the confluence area of the Dyle and Demer tributaries. They reveal a strong occupational signal (at 6 out of 41 selected drilling locations) in the form of lithic microchips, in a depositional sequence of intercalated loams and aeolian sands sitting directly on top of late Eemian peats as revealed by their botanical analysis. Based on the geochemical comparison of sediments and diagenetic deposits on artefacts at the surface site of Rotselaar Toren-ter-Heide, the stratigraphic position of the latter was inferred to be related to this loam and sand sequence (Van Peer et al. 2017).

The Rotselaar Toren-ter-Heide assemblage exhibits techno-cultural similarity with the lithic assemblage from Remicourt on the watershed between the Scheldt and Meuse basins. At Remicourt, the industry belongs to the *Horizon de Momalle,* a redeposited whitish sand layer which also seems to be present in the loam and sand sequence at some of the Flemish Valley coring locations. The Momalle horizon was originally dated to a stadial phase prior to the Saint Germain I

pedogenesis (Haesaerts et al. 1997), but subsequently revised to Saint-Germain II (Bosquet et al. 2011). The precise grounds for this are unclear, however, and given the emerging data from the Flemish Valley, I am of the opinion that the earlier interpretation of its chronostratigraphic position in MIS 5d still stands.

A combination of techno-typological traits similar to the Rotselaar and Remicourt assemblages can be recognized in many other assemblages from the northern Scheldt Basin, unfortunately all surface collections. Handaxes are well represented: mostly large cordiform or triangular specimens but a few small pieces with a thick base occur as well. Handaxe production flakes are present, hinting at handaxe maintenance procedures. Levallois and discoid production methods are attested, but a laminar component is also evident. Retouched flake tools occur but are rare. The variation in terms of exploited raw materials is large yet the sources seem to be restricted to the Scheldt Basin.

The overall techno-typological constellation is very reminiscent of the Micoquian variant variously referred to as KMG-A (Jöris 2003) or *Lebenstedt Gruppe* (Bosinski 1967). If on account of the cultural homogeneity observed, the northern Scheldt Basin open-air sites can be dated to the onset of the early Last Glacial, they represent an isolated cluster within the entire region of north-western Europe. The watershed ridge between the Meuse and the Scheldt basins then appears to be the southern frontier of this Micoquian open-air phenomenon. Outside of the northern Scheldt Basin, MIS 5d sites are extremely rare but they exhibit the same technological features.

### The 'Technocomplex of the Northwest' in France

The early Glacial interstadials in northern France, in contrast to MIS 5d, evidence a dense concentration of sites. Northern France is a well-studied region with a high resolution chronostratigraphical background, in which 86 Middle Palaeolithic levels in primary context are documented (Locht et al. 2016). They have been extensively studied from a techno-economic perspective on lithic production systems (e.g., Goval and Locht 2008), in part out of necessity due to the general paucity of retouched tools (Bordes 1984; Goval and Depaepe 2012).

This 'Technocomplex of the Northwest' (Depaepe 2007) has been characterised as follows:

*"Ces ensembles lithiques du Paléolithique de
France septentrionale et ceux des loess de
Moyenne Belgique présentent de fortes parentés
technologiques et typologiques [...] Le débitage
Levallois constitue un part importante du fond
commun technologique. Parallèlement, on constate
durant cette période la présence d'un outillage
faiblement retouché, la trace de quelques très rares
bifaces et, enfin, la présence en faible quantité
d'un débitage laminaire volumétrique. [...] Le
S.I.M. 5 [=MIS 5; note by the auhor] aurait ainsi pu
connaître une certaine homogénéité de la Seine au
Rhin," Locht and Depaepe (2011, 231).*

Some of these assemblages have been explicitly
identified as Micoquian (Blaser and Chaussé 2016).
Another striking observation about this open-air Middle
Palaeolithic phenomenon of the early Glacial is its broad
technological stability across tens of millennia. A good
example is the archaeological site of Bettencourt where
the same technological configuration is maintained
through five subsequent occupational levels spanning
the entire early Glacial (Locht 2002).

### The southern Aquitaine region

Throughout MIS 5, there seems to be sparse hominin
occupation in the entirety of south-western France.
Defleur *et al.* (2020, 3) symptomatically note:

*"[...] dozens of sites in the South of France that date
to the MIS 6/MIS 5 transition do not provide evidence
of human presence during MIS 5e. Examples include
la grotte du Lazaret, la Baume Bonne, la Baume des
Peyrards, le Bau de l'Aubesier, la grotte de Payre, la
grotte de Combe-Grenal, le Pech de l'Azé, la grotte
Vaufrey, and other sites of lesser importance."*

Early Last Glacial sites are thin on the ground as
well: barely 11 archeosequences provide evidence of
hominin occupation during this period, and even less
have chronometric dates (Jaubert 2012). Southwest
France during these times seems to have been
basically empty. At the onset of MIS 4 things change
dramatically: almost all of the key cave sites are now
occupied (Jaubert 2012).

### A case of demographic displacement?

This short review has shown that there is a clear
chrono-spatial gradient in the distribution of early
Upper Pleistocene Middle Palaeolithic sites in Western
Europe. For a period of over ~50,000 years, we witness

the core areas of Neanderthal occupation shifting
from continental central Germany to the Atlantic
coast, and further on to the south. As this pattern is so
clearly synchronized with the climatological timescale,
environmental change must be the prime driver of
this territorial shift. Regarding the end of the Eemian
interglacial in particular, it should thus be seriously
considered if not the Late Eemian Aridity Pulse (LEAP)
event (Sirocko *et al.* 2005) has triggered a then small
population to move into Atlantic regions.

We are of course far from understanding the
precise mechanisms of cultural change accompanying
this broader demographic phenomenon. In the
realm of lithic technology, it is clear that Eemian
lithic production is entirely different from what
we see in the early Glacial. Whereas the former is
concerned with opportunistic small flake production,
the latter seems to recapitulate many of the key
features of the late Middle Pleistocene Micoquian
among which extraordinarily large Levallois flakes
and blade production. This is very obvious when
comparing the northern Scheldt Basin assemblages
with, for example, Mesvin IV (Cahen 1984). The
apparent 'microlithisation' of lithic technologies
during interglacials versus 'macrolithisation' during
cold periods appears to be a long-term recurrent
phenomenon that will require close attention in
the future.

The general paucity of retouched flake tools that
is a persistent feature of the early Upper Pleistocene
industries constitutes a fundamental difference
with the Mousterian that I shall consider below. As
a matter of fact the absence of tools deprives the
Mousterian and *a fortiori* its facies from analytical
'visibility': they cannot exist by definition. Conversely,
the Micoquian is by definition as well the early-
stage Middle Palaeolithic of Western Europe during
which Neanderthals were open-air occupants of the
northern higher-latitudinal zones.

With the explosion of documented
archaeosequences in the Aquitaine region from
MIS 4 onward, we recognise the classic pattern of
Mousterian variability which then characterises
the record for another 30,000 years. The apparent
correlation of this techno-typological pattern with
population influx from the north and increasing
population density suggests a causal relationship.
The proximate consequence of this demographic
phenomenon in the technological realm then appears
to be that the respective late Neanderthals have
become 'flake tool producers'. It is only now that we

observe the presence of lithic assemblages with large numbers of such tools, providing the foundation for Bordes' analytical system and, hence, for the possibility to archaeologically identify and describe Mousterian assemblage-types. Based on the demographic scenario sketched thus far, the Mousterian becomes a distinct stage in an evolutionary sequence but the reasons for the associated cultural change – that is, the extensive production of flake tools – still need to be fully understood.

In stark contrast to the regionally clustered occupations from the Eemian through MIS4, MIS3 sites are distributed across the entire 850,000 km² of Western Europe again. In Germany, an unprecedented population density is inferred, with hominin populations seemingly collapsing again within only a few millennia at the end of the Middle Palaeolithic sequence (Richter 2016). We must thus envisage rapid re-colonisation of the north by Neanderthal populations, who had undergone a process of profound cultural change in their southern refuge. Next to having become 'flake tool producers', they now used caves as their residential bases. It is no wonder, from this vantage point, that we now register all the caves in the Belgian Meuse Valley as occupied. This historic scenario rekindles the taxonomic issue. Is the distinction at techno-complex level between the Mousterian and a contemporaneous late Micoquian legitimate and must we accept the challenge of explaining them under the proposed scenario? Or do we witness a case of formal systematics masking sameness? To address this question, I need to delve into the structure of Middle Palaeolithic variability.

## Variability structures

Recent research has seen an expansion of the classic Bordean facies of the Mousterian into numerous 'Lithic Technocomplexes' (LTCs) as a consequence of the incorporation of the *chaîne opératoire* idea (Faivre *et al.* 2014; Jaubert 2012). Fundamentally, however, this inflation of variability has not changed much as to its patterning and interpretation. To the contrary, it has only reinforced their apparently random occurrence in cave sequences. Also, up to the present day the variants, whether Bordean facies or LTCs, tend to conserve meaning as essentialist 'wholes', with a supposed one-on-one relationship to some kind of social entity. For example, one frequently sees reference being made to the 'long duration' of some of these wholes (*e.g.,* Guérin *et al.* 2016). Viewed as '*structured constellations of artefacts, reflecting*

*the behavioural patterns of a system and expressing its technological capacities*' (Clarke 1968, 102), these variants were and still are precociously promoted to the taxonomic level of Clarkian archaeological cultures even when it is admitted that '*the search for their 'meaning'* [quotes by the authors] *appears pre-mature*' (Faivre *et al.* 2017, 129). In the original Mousterian Debate as launched by the Binfords' seminal paper (1966), assemblage formation, *i.e.* the isolation of the basic components of such structured constellations, legitimately had been at stake. Soon, however, this methodological issue seemed forgotten and the facies acquired their quality as invariable assemblage-types with corresponding behavourial, social units. The nature and structure of the latter needed discussion in view of the non-directional structure of the record across time and space (Binford 1969; Bordes and De Sonneville-Bordes 1970; Mellars 1970; Rolland and Dibble 1990; Otte and Keeley 1990). This continues up to the present day and in this essentialist paradigm, the distinction between a northern late Micoquian culture and the Mousterian cultures of the south is bound to be maintained (*e.g.,* Ruebens 2013). Conversely, drawing such boundaries has prevented the recognition of patterns of sameness between these two contemporaneous phenomena.

## The Richter Model

In 2001, Jürgen Richter published a summary account of his earlier study (Richter 1997) of the late Micoquian sequence in the G-complex of Sesselfels Cave in south-eastern Germany. This gave way to an alternative model of late Neanderthal land-use, which I propose to call the 'Richter Model'. During the period between ca. 48,000 and 37,000 years ago, four recurrent cycles of land-use patterning are proposed to be reflected. First of all, Richter distinguished four analytical components of the G-complex as a whole: standard Mousterian tools, Upper Palaeolithic tool types, a distinct microlithic component, and a bifacial component comprising *Keilmesser* and other forms such as bifacial scrapers (Richter 2001, figure 4). Rather than dealing with this variability in Bordean fashion, he investigated the patterning of these lithic components relative to changing raw material diversities throughout the various occupational levels. A clear correspondence between raw material provisioning and typological composition appeared, in a surprising cyclic pattern that was repeated four times throughout the G-complex sequence. Richter explains these cycles in terms of shifting seasonal land-use, starting with a highly mobile context with *Initial inventories* made on a variety of raw materials. His model (2001, figure 11) indicates high frequencies of bifacial tools. This is followed by a radiating pattern with base camps containing *Consecutive Inventories* with many denticulates and *differential tools* among which scrapers. The bifacial portion evidences heavy curation and is reminiscent of Harold Dibble's (1988) scraper rejuvenation sequence. Richter postulates that they were used at special task sites away from the base camp. Microlithic tools are evidenced as well. He observes that they are always made on blanks from late stages of core reduction and connects them with plant exploitation in the neighbourhood of the base camp.

Presumably because of the stratigraphic palimpsest condition of some of the occupation events at Sesselfels Cave, Richter situates his land-use model at an ethnographic resolution. However, he also considers the possibility that these cycles are of much longer duration and represent the initial establishment of Neanderthal groups in new territories, when they lacked the environmental knowledge of the 'wise old men' who figure in the title of his contribution. How does this pattern of variability compare to the Mousterian in the south?

*Mousterian variability reconsidered*
However opposed the interpretations of Mousterian facies may be, the parties involved have always agreed on one issue: the absence of clear chronological order. This is in negation of rare efforts to demonstrate the opposite, for example based on consistent facies sequencing in local archaeological sequences (Mellars 1970). It needs to be kept in mind here that the regional pattern of facies-contemporaneities was derived from indirect sequence correlations in a time when chronometric age estimations were uncommon (Laville 1973). Now that a large set of chronometric dates has been assembled (Guibert *et al.* 2008; Vermeersch 2023), the time has come to critically re-evaluate this pattern using absolute chronologies with local stratigraphic sequences as 'Bayesian' constraints. Combe Grenal, with the longest archeosequence in the entire region (Bordes 1972) can serve as a stratigraphic constraint at regional scale. If Combe Grenal represents a transect of a regional chronological succession, it follows that the same order should appear in the chronological arrangement of the Aquitaine Mousterian. That is the hypothesis.

An exploration of the preliminary chronometric dataset (figure 1) leads me to three surprising observations:

1. The dates allow to replicate the stratigraphic order documented at Combe Grenal,
2. the chronometric-archeostratigraphic succession thus achieved is identical to the cyclic pattern in the Richter model and
3. the component typological groups of the Richter cycles and their succession in his land-use model recall the order of the Mousterian facies.

In the late Mousterian sequence of the Aquitaine region, three successive cycles of the 'Mousterian of Acheulean Tradition', 'Denticulate Mousterian', 'Typical/Ferrassie', 'Quina' and, finally, a laminar/microlithic phase of the Mousterian are recorded. The latter comprises unnamed assemblages such as Combe Grenal Layer 16 (Faivre 2012) showing affinities with the so-called 'Asinipodian' which Bordes identified on the basis of its diminutive lithic production (Bordes 1984; Dibble and McPherron 2006). The production of these small Levallois flakes appears to be an innovation during final MIS 5a which is already apparent in assemblages of the Techno-complex of the Northwest. Interestingly, in the Mousterian sphere, too, handaxes have been commonly characterised as highly mobile tools by several authors (Claud 2012; Soressi and Hays 2003; Turq 2000).

This pattern of changing settlement strategies over time in both the Mousterian and the late Micoquian fits the demographic scenario sketched above, wherein the north is forcefully recolonised during the Interpleniglacial. As Richter concludes himself, we have to come to the inevitable insight that the Mousterian and the late Micoquian are homologous archaeological signatures of one and the same metapopulation of late Neanderthals.

THE 70KA THRESHOLD
To improve our ability to properly address Neanderthal behaviour and cultural change, it seems necessary to abandon the analytical regionalism that has been in vogue for too long. The difference between Micoquian and Mousterian technocomplexes must be understood as variations on a chronogeographic gradient, the consequence of ecological shifts of Neanderthal groups (see Banks *et al.* 2021) across a Western European territory of small size when considered at a Pleistocene timescale. A much more important

| SOUTHWEST FRANCE | | | | | COMBE GRENAL ARCHEOSEQUENCE | | |
|---|---|---|---|---|---|---|---|
| Assemblage | Date (mean ka /method) | Facies | Descriptive comment | Reference | Culture-stratigraphic sequence | Descriptive Comment | Reference |
| Le Moustier K | 42 $^{14}$C mod | CHATELP. | | Higham et al. 2014 | | | |
| Regourdou L4 | 42 $^{14}$C cal | QUINA | | Pelletier et al. 2017 | | | |
| Le Moustier J | 44 $^{14}$C mod | TYP/FERR | with large side scrapers - Quina? | Higham et al. 2014 | | | |
| Le Moustier I | 46 $^{14}$C mod | DENTICULATE | | Higham et al. 2014 | | | |
| Le Moustier H | 47 $^{14}$C mod | MTA | | Higham et al. 2014 | L4-1 | | |
| | | | | | hiatus in distribution | | Dibble et al. 2009 |
| ? | | ? | | | L7-5 | 'A small-sized Typ. Moust. with plenty of Levallois flakes' | Bordes 1972:112 |
| Roc de Marsal L2-4 | 49 TL | QUINA | | Guérin et al. 2016 | L9-8 QUINA? | Moustérien indéterminé/typique pauvre | Turq 2000: Tab. 5 |
| Combe-Capelle Bas | 52 TL | TYP/FERR | | Valladas et al. 2003 | L10 | | Bordes 1972 |
| La Quina Amont L6a | 51 TL | DENTICULATE | | Frouin et al. 2017 | L14-11 | | Jaubert 2012; Turq 2000 |
| Le Moustier G1 | 56 TL | MTA | 386 handaxes; many denticulates | Guibert et al. 2008 | L15 MTA? | Denticulate (Bordes) but with handaxes (Turq) | Bordes 1972; Turq 2000 |
| | | | | | hiatus in distribution | | Dibble et al. 2009 |
| La Folie | 58 TL | ? | | Bourguignon 2010 | L16 | | Bordes 1972; Faivre et al. 2014; Faivre2012 |
| La Quina Amont LN-K | 63-55 IR$_{50}$/OSL | QUINA | | Frouin et al. 2017 | L26-17 | | Bordes 1972; Turq 2000 |
| Artenac L8-5 | 67 TL | TYP/FERR | | Guibert et al. 2008 | L35-27 | | Bordes 1972; Geneste et al. 1997 |
| Roc de Marsal L8 | 68-65 TL | DENTICULATE | | Guérin et al. 2012 | L37-36 | | Bordes 1972 |
| Grotte XVI | 65 TL | MTA | 19 handaxes - backed specimens | Soressi and Hays 2003 | L38 MTA? | 1 bifacial cleaver; blade production system | Bordes 1972; Turq 2000 |
| | | | | | hiatus in distribution | | Dibble et al. 2009 |
| Roc de Marsal L9 | 70 TL | ASINIPODIAN | | Richter 2017; Guérin et al. 2016 | L41-39? | No details on industry; first appearance of reindeer | Bordes 1972 |
| Start of dense occupation | | | | | thermoclastic éboulis - origin of shelter | | |

Figure 1. Chronological arrangement of selected lithic assemblages* from Southwest France (left) and proposed synchronisation with the Combe Grenal archeosequence (right). Note that the relative arrangement of assemblages in local archeosequences (Le Moustier *abri inférieur*; Roc de Marsal; La Quina Amont) has been respected. Available chronometric dates are cited as (ranges of) means rounded to the nearest ka unit**. For full chronometric data, see the provided references. Combe Grenal assemblages are grouped according to their conventional facies attributions (coloured). Those for which a facies revision may be in order are left blank. Hiatuses in the vertical distribution at CG are derived from Dibble and colleagues' piece-plotting of the CG data based on Bordes' fieldnotes. *This is a preview of the complete dataset of 113 dated lithic assemblages exhibiting the same pattern. **14C mod refers to modelled ages.

demarcation is found between early Glacial and Pleniglacial adaptations, where a sudden transition occurs from a long period of technological stasis to a condition of accelerated cyclic change. In the former lithic technology is oriented towards the manufacture of bifacial *façonnage* tools on the one hand and sizable debitage products with anticipated morphologies on the other. Rarely they seem to serve as blanks for retouched tool manufacture. The systematic incorporation of the latter in extended *chaînes opératoires* appears at the onset of the Pleniglacial and in tandem with the contraction of populations into the southern part of Western Europe. These longer lithic production sequences have greatly expanded the window of variability (see Dibble 1988), providing the empirical base for the Bordean system of measuring variation. Consequently, it is in this extended technological realm that something unprecedented emerges: rapid, directional change re-iterated in cycles of perhaps accelerating tempo (see figure 1) across the MIS3 middle palaeolithic, whether in its Mousterian form in the south or its late Micoquian form in the north. The Châtelperronian takes a predictable place in this pattern and may thus be considered a Middle Palaeolithic industry insofar as it inscribes in later Middle Palaeolithic long-term dynamics of cyclic technological change. In support of this assertion, it is enlightening to point out the remarkable appearance of the early Glacial assemblage from Seclin in Northern France, qualified by F. Bordes as *'une curieuse industrie'* (1984: 149). Taking its place in the suite of technological changes described above, it heralds all the techno-typological features of the Châtelperronian.

This brief review of and reflection on Middle Palaeolithic variability thus shapes the contours of a research question that seems to be of crucial importance: how does lithic diversity in the <70 ka Middle Palaeolithic precisely pattern chronospatially? For example, is the first-cycle MTA (see figure 1) in Aquitaine more different from the third-cycle MTA than the latter is different from the 'Initial Inventory' in Floor 11 at Sesselfels Cave? A quantitative analysis of this kind may inform us on the nature of cumulative culture in Neanderthals (Davidson 2016). Alternatively, given the fact that these late Neanderthals had undergone major behavioural change in their southern refuge and reached unprecedented population densities in MIS3, it is not unlikely that some diversity in their material productions, for example of bifaces, is stylistic (Ruebens 2013).

## Conclusion

The shape of the long-term pattern of variability sketched out here at least solicits the interesting hypothesis that the onset of MIS4 represents a significant evolutionary threshold in the Neanderthal lineage. Based on the patterning in their archaeological record, it is possible to view Neanderthals as limited top predators since Middle Pleistocene times and all through the early Upper Pleistocene. In MIS4 a suite of changes is set in motion, resulting in their escape from the Boserupian trap in which they had been caught up for so long (Bocquet-Appel and Degioanni 2013). These later Neanderthals had acquired the potential for growth and cultural change (Kline and Boyd 2011). They were behaviourally different from their predecessors and material cultures gained a novel status in their socioeconomic systems. In terms of historical change, the 70 ka threshold seems to delineate a more fundamental rupture than the conventionally accepted Neanderthal transition to the Upper Palaeolithic.

## Acknowledgements

The ideas expressed in this paper benefited from discussions with so many colleagues over the course of the years. Raymond Corbey was among the very first and our earliest exchanges go back to our student days in the early 1980s, when he came to Leuven to study Palaeolithic artefact collections. It was only a short period of time, but long enough to leave a mark. It is therefore with great pleasure that I have written this contribution to his *Festschrift*.

## References

Ashton, N., and B. Scott. 2016. The British Middle Palaeolithic. *Quaternary International* 411 Part A, 62-76.

Banks, W.E., M.-H. Moncel, J.-P. Raynal, M.E. Cobos, D. Romero-Alvarez, M.-N. Woillez, J.-P. Faivre, B. Gravina, F. d'Errico, J.-L. Locht, and F. Santos. 2021. "An ecological Niche shift for Neanderthal populations in Western Europe 70,000 years ago." *Scientific Reports* 11, 5346.

Binford, L.R. 1962. "Archaeology as Anthropology." *American Antiquity* 28, 217-225.

Binford, L.R. 1969. "Comment on 'Culture traditions and environment of Early Man' by D. Collins." *Current Anthropology* 10, 297-299.

Binford, L.R. and S. Binford. 1966. "A Preliminary Analysis of Functional Variability in the Mousterian of Levallois Facies." *American Anthropologist* 68, 238-295.

Blazer, F., and C. Chaussé. 2016. "Saint-Illiers-la-Ville and the Micoquian of Weichselian sequences of the Paris Basin." *Quaternary International* 411, 163-178.

Bocquet-Appel, J.-P. and A. Degioanni. 2013. "Neanderthal Demographic Estimates." *Current Anthropology* 54, 202-213.

Bordes, F. 1961. *Typologie du Paléolithique ancien et moyen*. Bordeaux: Publications de l'Institut de Préhistoire de l'Université de Bordeaux, Mémoire 1.

Bordes, F. 1972. *A Tale of two caves*. London: Harper and Row.

Bordes, F. 1984. *Leçons sur le Paléolithique, Tome II. Le Paléolithique en Europe*. Cahiers du Quaternaire N° 7. Paris: CNRS.

Bordes, F., and D. De Sonneville-Bordes. 1970. "The Significance of Variability in Palaeolithic Assemblages." *World Archaeology* 2 (1), 61-73.

Bosinski, G. 1967. *Die Mittelpaläolithischen Funde im Westlichen Mitteleuropa*. Köln: Böhlau Verlag.

Bosquet, D., P. Haesaerts, F. Damblon, J. Giner, P. Rsyssaert, and C. Rsyssaert. 2011. "Le gisement paléolithique de Remicourt-En Bia Flo I." In *Le Paléolithique moyen en Belgique. Mélanges Maegueritte Ulrix-Closset*, edited by M. Toussaint, K. Di Monica and S. Pirson, 375-384. Liège: Eraul 128.

Bourguignon, L. 2010. "Le Campement Moustérien de La Folie (Vienne)." In *Préhistoire entre Vienne et Charente. Hommes et sociétés du Paléolithique*, edited by J. Buisson-Catil and J. Primault, 169-174. Paris: Ministère de la Culture et Communcation Mémoire XXXVIII.

Cahen, D. 1984. "Paléolithique inférieur et moyen en Belgique." In *Peuples chasseurs de la Belgique préhistorique dans leur cadre naturel*, edited by D. Cahen and P. Haesaerts, 133-155. Brussels.

Clarke, D. L. 1968. *Analytical Archaeology*. London: Methuen.

Claud, E. 2012. "Les bifaces : des outils polyfonctionels ? Etude tracéologique intégrée de bifaces du Paléolithique moyen récent du Sud-Ouest de la France." *Bulletin de la Société préhistorique française* 109, 413-439.

Damas, D. 1968. "The Diversity of Eskimo Societies." In *Man the Hunter*, edited by R. B. Lee and I. Devore, 111-117. New York: Aldine the Gruyter.

Davidson, I. 2016. "Stone Tools: Evidence of Something in Between Culture and Cumulative Culture?." In: *The Nature of Culture*, edited by M.N. Haidle, N.J. Conard, N. and M. Bolus, 99-120. Dordrecht: Springer.

Defleur, A.R., E. Desclaux, R.S. Jabbour, and G.D. Richards. 2020. "The Eemian: Global warming, ecosystem upheaval, demographic collapse and cannibalism at Moula-Guercy." *Journal of Archaeological Science* 117, 105113.

Depaepe, P. 2007. *Le Paléolithique moyen de la Vallée de la Vanne (Yonne, France) : matières premières, industries lithiques et occupations humaines*. Paris: Mém. de la Société préhistorique française XLI.

Dibble, H.L. 1988. "The Interpretation of Middle Paleolithic scraper reduction patterns." *In L'Homme de Neandertal, vol.4: La Technique*, edited by M. Otte, 49-58. Liège: ERAUL 31.

Dibble, H.L. and S.P. McPherron. 2006. "The Missing Mousterian." *Current Anthropology* 47, 777-803.

Dibble, H.L., S.P. McPherron, D. Sandgathe, P. Goldberg, Paul, A. Turq, and M. Lenoir. 2009. "Context, curation, and bias: an evaluation of the Middle Paleolithic collections of Combe-Grenal (France)." *Journal of Archaeological Science* 36, 2540-2550.

Faivre, J.-Ph. 2012. "A material anecdote but technical reality: Bladelet and small blade production during the recent Middle Paleolithic at the Combe-Grenal rockshelter." *Lithic Technology* 37, 5-25.

Faivre, J.-Ph., E. Discamps, B. Gravina, A. Turq, J.-L. Guadelli, and M. Lenoir. 2014. "The contribution of lithic production systems to the interpretation of Mousterian industrial variability in south-western France: The example of Combe-Grenal (Dordogne, France)." *Quaternary International* 350, 227-240.

Faivre, J.-Ph., B. Gravina, L. Bourguignon, E. Discamps, and A. Turq. 2017. "Late Middle Palaeolithic lithic technocomplexes (MIS 5-3) in the northeastern Aquitaine Basin: Advances and challenges." *Quaternary International* 433, 116-131.

Frick, J.A. 2020. "Reflections on the term Micoquian in Western and Central Europe. Change in criteria, changed deductions, change in meaning, and its significance for current research." *Archaeological and Anthropological Sciences* 12, 38. DOI:10.1007/s12520-019-0967-5

Frouin, M., C. Lahaye, H. Valladas, T. Higham, A. Debénath, A. Delagnes, and N. Mercier. 2017. "Dating the Middle Paleolithic deposits of La Quina Amont (Charente, France) using luminescence methods." *Journal of Human Evolution* 109, 30-45.

Geneste, J.-M., J. Jaubert, M. Lenoir, L. Meignen, and A. Turq. 1997. "Approche technologique des Moustériens Charentiens du Sud-Ouest de la France et du Languedoc oriental." *Paléo* 9, 101-142.

Goval, E., and P. Depaepe. 2012. "Regards portés sur les travaux de François Bordes en France septentrionale." In *François Bordes et la Préhistoire. Colloque international François Bordes, Bordeaux 22-24 avril 2009*, edited by F. Delpech and J. Jaubert, 255-265. Paris: CTHS.

Goval, E. and J.-L. Locht. 2009. "Remontages, systèmes techniques et répartitions spatiales dans l'analyse du site weichsélian ancien de Fresnoy-au-Val (Somme, France)." *Bulletin de la Société préhistorique française* 106, 653-678.

Guérin, G., M. Frouin, J. Tuquoi, K. J. Thomsen, P. Goldberg, V. Aldeias, C. Lahaye, *et al.* 2016. "The complementarity of luminescence dating methods illustrated on the Mousterian sequence of the Roc de Marsal: A series of reindeer-dominated Quina Mousterian layers dated to MIS3." *Quaternary International* 433, DOI:10.1016/j.quaint.2016.02.063.

Guérin, G., C. Lahaye, N. Mercier, P. Guibert, A. Turq, H.L. Dibble, S.P. McPherron, D. Sandgathe, P. Goldberg, M. Jain, K. Thomsen, M. Patou-Mathis, J.-C. Castel, and M.-C. Soulier 2012. "Multi-method (TL and OSL), multi-material (quartz and flint) datinf of the Mousterian site of Roc de Marsal (Dordogne, France): correlating Neanderthal occupations with the climatic variability of MIS 5-3." *Journal of Archaeological Science* 39, 3071-3084.

Guibert, P., F. Bechtel, L. Bourguignon, M. Brenet, I. Couchoud, A. Delagnes, F. Delpech, L. Detrain, M. Duttine, M. Folgado, J. Jaubert, C. Lahaye, M. Lenoir, B. Maureille, P.-J. Texier, A. Turq, E. Vieillvigne, and G. Villeneuve. 2008. *Une base de données pour la chronologie du Paléolithique moyen dans le Sud-Ouest de la France.* Paris: Bulletin de la Société Préhistorique Française, Mémoire XLVII.

Haesaerts, P., H. Mestdagh, and D. Bosquet. 1997. "La séquence loessique de Remicourt (Hebaye, Belgique)." *Notae Praehistoricae* 17, 45-52.

Helm, J. 1968. "The Nature of Dogrib socioterritorial Groups." In *Man the Hunter*, edited by R. B. Lee and I. Devore, 118-125. New York: Aldine the Gruyter.

Higham, T., K. Douka, R. Wood, C. Bronk Ramsey, F. Brok, L. Basell, M. Camps, A. Arrizabalaga, J. Baena, C. Barroso-Ruíz, C. Bergman, C. Boitard, P. Boscato, M. Caparrós, N.J. Conard, C. Draily, A. Froment, B. Galván, P. Gambassini, A. Garcia-Moreno, S. Grimaldi, P. Haesaerts, B. Holt, M.-J. Iriarte-Chiapusso, A. Jelinek, J.F. Jordá Pardo, J.-M. Maíllo-Fernández, A. Marom, J. Maroto, M. Menéndez, L. Metz, E. Morin, A. Moroni, F. Negrino, E. Panagopoulou, M. Peresani, S. Pirson, M. de la Rasilla, J. Riel-Salvatore, A. Ronchitelli, D. Santamaria, P. Semal, L. Slimak, J. Soler, N. Soler, A. Villaluenga, R. Pinhasi, and R. Jacobi 2014. "The timing and spatiotemporal patterning of Neanderthal disappearance." *Nature* 512, 306-309.

Hublin, J.-J. and W. Roebroeks. 2009. "Ebb and flow or regional extinctions? On the character of Neandertal occupation of northern environments." *Comptes Rendus Palevol* 8, 503-509.

Jaubert, J. 2012. "Les archéoséquences du Paléolithique Moyen du Sud-Ouest de la France : quel bilan un quart de siècle après François Bordes?" In *François Bordes et la Préhistoire. Colloque international François Bordes, Bordeaux 22-24 avril 2009*, edited by F. Delpech and J. Jaubert, 235-253. Paris: CTHS.

Jöris, O. 2003. "Zur chronostratigraphischen Stellung der spätmittelpaläolithischen Keilmessergruppen. Der Versuch einer kulturgeographischen Abgrenzung einer mittelpaläolithischen Formengruppe." *Bericht der Römisch-Germanischen Kommission* 84, 51-153.

Kline, M. A. and R. Boyd. 2011. "Population size predicts technological complexity in Oceania." *Proceedings of the Royal Society B* 277, 2559-2564.

Laurat, T. and E. Brühl. 2021. "Neumark Nord 2 – A multiphase Middle Palaeolithic open-air site in the Geisel Valley (Central Germany)." *L'Anthropologie* 125, 102936.

Laville, H. 1973. "The relative position of Mousterian industries in the climatic chronology of the early Würm in the Périgord." *World Archaeology* 4, 323-329.

Locht, J.-L. 2002. *Bettencourt-Saint-Ouen (Somme). Cinq occupations paléolithiques au début de la dernière glaciation.* Documents d'archéologie française 90. Paris: Maison des sciences de l'Homme.

Locht, J.-L.. 2021. "Les Industries lithiques d'âge éemien du site de Caours (Somme)." *L'anthropologie* 125, 102903.

Locht, J.-L. and P. Depaepe. 2011. "Regards sur le Paléolithique moyen de France septentrionale et de Belgique." In *Le Paléolithique moyen en Belgique. Mélanges Maegueritte Ulrix-Closset*, edited by M. Toussaint, K. Di Monica, and S. Pirson, 229-237. Liège: Eraul 128.

Locht, J.-L., D. Hérisson, E. Goval, D. Cliquet, B. Huet, S. Coutard, P. Antoine, and Ph. Feray. 2016. "Timescales, space and culture during the Middle Palaeolithic in northwestern France." *Quaternary International* 411, 129-148.

Mellars, P. A. 1970. "Some Comments on the Notion of 'Functional Variability' in Stone-Tool Assemblages." *World Archaeology* 2, 74-89.

O'Brien, M. J. and R. L. Lyman. 2001. *Applying Evolutionary Archaeology. A Systematic Approach.* New York: Springer.

Otte, M. 2017. "The Mousterian with bifacial retouch in Europe: the fundamental historical error." *Quaternary International* 428A, 109-117.

Otte, M., and L. H. Keeley. 1990. "The Impact of Regionalism on Palaeolithic Studies." *Current Anthropology* 31, 577-82.

Pedersen, J. B., A. Maier, and F. Riede. 2018. "A punctuated model for the colonisation of the Late Glacial margins of northern Europe by Hamburgian hunter-gatherers." *Quartär* 65, 85-104.

Pelletier, M., A. Royer, T.W. Holliday, E. Discamps, S. Madeleine, and B. Maureille. 2017. "Rabbits in the grave! Consequences of bioturbation on the Neandertal "burial" at Regourdou (Montignac-sur-Vézère, Dordogne)." *Journal of Human Evolution* 110, 1-17.

Richter, D., S.P. McPherron, H.L. Dibble, P. Goldberg, and D. Sandgathe. 2017. "Additional chronometric data for the small flake assemblages ('Asinipodian') from Pech de l'Azé IV (France) and a comparison with similar assemblages at the nearby site of Roc de Marsal." In *Vocation à la Préhistoire. Hommage à Jean-Marie Le Tensorer*, edited by D. Wojtczak, M. Al Najjar, R. Jagher, H. Elsuede, F. Wegmüller, and M. Otte, 323-335. Liège: Eraul 148.

Richter, J. 1997. *Sesselfelsgrotte III: Der G-Schichten-Komplex der Sesselfelsgrotte. Zum Verständnis des Micoquien. 1st ed.* Stuttgart: Franz Steiner Verlag.

Richter, J. 2001. "For Lack of Wise Old Men? Late Neanderthal Land-Use Patterns in the Altmühl River Vallry, Bavaria." In *Settlement Dynamics of the Middle Paleolithic and Middle Stone Age*, edited by N.J. Conard, 205-219. Tübingen: Kerns Verlag.

Richter, J. 2016. "Leave at the height of the party: A critical review of the Middle Paleolithic in Western Central Europe from its beginnings to its rapid decline." *Quaternary International* 411 Part A, 407-428.

Rolland, N. and H.L. Dibble. 1990. "A New Synthesis of Middle Paleolithic Variability." *American Antiquity* 55, 480-499.

Ruebens, K. 2013. "Regional behaviour among late Neanderthal groups in Western Europe: a comparative assessment of late Middle Palaeolithic bifacial tool variability." *Journal of Human Evolution* 65, 341-362.

Sirocko, F., K. Seelos, K. Schaber, B. Rein, F. Dreher, M. Diehl, R. Lehne, K. Jäger, M. Krbetschek, and D. Degering. 2005. "A late Eemian aridity pulse in central Europe during the last glacial inception." *Nature* 436, 833-835

Soressi, M. and M. A. Hays. 2003. "Manufacture, Transport, and Use of Mousterian Bifaces: a Case Study from the Périgord (France)." In *Multiple Approaches to the Study of Bifacial Technologies*, edited by M. Soressi and H. L. Dibble, 125-148. Philadelphia: Museum of Archaeology and Anthropology, University of Pennsylvania.

Suttles, W. 1968. "Coping with Abundance: Subsistence on the Northwest Coast." In *Man the Hunter*, edited by R. B. Lee and I. Devore, 56-68. New York: Aldine the Gruyter.

Turq, A. 2000. *Paléolithique inférieur et moyen entre Dordogne et Lot.* Supplément Paleo 2. Les Eyzies: Société des amis du Musée national de Préhistoire et de la recherche archéologique.

Valladas, H., N. Mercier, J.-L. Joron, S.P. McPherron, H.L. Dibble, and M. Lenoir. 2003. "TL dates for the Middle Paleolithic site of Combe-Capelle Bas, France." *Journal of Archaeological Science* 30, 1443-1450.

Van Peer, Ph., M. Willems, P. Degryse, Ph. Claeys, and E. Marinova. 2017. "A reconstruction of the stratigraphic position of a former Middle Palaeolithic surface site at Rotselaar – Toren ter Heide (Flemish Valley, Belgium) using mechanical sounding and geochemical fingerprinting." *Journal of Archaeological Science: Reports* 16, 380-390.

Vermeersch, P. M. 2023. *Radiocarbon Palaeolithic Europe Database v30.* http://www.ees.kuleuven.be/geography/projects/14c-palaeolithic/index.html

In Hussain, S.T. and G.L. Dusseldorp (eds) 2025. Sitting on the fence: Negotiating archaeology, anthropology and philosophy. Festschrift for Prof. Dr Raymond H.A. Corbey in celebration of his 70th birthday. *Analecta Praehistorica Leidensia* 54. Leiden: Sidestone Press, pp. 163-178.

# Religious sacrifice in the Ice Age? Ritual finger amputation and the Gravettian hand images with incomplete fingers

Mark Collard, Brea McCauley

ABSTRACT

More than 200 hand images with incomplete fingers (HIIFs) have been found at cave sites in France and Spain that are associated with the Gravettian archaeological culture (27,000-22,000 BP). In 2018, we reported a cross-cultural study designed to shed light on the possibility that the Gravettian HIIFs reflect finger amputation. We concluded that, when the contexts and what we can infer about the sex and age of the participants are considered, the hypothesis that best fits the images is that they were produced by individuals whose fingers had been amputated in religious rituals. In this paper, we respond to the criticisms that have been levelled at our study in the intervening period. Drawing on the results of an expanded cross-cultural study, we show that the critics' arguments are unfounded. We also explain why amputation deserves to be taken seriously as a potential explanation for the Gravettian HIIFs, and why religious sacrifice is the motivation that best fits the currently available data pertaining to the images. Lastly, we outline the potential implications of the Ritual Amputation Hypothesis for our understanding of Gravettian social life and the evolution of human cognition.

*Keywords: Rock art; parietal art; cave painting; Upper Palaeolithic; permanent body modification; finger amputation.*

## INTRODUCTION

Over 200 hand images with incomplete fingers (HIIFs) have been found among Europe's Ice Age cave paintings. These images are in France and Spain and are thought to be associated with the Upper Palaeolithic Gravettian archaeological culture (27,000-22,000 BP) (Jaubert 2008). Some examples of Gravettian HIIFs at Cosquer Cave, France, are shown in figure 1A. The geographic distribution of sites with Gravettian HIIFs is depicted in figure 1B.

The term 'hand image' refers to both handprints and hand stencils. These can be thought of as positive and negative hand images, respectively (Snow 2006). To produce a positive hand image, the front of the hand is covered with pigment and then pressed on a surface. In contrast, a negative hand image is created by pressing the hand against a surface and applying pigment around it.

The Gravettian HIIFs vary along several dimensions. Both left and right hands were used to make the images, and it is believed that they represent the hands of both males and females (Barriére 1976). In addition, the number of incomplete fingers per image varies considerably between and within sites. Some images have just one incomplete finger, while others have only one complete finger (figure 1C).

**Mark Collard**

Department of Archaeology, Simon Fraser University, Canada

mcollard@sfu.ca

ORCID: 0000-0002-2725-4989

**Brea McCauley**

Department of Archaeology, Simon Fraser University, Canada

brea_mccauley@sfu.ca

ORCID: 0000-0002-2413-720X

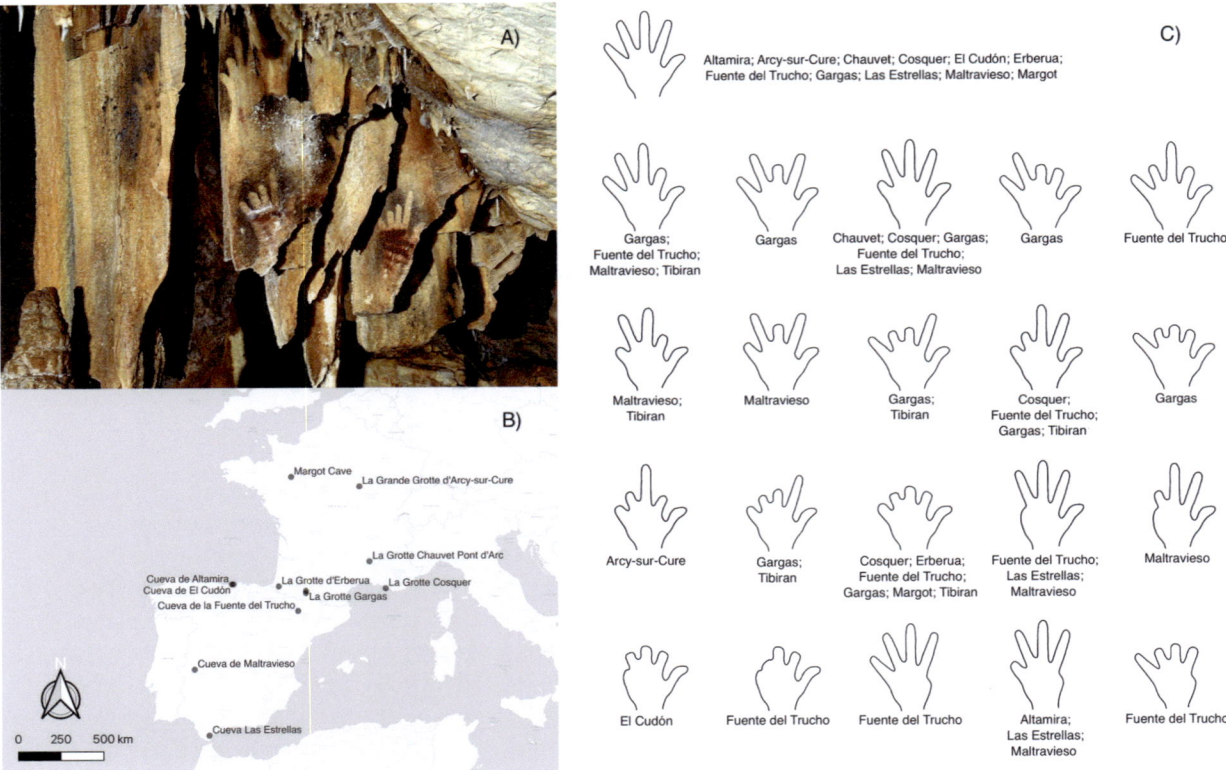

Figure 1. Gravettian hand images with missing finger segments. A) Photo of hand images from Cosquer Cave, France. Credit: Jean Clottes, used with permission. B) Geographic distribution of archaeological sites with Gravettian hand images with incomplete fingers. C) Drawings of hand images illustrating the variability in missing finger segments. All images drawn as left hands. The top left drawing lists sites with complete hand images. The incomplete hand drawings do not distinguish between one and two missing segments. Images redrawn from Sahly (1966), Leroi-Gourhan (1967), Baffier and Girard (1998), Clottes (2001), Clottes *et al.* (2005), Pigeaud *et al.* (2006), Larribau (2013), Groenen (2016), Collado Giraldo *et al.* (2018a-e), and Collado Giraldo *et al.* (2019).

Currently, the significance of the Gravettian HIIFs is unclear. Some authors have argued that the individuals who produced the images had all their fingers and simply manipulated their hands so that one or more finger segments were not visible. Others have argued that the images were produced by individuals who had undergone finger amputation.

In 2018 we reported a study designed to shed light on the possibility that the Gravettian HIIFs reflect finger amputation (McCauley *et al.* 2018). We identified 121 recent groups that practised finger amputation and distinguished ten motivations for the custom, nine of which did not involve a medical goal. We concluded that, when the contexts and what we can infer about the individuals' sex and age are considered, the hypothesis that best fits the Gravettian HIIFs is that the people who produced

them had undergone amputation in rituals intended to elicit help from supernatural entities.

Some colleagues have dismissed our study. Most notably, in media coverage of the study, Prof. Paul Pettitt called it "ill-informed" and argued that amputation cannot explain the Gravettian HIIFs because many lack more than just the little finger and that is not what is seen in the ethnographic record (Pappas 2018). In fact, Pettitt went beyond the claim that it is not seen ethnographically. He implied it is inconceivable, as can be seen in the following quotations:

*"Ethnographically, if amputations occur, they are typically of the little finger: It would be idiotic to amputate more!," Pettitt quoted in Pappas (2018).*

*"Nobody would be idiotic enough to remove every finger bar the thumb. That simply makes no sense,"* Pettitt quoted in Marshall (2018).

A similar argument can be found in a recent story for *New Scientist* by Dr. Alison George (2023). George's piece focused on the sites of Gargas and Cosquer in France. She noted that the most common HIIF pattern at these sites is an extended thumb with all other fingers incomplete and argued that this "extreme mutilation [...] would have been catastrophic for the recipient" (George 2023, 40). When combined with the fact that there are no incomplete fingers on the positive Upper Palaeolithic hand images, she suggested, this observation rules out "the mutilation idea [...] at least at Gargas and Cosquer" (George 2023, 40).

Inspired by Prof. Corbey's jousterly approach to the academic enterprise, the present paper is a response to Pettitt's and George's criticisms of our 2018 study. We begin with the basics – the definition of a HIIF and the geographic distribution of the Gravettian HIIFs. We then provide an overview of the hypotheses that have been put forward to explain the Gravettian HIIFs. Next, we evaluate Pettitt's and George's criticisms of the Ritual Amputation Hypothesis and show they are flawed. Thereafter, we explain why amputation deserves to be taken seriously as a potential explanation for the Gravettian HIIFs and why religious sacrifice is the motivation that best fits the available data pertaining to the Gravettian HIIFs. Subsequently, we outline the implications of the Ritual Amputation Hypothesis for our understanding of Gravettian social life and the evolution of human cognition. In the final section of the paper, we clarify what we are, and are not, arguing in relation to the Ritual Amputation Hypothesis.

## THE GRAVETTIAN HIIFS

We define a HIIF as a positive or negative image of a human hand in which more than one, but less than all, of the finger segments are visible. A finger segment comprises a phalanx and its associated soft tissues. The phalanges of the hand are the bones at the core of the fingers. Normally there are 14 phalanges in a human hand. The thumb has two – a proximal phalanx and a distal one. The forefinger, middle finger, ring finger, and little finger all have three – a proximal phalanx, a middle phalanx, and a distal phalanx. Thus, in principle, a HIIF can have between one and 13 finger segments visible.

We have specified that a HIIF must have at least one finger segment visible to exclude palm prints, which are uninformative regarding the absence of finger segments. Our definition of a HIIF also excludes the so-called crooked thumb images, which are stencils of flexed thumbs (Clottes 2008). It has been suggested to us that these may be a type of HIIF but we are not convinced. Crucially, it is unclear whether the hands featured in the crooked thumb images had all their other fingers.

In our 2018 paper we provided an overview of Gravettian HIIFs (McCauley *et al.* 2018). We have since identified additional sites and revised the number of HIIFs at some of the sites in our original list (McCauley and Collard, in press). Our current tally of Gravettian HIIFs is 203. These images are distributed among 12 sites in France and Spain (figure 1B). The 203 images are not evenly distributed among the sites (table 1). Ninety-three of them are found at Gargas Cave in southwest France, 42 occur at Maltravieso in western Spain, and 28 are found at Cosquer Cave in southern France. A further 23 occur at Fuente del Trucho, which is in northeast Spain. None of the remaining eight cave sites has more than ten HIIFs.

## POTENTIAL EXPLANATIONS FOR THE GRAVETTIAN HIIFS

A number of explanations have been put forward by those who believe the individuals who produced the Gravettian HIIFs manipulated their hands so that certain finger segments were not included. Several researchers have argued the Gravettian HIIFs reflect use of a sign language. Pettitt and George are proponents of this hypothesis (George, 2023). Support for the Sign Language Hypothesis can also be found in Patte (1960), Leroi-Gourhan (1967, 1986), Delluc and Delluc (1993), Clottes and Courtin (1994), and Etxepare and Irurtzun (2021). Van den Broeck (1950) proposed another explanation, which is that the Gravettian HIIFs were created as 'visiting cards'. Lastly, Rouillon (2006) and Overmann (2014) have posited that the Gravettian HIIFs represent a counting system.

As we mentioned earlier, in our 2018 paper we argued that the Gravettian HIIFs reflect finger amputation during life to appeal for supernatural assistance (McCauley *et al.* 2018). We were not the first researchers to support this hypothesis. Baudoin (1927), Casteret (1951), and Nougier (1963) all argued that Gravettian HIIFs were made by hands from which fingers had been removed as sacrificial offerings. Others have proposed related hypotheses. Breuil (1952)

| Site | Country | Complete | HIIF | Unclear | Total | Are the HIIFs positive or negative? | Source |
|---|---|---|---|---|---|---|---|
| Cueva de Altamira | Spain | 3 | 1 | 5 | 9 | Negative | Freeman and González Echegaray (2001); Collado Giraldo et al. (2018b) |
| Cueva de El Cudón | Spain | 0 | 1 | 1 | 2 | Negative | González Echegaray and Sáinz (1994); Collado Giraldo et al. (2018a) |
| Cueva de la Fuente del Trucho | Spain | 12 | 23 | 21 | 56 | Negative | Utrilla et al. (2013); Collado Giraldo et al. (2018c) |
| Cueva de Las Estrellas | Spain | 1 | 4 | 0 | 5 | Negative | Collado Giraldo et al. (2019) |
| Cueva de Maltravieso | Spain | 4 | 42 | 13 | 59 | Negative | López et al. (1999); Collado Giraldo and García Arranz (2018) |
| Grotte Chauvet Pont d'Arc | France | 10 | 1 | 0 | 11 | Positive | Clottes (2001) |
| Grotte Cosquer | France | 21 | 28 | 0 | 49 | Negative | Clottes and Courtin (1994); Clottes et al. (2005) |
| Grotte d'Erberua | France | 2 | 1 | 0 | 3 | Negative | Larribau (2013) |
| Grotte Gargas | France | 17 | 93 | 83 | 193 | Negative | Leroi-Gourhan (1967); Barrière (1976); Groenen (2016) |
| Grotte d'Arcy-sur-Cure | France | 7 | 1 | 1 | 9 | Negative | Baffier and Girard (1998) |
| Grotte Tibiran | France | 0 | 7 | 3 | 10 | Negative | Sahly (1966) |
| Margot Cave | France | 4 | 1 | 0 | 5 | Negative | Pigeaud et al. (2006) |

Table 1. Archaeological sites that contain Gravettian hand images with incomplete fingers. Complete = number of complete hand images. HIFF = number of hand images with incomplete fingers. Unclear = number of hand images where preservation does not allow for a designation as either complete or HIIF. Total = sum of complete, HIIF, and ambiguous. HIIFs positive or negative? = are the HIIFs at the site positive or negative hand images?

suggested that the HIIFs reflect ritual amputations carried out to ensure a successful hunt, and Narr (1966) argued that the HIIFs reflect voluntary amputation in the context of rites of illness and death. More recently, Lundborg (2014) argued that Gravettian HIIFs reflect finger amputation in connection with initiation rites.

Medical amputation has also been proposed as an explanation. Janssens (1957), for example, argued that the Gravettian HIIFs reflect Raynaud's syndrome. This medical condition involves a narrowing of the arteries that reduces blood flow to the fingers and toes and can, in severe cases, require amputation of the affected parts. Little is known about its etiology, but cold is thought to be one trigger, which is why Janssens (1957) suggested it might explain the Gravettian HIIFs. More recently, Gilligan (2010)

suggested the Gravettian HIIFs reflect amputation to deal with gangrene caused by frostbite.

In sum, then, the hypotheses that have been put forward to explain the Gravettian HIIFs can be divided into those that aver the missing finger segments were folded over and those that argue that they were amputated. The latter hypotheses can be divided into those that contend that the finger segments were amputated for ritual reasons and those that argue they were amputated to deal with a medical condition affecting the targeted segments.

## PETTITT'S AND GEORGE'S CRITICISMS OF THE RITUAL AMPUTATION HYPOTHESIS
As we explained earlier, Pettitt's rejection of the Ritual Amputation Hypothesis is based on two arguments. One is that amputation cannot explain

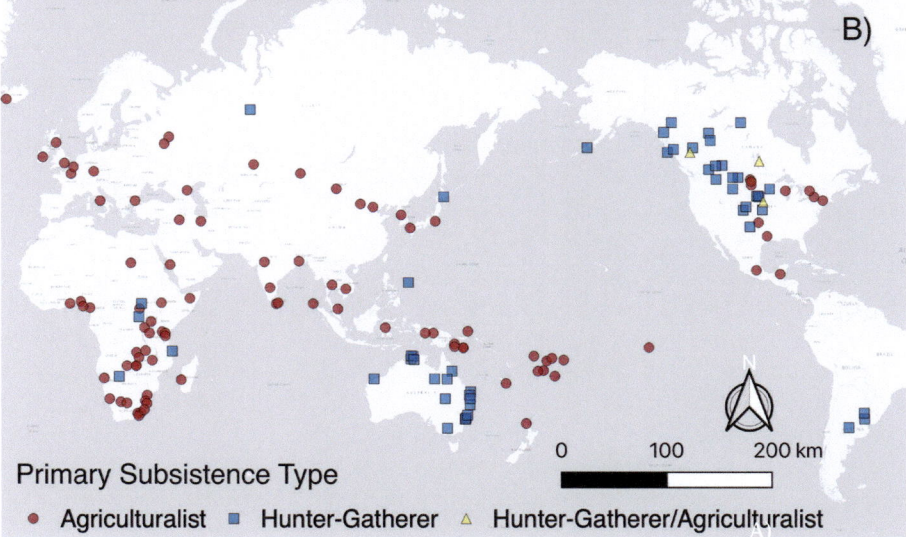

Figure 2. Finger amputation in the present and recent past. A) Hands of a Dani woman with missing finger segments. The Dani live in West Papua, Indonesia, and amputate finger segments to mourn deceased relatives (Credit: imageBROKER/R. Dirscherl/ Alamy). B) Distribution of 177 ethnographically-documented societies that engage(d) in finger amputation (McCauley and Collard, in press). Markers coloured based on the groups' mode of subsistence.

the Gravettian HIIFs because the latter tend to have multiple incomplete fingers whereas ethnographic cases of amputation usually involve just the little finger. The other argument that underpins Pettitt's rejection of the hypothesis is that amputation cannot explain the Gravettian HIIFs because removing multiple fingers is "idiotic" (see quotations from Pettitt in Pappas (2018) and Marshall (2018)).

George's (2023, 40) rationale for rejecting the Ritual Amputation Hypothesis as an explanation for the HIIFs at Gargas and Cosquer is similar to Pettitt's second argument. George noted that the commonest pattern of incomplete fingers at Gargas and Cosquer is an

extended thumb with all other fingers truncated, and she averred that this "extreme mutilation [...] would have been catastrophic for the recipient". Additionally, George contends the Ritual Amputation Hypothesis can be rejected because it is inconsistent with the fact that none of the positive hand images at European Upper Palaeolithic cave art sites has incomplete fingers.

These arguments do not withstand scrutiny. As part of the follow-up to our 2018 study, we expanded our search of the ethnohistoric literature for evidence of finger amputation, and one of the variables for which we collected data was the finger targeted (McCauley and Collard, in press). We found mentions of finger amputation unrelated to medical problems with the amputated finger in connection with 177 groups. Data on the finger that was targeted were available for 90 of these groups. Five groups focused on the thumb, seven targeted the forefinger, two selected the middle finger, one concentrated on the ring finger, and 48 focused on the little finger. A further four groups targeted all the fingers, and 20 focused on a combination of fingers. Three groups only amputated supernumerary fingers. Thus, contrary to what Pettitt averred, it is not the case that ethnographically documented groups limited amputation to the little finger. The little finger was the one most frequently targeted, but the other fingers were partially or completely amputated by multiple groups.

Similarly, the idea that the removal of multiple finger segments is "idiotic" and "catastrophic for the recipient" is not supported by our expanded sample. Data on the number of finger segments removed during an individual's life were available for 135 groups. Forty-four groups removed a single finger segment, while 41 amputated an entire finger. Of the remaining groups, 27 removed a variable number of finger segments, ranging from two to 20, and 23 removed a variable number of fingers, ranging from two to ten. Thus, while it was most common for just one finger segment to be amputated, it was not unknown for an individual to have more than ten finger segments removed in their lifetime. We have included figure 2A to illustrate this point. It shows the hands of an elderly female member of the Dani tribe in West Papua, Indonesia, who has had multiple fingers amputated in mourning rituals. The scars are manifestly old, from which we can infer that she lived for years without many of her fingers. How difficult she found it is unclear, obviously. But the loss of the fingers does not appear to have been catastrophic for her. While Pettitt and George may find it hard to comprehend that an individual would accept the loss of multiple finger segments for ritual purposes, it clearly occurred in several societies and evidently was not necessarily disastrous for the amputee.

George's argument against the Ritual Amputation Hypothesis is unconvincing for two reasons. First, it is not the case that all the Gravettian HIIFs are negative hand images. Most are, but the HIIF at Chauvet is a positive hand image (Clottes 2001: 154). Second, George's argument ignores the fact that negative hand images greatly outnumber positive hand images in Upper Palaeolithic cave art. A marked bias towards negative hand images among HIIFs is what we would expect given that negative hand images are much more numerous than positive ones. That the percentage of Gravettian HIIFs that are negative hand images is higher than the percentage of all Gravettian hand images that are negative can be explained by sampling effects. Work on genetic and cultural drift has shown us that we should not expect a small sample to have the same distribution for a given variable as the population from which the sample is drawn (*e.g.*, Neiman, 1995).

## REASONS FOR TAKING FINGER AMPUTATION SERIOUSLY AS AN EXPLANATION FOR GRAVETTIAN HIIFS

Having shown that Pettit's and George's arguments against the Ritual Amputation Hypothesis do not hold water, we will now outline the reasons why the hypothesis is worth taking seriously. The first is that amputation of finger segments from living people for reasons other than trying to resolve a medical problem with the amputated segment(s) was surprisingly common in the recent past. In the follow-up to our 2018 study (McCauley and Collard, in press), we identified mentions of finger amputation in documents pertaining to 181 societies. Four of these societies are only recorded as having engaged in finger amputation to try to resolve a medical problem with the amputated segment(s), which hereinafter we will refer to as 'surgical amputation'. Twenty-six of the societies only removed finger segments from recently deceased individuals. The remaining 151 societies had at least one custom that involved amputating finger segments from living people for non-surgical reasons. Importantly for present purposes, these societies are widely distributed (figure 2B). This precludes the possibility that non-surgical finger amputation is specific to a particular geographic region or language family. Instead, it is clear from the distribution of the 151 societies that non-surgical finger amputation was likely invented multiple times in different parts of the world. Equally importantly, there are hunter-gatherers among the 151 societies, which means that non-surgical finger amputation is not tied to food production (*e.g.*, via increased social hierarchy). Given that non-surgical finger amputation was carried out by over 100 societies, was clearly invented independently multiple times, and was engaged in by some recent hunter-gatherer societies, it is entirely possible, in our view, that some Gravettian groups engaged in the practice.

The second reason for taking seriously the possibility that the Gravettian HIIFs reflect finger

| Site | Country | Date | Complete | HIIF | Unclear | Total | Source |
|---|---|---|---|---|---|---|---|
| Abo Pueblo | USA | Pre 279 BP | 0 | 1 | 0 | 1 | Wellmann (1972) |
| Babamandil | India | ND | 0 | 1 | 0 | 1 | Dubey-Pathak and Clottes (2020) |
| Balaro | India | ND | 45 | 11 | 0 | 56 | Dubey-Pathak and Clottes (2020) |
| Ballawine (M86/6) | Australia | 23,000-18,000 BP | 15 | 1 | 0 | 16 | Harris et al. (1988) |
| Blood of the Ancestors Grotto | USA | 450-150 BP | 0 | 1 | 0 | 1 | Stelle (2012) |
| Hamtha | India | ND | 35 | 11 | 0 | 46 | Dubey-Pathak and Clottes (2020) |
| Jabbaren | Algeria | 8,000-7,000 BP | 1 | 1 | 0 | 2 | Sansoni (1994) |
| Jogdadeo | India | ND | 29 | 12 | 0 | 41 | Dubey-Pathak and Clottes (2020) |
| Karnasahi 06 | Chad | ND | ND | >1 | ND | ND | Zboray (2018) |
| Kejimkujik Lake | Canada | ND | 62 | 2 | 0 | 64 | Lenik (2016) |
| Leang Lompoa | Indonesia | 27,400-26,000 BP | 2 | 1 | 0 | 3 | Aubert et al. (2014) |
| Mackerel Beach Rockshelter | Australia | ND | ND | 1 | ND | ND | McDonald (2008) |
| Middle Park Highland Province Sites | Australia | 28,000-4,800 BP | 1282 | 5 | 2 | 1289 | Wade et al. (2011) |
| Ramel Pahar | India | ND | ND | 1 | ND | ND | Dubey-Pathak and Clottes (2020) |
| Sefar | Algeria | 8,000-7,000 BP | 0 | 1 | 0 | 1 | Sansoni (1994) |
| Texas Rock Art Site 2 | USA | ND | 2 | 3 | 0 | 5 | Jackson (1938) |
| Texas Rock Art Site 42 | USA | ND | 5 | 1 | 0 | 6 | Jackson (1938) |
| Texas Rock Art Site 51 | USA | ND | 1 | 1 | 0 | 2 | Jackson (1938) |
| Texas Rock Art Site 56 | USA | ND | 14 | 4 | 0 | 18 | Jackson (1938) |
| Texas Rock Art Site 142 | USA | ND | 2 | 1 | 0 | 3 | Jackson (1938) |
| Texas Rock Art Site 150 | USA | ND | 0 | 2 | 0 | 2 | Jackson (1938) |
| Wadi Sura/Sora Site WG45 | Egypt | 7,500-7,000 BP | ND | 25 | ND | 917 | Kuper (2013), Zboray (2013, 2018) |

Table 2. Hand images with incomplete fingers at archaeological sites outside of Europe. Complete = number of complete hand images. HIFF = number of hand images with incomplete fingers. Unclear = number of hand images where the preservation does not allow for a designation as either complete or HIIF. Total = sum of complete, HIIF, and ambiguous. ND = No data.

amputation is that there is other evidence of finger amputation that is thought to date to the same period. Sahly (1966) and Barrière (1976) both noted the presence of impressions of human hands in calcitic clay in the 'Chinese Pavilion' at Gargas. One of these impressions is of a right hand with a truncated little finger (Barrière 1976). The other impression is of fingertips with what Sahly (1966) interpreted to be evidence of scarring from amputation. The impressions are thought to be the same age as the cave art at the site (Barrière 1976). Impressions of hands with truncated fingers have also been found at the site of Lascaux, according to Sahly (1966). This author reports that one of the hands that created impressions in the clay at the site had undergone amputation of the index, middle, ring, and little fingers. He also reports that another hand impression at the site was made by a teenager who was missing a little finger. To these discoveries we can add evidence from Obłazowa Cave, Poland (Valde-Nowak et al. 1987; Valde-Nowak 2003). Two human finger bones have been found in the Gravettian layers at this site along with several objects that have been argued to be of symbolic significance including three Arctic fox tooth pendants, a bone needle, and what may be the world's oldest boomerang (Valde-Nowak 2003). It has been suggested these finds indicate that ritual activities were carried out at the site including finger amputation (Valde-Nowak 2009). Thus, we have reasons to believe that some Gravettian groups engaged in finger amputation that are independent of the HIIFs. Obviously, the HIIFs, the impressions, and the Obłazowa phalanges may not be contemporaneous. The Gravettian lasted for several thousand years, after all. But the most parsimonious explanation for the HIIFs, hand impressions, and Obłazowa phalanges is that they were produced by people who engaged in finger amputation. That the site with the largest number of HIIFs, Gargas, has yielded impressions of hands with incomplete fingers is especially compelling in this regard.

The third reason for taking seriously the possibility that the Gravettian HIIFs reflect finger amputation is that HIIFs are not limited to Europe. So far we have been able to identify HIIFs at a total of 22 archaeological sites outside of Europe. Four of these sites are in Africa, three are in Australia, nine are in North America, five are in South Asia, and one is in Southeast Asia (table 2). Not all the sites have been dated but those that have range in age between 27,400-26,000 BP and 450-150 BP. The occurrence of HIIFs at sites on multiple continents is consistent with the ethnographic evidence indicating finger amputation was practised by groups from all inhabited continents.

The fourth and final reason for taking seriously the possibility that the Gravettian HIIFs reflect finger amputation relates to the number of *incomplete* finger segments. Some sites, such as Gargas and Cosquer, have images with multiple incomplete fingers, but other sites, such as Chauvet and Maltravieso, have images that are only missing a small number of finger segments (figure 1C). This is in line with the results of our follow-up study (McCauley and Collard, in press). As we explained in the previous section, we found considerable cross-cultural variation in the fingers that were targeted, and the number of finger segments removed. Some groups only removed one segment from one finger, but other groups targeted multiple fingers and removed multiple segments per finger. Thus, the inter-site variation in the Gravettian HIIFs is like the inter-group variation in the ethnohistorical record.

## IS RELIGIOUS SACRIFICE STILL THE FINGER AMPUTATION MOTIVATION THAT BEST FITS THE GRAVETTIAN HIIFS?

To reiterate, in our 2018 study we identified ten motivations for finger amputation and concluded that, when the contexts and what we can infer about the characteristics of the amputees are considered, the hypothesis that best fits the Gravettian HIIFs is that they were produced by individuals who had undergone finger amputation as part of a religious ritual (McCauley et al. 2018). Given that in the intervening period we have expanded our sample of recent societies that engaged in finger amputation (McCauley and Collard, in press), an obvious question is, 'is religious sacrifice still the motivation that best fits the Gravettian HIIFs?'.

Based on the additional ethnographic and historical data, we have made a few changes to our taxonomy of motivations (McCauley and Collard, in press). To begin with, we have added eight motivations to the taxonomy. Second, we have dropped one motivation, *Veneration*, which we had defined as forced amputation to produce a magical object or worshipping device. This motivation was originally associated with the Sioux but additional sources we consulted in our follow-up study made it clear that the custom involved amputation of the whole hand rather than fingers. Third, we have subdivided the motivation type we had called *Medical* into *Surgery*, which we define as amputation to try to deal with a medical condition affecting the amputated finger segment(s) such as frost-bite-induced gangrene, and *Remedy*, which we define as amputation to try to resolve a medical condition that does not directly involve the amputated segment(s), such as bleeding sickness out of the amputee. Lastly, we have re-ordered the taxonomy so that the highest-level split is between surgical amputation and amputation for cultural reasons. The revised taxonomy, which includes 18 motivations, is shown in figure 3.

None of the newly identified motivations fits what we know about the Gravettian HIIFs better than sacrifice to try to elicit the assistance of supernatural entities. The newly identified motivations are 1) avoiding the draft, 2) expressing extreme love, 3) penance, 4) betting, 5) torture, 6) oppression, 7) confirming death, and 8) creating a charm. The last two of these motivations – confirming death and creating a charm – both involve the amputation of phalanges from recently deceased individuals. Previously we argued it is unlikely that the Gravettian HIIFs were

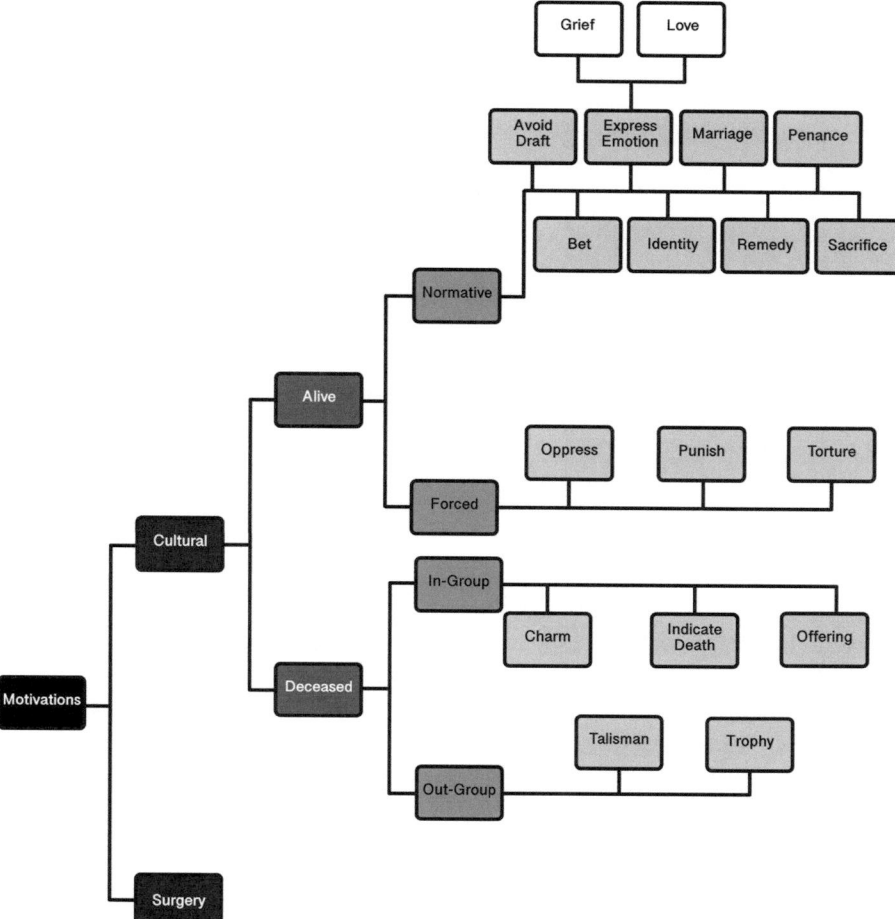

Figure 3. Revised typology of motivations for finger amputations presented by McCauley and Collard (in press).

produced after the death of the amputee because of the large number of individuals thought to have been involved in the creation of the images at some sites and the location of the images (*i.e.*, inside caves) (McCauley *et al.* 2018), and we think that argument still holds. As such, we believe we can discount confirming death and creating a charm as motivations for the acts of amputation reflected by the Gravettian HIIFs. Of the remaining six newly identified motivations, avoiding the draft can be dismissed. This is partly because forced military service is unlikely to have existed in the Upper Palaeolithic and partly because analyses suggest that the Gravettian HIIFs were produced by women as well as men (Groenen 1988). Among the ethnohistorically-documented cases, finger amputation to avoid the draft was only practised by men. Similarly, we think betting and penance can be discounted because they only involved men in the ethnohistorically-documented cases. Oppression also seems to be unlikely to have been a motivation for engaging in finger amputation in the Upper Palaeolithic, because in our ethnohistorical sample, the oppression involved members of a low status group undergoing forced amputation by members of a much higher status, and status differences of such magnitude are not thought to have existed during the Upper Palaeolithic. The remaining two newly-identified motivations – expressing extreme love and torture – were not restricted to a particular sex or class, which means that they could potentially explain the Gravettian HIIFs. However, they were much less common in our expanded ethnohistorical sample than religious sacrifice. Finger amputation to express extreme love was found in only one group, while finger amputation was a form of torture was practised by six groups. In contrast, amputating finger segments to appeal to a supernatural entity for assistance was normative in 33 groups. Thus, based on the ethnographic data we have been able to assemble to date, religious sacrifice is a much more likely motivation for finger amputation than expressing extreme love and torture.

There is another reason for considering religious sacrifice to be the finger amputation motivation that best fits the Gravettian HIIFs. As we explained in our 2018 study, the religious sacrifice motivation fits well with one of the major hypotheses concerning the nature of Upper Palaeolithic art in general – namely, that it is religious in nature. Numerous scholars have posited that the caves with Upper Palaeolithic rock art were places of ritual significance (*e.g.*, González 1985; Owens and Hayden 1997). The religion of the people who produced the art has been argued to have been animistic (Glory 1964; Sax 1994) and to have involved aspects of shamanism (*e.g.*, Clottes and Lewis-Williams 1996; Lewis-Williams 2002; Winkelman 2002; Hayden 2003).

## IMPLICATIONS OF THE RITUAL AMPUTATION HYPOTHESIS

If the Ritual Amputation Hypothesis is correct, there are some interesting implications for our understanding of social life during the Upper Palaeolithic and the evolution of human cognition.

In recent years, scholars in the interdisciplinary field known as the Cognitive Science of Religion have investigated the psychological and social consequences of rituals that elicit intense negative emotions through fear, pain, or temporary or permanent alteration of the body (*e.g.*, Whitehouse 2018; Xygalatas *et al.* 2013a; Fischer *et al.* 2014). These 'dysphoric rituals' tend to be extreme sensory and emotional experiences and have been suggested to be self-shaping and transformative events (Whitehouse 1992; Xygalatas *et al.* 2013b). In addition, it has been found that rituals of this type can create strong bonds among participants and related spectators (Konvalinka *et al.* 2011; Xygalatas *et al.* 2013a). The increased amygdala activation in states of fear and pain can result in the conditioned association of arbitrary stimuli with heightened emotional significance (Damasio 1998). This can have long-term effects on memory and is motivationally powerful (McCauley and Lawson 2002; Alcorta and Sosis 2005). Given these proposed social bonding effects, dysphoric rituals have been argued to be important when a high level of group cohesion is desired, such as in secret societies, military units, and terrorist cells (Whitehouse *et al.* 2014; Raffield *et al.* 2016).

Because of the proposed transformative nature of dysphoric rituals, it has been suggested they may cause the psychological phenomenon known as "identity fusion" (Swann *et al.* 2009, 2012; Whitehouse and Lanman 2014; Whitehouse 2018). Identity fusion involves group members identifying as if they are kin (Swann *et al.* 2014a; Buhrmester *et al.* 2015). This can happen due to a similar worldview within the group or through shared experiences, especially traumatic ones (Jong *et al.* 2015; Newson *et al.* 2016; Segal *et al.* 2018). Identity fusion can have important repercussions. For example, individuals who have fused to a group may feel motivated to act in what they perceive to be the best interests of the group even at considerable personal cost (Swann *et al.* 2010, 2012, 2014a, 2014b; Newson *et al.* 2022). Similarly, fused individuals may also be less trusting of, and hostile to, outsiders, whom they view as a threat (Sheikh *et al.* 2016; Vázquez *et al.* 2020; Newson *et al.* 2022).

Even with the use of effective anesthesia and pain relief, undergoing finger amputation is likely to be a dysphoric experience. Therefore, if the Gravettian HIIFs reflect ritual finger amputation, it is probable that the groups that produced them had exceptionally strong interpersonal bonds and may have even undergone identity fusion.

The people who produced the Gravettian HIIFs may not have been alone in seeking out dysphoric experiences. Pfeiffer (1982) argued that rituals during the Upper Palaeolithic likely involved the revelation of startling images in conditions of emotional and sensory arousal. He focused on caves as the most common surviving evidence of Upper Palaeolithic ritual activity. These environments, he averred, would be ideal for traumatic and mystical experiences. Whitehouse (1995) has also argued that cave art images were designed to provide an emotionally stimulating experience. According to this author, many of the images were placed in locations where they would appear abruptly out of the darkness. In a similar vein, Lewis-Williams and colleagues have raised the possibility that European Upper Palaeolithic groups were engaged in dysphoric ritual practice (*e.g.*, Lewis-Williams and Dowson 1982; Clottes and Lewis-Williams 1996; Lewis-Williams and Clottes 1998a, 1998b). They have suggested that much of the imagery used in Upper Palaeolithic cave paintings reflects features of altered states of consciousness related to shamanism (but see Bednarik 1990; Ross 2001; Kehoe 2002).

It is therefore possible that it was common for members of Upper Palaeolithic groups to engage in dysphoric rituals and hence to be both intensely bonded to one another and hostile towards other groups. We think it is worth considering whether this might help explain not only the ability of Upper Palaeolithic groups to outcompete non-modern hominins like the Neanderthals but also the emergence of the ethnolinguistic groups that appear to be reflected in the personal ornaments of the European Upper Palaeolithic (Vanhaeren and d'Errico 2006). Another interesting possibility is that finger amputation and other dysphoric rituals played a role in the evolution of what seems to be our psychological propensity for tribalism (Haidt 2012).

## Conclusions

The main goal of this paper was to respond to criticisms of a study we published in 2018 that focused on an intriguing feature of the rock art at several Gravettian sites – hand images with incomplete fingers or 'HIIFs' (McCauley *et al.* 2018). Since the early 1900s, several scholars have argued that these images were made by people who had undergone finger amputation. Some of these researchers have argued that the amputations were carried out to resolve medical conditions directly affecting the amputated fingers, while others have proposed that the amputations were performed for ritual reasons. In the study we published in 2018 we sought to shed light on these hypotheses via a cross-cultural survey of finger amputation. We found that the practice was surprisingly common in the recent past and was carried out not only to resolve medical problems but also for non-medical reasons. We concluded that, when the contexts and what we can infer about the identities of the participants were considered, the hypothesis that best fits the Gravettian HIIFs is that they were produced by individuals who had experienced amputation as part of a religious ritual.

Some colleagues have argued that the Ritual Amputation Hypothesis cannot explain the Gravettian HIIFs because the latter involve multiple fingers, and they think it is unlikely that people would have been able to survive after having multiple fingers amputated. It has also been argued that the Ritual Amputation Hypothesis is implausible because the HIIFs are all negative hand images when we would expect them to be both negative and positive hand images if the hypothesis were correct. In this paper, we have shown that neither argument withstands scrutiny. We have demonstrated that many recent societies engaged in the amputation of multiple fingers for cultural reasons. We have

also demonstrated that the Gravettian HIIFs are not limited to negative hand images.

In addition to showing that the arguments against the Ritual Amputation Hypothesis do not hold water, we have outlined evidence that suggests the hypothesis should be taken seriously as a potential explanation for the Gravettian HIIFs, and discussed some of the implications for our understanding of social life during the Upper Palaeolithic if the hypothesis is correct.

We want to end by stressing that we are not claiming the Ritual Amputation Hypothesis is the *only* explanation for the Gravettian HIIFs. Our position is that there are reasons to take seriously the Ritual Amputation Hypothesis as an explanation for Gravettian HIIFs, *not* that it is the only hypothesis to take seriously. We think it is too soon to decide which of the various hypotheses that have been put forward to explain Gravettian HIIFs is the correct one. Indeed, we urge our colleagues to allow for the possibility that there is more than one explanation for the absence of fingers on some Gravettian hand images. As Groenen (2011) has suggested, it is possible that multiple processes were involved in the creation of Gravettian HIIFs. This means that the best hypothesis for HIIFs at one site may differ from the best hypothesis for HIIFs at another site. It could even mean that the best explanation for one HIIF at a site may differ from the best explanation for another HIIF at the same site.

## Acknowledgements

We thank Shumon Hussain and Gerrit Dusseldorp for inviting us to contribute to this volume honouring Prof. Corbey, and for helping to improve our chapter via their comments. MC also thanks Prof. Corbey for many years of friendship and for convincing him that palaeoanthropologists should pay more attention to philosophy. Our work on this paper was supported by the Social Sciences and Humanities Research Council of Canada, the Canada Research Chairs Program, the Canada Foundation for Innovation, the British Columbia Knowledge Development Fund, and Simon Fraser University.

## REFERENCES

Alcorta, C.S., and R. Sosis. 2005. "Ritual, emotion, and sacred symbols." *Human Nature* 16 (4), 323-359.

Aubert, M., A. Brumm, M. Ramli, T. Sutikna, E.W. Saptomo, B. Hakim, M.J. Morwood, G.D. van den Bergh, L. Kinsley, and A. Dosseto. 2014. "Pleistocene cave art from Sulawesi, Indonesia." *Nature* 514, 223-227.

Baffier, D., and M. Girard. 1998. *Les Cavernes d'Arcy-sur-Cure*. Paris: La maison des Roches.

Barrière, C. 1976. *L'Art Pariétal de la Grotte de Gargas, Parts I and II*. Oxford: British Archaeological Reports.

Baudouin, M. 1927. "L'opération culturelle du sacrifice de doigt." *Journal des Practiciens* 1927, DXXXI-DXLVIII.

Bednarik, R.G. 1990. "On neuropsychology and shamanism in rock art." *Current Anthropology* 31 (1), 77-84.

Breuil, H. 1952. *Quatre cent Siècles d'art Pariétal*. Montignac: Centre d'études et de Documentation Préhistoriques.

Buhrmester, M.D., W.T. Fraser, J. A. Lanman, H. Whitehouse, and W.B. Swann Jr. 2015. "When terror hits home: Identity fused Americans who saw Boston bombing victims as "family" provided aid." *Self and Identity* 14 (3), 253-270.

Casteret, N. 1951. *Dix ans Sous Terre*. Paris: Librairie Académique Perrin.

Clottes, J. 2001. *La Grotte Chauvet. L'Art des Origines*. Paris: Seuil.

Clottes, J. 2008. *Cave Art*. London: Phaidon.

Clottes, J., and J. Courtin. 1994. *La Grotte Cosquer: Peintures et Gravures de la Caverne Engloutie*. Paris: Seuil.

Clottes, J., J. Courtin, and L. Vanrell. 2005. *Cosquer Redecouverte*. Paris: Seuil.

Clottes, J., and D.J. Lewis-Williams. 1996. *Les Chamanes de la Préhistoire: Transe et Magie dans les Grottes Ornées*. Paris: Seuil.

Collado Giraldo, H., M. Bea, J. Ramos-Muñoz, P. Cantalejo, S. Domínguez-Bella, J.R. Bello, J. Angás, J. Miranda, F.J. Gracia Prieto, D. Fernández-Sánchez, A. Aranda, A. Luque, J.J. García Arranz, and J.C. Aguilar. 2019. "Un nuevo grupo de manos paleolíticas pintadas en el sur de la Península Ibérica. La cueva de Las Estrellas (Castellar de la Frontera, Cádiz)." *Zephyrus* 83, 15-38.

Collado Giraldo, H., and J.J. García Arranz. 2018b. "Cueva de Maltravieso." In *HANDPAS: Manos del Pasado. Catálogo de Representaciones de Manos en el Arte Rupestre Paleolítico de la Península Ibérica*, edited by H. Collado Giraldo, 367-468. Mérida: Consejería de Cultura e Igualdad de la Junta de Extremadura.

Collado Giraldo, H., J.J. García Arranz, and R.M. Barquín. 2018c. "Cueva de Cudón (Cudón / Miengo, Cantabria)." In *HANDPAS: Manos del Pasado. Catálogo de Representaciones de Manos en el Arte Rupestre Paleolítico de la Península Ibérica*, edited by H. Collado Giraldo, 119-126. Mérida: Consejería de Cultura e Igualdad de la Junta de Extremadura.

Collado Giraldo, H., J.J. García Arranz, P. Fatás, C. de las Heras, A. Prada, L.M. Diaz, and D. Ordás. 2018d. "Cueva de Altamira." In *HANDPAS: Manos del Pasado. Catálogo de Representaciones de Manos en el Arte Rupestre Paleolítico de la Península Ibérica*, edited by H. Collado Giraldo, 93-118. Mérida: Consejería de Cultura e Igualdad de la Junta de Extremadura.

Collado Giraldo, H., J.J. García Arranz, P. Utrilla, and M. Bea. 2018a. "Cueva de la Fuente del Trucho." In *HANDPAS: Manos del Pasado. Catálogo de Representaciones de Manos en el Arte Rupestre Paleolítico de la Península Ibérica*, edited by H. Collado Giraldo, 289-366. Mérida: Consejería de Cultura e Igualdad de la Junta de Extremadura.

Damasio, A.R. 1998. "Emotion in the perspective of an integrated nervous system." *Brain Research Reviews* 26 (2-3), 83-86.

Delluc, B., and G. Delluc. 1993. "Images de la main dans notre préhistoire." *Dossiers d'Archéologie* 178, 32-45.

Dubey-Pathak, M., and J. Clottes. 2020. "Hands in Chhattisgarh rock art." *Adoranten* 2020, 1-21.

Echegaray, J.G., and C.G. Sáinz. 1994. "Conjuntos rupestres paleolíticos de la cornisa cantábrica. Arte Paleolítico." *Complutum* 5, 21-43.

Etxepare, R., and A. Irurtzun. 2021. "Gravettian hand stencils as sign language formatives." *Philosophical Transactions of the Royal Society B* 376 (1824), 20200205.

Fischer, R., D. Xygalatas, P. Mitkidis, P. Reddish, I. Konvalinka, and J. Bulbulia. 2014. "The fire-walker's high: affect and physiological responses in an extreme collective ritual." *PLoS ONE* 9, e88355.

Freeman, L.G., and J. González Echegaray. 2001. *La Grotte d'Altamira*. Paris: La Maison des Roches.

George, A. 2023. "Cave paintings of mutilated hands could be a Stone Age sign language." *New Scientist*, March 15, 2023. https://www.newscientist.com/article/mg25734300-900-cave-paintings-of-mutilated-hands-could-be-a-stone-age-sign-language/.

Gilligan, I. 2010. "The prehistoric development of clothing: archaeological implications of a thermal model." *Journal of Archaeological Method and Theory* 17, 15-80.

Glory, A. 1964. "L'énigme de l'art quaternaire peut-elle être résolue par la théorie du culte des Ongones?" *Revue des Sciences Religieuses* 38 (4), 337-388.

González García, G. 1985. "Aproximació al Desenvolupament i Situació de les Manifestacions Artístiques Quaternàries: a les Cavitats del Monte del Castillo." Unpublished Doctoral Dissertation., University of Barcelona.

Groenen, M. 1988. "Les représentations de mains négatives dans les grottes de Gargas et de Tibiran (Hautes-Pyrénées). Approche méthodologique." *Bulletin de la Société Royale Belge d'Anthropologie et de Préhistoire* 99, 81-113.

Groenen, M. 2011. "Images des mains dans la préhistoire." *La Part de L'œil: Revue de Pensée des Arts Plastiques* 25-26, 56-69.

Groenen, M. 2016. *L'Art des Grottes Ornées du Paléolithique Supérieur.* Brussels: Académie Royales des Sciences, des Lettres, et des Beaux-Arts de Belgique.

Haidt, J. 2012. *The Righteous Mind: Why Good People are Divided by Politics and Religion.* New York: Vintage.

Harris, S., D. Ranson, and S. Brown. 1988. "Maxwell River archaeological survey 1986." *Australian Archaeology* 27, 89-97.

Hayden, B. 2003. *Shamans, Sorcerers, and Saints.* Washington, DC: Smithsonian Institution.

Jackson, A.T. 1938. *Picture-Writing of Texas Indians.* Austin, TX: University of Texas Press.

Janssens, P.A. 1957. "Medical views on prehistoric representations of human hands." *Medical History* 1, 318.

Jaubert, J. 2008. "L'«art» pariétal gravettien en France: éléments pour un bilan chronologique." *Paléo: Revue d'Archéologie Préhistorique* 20, 439-474.

Jong, J., H. Whitehouse, C. Kavanagh, and J. Lane. 2015. "Shared negative experiences lead to identity fusion via personal reflection." *PloS ONE* 10, e0145611.

Kehoe, A.B. 2002. "Emerging trends versus the popular paradigm in rock art research." *Antiquity* 76, 384-385.

Konvalinka, I., D. Xygalatas, J. Bulbulia, U. Schjødt, E.-M. Jegindø, S. Wallot, G. Van Orden, and A. Roepstorff. 2011. "Synchronized arousal between performers and related spectators in a fire-walking ritual." *Proceedings of the National Academy of Sciences* 108 (20), 8514-8519.

Kuper, R., ed. 2013. *Wadi Sura – Cave of Beasts: A Rock Art Site in the Gilf Kebir (SW Egypt).* Cologne: Heinrich-Barth-Institut.

Larribau J.-D. 2013 *La Grotte d'Erberua: Art Pariétal Préhistorique du Pays Basque (Isturitz-Oxocelhaya-Erberua).* Orthez: Jean-Daniel Larribau.

Lenik, E.J. 2016. "The human hand in northeastern rock art: communicating with the spirits." *Bulletin of the Massachusetts Archaeological Society* 77 (1), 1-11.

Leroi-Gourhan, A. 1967. "Les mains de Gargas: essai pour une étude d'ensemble." *Bulletin de la Société Préhistorique Française* 64 (1), 107-122.

Leroi-Gourhan, A. 1986. "The hands of Gargas: toward a general study." *October* 37, 19-34.

Lewis-Williams, J.D. 2002. *The Mind in the Cave.* London: Thames and Hudson.

Lewis-Williams, J.D., and J. Clottes. 1998a. "The mind in the cave – The cave in the mind: Altered consciousness in the Upper Paleolithic." *Anthropology of Consciousness* 9 (1), 13-21.

Lewis-Williams, J.D., and J. Clottes. 1998b. "Shamanism and Upper Palaeolithic art: a response to Bahn." *Rock Art Research* 15 (1), 46-50.

Lewis-Williams, J.D., and T.A. Dowson. 1982. "The signs of all times: entopic phenomena in Upper Palaeolithic art." *Current Anthropology* 29 (2), 201-245.

López, S.R., E.R. Perelló, H. Collado Giraldo, M.M. Cornélla, and J.F. Jordá Pardo. 1999. "Maltravieso. El santuario extremeño de las manos." *Trabajos de Prehistoria* 56, 59-84.

Lundborg, G. 2014. *The Hand and the Brain: From Lucy's Thumb to the Thought-Controlled Robotic Hand.* London: Springer.

Marshall, M. 2018. "Stone Age people may have ritually cut off their own fingers." *New Scientist* November 30, 2018. https://www.newscientist.com/article/2186994-stone-age-people-may-have-ritually-cut-off-their-own-fingers/

McCauley, B., and M. Collard. in press. "Finger amputation in cross-cultural perspective." In *The Oxford Handbook of the Archaeology and Anthropology of Body Modification,* edited by F. Manni and F. d'Errico. Oxford: Oxford University Press.

McCauley, R.N., and E.T. Lawson. 2002. *Bringing Ritual to Mind: Psychological Foundations of Cultural Forms.* Cambridge: Cambridge University Press.

McCauley, B., D. Maxwell, and M. Collard. 2018. "A cross-cultural perspective on Upper Palaeolithic hand images with missing fingers." *Journal of Palaeolithic Archaeology* 1, 314-333.

McDonald, J. 2008. *Dreamtime Superhighway (TA27): Sydney Basin Rock Art and Prehistoric Information Exchange.* Canberra: ANU Press.

Narr, K.J. 1966. *Handbuch der Urgeschichte*, Volume 1. Bern: Francke Verlag.

Neiman, F.D. 1995. "Stylistic variation in evolutionary perspective: Inferences from decorative diversity and interassemblage distance in Illinois Woodland ceramic assemblages." *American Antiquity* 60 (1), 7-36.

Newson, M., M. Buhrmester, and H. Whitehouse. 2016. "Explaining lifelong loyalty: The role of identity fusion and self-shaping group events." *PloS ONE* 11, e0160427.

Newson, M., F. White, H. Whitehouse. 2022. "Does loving a group mean hating its rivals? Exploring the relationship between ingroup cohesion and outgroup hostility among soccer fans." *International Journal of Sport and Exercise Psychology* 2022, 1-19.

Nougier, L.-R. 1963. *La Préhistoire: Essai de Paleo-Sociologie Religieuse.* Paris: Bloud et Gay.

Overmann, K.A. 2014. "Finger-counting in the Upper Palaeolithic." *Rock Art Research* 31 (1), 63-80.

Owens, D'A., and B. Hayden. 1997. "Prehistoric rites of passage: a comparative study of transegalitarian hunter-gatherers." *Journal of Anthropological Archaeology* 16 (2), 121-161.

Pappas, S. 2018. "Were paleo artists also self-mutilators?" *Live Science* December 4, 2018. https://www.livescience.com/64228-paleo-artists-cut-off-fingers.html.

Patte, E. 1960. *Les Hommes Préhistoriques et la Religion.* Paris: Picard.

Pfeiffer, J.E. 1982. *The Creative Explosion: An Inquiry into the Origins of Art and Religion.* New York: Harper and Row.

Pigeaud, R., J. Rodet, T. Devièse, C. Dufayet, E. Trelohan-Chauve, J.-P. Betton, and P. Bonic. 2006. "Palaeolithic cave art in West France: an exceptional discovery: the Margot cave (Mayenne)." *Antiquity* 80, 81-92.

Raffield, B., C. Greenlow, N. Price, and M. Collard. 2016. "Ingroup identification, identity fusion and the formation of Viking war bands." *World Archaeology* 48, 35-50.

Ross, M. 2001. "Emerging trends in rock-art research: hunter-gather culture, land and landscape." *Antiquity* 75 (289), 543-8.

Rouillon, A. 2006. "Au Gravettien, dans la grotte Cosquer (Marseille, Bouches-du-Rhône), l'Homme a-t-il compté sur ses doigts?" *Anthropologie* 110, 500-509.

Sahly, A. 1966. *Les Mains Mutilées dans l'Art Préhistorique.* Toulouse: Ministère des Affaires Culturelles.

Sansoni, U. 1994. *Le Più Antiche Pitture del Sahara: L'Arte delle Teste Rotonde.* Milan: Jaca Book.

Sax, B. 1994. "Animals in religion." *Society & Animals* 2, 167-174.

Segal, K., J. Jong, and J. Halberstadt. 2018. "The fusing power of natural disasters: an experimental study." *Self and Identity* 17 (5), 574-586.

Sheikh, H., Á. Gómez, and S. Atran. 2016. "Empirical evidence for the devoted actor model." *Current Anthropology* 57 (S13), 204-209.

Snow, D.R. 2006. "Sexual dimorphism in Upper Palaeolithic hand stencils." *Antiquity* 80, 390-404.

Stelle, L.J. 2012. "The rock art of the blood of the ancestors' grotto (11SA557): the archaeology of religious theater". *Illinois Archaeology* 24, 1-70.

Swann Jr., W.B., M. D. Buhrmester, Á. Gómez, J. Jetten, B. Bastian, A. Vázquez, A. Ariyanto, T. Besta, O. Christ, L. Cui, G. Finchilescu, R. González, N. Goto, M. Hornsey, S. Sharma, H. Susianto, and A. Zhang. 2014a. "What makes a group worth dying for? Identity fusion fosters perception of familial ties, promoting self-sacrifice." *Journal of Personality and Social Psychology* 106 (6), 912-926.

Swann Jr, W.B., Á. Gómez, J.F. Dovidio, S. Hart, and J. Jetten. 2010. "Dying and killing for one's group: Identity fusion moderates' responses to intergroup versions of the trolley problem." *Psychological Science* 21 (8), 1176-1183.

Swann Jr., W.B., Á. Gómez, D.C. Seyle, J.F. Morales, and C. Huici. 2009. "Identity fusion: the interplay of personal and social identities in extreme group behavior." *Journal of Personality and Social Psychology* 96 (5), 995-1011.

Swann Jr., W.B., Á. Gómez, M.D. Buhrmester, L. López-Rodríguez, J. Jiménez, and A. Vázquez. 2014b. "Contemplating the ultimate sacrifice: Identity fusion channels pro-group affect, cognition, and moral decision making." *Journal of Personality and Social Psychology* 106 (5), 713-727.

Swann Jr., W.B., J. Jetten, Á. Gómez, H. Whitehouse, and B. Brock. 2012. "When group membership gets personal: a theory of identity fusion." *Psychological Review* 119 (3), 441-456.

Utrilla, P., V. Baldellou, M. Bea, and R. Viñas. 2013. "La cueva de la Fuente del Trucho (Asque-Colungo, Huesca). Una cueva mayor del arte gravetiense." In *Pensando el Gravetiense: Nuevos Datos Para la Región Cantábrica en su Contexto Peninsular y Pirenaico*, edited by C. de las Heras, J.A. Lasheras, Á. Arrizabalaga, and M. De la Rasilla, 526-537. Madrid: Monografías del Museo Nacional y Centro de Investigación de Altamira.

Valde-Nowak, P. 2003. "Obłazowa Cave: Nouvel éclairage pour les mains de Gargas?" *International Newsletter on Rock Art* 35, 4-6.

Valde-Nowak, P. 2009. "Obłazowa and Hłomcza: two Paleolithic sites in the north Carpathians province of southern Poland." *Lithic materials and Paleolithic Societies*, edited by B. Adams and B. S. Blades, 196-207. Hoboken: Wiley-Blackwell.

Valde-Nowak, P., A. Nadachowski, and M. Wolsan. 1987. "Upper Palaeolithic boomerang made of a mammoth tusk in south Poland." *Nature* 329, 436-438.

Van den Broeck, A.J.P. 1950. *De Dageraad der Mensheid*. Utrecht: Ossthoek's Uitg.

Vanhaeren, M., and F. d'Errico. 2006. "Aurignacian ethno-linguistic geography of Europe revealed by personal ornaments." *Journal of Archaeological Science* 33 (8), 1105-1128.

Vázquez, A., L. López-Rodríguez, M. Martínez, S. Atran, and Á. Gómez. 2020. "Threat enhances aggressive inclinations among devoted actors via increase in their relative physical formidability." *Personality and Social Psychology Bulletin* 46 (10), 1461-1475.

Wade, V., L.A. Wallis, and Woolgar Valley Aboriginal Corporation. 2011. "Style, space and social interaction: an archaeological investigation of rock art in inland north Queensland, Australia." *Australian Archaeology* 72, 23-34.

Wellmann, K.F. 1972. "New Mexico's mutilated hand: finger mutilation and polydactylism in North American Indian rock art." *JAMA* 219 (12), 1609-1610.

Whitehouse, H. 1992. "Memorable religions: transmission, codification and change in divergent Melanesian contexts." *Man* 27 (4), 777-797.

Whitehouse, H. 1995. *Inside the Cult: Religious Innovation and Transmission in Papua New Guinea*. Oxford: Oxford University Press.

Whitehouse, H. 2018. "Dying for the group: towards a general theory of extreme self-sacrifice." *Brain and Behavioral Sciences* 41, E192.

Whitehouse, H., and J.A. Lanman. 2014. "The ties that bind us: ritual, fusion, and identification." *Current Anthropology* 55 (6), 674-695.

Whitehouse, H., B. McQuinn, M. Buhrmester, and W.B. Swann Jr. 2014. "Brothers in arms: Libyan revolutionaries bond like family." *Proceedings of the National Academy of Sciences* 111 (50), 17783-17785.

Winkelman, M. 2002. "Shamanism and cognitive evolution (with comments)." *Cambridge Archaeological Journal* 12 (1), 71-101.

Xygalatas, D., P. Mitkidis, R. Fischer, P. Reddish, J. Skewes, A.W. Geertz, A. Roepstorff, and J. Bulbulia. 2013a. "Extreme rituals promote prosociality." *Psychological Science* 24 (8), 1602-1605.

Xygalatas, D., U. Schjoedt, J. Bulbulia, I. Konvalinka, E.-M. Jegindø, P. Reddish, A.W. Geertz, and A. Roepstoff. 2013b. "Autobiographical memory in a fire-walking ritual." *Journal of Cognition and Culture* 13 (1-2), 1-16.

Zboray, A. 2013. "Wadi Sura in the context of regional rock art." In *Wadi Sura – The Cave of Beasts: A Rock Art Site in the Gilf Kebir* (*SW-Egypt*), edited by R. Kuper, 18-23. Cologne: Heinrich-Barth-Institut.

Zboray, A. 2018. ""Korossom Fantastic" and the Karnasahi pastoralists, the principal rock art styles of the Eastern Tibesti." In *What Ever Happened to the People? Humans and Anthropomorphs in the Rock Art of Northern Africa*, edited by D. Huyge and F. Van Noten, 25-34. Brussels: Royal Academy for Overseas Sciences.

In Hussain, S.T. and G.L. Dusseldorp (eds) 2025. Sitting on the fence: Negotiating archaeology, anthropology and philosophy. Festschrift for Prof. Dr Raymond H.A. Corbey in celebration of his 70th birthday. *Analecta Praehistorica Leidensia* 54. Leiden: Sidestone Press, pp. 179-192.

# Three for playing, three for straying and three for staying. Exploring the changing role of cats in Pleistocene and Holocene Europe

Luc Amkreutz

## ABSTRACT

The origins of cat domestication lie in the Fertile Crescent about 10.000 years ago. The Near Eastern wildcat was domesticated in this region and the domesticated house cat subsequently spread over the world, including Europe. Before and during the arrival of the domesticated cat on the European continent, however, groups of hunter-gatherers also encountered, caught, and used wild cats. In this short contribution, I argue that the role of cats, both wild and domesticated, in communities of hunter-gatherers and farmers was very different and to some extent diametrically opposed. I then argue that the role of cats in our contemporary lives, by contrast, appears to have taken on a new identity that is based on a synthesis of both roles and simultaneously throws light on larger ecological questions of our time.

*Keywords: Cats, pets, prehistory, ecology, human-animal relations, commensalism*

## INTRODUCTION

Cats belong to the most popular pets world-wide. In the Netherlands, a human population of ca. 17.5 million, cats are the most popular pets and count up to 3 million individuals, apart from about half a million stray cats and an unknown number of feral ('rewilded') cats.[1] This is a gigantic number that has been argued to cause serious issues regarding the conservation of, in particular, avian wildlife, as well as herpetofauna, invertebrates, and small mammals, especially in rural or urbanized ecologies (*e.g.*, McDonald *et al.* 2015). The popularity and omnipresence of the domestic cat and its stray and feral counterparts makes it worthwhile to investigate the development of human-cat relations in the past, also to situate the psychology and choices of present-day cat-owners and reflect on their role. To do so, I want to throw a brief spotlight on three different stages or contexts of human-cat interaction. The first is wild cats in the Pleistocene and Early Holocene, focusing on our human fascination for felines. The second deals with domesticated cats in the Neolithic and in antiquity and their diverse roles in human communities. The third focuses on domesticated cats in modern times, in essence from the 19th century onwards, the ecological challenges they present and the mirror they are to human

**Luc Amkreutz**
National Museum of Antiquities & Faculty of Archaeology,
Leiden University, The Netherlands
l.amkreutz@rmo.nl
ORCID: 0000-0003-4664-5552

1    https://www.vogelbescherming.nl/over-ons/standpunten/standpunt-huisdieren-en-wilde-vogels.

society. I will present these timeframes as separate 'vignettes' that provide contrasting perspectives on the issues I wish to raise and discuss. These windows of course are imperfect in the sense that they do not offer a complete and exhaustive historical perspective, but in sequence they provide an interesting long-term contextualization of shifting interactions between humans and cats. I will conclude this survey by offering some stray thoughts on the nature and future of human-cat interaction.

Due to the scope of this contribution, I am fully aware that my perspective is centred on developments in the modern Western world and that as such unavoidably nuance and alternative perspectives will be missed. However, I hope my endeavour can supply some thought-provoking elements that serve future interests in this topic, especially for cat owners.

## THREE FOR STRAYING: (BIG) CATS IN THE PLEISTOCENE AND EARLY HOLOCENE

The character of interaction between humans and feline species such as cave lion (*Panthera speleae*) and sabre-toothed cat (*Homotherium latidens*) during the Ice Ages is difficult to grasp. While bones of these animals occasionally occur in archaeological faunal assemblages produced by hominins such as Neanderthals and anatomically modern humans (AMH/*Homo sapiens*), they do not seem to have been prey species of significance. Good examples are the Neanderthal open-air site of Biache St.-Vaast (MIS 7-6) and the travertine Eemian site of Taubach (MIS 5), where a small number of cave lion remains were identified (see Dusseldorp 2009, 75 and 119). Dusseldorp (2009, 122) argues that such dangerous species incur increased handling costs due to their 'weapons' such as claws and large teeth (although the author, remarkably, does not consider the large size of cave lion as an additional factor increasing its danger). For Taubach, Bratlund (1999, 150-151) originally proposed that the hunting of dangerous animals such as rhinos and brown bears may be related to prestige (also see Speth 2010). While (brown) bears about to enter hibernation may additionally provide a rich source of body fat, big cats are probably only dangerous and are not worth the risk as hunting targets, although additional reasons for hunting them, such as for personal or community protection may have existed. Nevertheless, this seems to be confirmed by the absence of cut marks on the bones of feline species at Biache and Taubach (Auguste 1992, 64; Bratlund 1999, 84, 86).

While hunting these dangerous animals may not have been a regular activity for Neanderthals and early AMHs in Europe, their presence in bone assemblages indicates that they were an integral part of the environment and were thus regularly encountered. Evidence for this comes from parietal and mobile art. It is remarkable that in particular early cave art at Chauvet (c. 32.000-30.000 BP) and pictorial expressions of the Aurignacian in general (*e.g.*, Floss 2018) host a large number of depictions of dangerous animals, large cats in particular. Clottes and Azéma (2005, 173) note that next to mammoth and rhinoceros, felines are among the most frequently depicted animals in Chauvet cave, in total representing over 60% of the known depictions of felines in Palaeolithic cave art (as to 2005). At Chauvet, felines are often depicted 'animated', sometimes in actual scenes such as a bison hunt (ibid., 180). This indicates that rather than embodying prey animals, they may have been seen as true, proficient hunters themselves, perhaps in a collegial manner, or rather as competitors that posed a direct or indirect threat to successful foraging. Hussain and Floss (2015) also comment upon the general complementarity between lions and humans in the Early Upper Palaeolithic. The authors note that this contrasts starkly with later Upper Palaeolithic depictions focusing much more on animals such as horses, bovids and various deer species (ibid.). Would it thus be fair to suggest that in the early stages of finding a niche in Ice Age Europe, the predatory species encountered would be seen as a strong and potent symbol of survival and success? In other words: a good animal to 'think with', as has been argued for depictions of animals in Upper Paleolithic art in general (*e.g.*, Clottes and Lewis-Williams 1996; Sauvet *et al.* 2009).

An important archaeological object from the early Aurignacian seems to support this suggestion, the so-called 'Lion Man' found in 1939, although only identified later upon re-assembly, in the Stadel cave in Hohlenstein, southern Germany, which is between 41,000 and 39,000 years old. The figurine was laboriously carved from mammoth ivory. It represents a therianthrope figure consisting of the upper body part of a cave lion and the lower body part and legs of a human, probably a male individual (Kind *et al.* 2014, 129, 140). As cave lions were the largest and most dangerous predators of the Late Pleistocene in Europe, it is assumed the figure could represent a deity or perhaps shaman pointing to a religious function (Kind *et al.* 2014, 142). Although it is probable that the

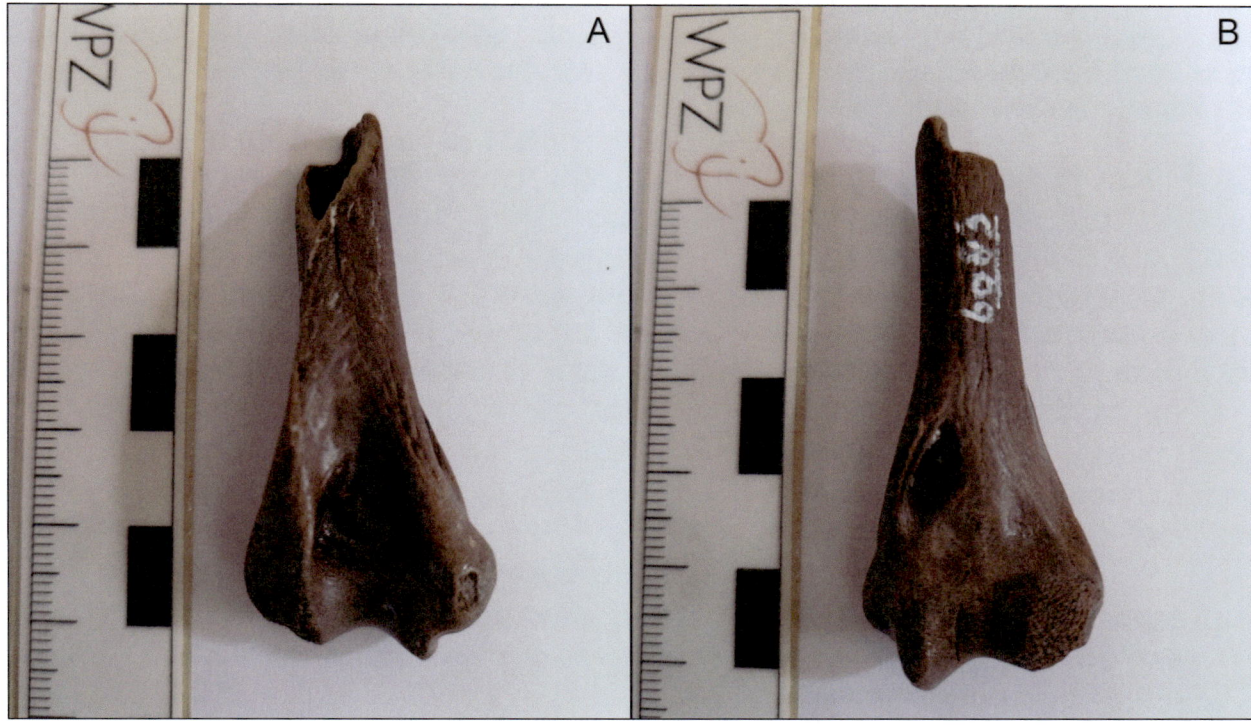

Figure 1. *Humerus* of the European wild cat (A: front; B: back) from Maasvlakte 2 (Kommer Tanis).

diverse eco-behavioural relationships and interactions between animals such as the cave-lion and humans may have led to more complex systems of animal personhood going beyond simple animal-human dichotomies (see Hussain and Floss 2015, 85).

The special position of this object in early human societies is supported by the fact that the statuette was found in a secluded area at the back of the cave, where it was probably buried (Kind *et al.* 2014). Although slightly conjectural, it is thus possible that these depictions of big cats served to impress, were held in awe, and were revered.

A different perspective is offered by some of the last hunter-gatherers in Europe from the Late Mesolithic (ca. 7000 BP). For this we travel to the North Sea basin. In 2020, the author picked up a fragment of a humerus of the European wildcat (*Felis silvestris silvestris*) on the artificial beach of Maasvlakte 2 (figure 1). This beach was constructed from marine sand from a submarine quarry several kilometers off the Dutch coast. As a temperate species, the cat may date to the Eemian but a placement in the Early Holocene before the submergence of Doggerland is also possible (Tanis and Amkreutz 2022, 40). Although the European wildcat is perhaps less impressive when

compared to the cave lion, it, too, is a formidable hunter, although mainly targeting mice, birds, fish, rabbits, hare and even small roe deer, at least as a scavenger (Ruiz-Villar *et al.* 2020). It is a solitary hunter and unlike the housecat typically goes for the direct kill, often biting the neck of its prey (Tanis and Amkreutz 2022, 43). Wildcats regularly occur in faunal assemblages of Mesolithic hunter-gatherer sites in northwest Europe, especially sites situated on ecotones where different habitats could be exploited. Another wildcat find from Doggerland was also discovered at the Maasvlakte 2 (collection Houtgraaf): a mandible which is assumed to be Early Holocene in age and is characterised by a perforation through the *ramus*. The perforation suggests that it may have been worn as a talisman (ibid.; Zeiler 2021). The wetland sites of Hardinxveld-Polderweg and De Bruin, dating to the Late Mesolithic and Early Neolithic Swifterbant culture, provide further information on human-cat relations. Both yielded bones of wildcats. At Polderweg, one of the 24 bones of wildcat yielded evidence for cutmarks associated with skinning (Van Wijngaarden-Bakker *et al.* 2001, 209). At De Bruin, 48 bones were found representing a period of roughly 1000 years. These bones have yielded evidence for cut-marks, gnawing, and charring. Remarkably, one of the bones was transformed into an awl (Oversteegen *et al.* 2001, 248). This could perhaps provide a link between the wild cat, its pelt, and the fabrication of clothing. Later Neolithic sites with a more distinct agricultural signature also produced low numbers of wildcat remains (see Tanis and Amkreutz 2022). It therefore appears that these felines were occasionally hunted by the hunter-fisher-farmers occupying these landscapes, and it appears their pelts were sought after. In order not to damage the pelt, it is likely, as probably also the case for otter, beaver, and pine marten, that wildcats were trapped and snared (ibid., 48-49).

Based on these limited sources, we may argue that the role of wild felines in Pleistocene and Early Holocene hunter-gatherer communities in Europe was not primarily related to their role in food economy. Rather, the animals were likely revered for their intrinsic qualities as they too were formidable hunters. They were thus animals to 'think with', as has also been argued by proponents of shamanistic interpretations of early cave art in relation to an animated environment (*e.g.*, Clottes and Lewis-Williams, 1996; Sauvet *et al.* 2009). These early cats were likely part of the complex and multifaceted human-animal relations of this time (see Hussain and Floss 2015), perhaps most aptly demonstrated by hybrid objects such as the Aurignacian lion man. Their specific physical characteristics perhaps formed important qualities in this respect. The use of pelts, claws and teeth, but also the use and transformation of mandibles such as that of the Early Holocene wild cat mentioned above may serve as a case in point here. Such cat-oriented human behaviours are also attested for other animal categories. For instance with regard to the importance of bears in early Neolithic wetland sites (Zeiler 2010), the use of raptor claws as jewellery as evidenced at the Neanderthal site of Krapina (Radovčić *et al.* 2015), or the well-known inventory of white-tailed eagle bones at Mesolithic and Neolithic wetland sites discussed by the author and esteemed colleague Corbey (Amkreutz and Corbey 2008). Like felines, these are all animals that 'strayed', that freely roamed the land and were perhaps envisaged as equally successful hunters by the hominins observing them. They were something to behold, their powers and qualities something to admire and appropriate. But in no way to own, control or domesticate. This would soon change, though.

## THREE FOR STAYING: CATS AND CAT DOMESTICATION THROUGHOUT THE HOLOCENE

Unlike the European wildcat, the domestic cat (*Felis catus*) is a different beast and for its origins we turn to the Near East and to the emergence of farming, and later on to Egypt. Recent analysis of genetic data from extant wild and domesticated cats indicates that only one of the five known species of Old World wildcats, *Felis silvestris lybica*, was domesticated in prehistoric times (Ottoni *et al.* 2017, 1). This initial domestication of cats is closely related to the process of Neolithization and the transition to agriculture. In sedentary societies, where livestock, crops and waste attract unwanted visitors, cats play an important role in barns, sheds, and for instance on ships, countering vermin and in particular rodent pests[2] (ibid.; see also Engels 1999). Interestingly, cats as solitary territorial hunters are not very suitable for domestication and archaeological evidence points to a prolonged period of commensal human-cat interaction, during which cats frequently became feral or intermingled with wildcats, which, in contrast to dogs, led to limited changes in their morphological, physiological, ecological and behavioural features (Montague *et al.* 2014; Ottoni *et al.* 2017, 2 and references therein).

Recent aDNA analyses by Ottoni *et al.* (2017) yielded further insights into the domestication process, albeit hampered by the limited and uneven distribution of faunal cat remains. Apart from discovering the *lybica* subvariant in southwestern Europe, indicating that these cats crossed the Bosporus, Ottoni *et al.* (2017, 2) demonstrate that the modern domestic cat's mtDNA pool can be traced back to five deeply divergent subclades (IV-A to IV-E) of the *F. s. lybica* clade, thus likely representing multiple wildcat lineages incorporated over time and space into domestic populations (also see Driscoll *et al.* 2009). The domesticated mitotype (IV-A; based on the *lybica* wild cats) was present in Anatolia from at least 8000 BCE onwards and in southeastern Europe (Bulgaria and Romania) around 4400 and 3200 cal BCE (Ottoni *et al.* 2017, 2). This postdates the advent of the Early Neolithic in southeastern and central Europe by one

---

2    It should be noted that 'pest' is an ascription, not an essential species-level quality – the status of an animal as 'pest' is thus to be demonstrated and may historically vary. Pre-casting certain animals as pests or even 'pest-species' may thus introduce Western/modernity biases (pers. comm S.T. Hussain 2023).

to two millennia, but according to the authors (ibid.) suggests a human role in the formation of this pattern. Earlier taming of the cat may also be inferred from a Neolithic human burial with wildcat remains on Cyprus dating to around 7500 BCE (Vigne *et al.* 2004). Due to limited data, the distribution of domesticated cats further east is more difficult to grasp. This being said, subclade IV-C appears most prominent and has a distribution from Egypt along the Nile towards the south (ibid.). It is one of the lineages of present-day domestic cats with an African origin (Ottoni *et al.* 2017, 5), also being the most frequent subclade among analyzed Egyptian cat mummies that were worshipped and during Greco-Roman times kept in precincts for mummification (ibid.; Màlek 2006).

Based on a range of other sources, Ottoni *et al.* (2017, 5) sketch the subsequent distribution of domesticated cats and argue that despite Egyptian bans on cat trading as early as 1700 BCE, the popularity of domesticated cats quickly increased in the wider Mediterranean. Type IV-C became especially popular and occurred twice as much in Western Anatolia during the 1st millennium CE compared to the IV-A type, suggesting the former had properties that rendered it more attractive to humans. These properties may have developed as a consequence of intensified human-cat relations in the Middle and New Kingdoms (ibid; also see Málek 2006). North of the Alps, the domesticated cat mostly made its appearance in relation to the Roman conquest, but the rule that sailors were to be accompanied by cats on their ships to control for vermin during Medieval times, may be responsible for an Egyptian IIV-C1 cat found at the Ralswiek Viking port in northern Germany, as early as in the 7-11th century CE (Ottoni *et al.* 2017, 5; also see Johansson and Hüster 1987). Cats may have benefited from other human-facilitated dispersal, related to for instance the trade in domestic cat pelts, or in relation to their role in pest control, following the distribution of the house mouse and black rat, already evidenced along Iron Age sea-routes (ibid., 5; also see Jones *et al.* 2015). An interesting finding by Ottoni and colleagues (2017, 5) is the development of a particular type of tabby cat with blotched coat, typical for house cats but very distinctive from the classic 'mackerel' pattern found in wildcats. The comparatively late emergence of this cat form in the Ottoman period indicates, in conjunction with, for instance, Egyptian depictions of cats sporting the mackerel striped pattern, that selection for these phenotypic traits occurred only relatively late in human history. This clearly indicates that cat domestication and the distribution of the domestic cat involved complex processes involving different types of human behaviour, with distinct contributions by Near Eastern and Egyptian cat lineages to the maternal genetic pool of modern domestic cats (ibid.).

More recent research adds further detail to the history of the cat, in particular in Central Europe. Krajcarz *et al.* (2020, 17710) present the so far earliest evidence for the dispersal of the Near Eastern wildcat into Europe, preceding the arrival of domesticated housecat populations by several millennia. Using stable isotope analysis, the authors investigated whether these wild cats followed the migration of farmers as early synanthropes, benefiting from human-shaped feeding opportunities and environmental contexts. The obtained dietary profiles of these cats indeed differed from those of contemporary European wildcats, with free-living feral individuals occupying a niche less wide than that of contemporaneous European wildcats. On the other hand, their profiles also differed from, much younger, Roman domesticated cats living in an agricultural environment, in fact taking up an intermediate position both. Human agricultural activity had thus apparently already impacted the availability and abundance of other synanthropic pest animals, in particular rodents, on which the cats could feed. These prey animals began to form an important dietary component of the Near Eastern wild cat. Krajcarz and colleagues (2020, 17715-17716) argue that while sharing an ecological niche with European wildcats, Near Eastern wildcats were thus probably synanthropes exploiting both natural and anthropogenic ecosystems. How close this relationship between humans and cats in the Neolithic of Central Europe was remains unclear (ibid.).

In general, it may therefore be concluded that the intensifying relationship between humans and domesticated cats in Europe is broadly evident, in particular from Neolithic times onward. Yet the somewhat ambivalent role played by early Near Eastern wild cats, seen from the perspective of a wild-domestic dichotomy, indicates that relationships were complex and involved a range of more or less pronounced synanthropic behaviours such as commensalism (*e.g.*, O'Connor 2013, ch. 7). Such a widening of the scope and intensity of cat-human interaction is of importance for grasping the nature of the relationship from this time onwards. It can, however, also be stated that domesticated cats in particular served the human niche from the transition to agriculture onwards, as human societies became sedentary. Cats provided a powerful tool in fighting pests, safeguarding seeds and harvested crops, and preventing the spread of disease.

From an anthropocentric perspective, these 'staying cats' then appear to have been functional to human needs and concerns. Without delving deeper into this matter, however, it is clear that the relationship between humans and domesticated cats also often had social, affective and even religious significance. The most well-known example is the special position held by cats in Ancient Egypt. Cats were venerated for killing snakes and protecting the pharaoh from the First Dynasty onwards, and the animals kept a special position until Roman times (Málek 2006). Several Egyptian deities such as Sekhmet, Bastet and Mafdet were depicted with cat heads, embodying power, fertility and justice. From the New Kingdom (c. 1570-1544 BCE) onwards, cat cults also became increasingly popular in Egyptian daily life, and from the 22nd Dynasty (c. 950 BCE) onwards the deity Bastet was believed to be embodied by domestic cats. Cats were worshipped as sacred animals, inter alia protecting households against rodents and other evils (ibid.). Interestingly, more 'powerful' cats such as the lion-headed Sekhmet served as protector of the pharaohs (Engels 1999). While cats were already embalmed and buried in cemeteries earlier, the animals were increasingly mummified and used as votive offerings from the 7th century BCE onwards (Ikram 2015; figure 2). Well known catacombs such as at Saqqara were re-used at this time as cat cemeteries for such offerings to Bastet (Ikram 2015; Zivie and Lichtenberg 2005).

Cats were deemed important in other human cultures too. In Islam for instance, it is believed that 'Muezza' was Mohammed's favourite cat (Geyer 2004), and cats are considered ritually clean and thus allowed to enter homes and mosques (Campo 2009, 131). In his study of the Marsh Arabs, Thesiger (1964) similarly highlights how cats are allowed to roam freely and enter community buildings. A recent study of the diet of cats in two mediaeval harbours in the Arabian Gulf and the Gulf of Oman seems to confirm this intersection of cats and human places (Brozou *et al.* 2023). The cats in these early historical towns probably roamed freely and scavenged the waste of human food consumption as well as fishing-related refuse. As such they also act as a proxy for the marine component in human diets and demonstrate the many often loose ways of human cat co-habitation (ibid.). Such an intermediate dietary profile was also already typical for the Near Eastern wildcats mentioned above.

In Christian Europe, cats appear to have sometimes had a less unencumbered role. They were associated with images of the annunciation and the Holy Family (Beadle 1977), but do not appear prominently in the bible, and medieval and post-medieval traditions such as cat-burning and the *Kattenstoet* in Ypres largely point to the association of cats with negative powers, witchcraft, and even the devil (McDonald 2007). Metzer (2009, 27-28) notes that medieval cats were perhaps seen as intruders into human society standing at the threshold between the familiar and the unfamiliar or malevolent. They as such could occupy a more liminal position.

In conclusion, we may argue that synanthropic and domesticated cats were invaluable companions and critically accompanied the developments that started with the transition to agriculture and that continue to shape our society until this day. In the course of this relationship, there appears to be a structural coupling between cats and specific human lifeforms. Over time a co-dependency between both species developed and such bonds often favoured strong affective ties as documented in many cases at the human-cat interface. The fact that cats were also venerated and even took on the shape of deities as exemplified by the role of the cat in Ancient Egypt, may have taken this affective relationship one step further, and perhaps even changed the relationship from co-dependency to the cat as a caretaker of human interests. The roots of this conceptualisation appear to lie with particular qualities of cats such as power, fertility and protection offered against unwanted pests – aspects of cats that tap especially into what could have been perceived as their wild and original characteristics. In a similar vein, medieval and post-medieval contexts highlight the ambiguous position of cats as both useful 'embodied mousetraps' and animals that relate to negative or perhaps non-Christian values because of their wild and uncontrollable qualities. It is this peculiar tension between a domesticated animal and its supposedly 'wild' behavioural expressions that still colours human-cat relations in the modern West. The study of human-cat interaction may therefore benefit from an 'agency' approach (Latour 2005): the characteristics and behaviours of cats affecting specific ways of how humans perceived their interaction with them. Such a perspective offers a more fluid and mutuality-emphasising understanding of human-cat interaction (see Poole 2015). These kinds of approaches allow us to rethink human-cat relations from a wider perspective and to re-assess the often-strict biological determinisms that govern much archaeological discussion on domestication and Neolithization in general.

A

B

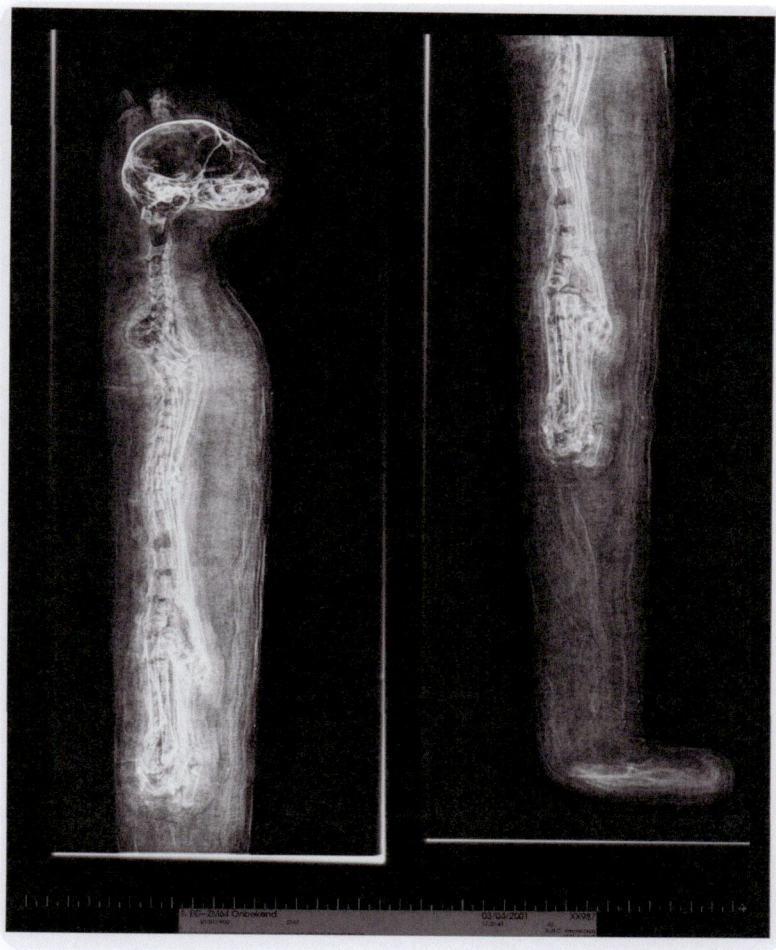

Figure 2. A: Cat mummy (AMM 16b), Egypt, Roman period, and B: X-Ray image of another cat mummy (National Museum of Antiquities).

## THREE FOR PLAYING

In modern-day Western society of the 20th and 21st centuries, cats combine the roles of companions and wild animals. Numerous studies have described the characteristics of human-cat relations and the positive impacts of owning cats on the lives of their owners (*e.g.*, Mahalski *et al.* 1988; Evans *et al.* 2019). Based on my own experience, I know more friends and colleagues with cats than without, and the fact that in the Netherlands cats amount to three million individuals forms a case in point. In numerous cities, one can now visit *cat cafés* to enjoy a hairy cappuccino and the company of cats. Cats and kittens are omnipresent in art (figure 3) as symbols of affection and endearment, and apart from their companion status have also become diverse icons of our society (*e.g.*, Rogers 2001). Cats

also continue to play an important, though perhaps imaginary, part in pest control, catching or deterring mice and rats (see Parsons *et al.* 2018). At the same time, an increasing number of studies suggests that this combination of traits is an ecological problem. Estimates of the numbers of native wild animals ranging from birds over small mammals and invertebrates to herpetofauna killed by domestic cats every year is estimated in the millions in the UK and in the billions in the United States (see McDonald *et al.* 2015, 2745 and references therein). Arguably, these cats most of the time do not kill primarily for food as, with the exception of self-sustaining feral cats, their food is to some extent based on what is provided to them by human individuals or communities (ibid.). As such these killings are part of their hunting and playing behaviour. Cat-owners in turn often do not or only to a limited extent acknowledge this problem. McDonald *et al.* (2015, 2745) point out:

> "Cat owners generally disagreed with the statement that cats are harmful to wildlife, and disfavored all mitigation options apart from neutering. These attitudes were uncorrelated with the predatory behaviour of their cats. Cat owners failed to perceive the magnitude of their cats' impact on wildlife and were not influenced by ecological information."

Crowley *et al.* (2019, 18) similarly highlight this problem and suggest that hunting is widely understood as a normal, natural component of cat behaviour, with owners rarely recognising individual responsibilities for preventing or reducing it. This is interesting. One would expect dog owners to be aware of the various transgressions of their four-legged friends, for instance when attacking other dogs, humans, cats or sheep and to act accordingly. As one can easily imagine, this would quickly be seen as unwanted behaviour, as a form of 'aggression' and not in line with the domestic status of dogs. As behaviour that should be avoided and controlled for, in some cases even motivating euthanisations. Not so for cats, however. There, predatory behaviour is typically accepted. Crowley *et al.* (2019, 28) thus argue that it would be wise to, next to other measures, invest in promoting responsible pet ownership by encouraging greater attentiveness and accountability in these matters.

Crowley and colleagues (2020, 477) point out that by having retained their behavioural and reproductive independence, cats maintain a liminal status as both domestic and wild animals with concurrent traits and dual roles as companions and pest controllers. These authors assert that the growing ecological conflict over the management of cats and the threat they incur to native wild species is linked to the difficulty of reconciling 'wild' and 'domestic' qualities. They (idem) argue that:

> "the fraught contemporary relationships between cats and human societies reflect a longstanding, important symbiosis that is both maintained and challenged by the resistance of the 'domestic' cat to complete domestication, and by the duality of its roles as autonomous predator and ostensibly dependent companion."

It is of course questionable to what extent the cat resists complete domestication. I would argue that the question rather is what domestication means and when it is 'complete'. In addition, the fundamentally different behavioural dispositions of animals such as cats in a way demonstrate that a discussion in terms of domesticated vs. non-domesticated may be of little use and would benefit from a more targeted approach that instead focuses on the dynamics and historical contexts of human-cat relationships. Indeed, as the authors suggest, in order to move beyond the impasse of conceptualising cats either as social pets or environmental pests, we have to acknowledge that their role is inextricably bound to our human role and how we share the world with them. They argue (ibid. 481) that due to our enduring symbiotic relationship with these animals, cats cannot be classified as a wild animal for purposes of management and we humans are thus jointly implicated with them in the major environmental disturbances of our time. In order to move forward, it is therefore necessary to *"recognize and work with the messy, difficult, multispecies histories and legacies of human-cat relations."* In this way (ibid. 477, 481), we may be able to arrive at more sustainable solutions of co-living and ecosystem management, but these require a novel 'companion animal ecology'. Such ecologies are grounded in what Haraway (2013) identified as a companion species, in fact stressing the mutually dependent or 'obligatory' relationships between human and non-human animals. Such relationships must strive to integrate both the wild and domesticated nature of cats, while acknowledging that these are Western, situated categories, and aim to elucidate the unique and diverse, multi-stranded relationships between cats and humans. Such a non-dichotomic approach would also be more attuned to understanding these relationships within the context of the Anthropocene as we head towards ever increasing human-shaped landscapes and anthropogenic ecologies (also see the *Feral Atlas*: https://feralatlas.org/). In dealing with these situations, it may be instructive to draw on our past relationships with cats and to interrogate the archaeological record for alternative modes of interaction.

## DISCUSSION: STRAY THOUGHTS
In recent years, numerous studies have foregrounded the role of archaeology and deep history in addressing the key challenges of today (Boivin and Crowther 2021). While not providing concrete answers to today's problems, the vast spatio-temporal

Figure 3. Indian and Abyssinian cats. From a painting by W. Luker junior from "The Book of the Cat" by Frances Simpson (1903, plate 12).

reservoir that we as archaeologists can access and use showcases the diversity of possible relationships between humans and nonhumans and the fact that there are multistranded avenues to address these and similar problems. An instructive popular example is given by some of the perspectives offered in *The Dawn of Everything* by Graeber and Wengrow (2021), in particular demonstrating non-linear developments in the social organisation of early human societies and the fact that there always were and therefore are many viable alternatives to how we want to build our human communities and live together with other species. Such new perspectives may also be of help when we attempt to understand seemingly small issues or supposedly marginal topics such as human-cat relations, and in doing so help us to develop 'new companion animal ecologies'. Here are some preliminary thoughts (and questions) that may be helpful in achieving this.

### The lure of the wild?

With regard to the place of bigger and smaller wildcats in Pleistocene and Early Holocene communities, I would argue that there is much to be learned from the fact that we as humans have always thought with and through animals, whether in adorning ourselves, by means of cave art, or in close observation of what at times would have been tension-ridden and competitive relationships. Such a connection can be attested from the Palaeolithic onwards (*e.g.*, Clottes and Lewis-Williams 1996), for instance in referencing the animals in art. It also continues to the present day in which there is a vast and lively debate regarding human-animal relationships and their anthropological and philosophical connotations (*e.g.*, Breyer and Widlok 2018). The essence of this human-animal connection may be formed by the fact that animals, in a way, can hold up a mirror to ourselves. What may be gleaned from the early stage of human-cat interaction in particular is therefore that there was a time when we did not see ourselves as separate from the natural environment encompassing felines and rather regarded everything in it from a connected and engendered perspective (Bird-David 1990; Ingold 2000). Rich ethnographic accounts of human-animal relations here provide a powerful remedy in providing new incentives to review our current interaction with these animals. As such these may help to develop thinking that goes beyond a Cartesian distinction of nature and culture, by not placing ourselves in a separate category from animals. In this respect, deep-time archaeology has recently made us reconsider how we approach multispecies relationships including past humans, also regarding the uniqueness of our own species (*e.g.*, Hussain and Floss 2015; Shipman 2010). From this perspective, one could argue that an important reason why we are attracted to cats is perhaps not so much their ambivalent social behaviour, their tactile qualities, or because they excel at catching mice, but because something in our mind connects to and admires their wild qualities. These can so come into play as a distant reminder of the way we spent most of our evolutionary existence. This may then position cats as a form of nostalgic, but also as essentially human 'portable wildness'. Given all the recent attention to 'rewilding' and embracing nature in the Anthropocene and especially in the West, is this not also fundamentally the attractivity of cats? The fact that we can tap into wildness in a safe and pleasurable manner?

### Domesticating

With regard to cats 'staying' with us, the interest mostly lies in the question what domestication is and to what extent we as humans domesticated wild animals by capturing, taming and breeding, or whether animals also domesticate themselves? For both cats and dogs, it has been argued that the start of their domestication process is linked to synanthropic relationships with human communities (*e.g.*, Perri *et al.* 2021; Yu *et al.* 2014). This dynamic eventually led both species to change their biological make-up, albeit on rather different ends of the spectrum of possibilities. Does this warrant the argument as stated above that cats have resisted completing their own domestication, or have both species (cats and dogs) and humans simply navigated the domestication process in ways that were optimal to their respective

relationships? It thus seems that there is always the question of intention and outcome and that this can only partially be controlled by humans, it is at least not controlled by humans *alone*. The process set in motion by domestication also has distinct repercussions for human societies. In contrast to what Hodder (1990) proposed for the Neolithic, juxtaposing the *domus* and the *agrios*, there is no absolute distinction between wild and domesticated. Free-roaming cats and their diet in the Medieval harbours of Iranian and Oman towns significantly overlapping with human diets forms a clear example (Brozou *et al.* 2023). So, if an animal is not bound to a human community, or when an animal rewilds itself and becomes feral, what does this tell us about the impact of domestication and would it also throw new light on taming versus domesticating? Perhaps approaching these issues from an experimental 'Neolithic mindset' would be interesting, instead of foregrounding the benefits for humans within an unilinear process of domestication. Focusing on creating the right conditions and boundaries for certain traits to develop – on issues of trust and mutual benefit – is perhaps a more interesting and productive way to understand domestication and how humans and cats have co-shaped each other over the course of human history.

### Pets or pests?

Building on the previous two sections, another avenue to explore could be how humans have dealt with other animals in the past and what this role entailed for notions and understandings of power-relations. Clearly, somewhere on the way, humans have changed their position in the matrix of power governing at least some human-animal relationships. There are numerous ethnographic accounts on how in a 'giving environment' taking an animal is often something reciprocal. In order to take, one has to ask permission and also to give something back in return (*e.g.*, Bird-David 1990). The question is to what extent this changed with the Neolithic, at least in the sense as it is often traditionally perceived, as the period in which livestock becomes an integral part of human worlds. Does it rhyme with 'in order to own an animal you have to care for it'? If this is so, it may also open up alternative viewpoints, for instance as argued by Oma Armstrong (2019, 171): the intensification of human-animal bonds throws processes of domestication into a perspective of reciprocity, foregrounding commitment and even co-authored lifeways within an ethics of a duty of care. And what does care then mean? The intimate relationship with farm animals in the past created very different ways of interacting than the detached and anonymous food industry of the capitalist West, which currently casts animals as mere economic entities and hardly as living creatures of flesh and mind. How does this influence which animals are used for food and which are kept as companions and how does it impact our understanding of these terms in the first place? What is the role of genetic adaptation and change with regard to important physical and social characteristics of animals, and how do certain rules in society such as taboos and religion come into play here? And are we as humans, in the light of zoonoses such as the recent COVID pandemic and the current climate crisis, in the end not the only species to blame? And do the same implications hold for the controversial discussion on the ecological pressure incurred by our beloved cats? And why is this so? Have we become a wayward species and what would be a possible way forward?

## CONCLUSION

As has been argued above animals can help us think, and in the past and present have often offered diverse avenues of doing so. Some of them have been briefly touched upon here, ranging from the way animals may have played a role as shamanistic and totemistic beings, or hybrids, for instance in the remote Palaeolithic past, to their veneration as gods as demonstrated in ancient Egyptian contexts, or the current position they assume and controversies they spark in the Anthropocene. Cats in particular form an interesting example as they seem to elude fitting into neat dichotomous perspectives of 'wild' or 'nature' versus 'domesticated' or 'culture'. As such, they serve as a mirror to us, questioning us in our own animality and our changing relationship to other animals and the wider environment around us. In order to better understand human-animal relationship, researchers can benefit from closer cooperations between the fields of philosophy, anthropology and archaeology, which is something our respected colleague has demonstrated throughout his career. This also goes for thinking about cats.

Thoughts, however, also need to be groomed, and that also goes for cats, those creatures with which we will have to find new and better ways to form a 'companion animal ecology'. Interestingly, and apart from their many other roles, they are also creatures that in many ways appear very conducive to stimulating an academy career, as my esteemed colleague living with two of them will probably know well. This is

why I would like to end with a 9th century Irish poem of a monk and his cat (originally in the *Reichenauer Schulschrift*), its popular translation, and a version composed by the British poet Wystan. H. Auden:

*Messe ocus Pangur Bán*
*cechtar náthar fria saindán:*
*bíth a menma-sam fri seilgg,*
*mu menma céin im saincheirdd.*

Popular translation:

*I and Pangur Ban my cat,*
*'Tis a like task we are at:*
*Hunting mice is his delight,*
*Hunting words I sit all night.*

The version written by the poet Wystan H. Auden:

*Pangur, white Pangur, How happy we are*
*Alone together, scholar and cat*
*Each has his own work to do daily;*
*For you it is hunting, for me study.*
*Your shining eye watches the wall;*
*My feeble eye is fixed on a book.*
*You rejoice, when your claws entrap a mouse;*
*I rejoice when my mind fathoms a problem.*
*Pleased with his own art, neither hinders the other;*
*Thus we live ever without tedium and envy.*

## ACKNOWLEDGEMENTS

The author wishes to thank the editors for their patient review and in particular Shumon Hussain for his valuable comments and references. I also wish to thank Raymond for his many years of inspiration during and after his studies, and for his sociable companionship. As a fellow member of *Het Limburgs Genootschap van Intellectuelen in Ballingschap* (LGIB/ the Limburg Society of Intellectuals in Exile), Raymond was always a kindred spirit with an inquisitive mind and often unexpected new perspectives on archaeological questions. I hope our friendship will remain and retain both the social and intellectual components for many years to come!

190 ANALECTA PRAEHISTORICA LEIDENSIA 54

## REFERENCES

Amkreutz, L. and R.H.A. Corbey. 2008. "An eagle-eyed perspective: Haliaeetus albicilla in the Mesolithic and Neolithic of the Lower Rhine Area." In *Between foraging and farming: An extended broad spectrum of papers presented to Leendert Louwe Kooijmans,* edited by H. Fokkens, B. Coles, A. van Gijn, H.H. Ponjée and C.G. Slappendel, 167-180. Leiden: Leiden University (Analecta Praehistorica Leidensia 40).

Armstrong Oma, K. 2019. "First Encounters: Domestication as Steps of Becoming." In *Animal Encounters. Cultural Animal Studies, vol 4.,* edited by A. Böhm and J. Ullrich, 171-85. Stuttgart: J.B. Metzler.

Auguste, P. 1992. "Étude archéozoologique des grands mammifères du site pleistocène moyen de Biache Saint-Vaast (Pas-De-Calais, France): apports biostratigraphiques et palethnographiques." *L'Anthropologie* 96, 49-70.

Beadle, M. 1977. *Cat.* New York: Simon & Schuster.

Bird-David, N. 1990. "The giving environment: Another perspective on the economic system of gatherer-hunters." *Current Anthropology* 31 (2), 189-96.

Boivin, N. and A. Crowther. 2021. "Mobilizing the past to shape a better Anthropocene." *Nature Ecology and Evolution* 5, 273-284. DOI: 10.1038/s41559-020-01361-4

Bratlund, B. 1999. "Taubach revisited." *Jahrbuch des Römisch-Germanischen Zentralmuseums Mainz* 46, 61-174.

Breyer, T. and T. Widlok, eds. 2018. *The situationality of human -animal relations. Perspectives from anthropology and philosophy.* Bielefeld: Transcript.

Brozou, A., B.T. Fuller, B. de Cupere, A. Marrast, H. Monchot, J. Peters, K. van de Vijver, O. Lambert, M.A. Mannino, C. Ottoni and W. van Neer. 2023. "A dietary perspective of cat-human interactions in two medieval harbors in Iran and Oman revealed through stable isotope analysis." *Scientific Reports* 13, 12316. DOI: 10.1038/s41598-023-39417-7

Campo, J.E. 2009. *Encyclopedia of Islam.* New York: Facts On File, Inc. An imprint of Infobase Publishing.

Clottes, J. and M. Azéma. 2005. "Les images de félins de la grotte Chauvet." *Bulletin de la Société Préhistorique Française* 102 (1), 173-82.

Clottes, J., and J.D. Lewis-Williams. 1996. *Les Chamanes de la Préhistoire: Transe et Magie dans les Grotes Ornées.* Paris: Éditions Seuil.

Crowley, S.L., M. Cecchitti, and R.A. McDonald. 2019. "Hunting behaviour in domestic cats: an exploratory study of risk and responsibility among cat owners." *People and Nature* 1, 18-30. DOI: 10.1002/pan3.6

Crowley, S.L., M. Cecchitti, and R.A. McDonald. 2020. "Our wild companions: domestic cats in the Anthopocene." *Trends in Ecology and Evolution* 35 (6), 477-483. DOI: 10.1016/j.tree.2020.01.008

Driscoll, C.A., D.W. Macdonald, and S.J. O'Brien. 2009. "From wild animals to domestic pets, an evolutionary view of domestication." *Proceedings of the National Academt of Sciences* 106, 9971-78. DOI: 10.1073/pnas.0901586106

Dusseldorp, G.L. 2009. *A view to a kill: investigating Middle Palaeolithic subsistence using a optimal foraging perspective.* Leiden: Sidestone Press.

Engels, D.W. 1999. *Classical Cats: The Rise and Fall of the Sacred Cat.* New York: Routledge.

Evans, R., M. Lyons, G. Brewer, and S. Tucci. 2019. "The purrfect match: The influence of personality on owner satisfaction with their domestic cat (Felis silvestris catus)." *Personality and Individual Differences* 138, 252-56. DOI: 10.1016/j.paid.2018.10.011.

Floss, H. 2018. "Same as it ever was? The Aurignacian of the Swabian Jura and the origins of Palaeolithic art." *Quaternary International* 491, 21-29. doi.org/10.1016/j.quaint.2016.12.044

Geyer, G. A. 2004. *When Cats Reigned Like Kings: On the Trail of the Sacred Cats.* Kansas City, Missouri: Andrews McMeel Publishing.

Graeber, D. and D. Wengrow. 2021. *The Dawn of Everything. A new history of humanity.* New York: Picador and Farrar, Straus and Ginou.

Haraway, D.J. 2003. *The companion species manifesto. Dogs, people and significant otherness.* Chicago: Prickly Paradigm Press.

Hodder, I. 1990. *The domestication of Europe.* New Jersey: Wiley-Blackwell.

Hu Yaowu, S.H., W. Wang, X. Wu, F.B. Marshall, X. Chen, H.L. Lianliang, and C. Wang. 2014. "Earliest evidence for commensal processes of cat domestication." *Proceedings of the National Academy of Sciences* 111 (1), 116-20. DOI: 10.1073/pnas.1311439110

Hussain, S.T., and H. Floss. 2015. "Sharing the world with mammoths, cave lions and other beings: Linking animal-human interactions and the Aurignacian "belief world"." *Quartär* 62, 85-120. DOI: 10.7485/QU62_4

Ikram, S. 2015. "Speculations on the role of animal cults in the economy of Ancient Egypt." In *Apprivoiser le sauvage / Taming the Wild,* edited by M. Massiera, B.

Mathieu, and F. Rouffet, 211-28. Montpellier: Cahiers de l'Égypte Nilotique et Méditerranéenne 11.

Ingold, T. 2000. *The Perception of the Environment: Essays on Livelihood, Dwelling and Skill*. New York: Routledge.

Johansson, F., and H. Hüster. 1987. *Untersuchungen an Skelettresten von Katzen aus Haithabu (Ausgrabung 1966 – 1969) 86*. Neumünster: Wachholtz (Ausgrabungen in Haithabu Bd. 24).

Jones, E.P., Eager, H., Gabriel, S., Johannesdottir, F. and J. Searle. 2013. "Genetic tracking of mice and other bioproxies to infer human history." *Trends in Genetics* 29, 298-308.

Krajcarz, M., M.T. Krajcarz, M. Baca, C. Baumann, W. Van Neer, D. Popović, M. Sudoł-Procyk, B. Wach, J. Wilczyński, M. Wojenka, and H. Bocherens. 2020. "Ancestors of domestic cats in Neolithic Central Europe: Isotopic evidence of a synanthropic diet." *Proceedings of the National Academy of Sciences* 117, 17710-19. DOI:10.1073/pnas.191888411

Krajcarz, M., W. van Neer, M.T. Krajcarz, D. Popović, M. Baca, B. De Cupere, Q. Goffette, H.C. Küchelmann, A. Gręzak, U. Iwaszczuk, C. Ottoni, K. Van de Vijver, J. Wilczyński, A. Mulczyk, J. Wiejacki, D. Makowiecki, and H. Bocherens. 2022. "Stable isotopes unveil one millennium of domestic cat paleoecology in Europe." *Scientific Reports* 12, 12775. DOI:10.1038/s41598-022-16969-8

Kind, J., N. Ebinger-Rist, S. Wolf, T. Beutelspacher, and K. Wehrberger. 2014. "The smile of the lion man. Recent excavations in Stadel cave (Baden-Württemberg, south-western Germany) and the restoration of the famous upper palaeolithic figurine." *Quartär* 61, 129-145.

Latour, B. 2005. *Reassembling the Social: An Introduction to Actor-Network-Theory*. New York: Oxford University Press.

Mahalski P.A., R. Jones, and G.M. Maxwell. 1988. "The Value of Cat Ownership to Elderly Women Living Alone." *The International Journal of Aging and Human Development* 27 (4), 249-260. DOI:10.2190/N40Y-68JW-38TD-AT9R

Màlek, J. 2006 (1997). *The Cat in Ancient Egypt*. London: British Museum Press.

McDonald, G. 2009. *Frommer's Belgium, Holland and Luxemburg*. Hoboken: Wiley.

McDonald, J.L., M. Maclean, M.R. Evans, and D.J. Hodgson. 2015. "Reconciling actual and perceived rates of predation by domestic cats." *Ecology and Evolution* 5 (14), 2745-53. DOI:10.1002/ece3.1553

Metzer, I. 2009. "Heretical Cats: Animal Symbolism in Religious Discourse." *Medium Aevum Quotidianum* 59, 16-32.

Montague, M.J., G. Li, B. Gandolfi, R. Khan, B.L. Aken, S.M.J. Searle, P. Minx, L.W. Hillier, D.C. Koboldt, B.W. Davis, C.A. Driscoll, C.S. Barr, K. Blackistone, J. Quilez, B. Lorente-Galdos, T. Marques-Bonet, C. Alkan, G.W.C. Thomas, M.W. Hahn, M. Menotti-Raymond, S.J. O'Brien, R.K. Wilson, L.A. Lyons, W.J. Murphy, and W.C. Warren. 2014. "Comparative analysis of the domestic cat genome reveals genetic signatures underlying feline biology and domestication." *Proceedings of the National Academy of Sciences* 111, 17230-35.

O'Connor, T. 2013. *Animals as Neighbors: The Past and Present of Commensal Animals*. East Lansing: Michigan State University Press.

Ottoni, Claudio, Wim Van Neer, Bea De Cupere, Julien Daligault, Silvia Guimaraes, Joris Peters, Nikolai Spassov, Mary E. Prendergast, Nicole Boivin, Arturo Morales-Muñiz, Adrian Bălăşescu, Cornelia Becker, Norbert Benecke, Adina Boroneant, Hijlke Buitenhuis, Jwana Chahoud, Alison Crowther, Laura Llorente, Nina Manaseryan, Hervé Monchot, Vedat Onar, Marta Osypińska, Olivier Putelat, Eréndira M. Quintana Morales, Jacqueline Studer, Ursula Wierer, Ronny Decorte, Thierry Grange, and Eva-Maria Geigl. 2017. "The palaeogenetics of cat dispersal in the ancient world." *Nature Ecology & Evolution* 1 (7): 0139. DOI:10.1038/s41559-017-0139.

Oversteegen, J.H. S., L.H. van Wijngaarden-Bakker, C.H. Maliepaard, and T. van Kolfschoten. 2001. "Zoogdieren, vogels en Reptielen". In *Hardinxveld-Giessendam De Bruin. Een kampplaats uit het Laat-Mesolithicum en het begin van de Swifterbant cultuur (5500-4450 v. Chr.)*, edited by L. P. Louwe Kooijmans, 209-298. Amersfoort: Rijksdienst voor het Oudheidkundig Bodemonderzoek (Rapportage Archeologische Monumentenzorg 88).

Parsons, M.H., P.B. Banks, M.A. Deutsch, and J. Munshi-South. 2014. "Temporal and Space-Use Changes by Rats in Response to Predation by Feral Cats in an Urban Ecosystem." *Frontiers in Ecology and Evolution* 6 (146), 1-8. DOI:10.3389/fevo.2018.00146

Perri, A.R., T.R. Feuerborn, L.A.F. Frantz, and K.E. Witt. 2021. "Dog domestication and the dual dispersal of people and dogs into the Americas." *Proceedings of the National Academy of Sciences* 118 (6), 1-8. DOI:10.1073/pnas.201008311

Poole, K. 2015. "The Contextual Cat: Human – Animal Relations and Social Meaning in Anglo-Saxon

England." *Journal of Archaeological Method and Theory* 22, 857-882 DOI:10.1007/s10816-014-9208-9

Radovčić D., A.O. Sršen, J. Radovčić, and D.W. Frayer. 2015. "Evidence for Neandertal Jewelry: Modified White-Tailed Eagle Claws at Krapina." *PLoS ONE* 10 (3), e0119802. DOI:10.1371/journal.pone.0119802.

Rogers, K.M. 2001. *The Cat and the Human Imagination. Feline Images from Bast to Garfield.* Ann Arbor: University of Michigan Press.

Ruiz-Villar, H., J. Vicente López-Baoand, and F. Palomares. 2020. "A small cat saving food for later: caching behavior in the European wildcat (Felis silvestris silvestris)." *European Journal of Wildlife Research* 66, 1-13. DOI:10.1007/s10344-020-01413-x

Sauvet, G., R. Layton, T. Lenssen-Erz, P. Taçon, and A. Wlodarczyk. 2009. "Thinking with Animals in Upper Palaeolithic Rock Art." *Cambridge Archaeological Journal* 19 (3), 319-336. DOI:10.1017/S0959774309000511

Shipman, P. 2010. "The animal connection and human evolution." *Current Anthropology* 51 (4), 519-538.

Simpson, F. 1903. *The book of the cat.* London: Cassell and company.

Speth, J. 2010. *The Paleoanthropology and Archaeology of Big-Game Hunting.* New York. Springer.

Tanis, K., and L. Amkreutz. 2022. "Zeldzame vondst van een opperarmbeen van een Europese wilde kat – Felis silvestris silvestris Schreber, 1777, op Maavlakte 2." *Cranium* 39 (2), 40-49.

Thesiger, W. 1964. *"The Marsh Arabs."* London: Longmans.

Van Wijngaarden-Bakker, L.H., C. Cavallo, T. van Kolfschoten, C.H. Maliepaard, and J.H.S. Oversteegen. 2001. Zoogdieren, vogels, reptielen. In *Hardinxveld-Giessendam Polderweg. Een mesolithisch jachtkamp in het rivierengebied (5500-5000 v. Chr.),* edited by L. P. Louwe Kooijmans, 181-242. Amersfoort: Rijksdienst voor het Oudheidkundig Bodemonderzoek (Rapportage Archeologische Monumentenzorg 83).

Vigne, J.-D., J. Guilane, K. Debue, L. Haye, and P. Gérard. 2004. "Early Taming of the Cat in Cyprus." *Science* 304, 259-259. DOI:10.1126/science.1095335

Vogelbescherming. n.d. "Standpunt huisdieren en wilde vogels."Accessed May 2023. https://www.vogelbescherming.nl/over-ons/standpunten/standpunt-huisdieren-en-wilde-vogels.

Zeiler, J. 2010. "Sometimes you eat the bear...Bruine beren en mensen in het neolithicum." *Westerheem Special nr. 2.* Veghel: AWN.

Zeiler, J. 2021. "Aangespoeld en opgeraapt. Archeozoölogisch onderzoek van bewerkt bot en gewei van Maasvlakte 1 en 2 en Hoek van Holland: een eerste inventarisatie" In *Doggerland en Rotterdam. Een inventarisatie van opgespoten paleolithische en mesolithische artefacten van (vuur)steen, bot en gewei van Maasvlakte (1 en 2) en Hoek van Holland (gemeente Rotterdam): een aanzet voor vervolgonderzoek,* edited by A. Carmiggelt and D. E. A. Schiltmans, 125-50. Rotterdam: Gemeente Rotterdam (Boornotitie 41).

Zivie, A., and R. Lichtenberg. 2005. "The Cats of the Goddess Bastet." In *Divine Creatures: Animal Mummies in Ancient Egypt,* edited by S. Ikram, 106-119. Cairo: Cairo Scholarship. DOI:10.5743/cairo/9789774248580.003.0005

In Hussain, S.T. and G.L. Dusseldorp (eds) 2025. Sitting on the fence: Negotiating archaeology, anthropology and philosophy. Festschrift for Prof. Dr Raymond H.A. Corbey in celebration of his 70th birthday. *Analecta Praehistorica Leidensia* 54. Leiden: Sidestone Press, pp. 193-204.

# Rediscovering the archaeological terrain

## Dimitri De Loecker, Jan Kolen

**ABSTRACT**

With this article we to aim to put the topic of landscape on the archaeological agenda again, this time emphasising its properties as a terrain and taskscape (following Ingold 1993). After having been seen as essentially belonging to the domain of geomorphology, the archaeological landscape has been subject to in-depth theoretical reflection over the past half century. Inspired by cultural materialism and human ecology, cultural geography and philosophical phenomenology, landscape has been redefined in archaeology in terms of human adaptation, cultural process, meaning and experience. As a result, the topic has become somewhat over-theorised and the landscape as terrain has been overlooked. Where this has not been the case, more or less traditional geomorphological, taphonomic and site-based approaches still prevail. We therefore stress the importance of an integral approach that links (archaeological) hotspots and "marginal" spaces, and the (seemingly) durable and (seemingly) ephemeral within the landscape as an extensive terrain in which people concretely live, work and move. After all, it is also the landscape as terrain that forms the natural habitat of the exploring archaeologist. Two very different examples are discussed to illustrate our argument: the landscape of early prehistoric foragers and the archaeology of twentieth-century terrorscapes.

*Keywords: Landscape archaeology, archaeological terrain, off-site, taskscape, palaeolithic foragers, terrorscape*

## INTRODUCTION: THE ARCHAEOLOGICAL TERRAIN

Although a theorist, philosopher and anthropologist, Raymond Corbey takes great pleasure in exploring the "archaeological terrain" – also in the most concrete and physical sense of the word. He is an exceptionally broadly interested researcher who not only likes to participate in the fieldwork of others, but also explores archaeological and geological landscapes himself on an individual basis – in the Netherlands, France, and during his many visits to colleagues and conferences abroad. Therefore, in this paper, we discuss a classical archaeological problem: How to take the step from the study of archaeological patterns and materials in the present-day landscape to an understanding of human activity in the past. In this way, we would like to reactivate, in a sense, the longstanding discussion about "off-site" archaeology.

By now many years ago, scholars like Robert Foley (1981) and Glynn Isaac (1981) signalled the understandable but problematic appeal of archaeological "hotspots", like ancient settlements and cemeteries, and rich "outcrops" of artefacts, to those who study the deep human past. Instead, they suggested to curb this traditional practice and to challenge our "short-sited" reflex by looking beyond the clearly

**Dimitri De Loecker**

Faculty of Archaeology,
Leiden University, The Netherlands
dimitri.loecker@pandora.be

**Jan Kolen**

Faculty of Archaeology,
Leiden University, The Netherlands
j.c.a.kolen@arch.leidenuniv.nl

visible, the dense and the seemingly unambiguous. Archaeologists should explore the margins of former cultural landscapes, where other aspects of human living space have escaped the archaeological attention for decades. Robert Foley (1981) defined the value of what he called "off-site" archaeology; in the same volume, the late Glynn Isaac asked for more attention for the "scatter between the patches" in Stone Age archaeology, (Isaac 1981). Nonetheless, in the meantime, the typical archaeological reflex has proved to be stubborn, as the "marginal landscapes" largely remained unexplored and – therefore – vulnerable and threatened.

With the exception of modern survey archaeology, the art of meticulous large-scale archaeological field research, resulting in highly detailed reconstructions of past environments and often involving valuable thought experiments with new geographical concepts, has somehow disappeared from the archaeological scene. This observation needs some explanation. Since the 1990s, landscape archaeology increasingly focused on theoretical reflection and on the re-conceptualisation of "landscape" as a social construct (see Ingold 1993 for critique). Instead of viewing landscape simply and uncritically as the backdrop to human action or as the natural world "out there", archaeologists now propagated the "humanisation" of landscape as a basic concept for research, interpretation, and societal engagement. Since the appearance of the first humans ca. 2.8 million years ago, humans have continuously impacted the outlook and development of natural landscapes and ecosystems – and have transformed these into deeply socialised worlds. Additionally, as cultural geographers, phenomenologists and post-processual archaeologists have consistently argued, all landscapes, past and present, are in fact social constructs "modelled" by human experience. In the process, landscape archaeology has become somewhat over-theorised and the archaeological terrain itself has moved to the background of the study of past landscapes, which has become extremely associative and interpretive. In doing so, archaeologists seem to have overlooked the particularities of the archaeological terrain itself.

The archaeological terrain is more than our primary source of information. It is more than the natural habitat of the archaeologist, so to speak, and for this reason it is also much more than the scene for romantic fieldwork experience. Through time, the archaeological terrain has been an integral part of the spatial setting within which humans used and ordered their living

space. The archaeological terrain appears fragmented and incomplete if viewed and analysed in terms of separate time slices, depositional events or "horizons" (Bailey 2007). However, if we do not consider it a set of eroded surfaces or frozen stages but as a dynamic whole, we might be able to follow path dependent changes that constantly reworked the material qualities and human legacies of environments through time.

In this paper we argue that to better understand this dynamic setting, archaeologists should dig deeper into the structures, patterns and spatial relationships that characterise and redefine the landscape as a terrain with archaeological substance. This is not only necessary for reconsidering the complex relationships between "site" and "off-site", but also – as will be shown – for empirical and theoretical reflections on the limitations of the landscape concept itself and of the ways in which it has been used in archaeology over the past few decades. Rediscovering the archaeological terrain may furthermore increase our understanding of how human environments have evolved over the long term as a kind of *process totalized* (Kobayashi 1989), at least at the local level. Finally, such an exercise will enable archaeologists to create new or better narratives about the environment *as heritage*, of which the archaeological terrain forms an integral part.

We will illustrate the potential of such a project by discussing two very different examples. First, we discuss the characteristics of a very old human environment dating to the Middle Pleistocene, some 250,000 years ago. This example is based on innovative research that was conducted already more than 30 years ago. The second case study deals with the archaeology of very young landscapes (or "terrorscapes") dating from the Second World War (Van der Laarse 2015). These landscapes are currently being transformed rapidly into cultural heritage, although their spatial scale and historical complexity is not fully understood yet. In this context, archaeology itself is quite a new phenomenon.

## A PLEISTOCENE "TASKSCAPE"
For the first example we go to southern tip of the Netherlands and inspect a snapshot of the landscape's history around 250.000 years ago. Here, in a hilly and urbanised environment, we find the Belvédère pit near Maastricht (southern Limburg, the Netherlands): a loess and gravel quarry where flint artefacts of early Neanderthals were discovered during the 1980s in fine-grained river sediments (Roebroeks 1988; De Loecker 2004). When Leiden-based archaeologist

Wil Roebroeks and his team started excavating these sites, Palaeolithic archaeology in Europe had gone through a rather turbulent period of theoretical debate and methodological innovation. In fact, Palaeolithic archaeology can almost be blamed for inventing site-based, or even site-*biased*, approaches in archaeology, as it has been searching consistently for the clearly visible, the massive living floors and the rich "base camps" in caves and abris (Binford 1987).

Well into the 1970s, the research of these sites was dominated by the excavation and analysis of single stratigraphical columns, with the aim of building detailed typo-chronologies of distinctive Palaeolithic cultures, which at the time were believed to fully represent former ethnic groups. The work of the late François Bordes at sites like Combe Grenal (Bordes 1972) was of paradigmatic importance in this respect. However, in the 1970s, the American archaeologist and anthropologist Lewis Binford claimed that archaeologists needed multi-dimensional information about these levels to better understand the *behaviour* of Palaeolithic hunters and gatherers. This also required detailed information of the horizontal distribution of artefacts within the levels themselves. The emphasis was on the reconstruction of activity areas, based on a functionalist explanation of artefact types, the spatial distribution of tools and waste, and where possible based on the results of micro-wear analysis. Sites were now explained as the remains of temporary camps, consisting of spatial agglomerations of specific activity areas. The wider variation of settlement types of one period within a specific region could then be seen as indicative of the land-use system practiced by the groups involved. This land-use system, in turn, should be analysed in relation to its former environmental setting to judge its adaptive success (Binford 1980).

It is against the background of this debate that we can place the start of the excavations in the Belvédère quarry at Maastricht. The team formulated research questions that were quite typical for the New (Palaeolithic) Archaeology of that time. These included questions like:

- What was the function of the sites discovered? What activities were carried out at these places in the past?
- What did the early Neanderthal system of land-use in the region looked like?
- Which food resources did they exploit?
- How did they organise their (lithic) technology?

- To what extend did early Neanderthals anticipate future events?

To answer these questions, it was initially believed that a classical site-based approach would work best. For this reason, the excavations focused on the clearly recognisable patches where most materials – stones and bones – had accumulated in the past. Notwithstanding the fact that these accumulations must have "grown" in complex ways, resulting from combinations of many different natural and cultural factors, the historical and behavioural integrity of the sites was implicitly considered "high", as they were all embedded in a fluvial so-called "low energy" sedimentary environment. This suggested that the time depth of the archaeological snapshots was limited, although the excavators could not give any reliable indication in terms of absolute time intervals.

After several field campaigns and after closer inspection, the Maastricht-Belvédère sites seemed to be characterised by a consistent number of features (Roebroeks 1988; Roebroeks *et al.* 1992; De Loecker 2004; De Loecker and Roebroeks 2012):

- They contained large numbers of artefacts in high densities, which mostly consisted of the waste of flint knapping activities;
- the flint nodules were relatively large and heavy and (for this reason) seem to have been transported to the sites over relatively short distances. The nodules were only slightly prepared before being brought to the sites (particularly at "Site K");
- refitting of the artefacts revealed that the assemblages represented rather complete sequences of flint knapping;
- most flint was left behind unused (at "Site K");
- selected pieces, most probably tools (and cores), seem to have been transported away from the sites to elsewhere, as can be inferred for refitting programs, particularly at "Site C";
- additionally, the sites also contained some tools that were not made on the site itself but were discarded on the spot in a worn-out state, such as at sites "G" and "K".

Yet, despite the large quantities of lithic material found, it remained almost impossible to adequately answer most of the research questions. The site-assemblages appeared to be too specific, too biased – almost as if important information was consistently missing.

In 1988, Roebroeks and his team decided to conduct a new experiment, this time excavating a large part of the old land surface randomly, even where clear indications for rich archaeological levels were absent ("Site N"; figure 1). All artefacts, stones and bone fragments were recorded individually to get as much spatial and cultural information as possible. In this way, after two campaigns of excavating, the team had uncovered almost 800 square meters, which was a milestone in the European research of a palaeo-landscape of this age. The randomly excavated surface was quite different from the high-density "hotspots" that they had excavated in the years before. First, and not surprisingly, the overall density of artefacts was much lower (table 1). Yet, this low-density scatter covered the entire area. Virtually no empty zones were detected, suggesting that the archaeologists could have continued excavating this ancient land surface for years over large areas, if only it had been preserved across the landscape. A second striking feature was the high percentage of worked tools within the scatter (table 1). This sharply contrasted with the nature of the high-density patches, which largely consisted of the unused waste of flint knapping and tool production. Moreover, many of the worked tools were broken and appeared to be worn-out. Thirdly, refits of flint artefacts were minimal, consisting mainly of refits of breaks instead of "dorsal-ventral-refits", and only occurred on a local scale, marking short episodes of land use. This also indicated that the technology was of a curated nature, being carried by the foragers as a kind of mobile technology through the landscape and probably also over larger distances.

Additionally, the low-density scatters contained larger numbers of bone fragments, which now and then showed a clear relationship with tools that were discarded nearby. In a similar low-density scatter in another level ("Site G"), the remains of a young rhino were found near a large backed flint knife, that was produced by means of a specific core preparation technique similar to the *Levallois*-technique. Micro-wear analyses independently showed that this knife was used for dissecting a thick-skinned animal, like an elephant or rhino (van Gijn 1988).

The team concluded that the low-density scatter, which they characterised as a "veil of stones and bones" (Roebroeks *et al.* 1992), reflected the zones in the landscape where Neanderthals *used* their toolkits in the context of their everyday hunting and gathering activities, whereas the clearly visible patches with high artefact densities marked the spots where the toolkits were produced or systematically maintained. Consequently, the classical "sites" had to be seen as the very-short term outcomes of a specific activity, whereas the widespread scatters were complex palimpsests that reflected a whole range of different activities that took place within a stretched-out window of time. The team also concluded that the sites were not clearly delineated, but in fact had a patchy nature and were an integral part of the veil of debris that covered the riverside landscape.

Now, what precisely are we looking at in the case of Maastricht-Belvedere? Do we see a true *landscape*? Is the concept of landscape appropriate and suitable to describe, analyse and interpret this ancient surface? Most archaeologists would probably say that it is a *section* of a landscape, or to be more precise, a section from the widespread archaeological *relics* of a former landscape, which has been taken up as a fossilised element in the living landscape of today. Some would probably remark that the pattern of debris was certainly more than just "litter", as the frequent deposition of artefacts and food remains, together with other traces left behind (like human footprints; see Happisburgh: Ashton *et al.* 2014), had the accumulative effect of gradually transforming the natural land surface into a truly *cultural* landscape. However, and although we used the term so far, we are not sure that the landscape concept covers this kind of spatial phenomena best.

The notion and perspective of "landscape" is strongly tied to the economic and social history of Europe, where it developed within a specific context of people's relationship to the land and in relation to the visual arts and enlightenment science – including the invention of the mathematical perspective *sensu stricto* (*e.g.*, Lemaire 1970; Cosgrove 1985). In this historical context, the landscape came to refer to a strong sense of territoriality and visual perception. Yet we can safely assume that territoriality and scenic qualities did not characterise human living space in the same way in prehistory. It is in such cases that we, as landscape archaeologists, must consider the cultural and historical limits of the landscape concept and should explore other options as well. What has been discovered in the Maastricht-Belvédère quarry, we believe, is not so much a landscape, but something more akin to the so-called "taskscape", a term which has famously been coined by Tim Ingold (1993). It refers to the landscape as an array of inter-related activities that is constantly a work in progress.

Figure 1. Maastricht-Belvédère. Map of the excavation area of "Site N", showing the horizontal distribution of flint artefacts (triangles represent tools and dots artefacts, including tiny chips). Coordinate system in m². After: Roebroeks *et al.* (1992, 7).

| Area | Number of artefacts | | | | | | Ratio | | | |
|---|---|---|---|---|---|---|---|---|---|---|
| Site | Area dug (m²) | All tools and fragments | Tools and fragments *sensu stricto* | Cores | Flakes and chips | Total | Tool:waste | Tool *sensu stricto*:waste | Core:waste | Core:tool |
| A | 5 | 2 | 1 | 1 | 77 | 80[2] | 1:39 | 1:78 | 1:77 | 1:2 |
| B | 20 | - | - | - | 6 | 6 | - | - | - | - |
| C | 264 | 23 | 5 | 4 | 3,040 | 3,067[3] | 1:132 | 1:609 | 1:760 | 1:6 |
| D | - | - | - | 1 | 10 | 11 | - | - | 1:10 | - |
| F | 42 | 8 | 3 | 2 | 1.167 | 1,177 | 1:146 | 1:389 | 1:584 | 1:4 |
| G | 50[1] | 8 | 3 | - | 67 | 75 | 1:8 | 1:22 | - | - |
| H | 54 | 10 | 4 | - | 260 | 270 | 1:26 | 1:65 | - | - |
| K | 370 | 137 | 111 | 91 | 10,684 | 10,912 | 1:79 | 1;97 | 1:117 | 1:2 |
| N | 765 | 26 | 12 | 1 | 423 | 450 | 1:16 | 1:35 | 1:423 | 1:26 |
| July '90 | 7 | 1 | 1 | - | 14 | 15 | 1:14 | 1:14 | - | - |
| L | - | - | - | - | 8 | 8 | - | - | - | - |
| M | - | 3 | 2 | - | 41 | 44 | 1:14 | 1:21 | - | - |
| O | - | - | - | - | 10 | 10 | - | - | - | - |
| Site N, Level X | - | - | - | - | 29 | 29 | - | - | - | - |
| Section finds | - | 4 | 3 | 1 | 62 | 67 | 1:16 | 1:21 | 1:62 | 1:4 |

Table 1. Maastricht-Belvédère. Comparison (basic count and ratios) of the primary context sites of Unit IV and section/test pit assemblages. After: De Loecker 2004, 239 ([1] The excavated Site G area together with the test pit measures 61 m²; [2] within the excavated Site A area only 34 artefacts were found; [3] site C, figures after Roebroeks (1988; n=3,067)).

According to Ingold (1993), the formation and change of human living space is always embedded in bodily action and the execution of concrete activities. Getting to know one's environment is never just a matter of pre-ordained cultural schemes, abstract learning or visual experience, but in the end always depends on hands-on training and the execution of tasks. The Maastricht-Belvédère patterns reveal how early Neanderthals did this some 250,000 years ago. The patterns at the same time show that they were not always fully and consciously planned, but that many actions were an outcome of path-dependency – almost imperceptibly "prepared" by chains of former actions and outcomes, or the need to invent local tactics, so that living space was consciously ordered and organically grown at the same time.

Like in all hunter-gatherer landscapes – indeed in *all* cultural landscapes – human activities in this Pleistocene taskscape produced traces and patterns that in *their* turn created possibilities or constraints for further action. For instance, a place where flint was worked became a suitable procurement site that influenced people's movements and choices at a later stage. Old tools could be picked up to fulfil an unexpected task on the spot. To quote Ingold (1993) freely, there were no "holes" in the living space of early Neanderthals, so that every change was not a matter of filling in empty space, but in fact a constant *reworking* of patterns in an already existing taskscape. In this way, and archaeologically speaking, the taskscape became a palimpsest that was subject to continuous transformation by human hands.

To conclude, the spatial patterns discovered by archaeologists at Maastricht-Belvédère may best be understood as an early expression of the human taskscape. We need an insight into the world *between* the archaeological hotspots to complete our picture of this taskscape. We now know, after several years of research in other regions such as Northern France (*e.g.*, Locht & Depaepe 2011) that these Middle Palaeolithic taskscapes were spatially extensive. They covered large areas and transformed the environment accordingly. To what extend these

Figure 2. Rubbish dump outside Camp Westerbork (courtesy Camp Westerbork Memorial Centre, the Netherlands).

early taskscapes were formed or influenced by the frequent or even controlled use of fire, is currently being investigated by a team of Leiden University (Roebroeks *et al.* 2021).

## "Terrorscapes" as "heterotopias"

For our second example we take a big step forward in time. We will now reflect upon an entirely new field of research, which is the archaeology of so-called "terrorscapes" (Van der Laarse 2015), most notably of the former Nazi-managed/administered extermination camps from the Second World War. The term "terrorscape" is generally used for landscapes that exhibit explicit political, moral and organised aspects of terror, such as the systemised use of violence by organised groups against civilian targets. The potential value of this kind of archaeological research was illustrated in the summer of 2014, when archaeologists finally traced the gas chambers of the Sobibor extermination camp (Schute 2020). The importance of this discovery in light of concerted efforts by the Nazis to hide the evidence after they dismantled the camp, and not to forget the recent spreading of disinformation by Holocaust-deniers, cannot be underestimated.

However, against the background of its recent development, it is somewhat surprising to see that the archaeological research of concentration camps again exhibits the traditional focus on the hotspots, on the clearly visible and durable, on the places with high densities of materials and building volumes, and much less so with the terrorscape as a spatially continuous and partly ephemeral phenomenon. Until now, by far most archaeological research projects have taken place within the limits of the concentration camps themselves. There is nothing wrong, of course, with an initial focus on the terrorscape in such a limited sense. In fact, archaeological research in these areas *has* generated valuable, additional information. This is again highlighted by the recent archaeological discoveries at the Sobibor extermination camp, where archaeologists have now gathered proof of the former existence of crematoria that were used to get rid of masses of human bodies. In many concentration camps, objects and personal possessions were re-discovered that identify individual camp prisoners or were even recognised by survivors. In other cases, archaeology has provided crucial information about the former existence of concentration camps as such. More than twenty years ago, in 2004, archaeologists of the *Landesamt Brandenburg* discovered the remains of camp Rathenow, a so-called *Außenlager* of concentration camp Sachsenhausen (Kolen 2009). The present community of the city of Rathenow stated to be unaware of the former existence of a camp, and some even concluded that archaeological research therefore was unnecessary. But the archaeological finds of watchtower foundations, double-row barbed wire and ceramics from SS factory '*Bohemia*' undoubtedly point to the former existence of an SS concentration camp, which was confirmed by personal testimonies and aerial photographs.

Notwithstanding these observations, it remains puzzling that archaeologists have been so reluctant to investigate terrorscapes as spatially extensive and temporally layered fabrics – that is, as true terror*scapes*. They could, for instance, shift their interest towards the fences and zones around the former camps, in this way adding a specific dimension to the study of space, material culture and heritage. Fortunately, archaeologists are now indeed gradually starting to discover the historical nature and informative potential of this zone. At Westerbork in The Netherlands, archaeologists for example mapped and excavated the garbage dumps around the former camp (figure 2). Similarly, Caroline Sturdy Colls' (2015) research at Treblinka aims at tracing and mapping the eroded margins and fences that once delineated the death camp.

From an interdisciplinary viewpoint, there are good reasons to exchange the inward archaeological perspective on the camps for a more outward perspective on the surrounding landscape. We are probably much better informed about the concentration camps by other sources and the research of other disciplines than archaeology. The literary works and autobiographical accounts of camp survivors, such as Primo Levi (1959), painstakingly describe the impact of terror on the daily lives of the prisoners, more particularly within the barracks, which functioned more or less as autonomous households. In addition, archival sources inform us about the organisation, administration and infrastructure of deportation, internment and of work in the camps. Architectural history, moreover, highlights the planned design and layout of the camps.

The pioneering work of the artist Hans Citroen shows what "looking outside" – as an archaeologist – may yield in terms of new insights. In and around Auschwitz-Oswiecim, Hans Citroen and his wife Barbara Starzynska (born in Oswiecim) are discovering more and more traces of the Holocaust and structures erected under Nazi rule (Citroen & Starzynska 2011). They exposed the logistics system by unravelling the "archaeology" of this terrorscape extensively and down to its individual fibers. They for example traced the *Judenrampe* – the train station that was "forgotten" but played a crucial role in the administrative and physical organisation of the mass murder of at least 800,000 of the 1,3 million Jews who were killed in Auschwitz (Citroen 2014). With hindsight, their project has revealed an extensive territory that was based on an ambitious German colonisation program with plans for a new city, a train station, three concentration camps, eight forced labor camps, and a huge industrial area within a logistical

web of access and transport routes, now only visible as a universe of isolated buildings, scattered material traces, and archaeological remains.

Others have highlighted how *outside* the fences of the World War II concentration camps, but still far removed from the world then occupied by distant witnesses and bystanders of the neighboring villages, which in a sense also belonged to the terrorscape of course, there was an interstice that nowadays can best be revealed by archaeologists. This space expressed the dual nature of terrorscapes as both emphatically designed and – again – organically grown. It is important to stress that landscapes were converted into terrorscapes not only because organised terror was exercised there in the past, but also because these landscapes were used as a facility, or even as a spatial technology for genocide in an active way, both practically *and* symbolically. The use of space in the surroundings of the camps was both formally planned and spontaneous and informal. Even today, its material dimension consists of a combination of explicit and immanent traces. We encounter roads and tracks, the remains of entrances, watchtowers, sequences of fences, small buildings, trenches and shooting ranges – all planned items and devices. But the interstice between the camp and the surrounding villages is also constituted by an extensive fabric of small artifacts and shallow imprints – an extensive veil of differentiated archaeological debris, consisting of stone bricks, iron fragments, ceramics, pieces of barbed wire, holes and pits, and unexpected graves. Here, we also encounter a thin but widespread layer of artifacts and traces that are seemingly uninteresting, anonymous and randomly distributed over the surface, but on closer inspection could mark distinct and meaningful events. This part of the landscape was not only a well-designed spatial technology for exercising terror, but also an *unplanned* palimpsest of silent witnesses.

This brings us to the second characteristic, as this also explains why the zones around the concentration camps were often forgotten after the war, keeping the immanent traces as a kind of treasure for themselves. In these zones, it was almost impossible to remove or erase all evidence of terror at the end of the war. The deeds of the wrongdoers were inscribed into a vast archaeological palimpsest, which could not be reset to an unwritten state anymore. In a sense, therefore, the terrorscapes remained best preserved within this transitional zone.

Thirdly, the area surrounding the concentration camps was betwixt and between. It was in this area that the perception of prisoners and bystanders might have met or interfered – the start of freedom for one and the beginning of horror for the other. At the same time, this space belonged to none of them, as it was the only section within the terrorscape that was almost exclusively controlled and dominated by the perpetrators – a strip where only the Nazis decided about the spatial ordering of matter, meaning, life and death.

In the landscape zone surrounding the concentration camps, mechanisms of inclusion and exclusion were constantly kept at work, and this gave this part of the landscape also a very specific but complex meaning. Here, the terrorscape was dissected by roads and railway tracks, which suggested *in*clusion, while at the same time being manipulated as mechanisms of *ex*clusion. Where fences indicated and symbolised closure, but also contained entrances that allowed free movement for the happy few. Strategies of *inversion* were practiced as well. Whereas the concentration and work camps where delineated and marked as *Fremdkörper* in the landscape, the houses of the camp commanders fitted the cultural and natural landscape outside the camps. They were often built from organic materials, natural stone and wood, and situated in idyllic environments, like at Ravensbrück and Natzweiler. Even where SS officers lived together in small villages, like at Dachau, trees and forests surrounded the houses and gardens. At Westerbork, the commander's villa was situated in this interstitial space as well, where he lived his private family life and realised his specific interest in landscaping and gardening. Recently, the layout of the original garden could be partly reconstructed on the basis of small-scale archaeological excavations.

As is evident from other instances and practices, such as the leisure activities of the Auschwitz officers and personnel represented by the recently discovered Höcker's album, the Nazi's systematically inverted terror into nature and harmony within their own life worlds (Van der Laarse 2015). Likewise, the nature and landscape surrounding the concentration camps functioned almost in a ritual way to normalise the working conditions in the camps into happy and harmonious family life outside the camps.

In a dark way, the terrorscapes of the Second World War combined all aspects of the taskscape discussed before. But their spatial, political and archaeological nature is best described by a geographical concept that was coined many years ago by Michel Foucault (1986). He used the term "heterotopia" to stress the dual, liminal and ambiguous aspects of those places. The concept was elaborated by Foucault to describe non-hegemonic spaces that cannot be classified easily in hierarchical terms or clear oppositions, like the here and there, public and private, urban and rural, self and other. Heterotopias do not create a clear spatial order, but a heterogeneous space, in which places are always ambiguous and multi-layered in terms of cultural and political meanings. This also relates heterotopias to systems of closing and opening, as we have seen in the case of terrorscapes.

Keeping all this in mind, the former concentration camps are eminent examples of heterotopias operating in political spaces, which were organised and dynamically sustained by means terror. Outside the fences of the camps, the terrorscapes continued while being characterised by activities, associations and material manifestations that referred to strategies of hiding or exposing, of the selective closing or disclosing, of ritual inversion and of the gradual "normalisation" of terror into nature. The fences and interstices between the concentration camps and the occupied world "outside" were literally filled with heterotopias that left their traces behind in the present-day landscape. Archaeology seems to be eminently suited to investigate these past material worlds. And like in the case of the early prehistoric forager landscapes, this could probably be done best by mapping and interpreting the worlds between the "classical" sites as detailed as possible.

## CONCLUSION

We draw the following conclusions from the foregoing discussion and examples:

1. Archaeologists have lost sight on the archaeological terrain, while over-theorising the landscape.
2. Better and more detailed knowledge of the archaeological terrain itself is important for reconstructing the precise environmental and cultural settings in which people in the past constituted and used their life worlds. This was not always done in well-ordered and unambiguous ways, as was highlighted with the example of the terrorscapes.
3. The landscape concept is not always a sufficient or appropriate concept for understanding how people have realised this. The concept has its limits, both from a cultural and a historical point of view.

4. Detailed knowledge of the archaeological terrain, as an area of cultural substance and a human biotope at the same time, may help us to better understand processes of change, as all human societies make a living in an environment that is already filled with the traces of previous generations. We should treat the archaeological terrain *not* as a fossilised "flat" land surface (Lorimer 2012), but as the expression of a multi-dimensional world were processes of path-dependency and constraint are important.

5. Lastly: there is nothing simply "positivistic" about returning to the landscape as an archaeological terrain. As a theoretically informed exercise, it is meant as an alternative for a discipline that seems to regularly get stuck in meanings and models.

It could be a challenge for international landscape archaeology to keep this topic on the agenda for several reasons. The kind of research that has been done in the Maastricht-Belvédère pit and around the former concentration camps can help us make better choices for field research and excavations in the future. This is important, as the archaeological terrain is a limited resource and future generations would like to investigate it from *their* own perspectives as well.

The archaeological terrain bears clear historical and spatial relationships with historic buildings, ruins and visible landscape elements in the cultural landscape of the present-day. It will be clear, therefore, that the archaeological terrain is always an integral part of the present-day landscape *as* heritage. Highlighting this dimension, as soon as we know more about it, may enable us to tell richer stories about the past. Because, in the end, as Tim Ingold (1993, 153) states, the archaeologist is a story-teller: "for both the archaeologist and the native dweller, the landscape tells – or rather *is* – a story. It is part of an archaeological training to learn to attend to those clues which the rest of us might pass over, and which make it possible to tell a fuller and richer story".

## REFERENCES

Ashton, N., S.G. Lewis, I. De Groote, S.M. Duffy, M. Bates, R. Bates, P. Hoare, M. Lewis, S.A. Parfitt, S. Peglar, C. Williams, and C. Stringer. 2014. Hominin Footprints from Early Pleistocene Deposits at Happisburgh, UK. *PLoS ONE* 9 (2), e88329. DOI: 10.1371/journal.pone.0088329

Bailey, G. 2007. Time perspectives, palimpsests and the archaeology of time. *Journal of Anthropological Archaeology* 26 (2), 198-223.

Binford, L.R. 1980. Willow smoke and dogs' tails: hunter-gatherer settlement systems and archaeological site formation. *American Antiquity* 45 (1), 4-20.

Binford, L.R. 1987. Searching for camps and missing the evidence? Another look at the Lower Paleolithic. In: *The Pleistocene Old World: regional perspectives*, edited by O. Soffer, 17-32. New York: Plenum Press.

Bordes, F. 1972. *A tale of two caves*, New York/Evanston/San Francisco-London: Harper & Row.

Citroen, H. 2014. *Auschwitz – de Judenrampe*. Hilversum: Verbum.

Citroen, H., and B. Starzyńska. 2011. *Auschwitz-Oswiecim*. Rotterdam: Post Editions.

Cosgrove, D. 1985. "Prospect, Perspective and the Evolution oft he Landscape Idea." *Transactions of the Institute of British Geographers* 10 (1), 45-62.

De Loecker, D. 2004. *Beyond the Site. The Saalian Archaeological Record at Maastricht-Belvedere (The Netherlands)*. Leiden: Analecta Praehistorica Leidensia 35/36.

De Loecker, D., and W. Roebroeks. 2012. "Beyond '15-minutes': revisiting the late Middle Pleistocene archaeological record of Maastricht-Belvédère (The Netherlands)." *Analecta Praehistorica Leidensia* 43/44, 349-367.

Foley, R. 1981. "Off-site archaeology: an alternative approach for the short-sited." In *Pattern of the past. Studies in honour of David Clarke*, edited by I. Hodder, G. Isaac, and N. Hammond), 157-183. Cambridge: Cambridge University Press.

Foucault, M. 1986. "Of Other Spaces, Heterotopias (Translated from French by Jay Miskowiec)." *Diacritics* 16 (1), 22-27.

Gijn, A. L. van 1988. "A functional analysis of the Belvédère flints." In *From Find Scatters to Early Hominid Behaviour. A Study of Middle Palaeolithic Riverside Settlements at MaastrichtBelvédère (The Netherlands)*, edited by W. Roebroeks, 151-157. Leiden: Leiden University Press.

Ingold, T. 1993. "The temporality of the landscape." *World Archaeology* 25 (2), 152-174.

Isaac, G.L. 1981. "Stone age visiting cards; approaches to the study of early land use patterns. In *Pattern of the Past: Studies in Honour of David Clarke*, edited by I. Hodder, G.L. Isaac, and N. Hammond, 131-155. Cambridge: Cambridge University Press.

Kobayashi, A. 1989. "A Critique of Dialectical Landscape." In *Remaking Human Geography,* edited by A. Kobayashi, and S. Mackenzie, 164-184. Boston, MA: Unwin Hyman.

Kolen, J. 2009. "The 'anthropologization' of archaeological heritage." *Archaeological Dialogues* 16 (2), 209-225.

Laarse, R. van der. 2015. "Fatal Attraction: Nazi landscapes, Modernity and Holocaust Memory." In *Landscapes: Biographical Approaches*, edited by J. Kolen, H. Renes, and R. Hermans, 345-376. Amsterdam: Amsterdam University Press.

Lemaire, T. 1970. *Filosofie van het landschap.* Baarn: Ambo.

Levi, P. 1959. *If this is a man.* New York: The Orion Press.

Locht J.L, and P. Depaepe. 2011. "Le Paléolithique inférieur et moyen. » *Revue archéologique de Picardie* 3-4, 65-84.

Lorimer, H. 2012. "Surfaces and Slopes." *Performance Research* 17 (2), 83-86.

Roebroeks, W. 1988. *From Find Scatters to Early Hominid Behaviour. A Study of Middle Palaeolithic Riverside Settlements at MaastrichtBelvédère (The Netherlands).* Leiden: Leiden University Press.

Roebroeks, W., D. De Loecker, P. Hennekens, and M. van Ieperen, 1992. "'A veil of stones': on the interpretation of an Early Middle Palaeolithic low density scatter at Maastricht-Belvédère (The Netherlands)." *Analecta Praehistorica Leidensia* 25, 1-16.

Roebroeks, J.W.M., K. MacDonald, F. Scherjon, C.C. Bakels, L. Kindler, A. Nikulina, E. Pop, and S. Gaudzinski-Windheuser. 2021. "Landscape modification by Last Interglacial Neanderthals." *Science Advances* 7 (51), eabj5567.

Schute, I. 2020. *In de schaduw van een nachtvlinder. Een archeoloog op zoek naar sporen van de Holocaust.* Amsterdam: Prometheus.

Sturdy Colls, C. 2015. *Holocaust Archaeologies. Approaches and Future Directions.* Cham: Springer.

In Hussain, S.T. and G.L. Dusseldorp (eds) 2025. Sitting on the fence: Negotiating archaeology, anthropology and philosophy. Festschrift for Prof. Dr Raymond H.A. Corbey in celebration of his 70th birthday. *Analecta Praehistorica Leidensia* 54. Leiden: Sidestone Press, pp. 205-214.

# Locating and analysing the Marginal in Archaeology

John Bintliff

## Abstract

This article illustrates the concept of marginality at increasing spatial levels from the house to the settlement and then the region and nation-state. Being marginal can be someone of inferior status within a wealthy household, or a whole community occupying a lower-class suburb within a town which is stratified spatially. On a much wider geographical scale, whole regions of poor farming populations within Early Modern nation-states have been characterised as 'primitive', marginal to urban civilisation and calling for radical intervention, a phenomenon known as 'internal colonisation'.

*Keywords: House studies, urban planning, marginality, internal colonialism, costume*

## Introduction

Between 2000 and 2014 I had the privilege and pleasure to be a colleague of Raymond Corbey in the Archaeology Faculty of Leiden University. I soon realized that he possessed an unparalleled interest in all the research being carried out across our wide range of staff, and was always the first to ask a challenging and intelligent question at guest lectures and seminars. His own interests spanned Archaeology, Social and Physical Anthropology, Psychology, Art History – and many other fields, and he published in them too. He is also an immensely kind and generous person, a wonderful source of goodness in a university environment where there were a surprising number of predatory sharks and narcissists. So it is a great delight to be able to offer a contribution to Raymond's Festschrift, to a scholar I greatly admire and a good friend. Suiting his breadth of interests, this paper links Archaeology to History, Anthropology, Architecture and the History of Costume.

In the following contribution I would like to give some examples of identifying the *Marginal* in Archaeology, with some insights they provide. Marginality is a relative term suggesting a distancing from an apparent 'centre', viewed for our purposes here as a subjective judgement linked to assumed inferior status. I will take us from the smaller spaces to the largest in scale, starting with the domestic house.

## The Marginal: A material culture approach

In Classical Greece the commonest house was a modular family type, iconically displayed in the 4th century BC by planned new suburbs at Olynthus in northern Greece (Cahill 2002) (figure 1A). It was favoured as it reflected publicly the ethos of most city-states towards citizen *'isonomia'* – not economic equality, but rather equality of status for all citizens under the laws of the state (Jameson 1990; Westgate 2007a; Bintliff 2010). Although nearly all homes had domestic slaves, they are invisible in the house-plans, since slaves were considered a part of the family

**John Bintliff**
School of History,
Classics and Archaeology,
Edinburgh University, Scotland, UK
johnlbintliff@gmail.com
ORCID: 0000-0001-5410-8832

unit. As Ruth Westgate (2007b) has shown, using the methodological tool of Access Analysis in the technical study of movement in the built environment known as Space Syntax, access to almost all the spaces of the home is easily granted once the door is passed (figure 1B*)*. The routes formalise navigation possibilities determined by doors and open spaces. Once invited in, there are no marginal spaces on the main groundfloor, but it is suggested that an upper floor provided privacy for the family (Bintliff 2010).

In the next, Hellenistic era, enhanced social and economic differentiation and a parallel rise in the role of homes as foci for social and economic networking and personal display, caused polarised, often very complex internal access sectors in people's homes (Bintliff 2010). Areas frequented by domestic servants/ slaves are now made remote to areas frequented by visitors and the family (Westgate 2007b), as also are the everyday household working areas which once were the major focus of family life – the domestic courtyard is less accessible compared to the display court to impress visitors (figure 2). However, marginality can also be observed between identical houses. Even in the Classical Greek period, the same house varied considerably in price if it lay marginal to the town centre, the core of urban life, as inscriptions from Olynthus reveal (Cahill 2002).

American Urban Theory in the 20th Century created models of the common division of space in modern cities, notably recognizing how different social classes were segregated into separate sectors (Haggett 1965; Beauregard 2007). In a sophisticated and wide-ranging study, the urban geographer Erwin Sabelberg (1983; 1985; 1986) has shown how the role of the elite house (*palazzo*) as a form of Renaissance and Baroque self-presentation differed fundamentally between northern and southern Italy, and this has led to dramatically contrasted townscapes in the modern era. In Florence the size and structure of Renaissance Palazzi, dominating the urban centre and the most significant streets, expressed contemporary socio-economics: they originated as elite residential, and at the same time as commercial premises of tradesmen, manufacturers and bankers, while each building was designed to meet the particular professional needs of its owner. On the groundfloors could be found stores, shops, offices, and manufacturing workshops for early industrial production. In contrast, on the first floor lay the magnificently furnished reception and other domestic rooms of the owners. Thus, Palazzi combined disparate functions: luxurious residences for wealthy families, accommodation for large households, as well as spaces for their crucial commercial and manufacturing activities.

Palazzi in the historic centres in Florence or Siena are still largely in the hands of the elite, and a high percentage of such families were in power before 1800. Also, banks and other institutions of culture and government prefer the use of the palazzi, as they still convey high status. The key shopping streets remain the same as in Medieval times today (figure 3A).

In southern Italy, however, we observe from the start a divergence from Tuscany. The Sicilian upper class were feudal landowners living on the proceeds of their agricultural great estates. Their town houses or *palazzi baronale* were without commercial roles, but also originally formed the facades of the chief thoroughfares in the city centre. The focus was on great entrance halls, broad stairways, and elegant living rooms. As palace fashions changed, this elite chose to construct new mansions increasingly more remote from the old town centre, and the key shopping streets moved with them (figure 3B). The historic centre is now dominated by lower-class residents, with the conversion of palazzi to poorly-maintained flats. So whereas the original high-status palace in Florence and Siena has retained its role and centrality to urban life, in stark contrast Sicilian palazzi have been converted into cheap apartments and restaurants. In Tuscany, the Renaissance house contained and exhibited to the public the means which *made* its resident elite, and this remains the function of palazzi today. In contrast in Sicily the Renaissance and Baroque house merely *expressed* the status of its elite residents whose wealth always lay elsewhere, and it has been easier to abandon – more than once – unfashionable houses for newer styles built in other parts of the city.

Let us finally move to the largest spatial scale, by looking at marginal rural communities in Early Modern Europe. By the late 18th and through the 19th century, the country peasantry distant from urban peripheries came to be universally characterised by the wealthier urban classes as akin to 'African savages' in the European colonies. Official and literary accounts categorize them as living in ignorance and squalor, incapable of economic progress, and survivals of a prehistoric way of life: "Revelling in the ignorance of peasants was a favourite pastime of the tiny, educated elite [in France], before and after the Revolution of 1789. Reports of half-human savages and grovelling

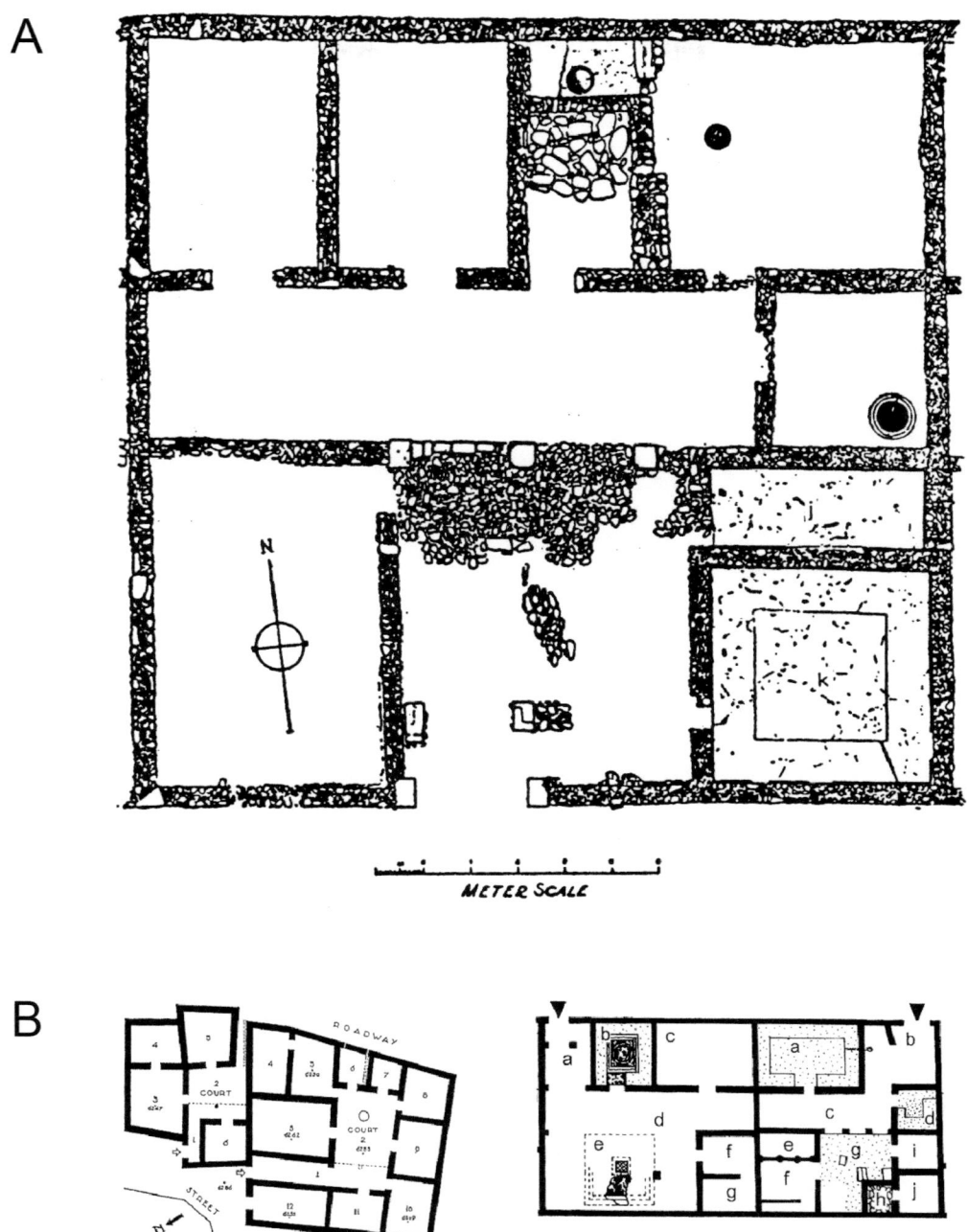

Figure 1. A: Plan of the typical Classical Greek family house. From: Jameson (1990, figure 7.6). B: Access routes inside Classical Greek homes. Initial access points are shown as dark circles, courtyards as grey circles, and individual roofed rooms as clear circles. The routes formalise navigation possibilities determined by doors and open spaces. From: Westgate (2007b, figure 1a-b).

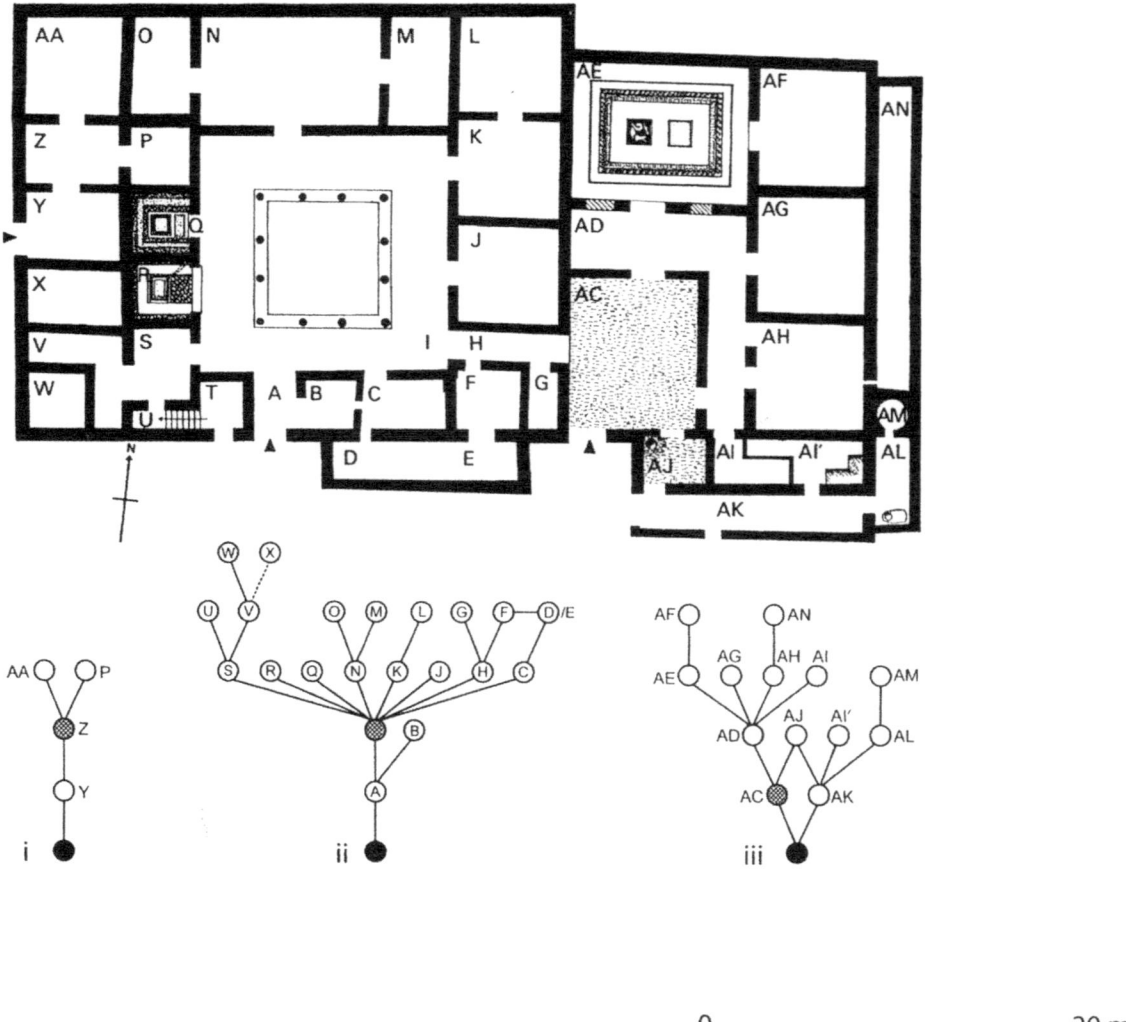

Figure 2. Access routes inside Hellenistic houses. Initial access points are shown as dark circles, courtyards as grey circles, and individual roofed rooms as clear circles. The routes formalise navigation possibilities determined by doors and open spaces. From: Westgate (2007b, figure 1c).

troglodytes lurking in thickets and holes in the ground gave the civilized minority a sense of its own sophistication" (Robb 2007, 6).

*Internal colonialism* is a notion of structural political and economic inequalities between regions within a nation state. The term is used to describe the uneven effects of economic development on a regional basis, and to describe the exploitation of minority groups within a wider society. This is held to be similar to the relationship between metropole and colony, in colonialism proper. Some other factors that separate the core from the periphery are: language, religion, physical appearance, types and levels of technology, and sexual behaviour (Howe 2002, 18-19). According to Nicholas Thomas (1994, 4), modernity can be understood as a colonialist project, wherein "societies internal to Western nations, and those they possessed, administered and reformed elsewhere" were framed as objects to be surveyed and regulated. The cultural and integrative nature of 'internal colonialism' is understood as a project of modernity.

How is Archaeology shedding light on the realities behind these consciously 'marginalized' rural communities and the enforced internal colonialism they became subjected to?

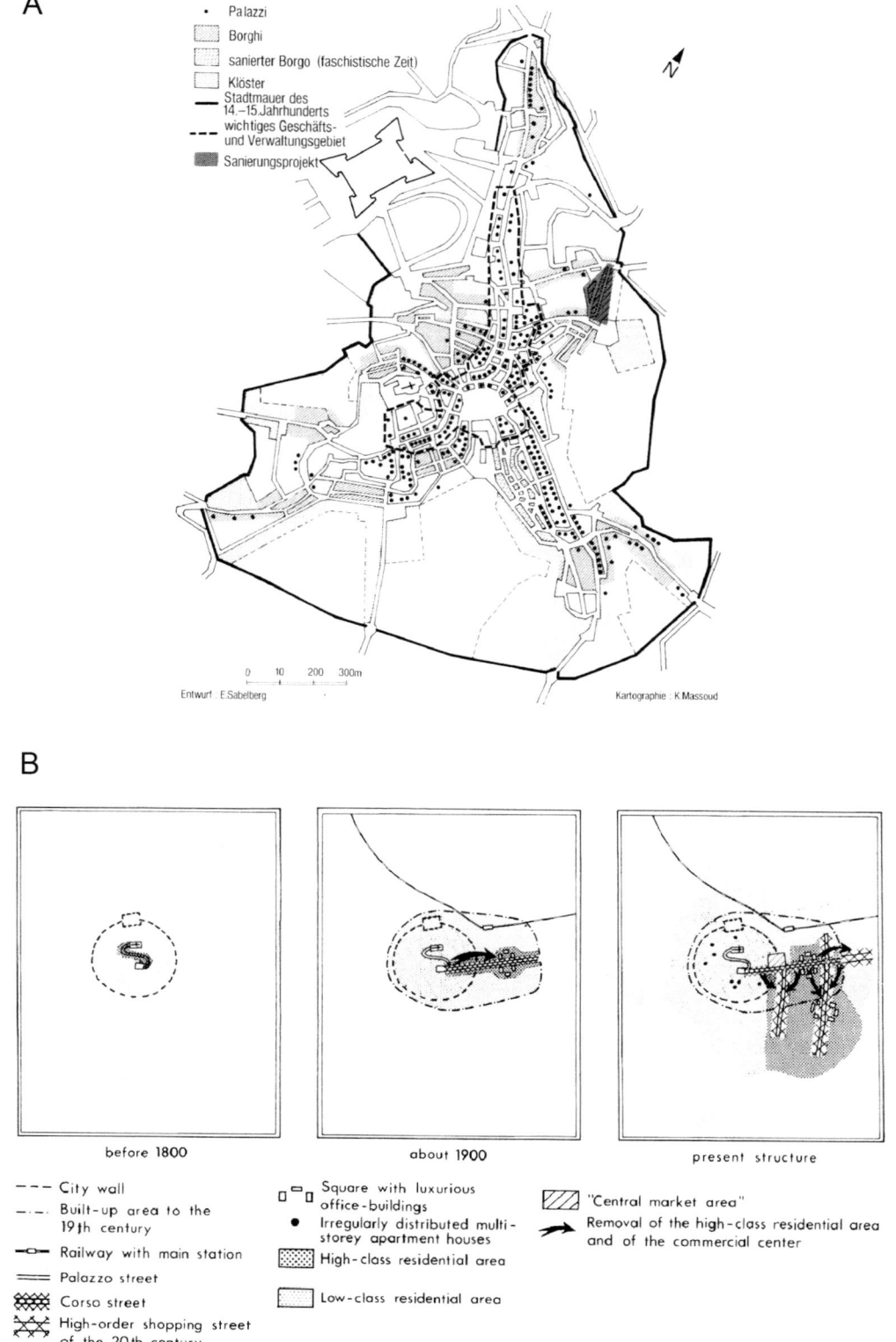

Figure 3. A: Modern Siena. The Renaissance palaces (black circles) are still in the key business and administration streets today (dashed line). From: Sabelberg (1985, figure 3). B: Displacement of the major economic and administrative zones over time from the original historic centre, a model for the South Italian city since the 19th century. From: Sabelberg (1986, figure 2).

Beginning in the late 18th century, new ways of thinking as well as demand from England for wool and food encouraged Scottish Highland landowners to "improve" their land so that it would be more productive and profitable (Devine 2006). The traditional ways in which the rural villages or townships belonging to these lairds (lords) worked the land were considered inefficient and an obstacle to progress. Over the course of about 100 years almost all of them were swept away in a process that changed the social order, culture, economy, and landscape, and created rural Scotland as we know it today. In some areas, people were relocated to new crofting townships, where everyone shared the land allotted to grazing but each family rented its own piece of land. This was not large enough to support a family, so people had to work elsewhere, typically in industries that would profit the landowner. In other cases, townships were absorbed into large farms let to a single tenant for whom others worked. Elsewhere, townships were removed entirely and the land was used to graze large numbers of sheep in the care of a few shepherds employed by the landowner. In some places, townships were turned into private sporting estates. From the 1830s onwards, a combination of economic factors, population pressure and famine led to whole communities progressively being removed from the land altogether. This sequence of events is usually known as the Highland Clearances.

In 1875, when Queen Victoria was staying at Inveraray Castle, she visited what she called the "primitive villages" of Auchindrain and nearby Achnagoul.[1] However, despite Victoria's preconceptions and superficial on-the-spot observation of Highland peasant lifestyle, excavations at the birthplace of Flora MacDonald, the Scottish heroine who saved Bonnie Prince Charlie, have revealed that poverty-stricken Highland farmers nonetheless aspired to some aspects of the finery of English wealthier society (Symonds 1997). In the decades around the time of the clearances, although many Highland farmers lived in deprivation in windowless, single-storey "black" houses made of stones and turf with earth or peat floors, archaeological work at the rural settlement where MacDonald had lived on South Uist has recovered fancy English and Chinese export pottery used for ostentatious display and taking tea

(figure 4A). The farmers' "conspicuous consumption" appears to have left the traditional house structure little changed with many spending what wealth they could mobilise in the form of portable objects like fine china, linen, and silver. Nonetheless by the 1860s only a few joint tenancy townships remained. Although all had adopted some of the principles of agricultural improvement, one by one they were modernised or abandoned. A small number of such settlements are now rebuilt as heritage sites (such as the restored Black House at Arnol, island of Lewis; figure 4B).[2]

Similar houses and lifestyles typify 'Uncivilized' Greece in the 18th-19th century, and my own project in Central Greece has been mapping deserted settlements and abandoned traditional longhouses and their lifestyle (Bintliff 2012; figure 5A). Here likewise, in the single-story longhouses and similar basic dwellings shared with domestic animals, a close parallel to the Highland Black Houses, poor peasants proudly displayed imported tableware and spent untold hours making traditional costumes for communal events – each distinctive for a particular village and hence marking its identity (Bintliff 2013; figure 5B).

## SOME CONCLUSIONS

In past built environments, marginality can be consciously created, as we saw made visible in changing domestic house-plans, the result of social changes that accompanied the transformation from Classical to Hellenistic Greece. In the case of Renaissance to Modern Italian town-plans, the contrasting fates of the historic city-centres in North-Central as opposed to Southern Italy, were an unintended consequence of contrasting forms of wealth-accumulation by the urban elite. Finally, the process of 'internal colonisation' that is observable in many European Early Modern nation-states, once more consciously adopts a model of inferiority – in this case for whole rural regions remote from the wealthy urban cores – to justify a process of radical social and economic engineering.

1 https://www.goindustrial.co.uk/our-blog/blog-post/auchindrain-our-first-visitors

2 https://www.historicenvironment.scot/visit-a-place/places/the-blackhouse-arnol/

A

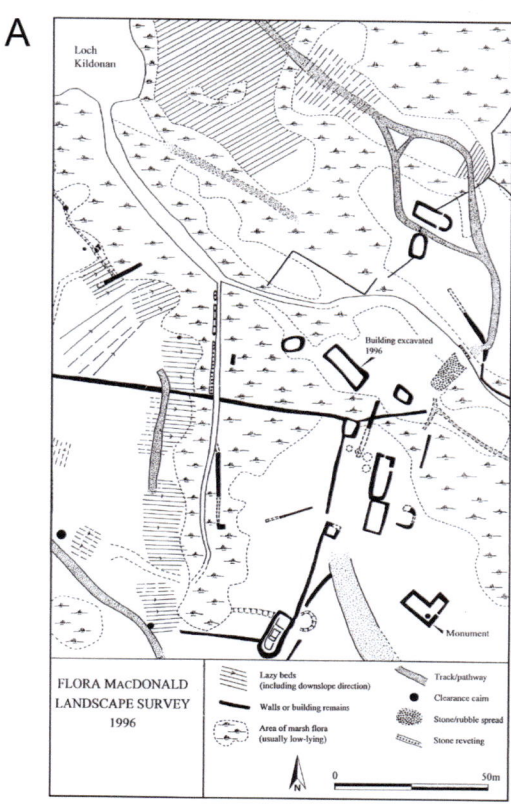

Figure 4. A: Archaeological plan of the scattered abandoned crofting settlement at Milton, on the island of South Uist, Scotland, associated with the historic figure of Flora MacDonald. From Symonds (1997, Fig. 1). B: Contemporary photograph of the restored Black House at Arnol, island of Lewis, Scotland, part of a heritage folk museum. Source: author.

B

A

B

Figure 5. A: Drawing of a traditional family longhouse in the village of Thespiai, believed to be 18th century in date. Drawn by N. Stedman in 1983, published in Bintliff, Farinetti *et al.* (2017, figure 3.87). B: Ladies ca.1900 AD wearing traditional regional dress and displaying imported ceramics from Çanakkale, N.W. Turkey. Left image from Sourpi, Thessaly; right image from Nea Anchialos in Thrace. From: Bintliff (2013, figure 2).

## REFERENCES

Beauregard, R. 2007. "More Than Sector Theory: Homer Hoyt's Contributions to Planning Knowledge." *Journal of Planning History* 6, 248-271.

Bintliff, J. 2010. "Classical Greek urbanism: a social darwinian view". In *Valuing Others in Classical Antiquity*, edited by R. Rosen and I. Sluiter, 15-41. Leiden: Brill.

Bintliff, J. 2012. *The Complete Archaeology of Greece, from Hunter-Gatherers to the Twentieth Century AD*. Oxford/New York: Blackwell-Wiley.

Bintliff, J. 2013. "Poverty and resistance in the material culture of Early Modern rural households in the Aegean". In *Pottery and Social Dynamics in the Mediterranean and Beyond in Medieval and Post-Medieval Times*, edited by J. Bintliff and M. Caroscio, 41-46. Oxford: British Archaeological Reports.

Bintliff, J., E. Farinetti, B. Slapšak, and A. Snodgrass, eds. 2017. *Boeotia Project, Volume II: The City of Thespiai. Survey at a Complex Urban Site*. Cambridge: McDonald Institute Monographs, University of Cambridge.

Cahill, N. 2002. *Household and City Organization at Olynthus*. New Haven and London: Yale University Press.

Devine, T. 2006. *Clearance and Improvement. Land, Power and People in Scotland 1700-1900*. Edinburgh: John Donald.

Haggett, P. 1965. *Locational Analysis in Human Geography*. London: Edward Arnold.

Howe, S. 2002. *Empire: A Very Short Introduction*. Oxford: Oxford University Press.

Jameson, M. 1990. "Domestic space in the Greek city-state". In *Domestic Architecture and the Use of Space*, edited by S. Kent, 92-113. Cambridge: Cambridge University Press.

Robb, G. 2007. *The Discovery of France*. London: Picador.

Sabelberg, E. 1983. "The persistence of palazzi and intra-urban structures in Tuscany and Sicily". *Journal of Historical Geography* 9, 247-264.

Sabelberg, E. 1985. "Die 'Suditalienische Stadt'". *Erdkunde* 39, 19-31.

Sabelberg, E. 1986. "The 'South-Italian City' – A cultural-genetic type of city". *Geojournal* 13, 59-66.

Symonds, J. 1997. "The Flora MacDonald Project". *Current Archaeology* 152, 304-307.

Thomas, N. 1994. *Colonialism's Culture: Anthropology, Travel and Government*. London: Polity Press.

Westgate, R. 2007a. "The Greek house and the ideology of citizenship". *World Archaeology* 39: 229-245.

Westgate, R. 2007b. "House and society in Classical and Hellenistic Crete". *American Journal of Archaeology* 111, 423-457.

In Hussain, S.T. and G.L. Dusseldorp (eds) 2025. Sitting on the fence: Negotiating archaeology, anthropology and philosophy. Festschrift for Prof. Dr Raymond H.A. Corbey in celebration of his 70th birthday. *Analecta Praehistorica Leidensia* 54. Leiden: Sidestone Press, pp. 215-228.

# Is there a Western *telos* and is it in danger? A rationalist critique of some recent challenges to the social sciences and humanities

Jon Abbink

## ABSTRACT

In this paper, I discuss some of the current challenges to the social sciences and contend that their impact, marked by epistemological confusion and unfounded accusatory discourse against the basics of open scientific debate and empirical methods, is damaging and undermining rational exchange. There is notable variety across disciplines, but contestation is rife. I argue for the existence and value of a historical Western telos, a scientific-epistemological 'project' driven both by basic curiosity and (material) interests. In the face of justified but also some grossly overstated accusations of science, especially during the past two decades, I plead for renewal and recalibration of a (Western or other) telos based on the intrinsic value of sound, evidence-based science and non-justificationist critical rationalism, not the least because the proposed 'alternatives' – slighting evidence-based reasoning and advocating the use of personal experience/bias as authoritative – hold little promise.

*Keywords: Western telos, epistemology, scientific method, rationalism, anti-science movement*

> *"Thoroughly conscious ignorance is the prelude to every real advance in science,"* James C. C. Maxwell (1831-1879).[1]

## INTRODUCTION: CONTESTATIONS ON THE *TELOS*

Western social science and humanities are (again) said to be in crisis, and there are indeed good reasons to be worried. In contrast to earlier waves of self-critique (Marxist in the 1960s and 1970s, and deconstructionist/post-modernist in the 1980s-1990s), the current critical moment is shaped by fragmented, subjectivist epistemology, by the transformative impact of social media use and discourses of 'identity politics' (*cf.* Fukuyama 2018), and of late also by the so-called 'decolonisation' of knowledge and/or intellectual forms of 'wokeism', the latter defined as an activist political attitude showing *awareness of inequalities, social*

**Jon Abbink**
African Studies Centre Leiden, Leiden University, The Netherlands
g.j.abbink@asc.leidenuniv.nl
ORCID: 0000-0003-1383-7849

---

1    Cited in Firestein (2012), 'What Science Wants to Know.' *Scientific American*, 1 April 2012.

*justice issues and the need for greater inclusivity (in academia, corporations, the job market, politics, etc.).*[2]

The growing impact of these critical tendencies – also notably fuelled by anti- or decolonialist protest in Africa (*e.g.*, most prominently since 2015 in South Africa: not only the 'Rhodes must fall'-'Fees must fall' protests but also the clamour for radical curriculum change; *cf.* Jansen 2019) – is partly a sound corrective to existing inequalities and discriminatory assumptions or practices in society and academia alike, that need to be addressed. But these tendencies now increasingly seem to evolve into problematic ideological contestation and even the rejection of evidence-based, critical science, not only by activists but also by academics (*cf.* Dreger 2015; Wayne 2022; Mund 2023). Yet, moves to make science directly subservient to moral-political agendas cannot satisfactorily deal with the indignities and pains of racism and minority denigration. To address the lasting effects of past inequities, I argue that we need evidence-based, comparative research and not selective subjectivism and relativism.

The emergence of science criticism, identity politics and related responses, especially since approx. 2014, is also a *generational* phenomenon and an *institutional* issue – they resonate among the student generations of today, impacted by overstressed 'social media' use (*cf.* Haidt 2022), and also in a problematic manner among university administrators in the US, the UK and Europe. As said, there are some legitimate reasons for the spread of this science criticism. One is an underlying desire for more 'inclusion, diversity and equality' (DEI) – scientific activity is open-ended and should be accessible to all capable of pursuing it – although the concepts of DEI are not straightforward and tend to become a new dogma (DEI 'evangelism'), for example in terms of 'equality of outcome'. Another is the sway of uncritically held assumptions in many academic fields,[3] although criticism of these

is currently too often extended into an ideological 'decoloniality' discourse with scholars pitched against each other on two sides (*cf.* Trisos, Auerbach and Katti 2021). The problem, however, is that the 'decoloniality' label is in danger of being generalized to apply to all scientific debate and discourse, way beyond its original political context. In that broad sense, it loses its meaning, because regardless of background we are all constantly influenced and challenged by other people's opinions and theories. As anthropologist Mary Douglas once said, (1975, xx) "[...] our colonization of each other's minds is the price we pay for *thought*". And as Nigerian-American academic O. Táiwò noted in the context of Africans: the 'decoloniality' approach tends to deny Africans agency and seriously harms scholarship in and on Africa (2022, 3-4) and he added that it can become an easy discourse of complaint.

The scientific endeavour of reasoned, evidence-based inquiry – in both the STEM fields and in social science and the humanities – is better not sacrificed to ideological elements external to good scientific practice itself. Otherwise, the intrinsic values of the scientific endeavour are traded for instrumental ones – at the whims of the day. I support Alice Dreger's view here, who in her 2015 book[4] said that in science, the critical pursuit and use of evidence is the most important ethical imperative of our time – *i.e.*, not ideology, collective identity concerns, notions of primarily serving 'social justice', or right-wing anti-science attitudes and conspiracy-thinking, etc. Particularly worrying to me is that this (epistemological) view on the value of evidence-based, open, critical science is now increasingly questioned even by many today's social scientists as well as university managers – although they often still posture as 'sharing' it.

Here I sketch some of the current challenges to the social sciences based on three recent 'cases' of such contestation and contend that the impact of the 'critical' tendencies just mentioned is damaging and subversive but varies across disciplines (*e.g.*, strong in anthropology, ethnic studies, etc.; less so in archaeology) and is always contested.

Similar to Doug Stokes (2019), I argue for the existence of a historical *telos* of the West, rooted in a scientific ethos, and plead for its renewal. What

---

2    See especially Rajasingam (2023). She refers to an entry in the OED on the meaning of 'woke'. Originally: 'well-informed, up-to-date'. Now chiefly: 'alert to racial or social discrimination and injustice'; frequently in 'stay woke'." This paper will not delve into the 'woke debates'. For more discussion on the issue, see Sage (2022) and Cofnas (2002).

3    For example, in psychology, *cf.* Schulson (2020) and Stanovich (2021).

4    And in many lectures available online, *e.g.*, www.sg.uu.nl/series/truth-or-dare-when-science-meets-activism and https://gwst.umbc.edu/korenman-2016.

exactly *is* the *telos* and is there one in the West? To begin with, it is a diverse 'civilisational' ethos, a core of shared, organising ideas or values, evident in law, religious tradition, national education, or politics developed and cultivated in the course of history. Although, as Karl Popper said, history has no meaning, a civilisational entity or society can produce one in certain subfields. Historian Niall Ferguson (2011) has argued that 'the West' (at the danger of over-generalising) has historically taken off from 'the Rest' via six 'killer apps',[5] as he calls them. One of these apps is *science*, understood as the quest for knowledge and investigation of phenomena and testing and verification (Ferguson 2011, 67-70). It no doubt has historical roots in the Greek worldview (*cf.* Cromer 1993) that, in modified form and via the Romans and Arabs became universalised in the West, and developed for real since the 17th century, in 'dialogue', or rather in opposition to, religious traditions (*cf.* Spinoza's magnificent 1670 *Tractatus Theologico-Politicus*). Of course, the view that since the onset of the scientific-economic revolutions of the mid-19th century everyone in western societies became 'modern' and scientifically-oriented is misleading at best (*cf.* Latour 1993). But one of the normative drivers of social, military, and economic development, led by a minority, and mostly elite, undoubtedly was science, which like in Greek antiquity since Thales set itself the *aim* to examine, explain, control, predict, and manage the human and non-human worlds. Science and its broad influences became part of our broader *cultural history*. Scientific efforts or techniques were not the monopoly of the West, however, as centuries *before*, other traditions were much more 'advanced': the Chinese (technology), Indians (mathematics) and Arabs (astronomy) (*cf.* Ferguson 2011, 11). But at least since the 17th century, a *telos* of basic, future-oriented inquiry – in the shadow of critiques on the dominant theological worldview – was culturally re-defined or reset by Western elites and became normative. Siegel (2017, 3) claims that the '*cultivation of reason*' was a fundamental intellectual ideal in Western tradition. All these lofty words do not deny that the ideal often

remained one of a minority and failed to prevent persecution and mass violence occurring often due to its instrumentalization. Indeed, 'the West' has one of the worst records of 'irrational' mass violence – due to politics. And as Jarvie (2001, 558) observed:

> *"[f]ar from always being socially positive, the pursuit of truth [science, J.A.] can be socially destructive."*

This being said, we nonetheless *can* identify the *telos* – a cumulative historical by-product (*not* a pre-set aim) of non-theological reflection, development of civic and political 'rights', and 'objectivist' scientific experimentation and development certainly since the late 17th century, which has had a tremendous wider societal impact since. In its early 21st century renewal moment, I would plead for seeing this *telos* as best embedded in re-affirming the attendant intrinsic values of critical, evidence-based science and ultimately, a self-critical, pancritical rationalist (PCR) epistemology (as developed by philosopher W. Bartley 1984; *cf.* Rowbottom and Bueno 2009) – with expanding circles of identification and inclusion. This PCR does not seek verification, is anti-positivist and holds every assertion, theory and knowledge claim open to criticism, refusing 'infinite regress' to ideological, fideist, or value positions (Bartley 1980).

The groundbreaking ideas underlying this approach, notably those of William Bartley, are still much discussed (*cf.* Rowbottom and Bueno 2009, Taliga 2022, Chmielewski 2022) but his basic insights on the matter are adopted here. Bartley defined it as 'pancritical rationalism' – an extension of Karl Popper's idea of the criterium of 'falsifiability' as marking scientific from non-scientific statements. Bartley's innovative and more radical view, used the principle of 'criticisablity', makes rationalism self-referential, and this obviates the need for 'faith in reason' as a founding principle (see Bartley 1984, 118; Gattei 2002, 246). A pancritical rationalist approach thus works with a non-hierarchical model of rationality that rejects any 'foundational authority' (*i.e.*, any ideological or 'belief' stance) and holds everything up for criticism – even the ideas of criticism and logic itself – but retains that what cannot (yet) be refuted.

---

5    These killer apps are the development and use of competition, science, property rights, medicine, consumer society, and work ethic. Science stands out as the key element of the *telos* due to its explicit future-oriented character.

## SCIENCE AND 'TRUTH'

Philosophically speaking, humans have *ratio*, but are clearly not consistently 'rational' in thought and action. They are more led by emotion, intuition, and feelings; scientists not excluded. But researchers ultimately (must) appeal to ratio and argument in making knowledge claims, which they then offer – in principle – for criticism, testing and improvement. In much of contemporary academic discourse, notably in the social sciences, this view is now contested, as people now often appeal to extra-scientific authority, fads, group interests or issues of identity as *justification* for backing claims.[6] This occurs both on the 'Left' and 'Right'. Needless to say, this position is difficult to accept because it tends to flout the aims of science and the critical appraisal of its claims, although it should not be forgotten that 'experience' can also be the basis for knowledge, in combination with other sources, and if held liable to critical appraisal. But nothing in science should be 'justified', all should be (able to be) criticised. In science one just cannot 'prove' anything – this idea is a remnant of justificationism. The core notion of justificationism is that 'knowledge is truth which is proven'. But this is a misconception (Weimer 1977, 2).

While the *telos* clearly exists and has shaped the Western scientific endeavour, it is often ignored in various waves of 'criticism' based on identity performance, social-psychological grievances or subjectivist positioning. Indeed, many critics are even loath to argue on facts and evidence – rejecting this form of discourse in favour of confessions and the use of arguments from personal 'authority' (see Mara and Thompson 2022). This approach might be seen as a hypertrophied development of 'interpretivism'. Interpretive methods are of course valid in social sciences such as anthropology, literary studies and sociology (*cf.* Little 1995), but the current emphasis on them has led many practitioners into a rejection of

'scientific', deductive, hypothesis-testing research and even of the ethical basics of science as an open-ended, honest quest for knowledge and truths established in critical, dialogic form.[7] While 'the truth' may not exist or not be knowable in full form, it is a regulative idea that leads curiosity-driven research about reality, about conditions that exist independent of our subjective minds. 'Truth' ultimately reflects the least persuasively criticized ideas and claims about 'what is the case'.[8] But as Cromer (1993, 3-4) succinctly said:

> *"science is 'analytic' and 'objective', and traditional human thinking is 'associative' and 'subjective'."*[9]

There is an over a century-old debate on such 'naturalist-scientific' vs. 'hermeneutic-interpretive' approaches to the study of humans and society, a problematic on which Raymond Corbey has frequently written in a range of always fascinating and inspiring publications, especially in his work on Scheler, Plessner, Kant and philosophical anthropology and on the possible *menschliche Sonderstellung* (Corbey 2007).

While the two camps may never be entirely reconciled and the temptation is great to resolutely choose one over the other, some efforts at dialogue are continuing, and no doubt a perspective based on complementarity ultimately seems the most fruitful. In anthropology, the hermeneutic approach has long been prevalent in the form of interpretivist, and more recently, subjectivist-witnessing-based accounts. As Descola *et al.* (2022, 317) have noted, in

---

6   A painful example is the attempted barring of Elizabeth Weiss (San José State University, USA) by indigenous researcher-activists of research on prehistoric North American skeletal remains, because she was not a 'native American' (even if she complied with all existing laws regarding this matter). See: https://quillette.com/2022/08/18/indigenous-activists-are-trying-to-end-my-academic-career-my-own-university-is-helping-them/. Another is Mara and Thompson (2022).

7   As seen in the correspondence of the 17th century Royal Society! A good example of critical debate resulting in better understanding, *i.e.* knowledge, might be M. Spiro's reinterpretation of Malinowski's theory on the absence of the 'Oedipus complex' among the matrilineal Trobriand people – a classic case in anthropology (Spiro 1982). Another recent example is G. Hanlon's (2023) fascinating study of infanticide in Europe: revising existing knowledge on the basis of a re-evaluation of all work done on it so far and producing a new explanation based on a host of new data.

8   Whether it would imply 'correspondence' to external reality, is opening up another discussion.

9   Cromer (1993, 21) interestingly said: "At its root, objectivity is simply respect for the critical opinions of others."

U.S. anthropology, *culturalism* has long dominated the discipline, making it

> "[...] *a branch of literary hermeneutics, and societies studied by ethnologists texts to be deciphered," (my translation, J.A.),*

which they regret. However, as Daniel Little (1995, 43) has shown years ago in an excellent paper, despite differences in framing and emphasis, the interpretive approach is also scientific (see below), and like the hard 'sciences' approach, relies on rational argument, testing, critiquing, and searching for the 'best possible explanation' of observed/experienced phenomena. Both approaches are thus necessary and legitimate, and a strict separation is often misguided. In addition, one could speak of a 'division of labour' rather than of an unbridgeable epistemological divide. There is no logical need to make the hermeneutic-interpretive approach subservient to explicitly subjective or 'witnessing' methods of 'proof' or evidence. But the debate often still proceeds along the rhetoric of two polar 'opposites'.

It could be claimed that what 'sound science' and critical thinking canons *are* has basically remained *the same* for years, certainly since the 1970s debates on epistemology and (critical) rationality (*cf.* Cromer 1993; Jarvie 2001). I here follow Little (1995, 42) in describing it as evidence-based research based on three epistemic features:

> "*an empirical-testability criterion, a logical coherence criterion, and an institutional commitment to intersubjective processes of belief evaluation and criticism.*"

While what sound science in practice *is* has indeed remained fairly stable, the responses to it have changed, as perhaps has the level of knowledge and openness of current student generations and the extent of marketing strategies of higher education institutions in the Western world – worst in the USA and the UK – to attract and process ever more students at all cost rather than safeguarding independent science.

## THREE CASES

In the following, I present three examples as 'cases' of contestation seemingly going against the Western *telos* as shaped by science. The academics discussed were doing their job as researchers/teachers but met with criticism that went beyond constructive

scientific evaluation. They became the issue of vehement contestation. This should have taken the form of scientific debates that should have proceeded without policing or 'cancelling' the contested authors by colleagues who theoretically disagreed and rejected empirical data. In the cases sketched, however, contestation often amounted to attacking the academics' legitimacy on questionable grounds and rejecting their data on primarily ideological motives (*cf.* also Boghossian 2022; Salzman 2021; Dreger 2015). Such an approach also prevents full debate and criticism of methods and evidence – and this kind of 'immunization strategy', based on irrational grounds, is scientifically hard to accept.

### Chagnon

A well-known case in anthropology centres on the figure of Napoleon Chagnon (1938-2019). His anthropological work among the Yanomamö people was widely known via his bestselling book, "Yanomamö: the Fierce People" (which went through six editions). A dispute on his work and his subsequent blacklisting by the American Anthropological Association fits into the long-standing debate mentioned above between the hermeneutic-*Verstehen* and more natural-science approach of *Erklären, e.g.,* via deductive testing and quantification. Napoleon Chagnon, as a 'hard science' anthropologist, was harshly attacked by a group of interpretive anthropologists, among them Leslie Sponsel, Terrence Turner and Marshall Sahlins, based on the falsely conceived journalistic account by Patrick Tierney in 2000 incorrectly accusing Chagnon and his co-researcher James Neel, among others, of 'genocide' (via allegedly spreading a measles epidemic among the Yanomamö). These anthropologists were led by their own restricted view on what anthropology should be: only a cultural-interpretive, not a deductive-explanatory enterprise using 'biological' variables, and used the faulty assertions by Tierney as evidence. The case turned into an enormous row in American anthropology (*cf.* Dreger 2015, 143-45). Chagnon had done work on Yanomamö violence – aggression, homicide, and village fights – and advanced evolutionary hypotheses on their behaviour in the light of their history, kinship, and sociocultural organisation. The origins and details of this row will not be discussed here (because it is well-documented; *cf.* also Dreger 2011, 2015; Jarvie 2015). But the case is telling because of the *institutional* efforts of negatively labelling him as a kind of 'heretic'. This went via the professional organisation, the American Anthropological Association,[10] which played a questionable role in taking the many dubious accusations at face value and, I argue, made Chagnon a scapegoat. Various investigations followed, including a damning but largely spurious AAA 'Taskforce' report in 2002 directed at Chagnon. His health seriously suffering under this decade-long barrage of critique, Chagnon had to take early retirement. He had also been prevented from doing further fieldwork among the Yanomamö in Venezuela-Brazil. The string of accusations, unsupported by Yanomamö amongst whom Chagnon had worked, was eventually refuted (*e.g.*, by Gregor and Gross 2004), and the Taskforce report was rejected by an AAA members' majority vote in 2005 (although the report stayed on the website until 2009; *cf.* Dreger 2015, 145). Chagnon eventually responded to his critics in his fascinating but unfortunately often-overlooked book *Noble Savages* (2013).

While Chagnon's sociobiology-inspired approach and data on the Yanomamö can certainly be criticised in their details, underlying assumptions, and have shown the need for more testing, the story of exaggerated accusations by a journalist and a questionable campaign by his 'culturalist' opponents is in fact a dismal one, led more by ideology than by evidence. In his 2013 book, Chagnon himself indicated that although an evolutionary anthropologist, he was *not* opposed to cultural interpretations to come to a more comprehensive theory of human behaviour (Chagnon 2013, 31). Today the chasm is still not bridged, neither in terms of the roles of the two 'epistemological' positions involved nor on the possibility of their combination and/or collaboration. The excessive culturalist critique foreclosed dialogue on contents, denied the idea of an academic 'division of labour', and was not open to adversarial collaboration efforts to try and assess the evidence from different points of view. The role played by 'colleagues' and by the AAA was more than dubious (see Jarvie 2015). The affair was perhaps a foreboding of things to come in American academic life in other scientific domains 20-25 years later.

## The Roland Fryer case

This second case on Roland Fryer garnered notable attention (Montz 2022). Fryer is a brilliant Black sociologist at Harvard, and his meticulous study of US police violence over a longer period (Fryer 2019) indirectly fitted into the ongoing debates on (racial) discrimination and inequality in the USA. His empirical research found that in many US cities Black suspects were *less likely* to be fatally shot by police than white suspects – in contrast to received opinion. He did not deny racial differences in police use of non-lethal force, but concluded also that there were "no racial differences in officer-involved shootings." The paper was a study of the empirical evidence and did not set out to make ideological points. Based on the data Fryer dismantled several misconceptions. In the heated media discourse in the wake of the George Floyd case – the indefensible killing in May 2020 of a Black man by bigoted Minneapolis police officers – his analysis of the evidence was 'politically incorrect' and not accepted by many – although it was scientifically sound. While matters of his sampling and other details could be argued with, the evidence criticized blanket ideological points made beforehand by partisan commentators on the US police. Critics – for example those allied to the 'Black Lives Matter' movement – tried to take the study down with such an ideological approach and by motivated reasoning (*i.e.*, reasoning geared to find evidence/arguments that support one's own opinion; in other words, explicit bias), also marshalling convenient sexual harassment charges to discredit him (see Montz 2022). He was demoted and barred from research. The point is: reality was more complicated than ideology suggested; the efforts to block such pioneer empirical research were unfair and misplaced. The proper answer would have been serious criticism; not trying to take him out of circulation. Disturbing was that Harvard University quickly gave in to the criticisms, demoted him from his position and cut his research funds.[11] A 'political' response to a scientific paper under the pressure of seemingly populist critique. Fryer's paper is certainly criticisable, but it led to sound debate about the evidence (see Fryer 2020), and without denying major problems in the US police force, it nuanced the preconceived public picture of it. After two years, Fryer was reinstated by Harvard to his previous position.

---

10   The AAA already had a problematic relation with the concept of science, see esp. Dreger 2010.

11   See https://quillette.com/2022/04/15/why-did-harvard-university-go-after-one-of-its-best-black-professors/.

*The Erica López Prater case*

In the Fall semester of 2022 in her art history class at Hamline University (USA), Erica López had shown – but with preliminary notification to students and pre-course distribution of the syllabus – artful depictions of the Prophet Mohammed, as known (also) from some Islamic traditions. One female Muslim student complained that such portrayal should not be done publicly, and had 'hurt' her feelings and cultural identity. López was subsequently vilified[12] and eventually fired. She was even accused by the university management of being 'Islamophobic' – a comment they later retracted (AAUP 2023, 6). This is a typical contemporary case of a university administration thoughtlessly giving in to ill-motivated, subjective complaints of a student 'feeling hurt', with the administration thereby betraying academic education and freedom[13]: as part of their academic education, students *have* to be confronted with different viewpoints, and in this case the idea of any justified feeling of insult was also refuted by other Muslims, who disagreed with the complaining young student. A massive groundswell of support for López emerged, and indeed included Muslim scholars, and she started a court case against Hamline University. The university administration was met with objections from the scholarly community with evidence and nuance (see, *e.g.*, AAUP 2023), and Hamline faculty eventually voted (71 to 12) in favour of the university president to step down due to her handling of the case. But the university management could not stand criticism and responded with denial, defending its anti-science attitude by denying the long tradition in art history debate *and* Muslim discourse on depictions of the Prophet Muhammad in manuscripts. The administration just bypassed these traditions (the first one academic) and thus did not care to uphold the Western *telos*. Dr. López Prater meanwhile found another job, while the court case is still pending (as of the time of editing).

## REASON AND RATIONALISM

The three cases briefly outlined above show that rationality and reasonableness can quickly get lost if the institutional environment betrays its own principles, for instance because of a certain 'business model'.

The creeping assault on some basics of science, as evident in the three above cases, tending to replace the quest for truth(s), as a general regulative mission (at the origins of science),[14] with concerns of an ideological nature, is one of the most discussed and headline-making developments in Western academia today. The response by many mainstream academics has been to just focus on their own work and hope reason will win out. But that is not guaranteed. Indeed, the anti-academic contestation and protest or what some even call 'cancel culture' (*cf.* Salzman 2021; Ben-Porath 2023) are seeping into the mainstream, and this is a challenge (Krylov and Tanzman, in press[15]) and a disturbance to deal with. A flight into more professional studies for a small audience, or into aestheticism, is fine but will not confront the challenges. The number of worrying cases of academic colleagues declared as 'beyond the pale' or even 'cancelled' or prevented from tenure is now too large to ignore, and in this respect the influence of American academia on the rest of the world is to be confronted and taken seriously.

At the same time, the critical moment that now animates academia – *i.e.*, the focus on inclusion, diversity, correction of biased recruitment, 'social justice' concerns and grievances/reparation – should not be denigrated. Everything is criticisable, including mainstream science and many of its automatisms and assumptions. But all claims, even if motivated by non-scientific intuitions and positions, should be studied, and addressed and tested/evaluated based on the facts, the evidence, and reasoning; not by personal 'witnessing' or ideological preference as a determining source of reliable data or persuasive argument. In science, the 'argument situation' is *default*, be it in the natural, life or social sciences.

---

12 See www.insidehighered.com/news/faculty-issues/academic-freedom/2023/05/22/report-adjunct-who-showed-images-prophet-was.

13 Jacques Berlinerblau, "Hamline University's free speech controversy shows the collapse of the professoriate", MSNBC.com blog, 14 January 2023 (www.msnbc.com/opinion/msnbc-opinion/hamline-professor-hamin-prophet-muhammad-rcna64949).

14 Here the pioneering work by Galileo (1564-1642), at the dawn of the scientific era, might perhaps provide the best example; notably his great 1632 book *Dialogue Concerning the Two Chief World Systems – Ptolemaic and Copernican.*

15 These authors provide a catalogue of how far the madness in scientific censoring (note, in chemistry) has gone.

Yet not all assumptions and statements – however criticisable – will and can be refuted; many will indeed be corroborated – and show considerable resilience to critique, such as Darwin's idea of evolution. What survives after critique is (for the time being) acceptable, as our best knowledge at time T[1]. In this process, the pursuit of 'truth' – as a regulative idea (*cf.* Jarvie 2001, 560) – remains as important as ever.

In view of today's epistemological contestation and the disarray caused by, inter alia, 'decoloniality' critiques and what some people refer to as 'wokeness', is science under threat? We cannot open a social science or humanities journal without encountering at least one paper using such concepts and questioning mainstream science – a tendency which begins to also engulf STEM fields, with even *Nature* editorials[16] occasionally tuning in to what many see as fashionable diversity and inclusivity discourse. In fact, decoloniality discourses and related critiques are even tending to become 'mainstream' in certain domains, notably in the USA. This is seen in job recruitment strategies – where DEI criteria sometimes are weighed heavier than professional qualifications. Threats to what were thought to be unassailable principles (*e.g.*, disciplinary qualifications, critical sense, balance, merit-based assessment) are serious (*cf.* Abbot *et al.* 2023). There are no doubt dangers to free, scientific thinking and the critical quest for truth (*cf.* Mac Donald 2022; Sage 2022; Sophalkalyan 2023[17]) Authors like Lukianoff and Haidt (2015) explain this primarily in terms of social-psychological and cultural problems in modern (USA) society.[18] They are probably right, but there is a real need to also recognise and understand the underlying *sociological* and *institutional* processes as well.

## GENERATIONAL AND INSTITUTIONAL ISSUES IMPACTING SCIENTIFIC PRAXIS

The debate continues on *why* academia is showing signs of derailment in its scientific *telos*, of over-concentration on so-called 'social justice' issues, on the possible 'hurting' of students, and on censoring and excluding of certain academics because of different or 'deviant' views that are beyond current political orthodoxies.

Apart from ignorance which almost always plays its part, there are at least two processes at work: a) the growing numbers and diversity of the student body and its generational dissent towards established higher education structures (as any generation does, in its own way), and b) the ever-increasing commercialisation of today's universities, notably in the USA, but also expanding globally.

First the generational issue. Students are animated by the issues of the day circulating in the public sphere, and these currently are multicultural diversity, inequality, social justice and of late issues of gender identity, often in inchoate forms. In curricula, universities have catered to such presumed students' interests and sensitivities. They have offered courses that address such issues – often selectively – but that also often teach students how to reason as 'victims' and confirm them in their own notions, rather than help them develop and do new, disinterested, open-minded research that academia is supposed to cultivate.[19]

We also must be open to the idea that many students may not (yet) entirely know what they are talking about, standing only at the beginning of a learning curve (I recall my own student days). A relative lack of knowledge and judgement is not to be condemned, but many are not familiar yet with the scientific ethos and procedures and their history. Often, ideological notions (as motives) and a politics of 'feeling' are followed, and their contributions to academic debate are often less compelling. The often-heard demand by students that they should be 'safe', and have 'safe spaces', is sometimes justified, but can be a demand to be 'spared' arguments and different views of those they themselves have – which is the opposite of an academic education.

This sociological phenomenon of a rebelling generation busy with social ideologies and social media-propelled, self-centred views, may be

---

16   See the well-meaning 2022 editorial "Perils for Science in Democracies and Authoritarian Countries", *Nature Human Behaviour* 6, 1029-1031 (www.nature.com/articles/s41562-022-01443-2). See also: https://quillette.com/2022/08/28/the-fall-of-nature/ and www.nature.com/articles/d41586-022-01536-y.

17   See also https://hxstem.substack.com/p/the-search-for-truth-at-cornell-university.

18   See also J. Haidt's article in *The Atlantic* (2022).

---

19   Lloyd (2023) describes this experience in a particularly shocking account.

characteristic of the current conjuncture in 'late' industrial-capitalist-societies. But the principles and canons of sound, criticisable and productive science mentioned above – empirical, evidence-based research, critical methods not dictated by moral/ideological preoccupations, holding all statements/claims open to criticism – remain the same and will ultimately survive the onslaught by its opponents. But this will not occur without sustained efforts at corrective debate, new policy and action. The Leftist and Rightist critiques may ultimately be *absorbed*[20] or transformed by the basic principles and demands of critical science, led by rationalist and critical-pragmatist procedures to continually test and advance plausible knowledge claims.

The second and decisive issue is that of university management. The strongly business-like running of universities today has led to a creeping reformulation of their *telos*: not primarily an open-minded, diverse, critical institution of learning and research dedicated to the pursuit of knowledge and truth, but a place that 'has to' attract and keep as many paying students as possible – students who are *customers* and must be 'served' in producing degrees a.s.a.p. Generally speaking, this has led to a watering down of the idea of curiosity-driven, evidence-based, and confrontational science (*i.e.*, serious debate and exchange of ideas of all kinds). University managers are prepared to go far here. The number of cases of faculty members forced to 'conform', apologise or resign in cases of so-called insensitive or 'politically incorrect' teaching or research now runs in to the hundreds.[21] Rarely were they accused of violating the canons of proper scientific research itself. Here we see a neglect among university managers of their responsibility to stimulate good science and solid academic education of today's students, in favour of material incentives: getting as many students as possible and 'marketing' their institution. This depressing let-down of science and truth-seeking in science by many university managers is the most troublesome issue to address, more than the generational criticisms alluded to above. The Erika López Prater case illustrates this

well. It recalls the Peter Boghossian case at Portland State University (Boghossian 2022). There *is* a certain backlash emerging, *e.g.*, via the American Association of University Professors, the 'Heterodox Academy' and the National Association of Scholars, and by numerous individual scientists (see also Friedersdorf 2023; Wayne 2023). But a general reform of the institutional setting of Western (notably US) university management is crucial for the overall regeneration of science and of the Western *telos*. While the commercially fuelled managerial misery in US and other Western higher education institutions has been diagnosed many times, reform, especially in the rich private universities, is slow.

## RETURNING TO SCIENCE AND DEBATE AS NON-JUSTIFICATIONIST CRITICAL DISCOURSE

The 'Western' scientific *telos* – or rather, the telos of scientific practice anywhere – must be restored. In order to do so, it first has to be *understood*. That is less and less the case among (undergraduate) students and among university administrators – for different reasons.

I repeat that the *telos* is a product, not a self-evident aim of any civilisational tradition, the West included. Humans indeed may not have evolved at all for 'rational thought' (*cf.* Marx 2017), but are more pragmatic, survival-oriented beings. A rationalist *telos* is a self-declared, regulative idea, evolved in a particular moment in history, but one that now works best, in a world dependent on science, engineering and evidence-based progress. It is aware of the context factors impinging on scientific practice but does not yield to relativist epistemology, which is morally and logically highly problematic.

As I have suggested above, it is worthwhile to re-emphasise a pancritical rationalist perspective as the epistemological basis for scientific research. Following Bartley (1984) we hereby appeal to a non-justificationist perspective that rejects the authoritarian metaphysics that underlies so much of Western philosophy and science. Evidence-based research and rational argument – especially needed in social science (*cf.* Little 1995) – recognise that all assertions are and can be held open to criticism without 'justifying' them with an appeal to an external authority or motives. Nothing in logic, which we

---

20  See Brooks' (2021) optimistic argument on the 'woke' section of the critical movement.

21  A recent painful example is that of Prof. Kathleen Stock, at Sussex University in the UK (www.spectator.co.uk/article/kathleen-stock-and-the-debate-over-gender-reality/).

use to argue and assess, prevents us from doing so (Bartley 1980, 76-77).[22]

Science on the basis of critical, rationalist methods and procedures is not flawless and immune to abuse (*cf.* Jarvie 2001, pleading for democratic control), but its self-correcting potential should be radically reinforced: to allow multiple testing and critique, allow more inclusion and diversity of approaches and viewpoints, not only based on gender, marginalised or 'race' criteria but also on ethical and political orientations, provided that the ideas, hypotheses and results are held open to criticism on rational grounds, *i.e.*, can be examined and refuted (if need be) with evidence and logic. Otherwise, it is one subjective view against another. That science in this sense is 'doubted' and 'distrusted' is only good: "Science deserves to be trusted in so far as it is based on a rigorous distrust of itself" (Chmielewski 2022, 1686). If, as alluded to above, the institutional environment and the societal regimes and pressure inhibit science from exercising its self-correcting practices and thus override its truth and knowledge claims by economic, political, or ideological interests, trouble is in store. We live in an era where 'truth' is again under threat or denied by politicians and ideologues, but as Lee McIntyre said (2018, 172) in his great study of contemporary denials of the value of seeking truth by efforts to politically subordinate reality: "Truth still matters, as it always has". It is a sign of the times that this elementary idea even has to be re-emphasised today.

## TOWARD RENEWAL OF THE *TELOS*

Stokes (2009) was right: we need to renew the *telos*. It is not only 'Western' but shared by all those interested in sound science and critical academic debate. Scientific progress – evidence-based, critical exploration of the nature and state of the cosmos, nature and humans via trial and error – is possible and largely obvious, as can be seen and traced across centuries.[23] Although the idea that science is a fully 'rational' undertaking is incorrect, its impact has been tremendous, with humans having even been 'too successful': science and (economically instrumentalised) rationality have begun to work against us (environmental destruction, climate change,

social media intimidation, certain AI applications) and – ironically – need reflexive, scientific-rational correction (*cf.* Wagenmakers 2023). But, as noted, science, as a quest for valid, corroborated knowledge, never gives us total 'proof' or certainty – all is open to correction or refutation.

James Maxwell's quote from the beginning of the paper may incite hope – from nothing *may* come something – but there is also reason to doubt whether those in the camp of the Western *telos* have the will or ability to take such steps if they undermine argument and debate. Further debate and dialogue – without precondition and without condescension – is critically needed but is only possible when higher education institutions and their management are reoriented – away from fads and ideological preoccupations as agenda-setting, and back to the institutionally grounded basics of free, ethical, open-ended, critical methods of research and debate geared to finding the best possible knowledge consensus. This may sound utopian, but there is no alternative, and without this procedural basis, scientific activity would lose its significance. One cannot advance scientific research and university education without institutionally recognising and protecting the value of debate, (dis)agreement and critical exchange. To restore the diversity of views and of free inquiry and academic culture, more is needed than good-natured calls to reason such as for example voiced by Ben-Porath (2023). Needed are serious institutional reform, more courageous personnel in defending free, rationality-based inquiry, de-emphasising the commercialisation of higher education, tempering of non-scientific (ideological) demands upon the practice of research and of 'oaths of loyalty' placed upon staff and newly hired faculty, more 'adversarial' research projects (*cf.* Stanovich 2021; Ceci, Kahn and Williams 2023), and public action to defend evidence-based, critical scientific research and policy. Backlash to attacks on non-ideological, primary evidence-based research has been emerging[24] and likely it will grow stronger,

---

22 I here skip the entire debate on the Popper-Bartley controversy as this is explored in detail by Artigas (1999).

23 Of course, not necessarily meaning human or moral progress.

---

24 See: www.dailymail.co.uk/news/article-12141319/ ROBERT-HARDMAN-recounts-cancel-culture-cancelled-Oxford.html?ico=topics_pagination_desktop; www.independent.co.uk/news/education/ education-news/professor-kathleen-stock-quits-university-gender-identity-b1947387.html; www.independent.co.uk/news/world/americas/kathleen-stock-transphobia-university-austin-b1954486.html.

with a chance of science eventually 'absorbing' the criticisms (Brooks 2021). An awareness of the potential of a pancritical rationalist approach (see above) can help here.

A final note on the current state of play in Western (social) science: the earlier cited paper by Abbot *et al.* (2023), entitled 'In defence of merit in science', was *refused* publication in the *Proceedings of the National Academy of Sciences* (*PNAS*) in the USA.[25] As this was an excellent paper making basic points about evidence-based science and about the standards of judging work on results regardless of authors' personal backgrounds, this suggests hypocrisy: the editors of this prestigious journal generally accept only papers that show the highest merit in their subfields. But they deny acknowledging the principle when it is explicitly and eloquently defended in an ethical and epistemologically sound manner. This, to some, looks like worrying institutional cowardice and fear of the 'woke crowd' (*cf.* Sage 2022), and may illustrate a corrosion of higher education establishments, which thereby needlessly subvert the Western *telos*. If the business model of journal publishing overrides the solid and critical evaluation of serious scientific papers then something seems wrong. Institutional courage and national policy to correct this therefore seem urgently needed, so that the pancritical attitude can flourish .

## ACKNOWLEDGEMENTS

Dedicated to Raymond Corbey, amicable colleague and ever-original, erudite scholar. Also my gratitude to Dr. Petr Kokaisl (editor of 'Critical Studies'). Final editing of this chapter was done in July 2024.

---

25 It appeared in the *Journal of Controversial Ideas*, while the merit idea is not so controversial at all.

## REFERENCES

Abbot, D., A. Bikfalvi, A.L. Bleske-Rechek, W. Bodmer, P. Boghossian, C.M. Carvalho, J. Ciccolini, J.A. Coyne, J. Gauss, P.M.W. Gill, S. Jitomirskaya, L. Jussim, A.I. Krylov, G.C. Loury, L. Maroja, J.H. McWhorter, S. Moosavi, P. Nayna Schwerdtle, J. Pearl, M.A. Quintanilla-Tornel, H.F. Schaefer III, P.R. Schreiner, P. Schwerdtfeger, D. Shechtman, M. Shifman, J. Tanzman, B.L. Trout, A. Warshel, and J.D. West. 2023. "In Defense of Merit in Science." *Journal of Controversial Ideas* 3 (1), https://journalofcontroversialideas.org/article/3/1/236.

Artigas, M. 1999. *The Ethical Nature of Karl Popper's Theory of Knowledge.* Bern: Peter Lang.

AAUP (American Association of University Professors). 2023. *Academic Freedom and Tenure: Hamline University (Minnesota),* May 22, 2023. Washington, DC: AAUP.

Bartley, W.W. 1980. "On the Criticizability of Logic – A Reply to A.A. Derksen." *Philosophy of the Social Sciences* 10 (1), 67-77.

Bartley, W.W. 1984. *The Retreat to Commitment.* LaSalle, Ill./London: Open Court (2nd ed.).

Ben-Porath, S. 2023. *Cancel Wars. How Universities Can Foster Free Speech, Promote Inclusion and Renew Democracy.* Chicago: University of Chicago Press.

Boghossian, P. 2021. "My University Sacrificed Ideas for Ideology. So Today I Quit." https://bariweiss.substack.com/p/my-university-sacrificed-ideas-for

Brooks, D. 2021. "This is how wokeness ends." *New York Times*, May 13, 2021.

Ceci, S.J., S. Kahn, and W.M. Williams. 2023. "Exploring Gender Bias in Six Key Domains of Academic Science: an Adversarial Collaboration." *Psychological Science in the Public Interest* 24, DOI:10.1177/15291006231163179.

Chagnon, N. 2013. *Noble Savages: My Life among Two Dangerous Tribes – The Yanomamö and the Anthropologists.* New York: Simon & Schuster.

Chiemelewski, A. 2022. "Critical Rationalism and Trust in Science." *Science & Education* 31, 1671-1690.

Cofnas, Nathan. 2022. "Four Reasons Why Heterodox Academy Failed." *Academic Questions* 35 (4), www.nas.org/academic-questions/35/4/four-reasons-why-heterodox-academy-failed.

Corbey, R.H.A. 2007. "Menschen, Menschenaffen, Affenmenschen – Zur Geschichte der Idee der menschlichen Sonderstellung." In *Tierrechte: Eine interdisziplinäre Herausforderung*, edited by Interdisziplinäre Arbeitsgemeinschaft Tierethik, 54-70. Erlangen: Harald Fischer Verlag.

Cromer, A. 1993. *Uncommon Sense. The Heretical Nature of Science.* New York/Oxford: Oxford University Press.

Descola, P., G. Lenclud, C. Severi, and A.-Ch. Tylor. 2022 [1988]. *Les Idées de l'Anthropologie. Nouvelle Édition.* Paris: Éditions EHESS.

Dreger, A. 2010. "No science, please. We're anthropologists." http://alicedreger.com/AAA_purges_science.

Dreger, A. 2011. "Darkness's Descent on the American Anthropological Association". *Human Nature* 22, 225-246.

Dreger, A. 2015. *Galileo's Middle Finger: Heretics, Activists, and One Scholar's Search for Justice.* New York: Penguin Press.

Ferguson, N. 2011. *Civilization: the West and the Rest.* London/New York: Allen Lane.

Friedersdorf, C. 2023. "The Hypocrisy of Mandatory Diversity Statements." *The Atlantic*, 3 July 2023. www.theatlantic.com/ideas/archive/2023/07/hypocrisy-mandatory-diversity-statements/674611/?taid=64a4b6075e50780001773784&utm_campaign=the-atlantic&utm_content=true-anthem&utm_medium=social&utm_source=twitter.

Fryer, R.G. 2019. "An Empirical Analysis of Racial Differences in Police Use of Force." *Journal of Political Economy* 127 (3), 1219-1261.

Fryer, R.G. 2020. "What the Data Say About Police". *The Wall Street Journal,* June 22, 2020.

Fukuyama, F. 2018. "Against Identity Politics: The New Tribalism and the Crisis of Democracy". *Foreign Affairs* 97 (5), 94, 96-102/104-114.

Gattei, S. 2002. "The Ethical Nature of Karl Popper's Solution to the Problem of Rationality." *Philosophy of the Social Sciences* 32 (2), 240-266.

Gregor, T. A., and D.R. Gross. 2004. "Guilt by Association: The Culture of Accusation and the American Anthropological Association's Investigation of 'Darkness in El Dorado'." *American Anthropologist* 106 (4), 687-98.

Haidt, J. 2022. "Why the Past 10 Years of American Life Have Been Uniquely Stupid." *The Atlantic*, May 2022. www.theatlantic.com/magazine/archive/2022/05/social-media-democracy-trust-babel/629369/.

Hanlon, G. 2023. *Death Control in the West 1500-1800: Sex Ratios at Baptism in Italy, France and England.* London/New York: Routledge.

Jansen, J.D., ed. 2019. *Decolonisation in Universities: The Politics of Knowledge.* Johannesburg: Wits University Press.

Jarvie, I.C. 2001. "Science in a Democratic Republic". *Philosophy of Science* 68 (4), 545-564.

Jarvie, I.C. 2015. "Noble Savages, Ignoble Colleagues." *Philosophy of the Social Sciences* 45 (2), 273-282.

Krylov, A. and J. Tanzman. forthcoming/2023. "Critical Social Justice Subverts Scientific Publishing". *The European Review*, special issue on *Perils for Science in Democracies and Authoritarian Countries*, edited by U. Deichmann.

Latour, B. 1993. *We Have Never Been Modern.* Cambridge, Mass.: Harvard University Press.

Little, D. 1995. "Objectivity, Truth, and Method. A Philosopher's Perspective on the Social Sciences." *Anthropology Newsletter* 36 (8), 42-43. DOI:10.1111/an.1995.36.8.42

Lloyd, V. 2023. "A Black Professor Trapped in Anti-Racist Hell". *Compact Magazine*, February 10, 2023. https://compactmag.com/article/a-black-professor-trapped-in-anti-racist-hell

Lukianoff, G., and J. Haidt. 2018. *The Coddling of the American Mind.* New York: Penguin Books.

MacIntyre, L. 2018. *Post-Truth.* Cambridge, Mass/London: The MIT Press.

Mara, K. and K.D. Thompson. 2022. "African Studies Keyword: Autoethnography." *African Studies Review* 65 (2), 372-398.

Marx, J. 2017. "What if the Human Mind Evolved for Nonrational Thought? An Anthropological Perspective." *Zygon* 52 (3), 790-806.

Montz, R. 2022. "Why Did Harvard University Go After One of Its Best Black Professors?" *Quillette*, April 15, 2022. https://quillette.com/2022/04/15/why-did-harvard-university-go-after-one-of-its-best-black-professors/

Mund, E. 2023. "Can Wokism Entail Damage to Industrial Society?" www.europeanscientist.com/en/features/can-wokism-entail-damage-to-industrial-society/

Rajasingam, S. 2021. "Woke Culture: The Good, The Bad, and The Ugly." *The Karyawan*, October 15, 2012. https://karyawan.sg/woke-culture-the-good-the-bad-and-the-ugly/.

Rowbottom, D.P. and O. Bueno. 2009. "Why advocate pancritical rationalism?" In *Rethinking Popper*, edited by Z. Parusniková and R.S. Cohen, 81-89. Cham: Springer.

Sage, R. 2022. "A New Woke Religion: Are Universities to Blame?" *Journal of Higher Education Policy and Leadership Studies* 3 (2), 29-51.

Salzman, P.C. 2021. "Why Professors Are Canceled." *Minding the Campus*, September 20, 2016.

www.mindingthecampus.org/2021/09/20/
why-professors-are-canceled/

Schulson, M. 2020. "Psychology Still Skews Western and Affluent. Can It Be Fixed?" *Undark Magazine*, January 2, 2020. https://undark.org/2020/01/20/psychology-bias-western/.

Sophalkalyan, J. 2023. "The Moral Myopia of Woke Culture." *Journal of Political Inquiry*, March 25, 2023. https://jpinyu.com/2023/03/25/perspective-the-moral-myopia-of-woke-culture/.

Spiro, M.E. 1982. *Oedipus in the Trobriands*. Chicago/London: University of Chicago Press.

Stanovich, K. 2021. "The social science monoculture doubles down." *Quillette*, August 30, 2021. https://quillette.com/2021/08/30/the-social-science-monoculture-doubles-down/

Stokes, D. 2019. "Forget about Decolonizing the Curriculum. We Need to Restore the West's *Telos* Before It's Too Late." *Quillette*, March 3, 2019.

https://quillette.com/2019/03/03/forget-about-decolonizing-the-curriculum-we-need-to-restore-the-wests-telos-before-its-too-late/.

Taliga, M. 2022. "How to Make Critical Rationalism Comprehensive and Non-Paradoxical." *Synthese* 200, 387. DOI:10.1007/s112229-022-03881-x

Trisos, C.H., J. Auerbach, and M. Katti. 2021. "Decoloniality and Anti-Oppressive Practices for a More Ethical Ecology." *Nature Ecology and Evolution* 5, 1205-1211.

Wagenmakers, E.-J. 2023. "How Science Breeds Nonsense." *Nature* 619, 669-670.

Wayne, R. 2023. "The Search for Truth at Cornell University". https://hxstem.substack.com/p/the-search-for-truth-at-cornell-university.

Weimer, W.B. 1977. "Science as a Rhetorical Transaction: Toward a Nonjustificational Conception of Rhetoric," *Philosophy and Rhetoric* 10 (1), 21-29.

In Hussain, S.T. and G.L. Dusseldorp (eds) 2025. Sitting on the fence: Negotiating archaeology, anthropology and philosophy. Festschrift for Prof. Dr Raymond H.A. Corbey in celebration of his 70th birthday. *Analecta Praehistorica Leidensia* 54. Leiden: Sidestone Press, pp. 229-236.

# What Language Are We Speaking Here? Λογος in a Post-Humanist Climate

Joep Leerssen

## ABSTRACT

Reflections on language and metalanguage highlight the systemic power of language to generate self-referentiality and meta-referentiality, even to the point where language can be used to negotiate the different contexts and codes within which language can function. These "indexial" and autopoietic capacities are often carried by unobtrusive (*e.g.*, "phatic") linguistic functions and can frequently express themselves in fleetingly subtle verbal interactions. Hence the reduction of language to its referential function – as habitually happens when comparing human language to other information-processing organisms and systems – ignores what is probably its most powerful systemic characteristic. This insight – the power of language and its users to become self-reflexively metacontextual – should not be overlooked in contemporary posthumanist discussions problematizing the distinction between humans and other animals, or humans and artificially intelligent machines.

*Keywords: Language, emic/etic, system theory, language functions, phenomenology*

## THE VEXED LANGUAGE/DIALECT DISTINCTION

### Limburgs not Dutch? The etic and the emic.

Raymond Corbey and I have since 1988 conducted our conversations in the regional language of our home province, Limburg. This is, we are aware, a little unusual; it certainly was unusual at the time. The use of regional "dialects" is considered something homely, informal, communitarian, and hardly suited to the issues of academic theory that are the substance of our exchanges. It feels a bit like translating Heidegger into Cockney. Raymond and I fell back on our native "Limburgs" in the late 1980s. Since then, Limburgs has been legally promoted to the status of a recognized regional language under the terms of a charter of the Council of Europe. One of the reasons Limburgs was eligible for such a recognition was the fact that it could be used for the type of professional, high-level conversations that Raymond and I conducted (*cf.* Werkgroep 1996).

This recognition process in turn opened up the old, vexed "Is it a dialect or is it a language?" debate. Linguists will roll their eyes in despair when hearing the question. There is, for them, no objective criterion to distinguish between the two: the diverging features and the mutual comprehensibility within a language (say between Glasgow English and "Black" Brooklyn English) can be more pronounced than between, say, Norwegian and Swedish. The Limburgs I speak is outlandish to people from Amsterdam, but comprehensible to people from Cologne or Luxembourg. No hard and fixed lines can be drawn between discrete sub-units of this linguistic tangle. Even so, in the debates sparked off by the recognition of Limburgs as a

**Joep Leerssen**
Universities of Amsterdam and Maastricht,
Mauritsstraat 95, 3583 HL Utrecht (NL), The Netherlands
leerssen@gmail.com
ORCID: 0000-0002-0456-0078

"regional language" the question would not simply go away. Even the eye-rolling linguists who said that it made no sense to differentiate between "dialect" and "language" went on to apply exactly that same opposition between the two by asserting that for that reason, Limburgs should not, repeat *not*, be reclassified as a language (*cf.* Leerssen 2002) Why not, if it made no difference anyway?

In dealing with these debates as a cultural scholar it struck me that despite the non-distinguishability between languages and dialects, the two categories were constantly and persistently applied as a binary opposition. My impression was (and still is) that variants used in public-sphere communication (literature; printed texts; cultural contexts valorised as prestigious; social contexts addressing non-private and non-communitarian issues; governance) are experienced as a "language", while "dialects" are experienced as private, domestic or communitarian, oral. The habitual distinction between language and dialect is thus made on the basis of *context*, not on the basis of intrinsic features. While there are no objective differences accounting for the dialect/language distinction, people habitually apply, invoke, and rely on that very distinction (Leerssen 2023).

As Raymond would surely have told me, this is a classic case of the etic/emic duality, so notorious among anthropologists (*cf.* Sahlins 2017). There are no objective etic features that set certain variants apart as different languages; yet there is, patently and pervasively, an emic distinction that is applied deliberately by speakers and even, sub-consciously, by some linguists. Is Limburgs a local dialect variant within the broader Netherlandic language area, or is it is a language used in the Dutch and Belgian provinces of Limburg and as such entangled with the adjacent Rhineland? The question cannot be decided on the basis of etic features (and so the linguists are right); but a constant choice navigated on emic grounds by the bilingual speakers of the respective area, like Raymond and me, involving the tell-tale crossover mechanism called "code-switching" (Backus and Eversteijn 2004 and sources cited there, esp. Auer 1998, Gumpertz and Hymes 1972, Gardner-Chloros *et al.* 2000). The reluctance of some linguists to acknowledge the operative presence of such an emic distinction was manifested in a 2018 survey by the *Nederlandse Taalunie* about "The State of Dutch" (*De staat van het Nederlands*). No allowance was made for respondents to indicate that for them, Limburgs was a separate and credible alternative to Dutch (*cf.* Leerssen *et al.* 2018).

## Language choice and Roman Jakobson: The metacontextual function.

The debate about the methodology of studying language/dialect preference made clear that a choice between linguistic variants is an intriguing and important process of communicative interaction. Raymond and I were first introduced to each other amongst Dutch-speaking company, and on becoming acquainted and recognizing our shared regional background, decided to switch from default Dutch to Limburgs. The process plays out much more swiftly and intuitively in superficial or even anonymous social gatherings within the Limburg area. Upon entering a shop in a Limburg village or town, or approaching a porter's desk in a hospital or office building, the initial salutation (saying hello, or the attendant asking how they can be of help) will carry the secondary function of indicating the speaker's gravitation towards either standard Dutch or Limburgs. The default assumption is Dutch, the official language of the country; the subsidiary alternative is Limburgs, the communitarian speech of the locals (which as a result has a more informal, companionable "feel" to it). If either of the speakers uses Limburgs, and the other is able and willing to respond in Limburgs, that will establish the usage from the outset. Even if the "official" default Dutch is used initially, an audible Limburg background may shift the language towards the more subsidiary level of the regional language; tell-tale indicators are intonation and accent (a "soft" or "hard" G, monophthong long vowels or diphthongized ones). The process is even more saliently noticeable in the trilingual Voerstreek, between Maastricht and Liège: strangers meeting will, in their salutation (*bonjour*, *goededag* or *goojedaag*) convey with which language community they identify. French and Dutch being antagonistic politically, Limburgs can here be a neutral middle ground since it is the local language of a large portion of French-speakers as well as Dutch-speakers.

Thus, the analysis of language choice and variant preference threw up a communicative feature that has interesting system-theoretical implications: language ("a" language) is used to negotiate a *choice* of language. The question in the title, "What language are we speaking here?" is paradoxically ambivalent, since the question is formulated within a given language to negotiate a choice between languages. "Within" and "between" collapse into a single communicative act. Language, of course, is uniquely a communicative or semiotic system where the "meta"-levels are dimensions within the system. We use language to talk *about* language, and even to talk about how we talk about language: language is its own meta-language.

We owe to the great linguist Roman Jakobson (1962) a classification of the various functions that language can have in human interaction. Jakobson classified these functions as follows: [1] referential (conveying information); [2] emotive (conveying an affect); [3] conative (giving an instruction, or order); [4] phatic (confirming one's ongoing presence as an interlocutor); [5] metalingual (discussing words and linguistic features); and [6] poetic (aiming for an aesthetic or rhetorical effect). At first sight, the interactions referred to here belong to the Jakobsonian "metalingual" category; but that is not quite the case. In the Jakobsonian scheme, the *a priori* assumption is that any linguistic exchange will take place on the basis of an established set of conditions ("factors of communication"), which include context, contact and a common code in which the sender and the receiver can exchange messages. On that *a-priori* basis, metalinguistic exchanges (in the Jakobsonian sense as usually understood) can be about the question whether one should use gendered pronouns, or when to use the present-perfect rather than the past tense, or whether a certain comment was used earnestly or ironically, or how best to phrase a letter of complaint. But what if language is not just about itself, but about a choice between different possible languages? Opting for either *bonjour* or *gojedaag* is used, not merely phatically ("I am here, and gently acknowledge your presence"), but also to establish context and a common code ("my language of preference is French/Limburgs; what about yours?"). For without such a common code, language can carry no meaning, cannot establish communication. The word *teangeolaíocht* is a meaningless abracadabra for people ignorant of Irish Gaelic (where it means "linguistics"), the word *verflucht* can be read, depending on context, either as "damned" (in German) or as "a smell of paint" (in Dutch). Indeed, even the etic features of that word pan out differently according to context, and hence can be established only once that context is clear: the morphemes divide between r and f in German, between f and l in Dutch; the stress falls either on one syllable or on the other, the grapheme <u> is rendered by different phonemes (as in *booze* or *buzz*).

Jakobson's functions are a strong and ingenious matrix for analysing linguistic functions within a given systemic context; but the *a priori* assumed monolingualism of that context (we know what language we are in, we are all in that language together, and that language as a system is a homogenous continuum for all those involved) needs to be relativized (*cf.* also Duranti and Goodwin 1992). Much of our language is about asking context- and code-negotiating questions like "what language are we speaking here?" – the sort of thing that is known as "handshaking" in IT circles – a "process of negotiation between two participants through the exchange of information that establishes the protocols of a communication link at the start of the communication, before full communication begins" (as the Wikipedia article phrases it). But even the process of handshaking itself requires an *a priori* set of established rules known as a Transfer Protocol (TCP, SMTP, etc.).

I propose to call this "handshaking" question of establishing a joint language choice the "metacontextual function" of language, as an addition to the six Jakobsonian ones. Jakobson's metalingual function seems to address, primarily, the features and operations of a given language: its lexicon, grammar, syntax, and rhetoric; what language is and what is does. The metacontextual function of language goes into the context within which a given language becomes a meaningful message-carrier. It is not as if linguists have not long been aware of this added power of language to signal its own context: the established term is "indexicality" (*cf.* Silverstein 1976, who already stressed the need for linguistic analysis to factor in more than the mere referential function.)

Widening the palette of Jakobsonian functions to include the *situational context* in which language gains its meaning is not just, I submit, a useful way to capture multilingual, multi-coded communicative exchanges; this metacontextual function is also, I think, a crucial characteristic of human communication more generally, and perhaps especially in non-state and possibly prehistoric contexts. After all, it is a condition of life that most people encounter, not infrequently, multilingual situations. Monolingualism is exceptional, code-switching happens everywhere all the time.

## COMMUNICATION AS (MORE THAN) INFORMATION EXCHANGE

### Language as definer of humanity

Many of my discussions with Raymond involved the problematic distinction between humans and other animals. What sentience, what self-awareness, what powers of reflection and cogitation, do we as Homo *sapiens* (yes, *sapiens*, that word so aptly chosen by Linnaeus) arrogate for our own species, and on what basis do we set ourselves apart from other living beings? The power of the word, as articulator and systematiser of our sensations and experiences, is traditionally central in that self-definition: the Platonic and Christian *logos* (a further teleology was imposed by the idea that the Word gains fresh powers, separating savages from civilized societies, once it moves from orality to literacy). With Herder and Wilhelm von Humboldt, who realized that different species had their own powerful organizing abilities, the emphasis shifted from "language" as such to the power of the human languages to *diversify*, which led, ultimately, to the Sapir-Whorff thesis, the "fifty words for snow" meme, and the Orwellian idea that by engineering language we can determine how we see the world. Strangely, however, these post-Humboldt developments were largely overlooked by phenomenologists like Heidegger, Merleau-Ponty and even by Foucault and Derrida (*cf.* Zhu 2013 and sources there), who address language as a single, uncountable and undifferentiated cognitive and experiential ambience, rather than as plurality of diversifying and even competing matrices for social interaction and "worlding".

Recently, the human-animal boundary has become overshadowed by discussions on the relationship between humans and machines. From the Turing Machine thought experiment, by way of Richard Dawkins's "Selfish Gene" to the development of *ChatGTP*, human beings are increasingly juxtaposed with the input-output dynamics of physiological or natural processes. Conversely, after a few decades of habitually ascribing sentience to non-human systems like genes ("selfish") or markets ("nervous"), artificial machines can now increasingly convincingly mimic human discourse and "intelligent" interaction.

The roots of this new boundary problem between humans and non-humans go back to nineteenth-century narratives like Mary Shelley's *Frankenstein* (1818; *cf.* Baldick 1990, Nagy *et al.* 2020). Western intellectual life is at present subjected to and shaped by a "post-humanist" paradigm (*cf.* Ferrando 2013, Hayles 1999). The privileged vantage point of a self-identifying humanity as inhabiting a common and cognitively sovereign outlook on the rest of the world is fundamentally being challenged from at least two sides: the animal world and the mechanical world. In the humanities, posthumanism means the emancipation of the animal as an autonomous experiencer of events and occurrences, and the role of humanity in the "Anthropocene" (understood as a recent, transient and possibly ruinous stage in the geological history of planet Earth) is one of disruption,

*caesura* and disturbance rather than one of ownership, mastery and organizing focus. In the life sciences, humans are often seen purely as organisms, in terms of their etic features, and language and culture are cast as evolutionary tools whose purpose and workings can also be analysed and generated as mechanically operating systems. Popularizing publications by researchers from the experimental sciences carry titles (provocatively phrased but becoming commonplace by now) such as *We Are Our Brain* and *Free Will Does Not Exist* (*cf.* Leerssen 2021).

In short: the human monopoly on the *logos* is now in a process of meltdown. Is not our vaunted, particularly human power of articulation, reflection, and communication a mere byproduct of evolutionary trial and error, our sapience and self-awareness a mere beguilement cloaking what are essentially physiologically determined and naturally selected stimulus-response mechanisms?

This is hardly the right moment to intervene in what is a fraught and confused debate. Nonetheless, two points seem to be worth making in the light of Raymond's anthropological interests and our shared penchant for a phenomenological understanding of the world around us. If we assume that language and the use of language form a core characteristic of what makes humans human in the first place, then language use must be something more than a mere carrier of information (Jakobson's "referential function"). Ironically, a model of "language as information transfer" is precisely the frame that human interaction is being reduced to in the human/animal or human/machine discussions.

If language is reduced to its mere referential function, to a process of information transfer, then we load the dice *a priori*, and it is a foregone conclusion that such information transfers, even complex ones, can happen equally successfully between non-human parties (animals or cybernetic machines). Language as *logos*, however, is multifunctional, and as I have argued elsewhere (Leerssen 2021) its non-referential functions (poetic, metalingual and metacontextual ones, most of all) are specifically apt to *signal* the emic experience as well as *conduct* the etic praxis of communication. In my view, the emic aspects of language and culture are crucial to communicate self-reflection (not just talking about things and doing things, but talking about *how* we experience things and *what* it is we think we are doing). And it is precisely these crucial functions that tend to be disregarded if we reduce the function of language to the referential.

## Humans as metacontextual, code-switching animals

In human exchanges, "phatic" language use tends to be seen as ambient and infrastructural – for instance, the occasional "uh-huh" noise we make during a telephone conversation, just to let the other know that we are still there and the line has not gone dead. The "referential function" of this "uh-huh" is almost nil, and it fits the most diverse contexts: gossip, a philosophical discussion, a military command – it is even used across different languages. Unobtrusively, however, this phatic signal also carries a context- and code-confirming message ("I am with you"). Other context- or code-querying messages are tucked away, equally unobtrusively, in utterances with low referential appeal, even as unreferential and unintentional as a melodic singsong intonation or an "accent". But once we are aware of their existence, we realize how very common they are in human communication, and how much more than just "noise on the line" they are. Interjected questions like "Really?" or "What do you mean?" serve as information control markers, and in many cases these markers address the meta-level of the ongoing communication: "Funny-haha or funny-peculiar?", "What do you mean by that?", "Why are you asking me?".

Since language then enfolds its own meta-language, it stands to reason that some linguistic acts will be indexical, concerned with establishing on what (meta-)level the communication is situated and ready to unfold. In everyday life we rely on "air quotes", and in written texts we rely on "scare quotes" (like the ones in this sentence) to signify that we do not just *use* a certain word but that we are *mentioning* it (Sperber and Wilson 1981) in order not just to convey its reference but to draw attention to it as a signifier. Language continually hops from base-level to meta-level, up and down and back again, and often yoyoing between multiple stacked levels of meta-reflection. The outermost meta-level is reached when the fundamental parameters of the communication itself are addressed, such as the context and the choice of language/code.

This means that a language, dynamically agreed upon from amidst other available registers and variants, is much more than a transactional code for communication. Its recursive systemic meta-loops (and the human capacity for navigating their scalarity) ensure that, emically, it makes self-reflection possible: using language to reflect, not just on language, but on the use of one language amidst a plurilingual menu, and to reflect on the act of reflection itself.

Autoreferentiality and recursively nesting meta-levels are the hallmarks of complex systems in Luhmannian system theory, and *autopoiesis* is a concomitant of that complexity (Luhmann 1986). The complexity of culture resides in its multiply-stacked scalarity of emic levels and meta-levels superimposed on the primary ("natural") function of behavioural practices. The way in which the Michelin Guide awards stars to chosen restaurants is separated, by many interposed systemic meta-levels, from the fundamental natural function of eating food. And this means that we can define "cultural literacy" (the ability to participate socially in complex cultural practices, *cf.* Murray 1992; Fokkema and Rigney 1993) as the implicit ability to negotiate the scalarity of all these levels and meta-levels, to read language in its referential function but also to intuit its obliquely implied meta-levels, its rhetorical registers, and its metacontextual indexicality. Or things like irony.

## TO CONCLUDE: WHAT DO I THINK I AM DOING HERE?

These reflections are not offered as a last-ditch defence of humanism against posthumanism. There would be something defensive in asserting, almost metaphysically, that there are still characteristics out there which make human cognition, cogitation and communication special, and set us categorically apart from animals and cybernetic problem-solving machines. But it would be equally misguided to make the opposite case on the basis of an inadequate understanding of what is involved in human cognition, cogitation and communication in the first place, stripping them of the systemic complexities which are essential to them. Whatever is central to the experience of being a human being (or what makes the *Anthropos*), it arguably cannot be divorced from being part of an *experience*. Humanity is an emic, experiential condition, and part of the latter is to reflect on what this means, what anything means, and why or how it should make sense.

## ACKNOWLEDGEMENTS

These reflections draw on the erudition and wisdom of Raymond Corbey, which I recalled during my discussions, in particular about "cultural evolution", with colleagues at the congenial Netherlands Institute of Advanced Studies (NIAS) during my 2018/19 fellowship there.

## REFERENCES

Auer, P. ed. 1998. *Code-switching in Conversation: Language, Interaction and Identity*. London: Routledge.

Backus, A., and N. Eversteijn. 2004. "Pragmatic Functions and their Outcomes: Language Choice, Code-switching, and Non-switching." In *Bilingual Socialization and Bilingual Language Acquisition. Proceedings from the Second International Symposium on Bilingualism*, edited by A.-M. Lorenzo Suárez, F. Ramallo, and X.-P. Rodríguez-Yáñez, 1393-1410. Vigo: Universidade de Vigo.

Baldick, C. 1990. *In Frankenstein's Shadow: Myth, Monstrosity, and Nineteenth-century Writing*. Oxford: Clarendon Press.

Duranti, A., and C. Goodwin, eds. 1992. *Rethinking Context: Language as an Interactive Phenomenon*. Cambridge: Cambridge University Press.

Ferrando, F. 2013. "Posthumanism, Transhumanism, Antihumanism, Metahumanism, and New Materialisms." *Existenz* 8 (2), 26-32.

Gardner-Chloros, P., R. Charle, and J. Cheshire. 2000. "Parallel Patterns? A Comparison of Monolingual Speech and Bilingual Codeswitching Discourse." *Journal of Pragmatics* 32 (9), 1305-41.

Gumperz, J.J., and D.H. Hymes, eds. 1972. *Directions in Sociolinguistics: The Ethnography of Communication*. New York: Holt, Rinehart & Winston.

"Handshake (computing)". 2023. In *Wikipedia, the Online Ecyclopedia*, https://en.wikipedia.org/w/index.php?title=Handshake_(computing)&oldid=1147501104 (Last changed 31 March 2023; last consulted 8 May 2023).

Hayles, N.K. 1999. *How We Became Posthuman: Virtual Bodies in Cybernetics, Literature, and Informatics*. Chicago, IL: Chicago University Press.

Hirsch, E.D. 1987. *Cultural Literacy: What Every American Needs to Know* Boston: Houghton Mifflin.

Jakobson, R. 1962 "Linguistics and Poetics." In *Style in Language*, ed. T.A. Sebeok, 350-376. Cambridge, MA: MIT Press.

Leerssen, J. 2002. "Streektaal en erkenning: een paradox en zes misverstanden." In *Hartstocht in contrapunt*, edited by M. Mathijsen, 169-181. Amsterdam: Bezige Bij.

Leerssen, J. 2021 "Culture, Humanities, Evolution: The Complexity of Meaning-Making over Time." *Philosophical Transactions of the Royal Society B* 376 (1828), DOI:10.1098/rstb.2020.0043

Leerssen, J. 2023. "Language or Dialect? A Crux in the History of Central European Nation-Building." In *Languages and Nationalism Instead of Empires*, ed. M. Nomachi and T. Kamusella, 10-23. London: Routledge.

Leerssen, J., H. Bloemhoff, L. Cornips, R. van Hout, and G. Jensma. 2018. "De Nederlandse Taalunie en het wegmoffeleffect." *Vaktaal* 31 (4), 4.

Lotman, J.M., and B.A. Uspenskij. 1978 "On the Semiotic Mechanism of Culture." *New Literary History* 9, 211-232. DOI:10.2307/468571

Luhmann, N. 1986 "The Autopoiesis of Social Systems." In *Sociocybernetic Paradoxes: Observation, Control and Evolution of Self-steering Systems*, edited by F. Geyer and J. Van der Zeuwen, 172-192. London: Sage.

Murray, D. E. 1992. *Diversity as Resource: Redefining Cultural Literacy*. Alexandria, VA: TESOL.

Nagy, P., R. Wylie, J. Eschrich, and E. Finn. 2020. "Facing the Pariah of Science: The Frankenstein Myth as a Social and Ethical Reference for Scientists." *Science and Engineering Ethics* 26, 737-759.

Rigney, A., and D. Fokkema, eds. 1993. *Cultural Participation: Trends since the Middle Ages*. Amsterdam: Benjamins.

Sahlins M. 2017. "In Anthropology, It's Emic All the Way Down." *HAU: Journal of Ethnographic Theory* 7, 91-128.

Silverstein, M. 1976. "Shifters, Linguistic Categories and Cultural Description." In *Meaning in Anthropology*, edited by K. Basso and H. Selby, 11-55. Albuquerque: University of New Mexico Press.

Sperber, D., and D. Wilson. 1981. "Irony and the Use – Mention Distinction." In *Radical Pragmatics*, edited by P. Cole, 295-318. New York: Academic Press.

Werkgroep Erkenning Limburgs als Streektaal. 1996. Advies inzake de erkenning van het Limburgs als streektaal. Online at https://leerssen.nl/publications/advies (last changed: 14 August 2019; last consulted: 8 May 2023).

Zhu, L. 2013. "Philosophy of Linguistics: The Phenomenological Perspective." *History and Philosophy of the Language Sciences*. 17 April 2013, https://hiphilangsci.net/2013/04/17/philosophy-of-linguistics-the-phenomenological-perspective/